Cavalry Operations in the
Ancient Greek World

Cavalry Operations in the Ancient Greek World

Robert E. Gaebel

UNIVERSITY OF OKLAHOMA PRESS : NORMAN

Library of Congress Cataloging-in-Publication Data

Gaebel, Robert E., 1937–
    Cavalry operations in the ancient Greek world / Robert E. Gaebel.
      p. cm.
    Includes bibliographical references and index.
    ISBN 0-8061-3365-1 (alk. paper)
    1. Cavalry—Greece—History. 2. Cavalry—Middle East—History. I. Title.

UE75 .G34 2002
357'.1'0938—dc21

2001034737

The paper in this book meets the guidelines for permanence and durability of the Committee on Production Guidelines for Book Longevity of the Council on Library Resources, Inc. ∞

Copyright © 2002 by the University of Oklahoma Press, Norman, Publishing Division of the University. All rights reserved. Manufactured in the U.S.A.

1 2 3 4 5 6 7 8 9 10

To my family,
Jaynie, Susie, Rob, and Deric

Contents

List of Maps and Battle Plans	ix
Preface	xi
Abbreviations	xiii
Introduction	3
PART 1. BACKGROUND: Circa 2000 to 500 b.c.	17
1. The Greek Horse	19
2. Horse-Drawn Chariots in the Near East and Greece during the Late Bronze Age: Circa 1550 to 1200 b.c.	32
3. Riding in the Near East and Greece: Late Bronze Age to 500 b.c.	44
PART 2. THE GREEK CAVALRY: 500 to 360 b.c.	61
4. The Persian Wars: 500 to 479 b.c.	63
5. From City-State to Empire: 479 to 432 b.c.	81
6. The Peloponnesian War: 431 to 404 b.c.	90
7. The March of the Ten Thousand: 404 to 399 b.c.	110
8. The Corinthian War: 395 to 386 b.c.	116
9. Interlude—Spartan Decline: 386 to 371 b.c.	124
10. Theban Ascendancy: 371 to 362 b.c.	129

PART 3. THE AGE OF PHILIP AND ALEXANDER: 359 TO 323 B.C.   141

  11. Timoleon and Philip: 359 to 336 B.C.   143
  12. Alexander: 336 to 323 B.C.   159

PART 4. THE AFTERMATH: 323 TO 150 B.C.   197

  13. The Successors from the Death of Alexander to the
      Battle of Ipsus: 323 to 301 B.C.   199
  14. The Hellenistic Period: 300 to 150 B.C.   230
  15. Hannibal: 218 to 202 B.C.   263

Conclusion   277
List of Battles Discussed in the Text   313
Note to the Maps and Battle Plans   315
Glossary   323
Bibliography   327
Index   341

List of Maps and Battle Plans

MAPS

Greece and the Lower Balkans	316
Battle Sites in Central and Southern Greece	317
Battle Sites in Northern Greece	318
Battle Sites in Lands to the East of Greece	319

BATTLE PLANS

Nominal Order of Battle in the Hellenistic Period	320
Battle of Chaeronea, 338 B.C.	321
Battle of Sellasia, 222 B.C.	322

Preface

ALTHOUGH I HAD READ military history for many years both from personal interest and from a need for insights into ancient history for courses I was teaching, my dissatisfaction with semipopular articles on Greek military history first drew my attention seriously to the subject. Perhaps a misplaced academic bias against the study of military history in the decade or so following the Vietnam War—an attitude that fortunately came to an end in the 1980s—had encouraged this less scholarly approach. In the years since then many fine works on Greek military history have appeared and our understanding of the subject has significantly improved, especially in regard to the fighting of infantry, thanks to work that was begun by V. D. Hanson. Although several works on Greek and Roman cavalry have appeared recently (which I discuss in the introduction), there is still room for a purely military study of the subject from the beginning of the Classical period to the end of Greek independence, especially since much of the content of recent works is devoted to social history.

One of the attractions of military history—particularly in the ancient world, when battles were of short duration and usually decisive—is the opportunity it affords to evaluate human decision making. The study of cavalry also provides a wonderful opportunity to immerse oneself in the vast subject of horses and horsemanship, not to mention that it offers the perfect excuse for spending more time in the saddle.

Yet there is a most regrettable element in this study as one comes to terms with the horrible wastage in human and animal lives that war demands. Sometimes the human combatants had a say in what happened, but the horses and other animals who were exposed to war never did. In 1812 Marbot, one of Napoleon's cavalry officers, departed from Prussia with seven horses of his own, but at the end of that disastrous campaign he walked out on foot. Now that the working days of the horse are past in the Western nations, it is used mostly for pleasure and sport. The care it generally receives is unmatched in history except for that given animals bred and used by the European nobility in recent centuries.

The initial work for this book was done at the Institut für Alte Geschichte at the University of Munich. There I experienced the splendid hospitality of the former director, Prof. Dr. Hatto H. Schmitt; the generosity of Prof. Dr. Jakob Seibert, who graciously shared his office; and the manifold helpfulness and personal hospitality of Kai Brodersen (now Prof. Dr. at the University of Mannheim).

Many thanks are also due to my late colleague Prof. Constantin Dimitriu, onetime reserve officer of the Royal Rumanian Cavalry and equestrian of vast knowledge and experience, for encouragement and advice; to Dr. Jeffrey Kaimowitz, rare book librarian at Trinity College, Hartford, Connecticut, for longstanding advice and encouragement; to my wife, Jayne, for loving support and the task of proofreading; to my daughter, Susan Wallace, who prepared the bibliography and the index; to Lois Henson for help with equitation and horse behavior; to Joe Stoll, who prepared the maps and plans; to Sarah Akers and John Ball of Bierce Library Interlibrary Loans, who insured that I had timely access to books and articles not locally available; to the two anonymous readers for their positive suggestions, obviously based on a careful reading of the manuscript; to the editors at the University of Oklahoma Press, especially copy editor, Sarah Nestor, and managing editor, Alice Stanton; and finally to my Trakehner mare, Dynamik, who embodies the superb riding qualities of her Prussian ancestors that made them perhaps the finest cavalry horses of modern Europe.

I would also like to record my debt to several of the great military historians of the twentieth century from whom I have absorbed countless ideas over many years of reading and study: J. C. Fuller, B. H. Liddell-Hart, Michael Howard, John Keegan, Edward Luttwak, and Martin van Creveld.

Abbreviations

Modern works frequently cited in the notes are identified by the following abbreviations.

AA 1, 2	P. A. Brunt. 1976-83. *History of Alexander and Indica.* 2 vols.
AAG	A. M. Snodgrass. 1967. *Arms and Armour of the Greeks.*
ACHS	R. A. Billows. 1990. *Antigonus the One-Eyed and the Creation of the Hellenistic State.*
AE	A. B. Bosworth. 1996. *Alexander and the East: The Tragedy of Triumph.*
AG	N. G. L. Hammond. 1980a. *Alexander the Great.*
AGH	J. K. Anderson. 1961. *Ancient Greek Horsemanship.*
AHA 1, 2	A. B. Bosworth. 1980-95. *A Historical Commentary on Arrian's History of Alexander.* 2 vols.
AJArch.	*American Journal of Archaeology.*
AJPhil.	*American Journal of Philology.*
CAH	*Cambridge Ancient History* [1923–39] 1961.
CCG	I. G. Spence. 1993. *The Cavalry of Classical Greece.*
CE	A. B. Bosworth. 1988. *Conquest and Empire.*
CLT	J. H. Crouwel. 1981. *Chariots and Other Means of Land Transport in the Bronze Age.*
CT 1-2	S. A. Hornblower. 1991–96. *A Commentary on Thucydides.* 2 vols.
EGW	P. A. L. Greenhalgh. 1973. *Early Greek Warfare.*
Fr. Gr. H.	F. Jacoby. [1923–58] 1954–69. *Die Fragmente der griechischen Historiker.*

GA	J. F. C. Fuller. 1958. *The Generalship of Alexander the Great.*
GRW	P. Connolly. 1981. *Greece and Rome at War.*
GSW 1-5	W. K. Pritchett. 1971–91. *The Greek State at War.* 5 vols.
HA	G. R. Bugh. 1988. *The Horsemen of Athens.*
HAW	H. Delbrück. 1975. *History of the Art of War.*
HB	J. Seibert. 1993. *Hannibal.*
HCAG	L. J. Worley. 1994. *Hippeis: The Cavalry of Ancient Greece.*
HCP 1-3	F. W. Walbank. 1957–79. *A Historical Commentary on Polybius.* 3 vols.
HCT 1-5	A. W. Gomme. 1945–81. *A Historical Commentary on Thucydides.* 5 vols.
HH	C. Chenevix-Trench. 1970. *A History of Horsemanship.*
HM 1-3	N. G. L. Hammond. 1972–88. *A History of Macedonia.* 3 vols.
HMND	W. W. Tarn. 1930. *Hellenistic Military and Naval Developments.*
HW	J. F. Lazenby. 1978. *Hannibal's Wars.*
IG	*Inscriptiones Graecae.*
JHS	*Journal of Hellenic Studies.*
MAT	M. M. Markle. 1982. "Macedonian Arms and Tactics under Alexander the Great." In *Studies in the History of Art* 10: 87–111.
RE	A. Pauly–G. Wissowa. *Real-Encyclopädie der classischen Altertumswissenschaft.*
SA	B. Bar-Kochva. 1976. *The Seleucid Army.*
SAGT 1-4	W. K. Pritchett. 1965–82. *Studies in Ancient Greek Topography.* 4 vols.
TAPA	*Transactions of the American Philological Association.*
TH	J. Buckler. 1980. *The Theban Hegemony 371–362 B.C.*
TS	N. G. L. Hammond. 1980c. "Training in the Use of the Sarissa and Its Effect in Battle, 359–333 B.C." *Antichthon* 14: 53–63.
WVRA	M. A. Littauer and J. H. Crouwel. 1979. *Wheeled Vehicles and Ridden Animals in the Ancient Near East.*
XIG	C. Hignett. 1963. *Xerxes' Invasion of Greece.*

Cavalry Operations in the Ancient Greek World

Introduction

WHEN I BEGAN WRITING this book on the use of cavalry in ancient Greece and Macedon, one of my principal concerns was to determine the place of Alexander in the evolution of Greek cavalry tactics. Consequently, one might expect the word *tactics* to appear in its title. The fact that it does not reflects my growing awareness that the concept of tactics would not be a good organizing principle around which to write military history of the sort that interested me. My reading of the sources suggested that it was not really tactics that evolved so much as the underlying principles of and attitudes toward fighting, including ideas about both the nature and the purpose of warfare. Tactics began to appear to me more as an epiphenomenon that arose from human reflection on the environment in which the fighting occurred. This environment possessed both animate and inanimate facets, ranging from human and animal behavior to the nature of the terrain. Although most familiar to me in the context of more recent military history, the term *operations* appeared to be a closer approximation of what I had observed in Greek and Macedonian warfare, especially for the period beginning with the Peloponnesian War. Whereas tactics have to do with specific battlefield techniques, operations refer to the attempt to apply broader goals that are reached through a "suitable combination of tactics."[1] The term *operations* is not used in antiquity, but it does seem to describe what happened, especially if a narrow definition of tactics is used as I have done here. The term may apply at more than one level of military activity. For example, it may be

---

1. Here I follow and quote Luttwak (1985), 175.

used in connection with a large army comprising several arms, in which the tactics of each arm are integrated into the overall plan, or with a single arm such as the cavalry, in which the different tactics of lancers, mounted javelinmen, and mounted archers must be blended for maximum effect.

Much of this should appear obvious, and it certainly is not original, but too often it seems to be ignored in the reconstruction of past military events. Successful military leaders do not borrow tactical ideas and expect success from them simply because those ideas are new or different. In the hands of poor leaders that course has proved to be disastrous. At least two things must precede a choice of tactics: a brutal grasp of reality and an understanding of the elements and principles that pertain to warfare. Among such elements and principles are those of the offensive, intelligence gathering, the need to protect the flanks, organization, discipline, training, the indirect approach, economy of force, concentration of force, surprise, security, ruthlessness, ability in a short war, resources in a long war, and adaptability. Simply to be aware of these, however, is not enough; to be effective, they must be applied in accordance with the subsuming principle of asymmetry.

Asymmetry occurs on the battlefield when one or more differences exist between two armies in such a manner that one side is able to exploit them for its own advantage.[2] Such differences may take a great variety of forms, including disparity in number; differences in levels of training, discipline, morale, organization, and fighting power; the level of technology, and so forth. Successful commanders recognize or create asymmetry and then employ tactics that allow them to exploit the difference. The last thing one wants on a battlefield is a head-on clash between two evenly matched armies, although the pages of history are full of such events, some due to force of circumstances, too many to the result of conscious decisions by generals. When this is the case, the adoption of new tactics by one side may still suffice to bring victory, so long as they play to the enemy's weakness and do not allow him time to adjust. This sort of advantage was enjoyed by the French in the 1790s, when they developed a drill whereby a battalion could deploy quickly from

---

2. See, for example, O'Connell (1989) 95: "As military confrontations go, the three Crusades were unusually asymmetric in tactics and weapons. . . . Under the circumstances, a premium was placed on experimentation and the exploitation of weakness." Luttwak (1985) 170 uses the term *maneuver* to describe the action that leads to asymmetry: "the purpose [that is to say, of *maneuver*] is to muster some localized or specialized strength against the identified points of weakness of an enemy that may have superiority overall." Modern definitions of military terms are not rigid and vary from country to country. See Margiotta (1994) 974–75 for operation, tactics, and so forth; 786–89 for principles.

a "broad column into a line of three ranks, ready for firing."[3] The new mobility enabled the French to be ready to attack before the enemy and gave them a better chance of striking the flank as well. In this century the most spectacular example of asymmetry is blitzkrieg, as practiced by the Wehrmacht between 1939 and 1942. Conversely, the trench battles of the First World War were "symmetrical brute force engagements not far removed from pure attrition."[4] Noteworthy is the fact that blitzkrieg succeeded even when the Germans did not have superiority in number and quality of armored vehicles, since their success "derived from the method of command" rather than from superiority in matériel or firepower.[5]

During the period under consideration, circa 500–150 B.C.,[6] it was precisely the ability of leaders to recognize and exploit asymmetry that produced consistent military success. The tactics that led to victory on any occasion were usually those which the immediate circumstances permitted or encouraged. There is, as we shall see, a good reason why Alexander's tactics against Porus in India differed from those that he used against Darius in the Near East. Likewise, when Hannibal fought Scipio at Zama, he correctly made no effort to employ the tactics that had been so successful at Cannae. The reality of battlefield circumstances there did not permit them.

It is the task of a commander, after having recognized the reality he faces, to employ any arm, singly or in combination, that fits the situation. Herein lies the importance both of intelligence gathering and deception, for once a general begins to lose the distinction between perception and actuality he is at a great disadvantage.[7] In order to understand the reasons for the task assigned to different arms and the particular tactics adopted, close scrutiny must be given to the nature of the two armies involved and particularly to their strengths and weaknesses. For example, the broad statement that both Alexander and Hannibal—almost alone among ancient generals—used cavalry as a striking force is true but rather irrelevant, since each used

---

3. Jones (1992) 252. The American Civil War offers a prime example of the difficulties that arise when very similar armies face each other in battle. The armies of the two sides were created out of much the same raw material, employed the same technology, and were led by a core of professional officers educated at the same institution, West Point.

4. Luttwak (1985) 179.

5. Ibid. (1985) 183.

6. All dates are B.C. unless otherwise noted or where an A.D. context is clear.

7. During the American Civil War this was precisely the problem that destroyed McClellan, who consistently overestimated the number of enemy opposed to him by making poor use of intelligence and succumbing to Confederate efforts to mislead him.

very different tactics for both infantry and cavalry, and these tactics were chosen after evaluating the differences between the armies they led and faced.

In spite of what has just been said about a commander's task, the genius and fame of individuals such as Alexander and Hannibal obscure the fact that many military leaders are incompetent; it remains an open question how much they, rather than their troops, contribute to victory. Almost every battle ends in success for one side or the other, and it is natural to look for decisions made by generals to explain it. Yet to concentrate on this alone is misleading, for mediocrity and downright incompetence are more normal than brilliance on the battlefield, where many a mistake has been made good by the steadiness, discipline, and courage of the rank and file. The British army in World War I offers an example of this, as can be seen in the noteworthy comment of British historian E. L. Woodward regarding the "lowness of professional competence. . . . No one doubted their [that is to say, the officers'] personal courage, their discipline, their coolness in difficult moments, their powers of endurance. Their trouble was lack of imagination and 'free intelligence.'" Winston Churchill himself confirmed this and gave the ranks their due: "As in the shades of a November evening, I for the first time led a platoon of Grenadiers across the sopping fields which gave access to our trenches. . . .The conviction came into my mind with absolute assurance that the simple soldiers and their regimental officers, armed with their cause, would by their virtues in the end retrieve the mistakes and ignorance of Staffs and Cabinets, of Admirals, Generals and politicians—including, no doubt, many of my own."[8]

While many of the military principles mentioned above have long been considered universal, that is not to say that they are applied with the same intensity at all times and in all places. The high value placed on organization, discipline, and training by the Greeks, Romans, and other Mediterranean peoples of Classical times gave them a distinct long-term advantage over many of their external enemies, as did the principle of the offensive, especially as it was employed by Alexander and Hannibal. Recent research suggests that the Romans too—despite appearances sometimes to the contrary—regularly employed an offensive strategy.[9]

The manner in which principles are applied is also subject to societal and cultural differences, since these have a strong influence on the purpose

---

8. Woodward (1967) xviii, Churchill (1931) 523.
9. Goldsworthy (1996) 114.

of war and its goals. In spite of the survival of many continuities between ancient and modern warfare based on physical laws and human nature, it is best to ignore the concept of *nation-state* that has dominated European history in recent centuries. Ancient Mediterranean societies were very different in political and social structure and thus should be studied on their own terms. In the Greek polis, for example, the army and the demos were one and the same. As demos, meeting in assembly, the male citizens voted to wage war under the guidance of elected magistrates, while the army, drawn from the same body of citizens, carried out the will of the assembly. Although the hoplite clash itself might be violent and bloody, until the time of the Peloponnesian War the goals of the conflict were, generally speaking, modest and limited. Broader and more intensive views of fighting grew out of the Peloponnesian War, and the mercenaries who appeared in numbers at this time and played an important role in the fourth century began the separation of army and demos.

The Macedonians, who became major players in the Balkan peninsula by the middle of the fourth century, represent a different cultural model. They seem to have retained more of the warrior ethos of their Indo-European ancestors, which was regularly exercised in their unintentional role as a buffer between the northern barbarians and the more civilized Greeks to the south. When this warrior ethos was joined with the organization and discipline from Greece and the Near East, the Macedonian kings, with their open-ended tenure of power and close personal bond with their people, effected significant changes in warfare. Common to both Greeks and Macedonians, however, were the merging of civil and military authority in the same individual; military units with a territorial basis; and the considerable degree of familiarity among soldiers in a unit and between them and their leaders that arose from the social and political setting. In the aftermath of Alexander's death in 323, further significant changes occurred. When the dust settled about 300, the territory comprising the Macedonian kingdom and the former Persian Empire devolved into several large, multiethnic kingdoms (Macedon largely excepted) under the control of military tyrants who transformed the use of the military. Armies became mostly separate from the civilian population—Macedon again being something of an exception—and were used to support the kings' struggles among themselves for power and aggrandizement. Their armies became professional forces that had little in common socially with the older city-state militias. Soldiers now fought because they were paid to do so, and their loyalty was much less reliable than that of the city-state citizen/

hoplite. This resulted in profound changes in the nature of war making, particularly in the reasons for fighting and the intensity and professionalism with which it was conducted. Yet there was no significant change in weapons technology or basic weapons skills, aside from an improvement in those skills that attends a higher level of training and experience.

Bedeviling any study of this sort is the inherent inaccuracy and incompleteness of all battle accounts, even those derived from eyewitnesses. As a result much effort has gone into attempts to reconstruct ancient battles by applying rational, scholarly principles and logic to the primary sources. Although this is a common and accepted practice, I avoided it in this book, lest any preconceptions of mine influence my battle descriptions. Instead, I have adopted as a working hypothesis the premise that examination of the original sources in the aggregate would reveal a sufficient amount of correct and consistent information about cavalry operations and fighting style to permit a reasonably clear understanding of the use of the mounted arm in antiquity. Once that understanding is achieved, perhaps it would be worth while to use it as an aid in the reconstruction of specific battles. The entire task is made appreciably easier by the fact that ancient battles were usually short and decisive.

Until recently there were no book-length treatments of ancient Greek cavalry, so one had to rely on general military histories, general histories of cavalry, works devoted to ancient military history in general, historical commentaries on ancient historians, and specialized articles in scholarly journals.[10] While these works were often quite good within their self-imposed limitations, they did not answer the need for a more comprehensive study of Greek cavalry. This seemed to change with the publication of three books on Greek cavalry between 1988 and 1994.[11] G. R. Bugh, nevertheless, confines himself to Athens and exhibits little interest in military events, while L. J. Worley and I. G. Spence barely touch upon Alexander, much less the Hellenistic period, which I view as essential to a full understanding of the Greek and Macedonian use of cavalry. Alexander's position in ancient military history, for example, cannot be appreciated without an awareness of both what followed and what preceded him. Worley, though he treats Alexander, devotes only four pages to his campaigns, whereas most historians require more pages to describe one of Alexander's battles. Spence's work is organized themati-

---

10. See, for example, Delbrück (1975); Denison (1913); Adcock (1957); Kromayer and Veith (1928); Tarn (1930); Gomme(1945–56); Gomme, Andrewes, and Dover (1960–81).
11. Bugh (1988); Spence (1993); Worley (1994).

cally and contains no narratives of battles. Thus, I feel that a need remains for a chronologically arranged study of battle narratives and commentary covering the period from circa 500 to 150.

Many works, with the exception of the commentaries, exhibit what may be considered a serious defect in methodology, concentrating on the highlights of ancient warfare, specifically those battles that had some immediate effect upon the political history of the ancient world. To be sure, this practice is valid in writing general political history, but not necessarily in writing military history. There is, for example, no a priori reason why major battles should contain more useful information on military operations than do battles of less political significance. Indeed, it is not unlikely that commanders of small expeditionary forces, out of touch with authorities at home, had opportunities for innovation that were denied to generals commanding full levies, who were subject to greater political pressure. Consequently, it seems important to examine every mention of military horsemen in the ancient sources and to evaluate this body of information for its intrinsic worth.

Clearly, modern historians tend to apply anachronistic judgments when evaluating ancient cavalry. A case in point is the tendency to judge all ancient cavalry by the standard set by Alexander the Great. There is also an implication that cavalry that did not employ "shock" tactics and that made no use of the treed saddle, stirrups, and iron horseshoes is somehow less worthy of notice. Such criticism is not only out of place but also belittles or ignores the genuine accomplishments of ancient cavalry and denies them their proper place in the history of warfare.

As for Alexander, I think it is fair to say that he was such a superior tactician and leader of genius, with enemies so different from those of his predecessors and successors, that there is little to be gained by comparing other military leaders to him. Too much of his ability seems to have come from native talent, a fact insuring that only part of his military legacy was transmitted to his successors. Unfortunately, many modern historians seem to have fallen under the influence of his charisma. The result is that they tend to attribute more tactical innovation to him than can be demonstrated by reference to the original sources. In fact it appears that many of the tactical ideas of which he was a master appeared gradually over the preceding century and finally came to fruition in the mid-fourth century with the rise of Macedon under his father, King Philip II. These two—father and son—possessed the rare ability to exploit the evolving military legacy of the preceding one hundred years to the fullest and, in the case of Alexander, to apply it to a very different enemy. The latter's military achievements are outstanding because he applied his inimitable personal leadership to this legacy.

By adopting the performance of Alexander as the standard, contemporary historians have also come to underestimate the use of cavalry before his time, while overestimating its importance subsequent to him. The relatively greater use of cavalry by Alexander and his successors in the lands to the east of Greece is due, at least in part, to the nature of the terrain and the traditional military practices of the peoples against whom they fought. It is impossible to demonstrate that cavalry per se were intrinsically superior to good infantry of the Greek type. The dominance of the mounted arm at certain times in history may even owe something to a bias toward a horsey way of life. In Greece itself in the period covered by this book, military victory was only assured by the defeat of heavy infantry and the capture of cities, accomplishments that cavalry alone could never achieve. Furthermore, the horse was never of great economic importance in Greece and Greek culture was never a horse culture as was the case among the nomads of the steppe. Nevertheless, the appeal of the horse was very strong, especially among the aristocracy, and the claim has been made that the Greeks "raised the esthetic appreciation of these animals to a pitch never surpassed."[12]

Indispensable to any discussion of the military use of horsemen is the subject of equitation, or the art of horsemanship. Quite apart from the obvious physical limitations involved (the speed and endurance of horses, the relative size of horse and rider, the distance a rider can hurl a javelin, problems of supply—with fodder and water for horses equivalent to fuel for engine driven vehicles, and so forth), the ability of cavalry to perform their tasks rests on the combined skills of man and horse, who are partners in an intimate, reciprocal relationship. Modern works make little mention of horsemanship, perhaps following the lead of the historians of the last century who founded the modern study of ancient history and who were as familiar with horses as we are with automobiles. J. K. Anderson's standard work, Ancient Greek Horsemanship (1961), is excellent but is restricted to the period prior to Alexander (for which the sources are admittedly fuller) and has only a brief discussion of cavalry tactics, since his subject is equitation in the broad sense.

Although difficult because of the lack of evidence, an evaluation of ancient horsemanship is essential for our understanding of ancient cavalry. This requires an appreciation of the level of skill of the bareback rider, since

---

12. Simpson (1961) 39.

treed saddles with stirrups were unknown in Europe until the Middle Ages.[13] Problems have been created where none exist by scholars who have greatly overvalued the importance of stirrups.[14] L. White, for example, has argued that the lack of stirrups severely limited the military effectiveness of ancient cavalry.[15] Yet such arguments are fundamentally wrong. Never having been exposed to the idea of stirrups and the advantages they bring, ancient horsemen developed skills such as a good, deep seat and more useful leg contact that more than made up for the lack of stirrups in most respects. It is essential to recognize the relative merits of riding with and without stirrups as well as the fact that no cavalryman in antiquity rode with stirrups, so that in this respect, at least, all cavalry fought on equal terms. It cannot be denied that stirrups offer genuine benefits. They greatly increase the ease of mounting, especially with taller varieties of horses. They improve lateral stability, though they do little to prevent the rider from sliding forward or backward. For that one needs a prominent pommel and cantle, which has been demonstrated recently by experiments with recreated imperial Roman saddles. These offered exceptional security for the rider without any benefit from stirrups.[16] Stirrups also provide leverage for using the slashing sword and offer stability for mounted archers at the gallop. When performed bareback, these actions require more skill and strength.

Modern cavalrymen and, indeed, all who take riding instruction today have been taught to ride without stirrups, both as an exercise and as a way of avoiding the problems arising from losing a stirrup in action or having a stirrup leather tear away. Balance, relaxed muscles, and the ability to "go with the horse" when it suddenly changes direction are essential for keeping one's seat. In some respects it is more difficult to ride well with stirrups than without them, since there is the tendency toward their overuse. For example, standing in stirrups raises the rider's center of gravity and eliminates the

---

13. Littauer (1981) 99–105. Scythian saddles, contemporary with Classical Greece, were found in the Pazyryk tombs. These comprised two jointed cushions; four wooden bows (one on either side, front and rear); occasional wooden spacers between the cushions; and girth, breast, and crupper straps. Nothing similar is known from Greece. Rudenko (1970) 129–37, pl. 75, 76.

14. For discussion see Junkelmann (1990–92) 3: 102–104.

15. White (1962) 13–14, 38.

16. Hyland (1990) 130–34. This is based on Connolly (1987) 7–27. For photographs of recreated combat with the Roman saddle, see Junkelmann (1990–92) 3. ill. 56, 59–61, 111, 115, 116, 133–36, 139–42. In the Middle Ages a high cantle, rising up behind the rider, prevented him from being swept off his horse when he was struck by a lance. When the tournament became more of a spectator sport, however, cantles were removed from the saddle so that a rider struck by a lance could roll backwards off the horse and thereby have less chance of sustaining serious injury. *HH*. 58, 100.

possibility of achieving the deep seat that is so important for applying the aids. It is clear from the type and variety of mounted skills that Xenophon takes for granted that a high level of riding ability was indeed possessed by ancient horsemen. His advice for evaluating a prospective cavalry mount is that the animal be "tested in all the particulars in which he is tested by war. These include springing across ditches, leaping over walls, rushing up banks, jumping down banks."[17] A more recent example of exquisite bareback riding is offered by the North American Plains Indians. Although they possessed saddles, which were used for everyday riding on the trail, they preferred to ride bareback into battle. The reasons given for this preference are the restricting effect of a girth on the horse's breathing and the saddle's interference with the rider's use of the "hang over" alongside the horse's neck in combat.[18] Even today, the level of horsemanship that can be attained riding without saddles, stirrups, or even bridles for that matter, is well demonstrated by the Foxfield Drill Team of Foxfield Stable, Westlake Village, California. The members of the team, twelve girls ranging in age from eight to nineteen years, perform a variety of movements at different gaits without any tack. Included are jumps up to four feet in height performed without hand control.[19] Equally impressive are the riding skills of the Hungarian horsemen of the Puszta, who use a leather and felt treeless saddle that has stirrups but no girth. Although the saddle merely rests on the horse's back like a pad, horsemen skillfully mount with the stirrup and ride with complete confidence.[20] The fact that such skill can still be mastered today enables us better to understand the ability of ancient horsemen. More specifically, it makes perfectly credible the description of the Numidian light cavalry of North Africa, who rode without saddle, bridle, or bit, having only a neck strap.[21]

Although the level of equitation described by Xenophon elicits admiration even from modern experts, the extent to which the typical cavalryman of his time exhibited the same skills is unknown. Xenophon himself criticizes his contemporaries for excessive harshness, because it produces the opposite of what it aims for.[22] A rough-and-ready style of riding that relies on compelling the horse to obey can be effective, but it is different from a high level

17. Xen. *On Hors.* 3.7.
18. Roe (1979) 230, 264.
19. Kilby (1987) 64–70.
20. Schiele (1975) 42–45.
21. *GRW* 149. A typical overvaluation of stirrups appeared recently in Keegan (1987) 38, where they are described as "the means of control thought essential by modern horsemen."
22. Xen. *On Hors.* 10.1–5.

of equitation that depends more on persuasion. Because the number of available cavalry horses in the Balkans was small compared to the great horse herds controlled, for example, by the Mongols on the Asiatic steppe, it is possible that Greek and Macedonian horsemen had a closer relationship with individual horses than the Mongols, who changed mounts frequently. Although evidence from the ancient sources is lacking, it is well known that the bond between horse and rider is important, for an animal that trusts its rider can be persuaded to do things when it is afraid that it would not otherwise do. If modern practice reflects the activities of the medieval Mongols, their horses were subject to less human handling than those of the Greeks and Macedonians and seem to have existed in a half-wild state. A Westerner who rode with contemporary Mongols in 1990 reports that they viewed horses as tools and, because of the many remounts, rarely even named individual horses. He was struck by the fact that there was "nothing graceful about the gait. It was the gait of completely unschooled horses, without any concessions for the rider's comfort."[23] The fact that Alexander rode Bucephalus for ten years shows a potential for bonding between horse and rider that may have been an element in the performance of Greek and Macedonian cavalry.

Of the varied evidence of ancient horsemanship, the figured evidence (for example, vase paintings, coins, and sculpture) is perhaps the most difficult to interpret, in spite of the fact that it exists in some quantity. It is inherently unlikely that ancient artists were good horsemen; they were good artists, however, and their increasing concern for anatomical realism throughout the Classical and Hellenistic periods is well documented. Thus it should come as no surprise that it is possible to identify different types of horses from representations on ancient art in spite of some inaccuracy and the standardization of types that was introduced by Greek artistic idealism. We are particularly fortunate that so many coins from widely separated parts of the Greek world survive, for they offer an opportunity to compare horse types from different geographical locales. If one compares, for example, horse types on coins of the Mediterranean region and the Parthenon horses with the animals depicted on gold objects and coins from Scythian graves, the distinction is clear. The Greek horses are generally a fine, longer-legged type, whereas the Scythian horses are the coarser ponies typical of the steppe.[24] This, to be sure,

---

23. Severin (1991) 48–57, esp. 50, 55–57. For a full description of the nomadic way of life see Vainshtein (1980).
24. Rice (1957) 72–74. For the most recent work on the Scythians see Davis-Kimball, Bashilov, and Yablonsky (1995).

is an oversimplification, since it seems clear that there were several types of horses in the Greek lands and at least two—perhaps three—different varieties among the Scythians. Nevertheless, this is clear evidence that Greek artists (by whom or under whose influence the Scythian work was also done) were conscious of the different horse types and, at least when they chose to do so, were capable of recording these differences in their artwork. One striking example of the accuracy of Greek artists is the appearance on the coins of Larissa in Thessaly of a broodmare, showing the characteristic belly shape. The artistic portrayal of riders on the coins also seems to be essentially correct insofar as the position of body and legs is consonant with observations of bareback riding today. The leg bent at the knee, with the heel back and the toe down, seems to be a natural position in active bareback riding. Greek art is also an invaluable source of information about armor, weapons, tack, and clothing.

A few words must be said about the meaning of the word *cavalry*. The *Oxford English Dictionary* defines it as "that part of a military force which consists of mounted troops." In the context of Near Eastern and Greek military history this definition is too broad, but one suggested by J. H. Crouwel fits the situation nicely: "mounted troops—trained to a degree where they can function with precision as a unit—advancing on command, changing gaits, turning, deploying and reassembling in their proper positions in the ranks."[25] The significance of this definition lies in the fact that simply placing one's soldiers on horseback is not enough to insure their effective use. The difference during antiquity is most noticeable when one compares the cavalry of the nomadic barbarians, who were often superb riders, with that of the more highly civilized peoples of the Near East and the Mediterranean lands. The latter clearly could not match the sheer riding ability of the steppe nomads, but they were frequently superior in organization, discipline, tactics, and supply. The quality and training of the horses and the differences in weapons and armor also played a role.

Another point to keep in mind is the fundamental difference between infantry and cavalry. In open battle a phalanx has to maintain its formation in order to have any hope of success. Once its ranks are broken, disaster usually follows. Cavalry formations are inherently more open due to their mobility, their speed, and the size and shape of the horses, and they exhibit a flowing quality emphasized by changes in direction. The size and motion of

---

25. *CLT* 23.

horses also limit the number of weapons that cavalrymen can bring into play in a given space. In this regard infantry would seem to have the advantage by projecting a veritable hedgerow of spearpoints in front of their more compact ranks. If the battle devolved into hand-to-hand fighting, formation was lost, and the capability to reform under combat conditions was essential if the unit's effectiveness was not to be lost. The Roman historian Tacitus, in his work *Germania*, offers an interesting perspective on the differences in fighting style between cavalry and infantry. Describing the Chatti, a tribe that fought relatively seriously, that is to say, like the Romans, he says: "Forays and casual fighting are rare with them: The latter method no doubt is part of the strength of cavalry—to win suddenly, that is, and as suddenly to retire; for the speed of cavalry is near allied to panic, but the deliberate action of infantry is more likely to be resolute."[26]

Over the centuries since the domestication of the horse humans have developed many different styles of riding, and we shall never have a complete understanding of the equestrian ability of the ancient Greeks. Nonetheless, personal experience with modern practices (in my case, hunter seat and dressage) offers insights into the bond between horse and rider and suggests some idea of what this combination is capable of achieving when an appropriate level of skill is present.

---

26. Tac. *Germ.* 30.

PART 1

Background:
Circa 2000 to 500 B.C.

Chapter 1

The Greek Horse

IN SPITE OF CONSIDERABLE amounts of figured evidence (vases, coins, sculptures, and so forth) it has proven impossible to identify the breed(s) or type(s) of ancient Greek horses. Indeed, the word *breed* may be an anachronism in this context, since it is inherently improbable that ancient breeding practices were as strict as is the case for many modern breeds. In the broad sense ancient Greek horses seem to belong to the Oriental type, which was common to the Mediterranean basin and the Near East. They were generally slender, fast, and rather small, though usually above pony size. Among surviving Greek horses and ponies, attention has been drawn to the similarity of the Skyros pony to the horses in the Parthenon sculptures.[1] Another modern Greek type, the Pindos of Thessaly, is said to have been bred since antiquity. Such claims cannot be accepted uncritically for at least two reasons. First, the movement into Greece by various peoples and their domestic animals over the last three thousand years must have altered the genetic make-up of the old types. Second, recent experience by breeders shows that horse and pony types can be and have been altered significantly in less than a century by the conscious introduction of new bloodlines. In the eastern Mediterranean similarity of type can be explained by prolonged exposure to a generally unfavorable environment and an obvious preference for speed and endurance rather than weight and power. Over time, by breeding for function, several originally different types could have been brought to resemble each other. The attractiveness of this view rests in the fact that the

---

1. Edwards (1980) 201. For more recent work on breed descriptions see Hendricks (1995).

conformation of the horse to a large degree determines its performance. Thus a breeding program that selects for performance becomes ipso facto a selection for conformation.[2]

There seems to be little doubt that most common color types familiar to us were also present in antiquity. Homer mentions bay, chestnut, white, dun, and some type of dapple.[3] Archaeological finds from a later date confirm this and add further information about cavalry horses in particular, the information coming from approximately 680 lead tablets that comprise part of the Athenian cavalry archives and date to the mid-fourth and mid-third centuries. These tablets, apparently recorded annually, contain the cavalryman's name, the color of his horse, a description of the horse's brand, and the replacement value of the horse.[4] The colors recorded on the tablets are red or chestnut (by far the most frequent), black, reddish brown (or perhaps bay), white, dapple gray, and spotted (without reference to color or size of spots). Dapple gray occurred only twice, and one color on a damaged tablet is unique. The word on this tablet began with *white* and the missing portion is presumed to be another color, so perhaps the animal referred to was a piebald.[5]

The appearance of brands on these documents is also quite useful, as they are indications of origin rather than ownership, thus providing information about breeding and trading. Among the twenty-five brands that appear on the tablets, it is known that the ox head (bucephalus) was associated with Thessaly, probably in the vicinity of Pharsalus; the centaur brand with Larissa; the axe with Pherae at the time of the tyrant Alexander (369–357); the caduceus with Macedonia under kings Alexander I (498–454) and Pausanias (390–389); the koppa (Ϙ) with Corinth; and the san (Σ) with Sicyon. These brands seem to be "trademarks of established stables and herds that provided the finer mounts for the whole of Greece."[6] From this type of information as well as other sources such as Xenophon's equestrian treatises, it is clear that horse management in Greece was a sophisticated enterprise. It was also expensive, as the replacement values for horses on the tablets show. The price of a cavalry horse ranges from 200 to 1,200 drachmas, with the greatest number costing about 500 drachmas each. By 400, a drachma

---

2. Simpson (1961) 47; Wagoner, Chalkey, and Cook (1978) 109–13.
3. Richter (1968) 73.
4. Kroll (1977) 83–140; Braun (1972) 129–269.
5. Kroll (1977) 86.
6. Ibid., 88.

represented a day's wages for a laborer and would purchase a gallon of domestic wine, five pounds of wheat, and one salted fish. A sheep or goat cost 10 to 15 drachmas, and a cow about 50. Human slaves might range from 140 drachmas for a donkey driver to 360 for a Carian goldsmith.[7] Obviously, each horse represented a substantial investment and was important as an individual because of its comparative rarity. The Greek environment, especially in the central and southern parts of the Balkan peninsula, precluded the raising of horses in large numbers, as was common on the Eurasian steppe. The comparative abundance or lack of pasturage in these two environments prompted the development of two distinct models of horse management. Geographically, Greece lies within the Near Eastern and European system characterized by stabling, feeding grain and cut hay, selective breeding, and—potentially at least—a relatively close bond between horse and rider.[8] On the Eurasian steppe—as well as later among the American Plains Indians—there was a much higher ratio of horse to rider, with large herds of almost feral animals that largely fended for themselves and ate what was available.

There is less available information regarding the size of these horses. Unfortunately, there is no way to judge the accuracy of proportions between man and horse depicted in Greek art. At times it is obvious that the size of the horse has been reduced because of the limitations of space.[9] It has been estimated that the average height of the Greek horse was from fourteen to fifteen hands at the withers (that is to say, fifty-six to sixty inches, since a hand equals four inches).[10] Extremely limited archaeological evidence suggests that this estimate may be too high by several inches.[11] But the point may be moot, since this height is more than sufficient for effective cavalry operations under ancient conditions, which included smaller riders. In fact it is primarily the horse's build, not its height (within certain reasonable limits) that determines the task for which it is best suited. Modern, massive draft horses are often no taller, and sometimes even shorter, than thoroughbreds.

It is worthwhile to note that two of the greatest conquering peoples in history rode horses no larger than this and, in the majority of cases, considerably smaller. The mounts of the Bedouin Arabs, in the harsh environment

  7. Ibid., 89; Frost (1997) 69–71; *CCG* 274–77.
  8. See *CCG* 39, 199, for comments on the affection of owners for their horses.
  9. See *EGW*, figs. 63, 64.
  10. *HH* 24 suggests about 15 hands. By modern definition a pony cannot exceed 14.2 hands (58 inches), irrespective of its bloodlines. Many ancient horses were below this standard, which is, in practical terms, arbitrary.
  11. *CCG* 282–83.

to which they were accustomed, probably averaged no more than 14 hands high, while the ponies ridden by the Mongols of the steppe were smaller yet, ranging from 12.2 to 14 hands. Skeletal evidence from elsewhere in Europe as well as from Asia suggests that horses of various sizes and types equivalent to the full modern range, except for the large draft breeds, have existed since Neolithic times.[12]

Anderson felt that there was no difference between riding and chariot horses before the fourth century, but this may not be the case.[13] M. B. Moore, who has studied the horses on sixth-century Greek vases, does distinguish between riding and chariot horses, at least in the work of the painter and potter Exekias. She detects in the chariot horses more slender and longer bodies, on which the withers are "scarcely noticeable."[14] Differences in the shape and proportions of riding and chariot horses are also noticeable on coins, where the chariot horses have lighter bodies and thinner legs. The workmanship on the many coins from all over the Greek world that carry horses is frequently remarkable. The degree of accuracy is very high in many cases, and this is strengthened by the artist's ability to capture a particular essence that could not have been created. A particularly good example of this is found on coins from Larissa in Thessaly from the first third of the fourth century. Thessaly was horse-breeding country, and these coins bear the images of a mare and her foal. What is so striking is that the mother of the foal has the characteristic shape of the broodmare. It seems reasonable, then, to accept some of the variations in the shape of horses on coins as evidence for the existence of several types of horse in the Mediterranean region during the fifth and fourth centuries. If the figured evidence is to be trusted, no one of these Greek or Mediterranean types differs as much from the others as they all differ from the characteristic Persian type found on the reliefs at Persepolis. In the scenes showing horses brought as tribute by subject peoples, three distinct varieties have been recognized.[15] The Persian type with its heavier build and Roman nose is quite unlike the Greek types, which are lighter and have a concave profile.[16] It may be an example of the famous "Nisean" breed, well known from literature.[17]

12. Engels (1980) 127.
13. *AGH* 11.
14. Moore (1968) 357–68.
15. Afshar and Lerner (1979) 44–47.
16. *AGH* pl. 8, 39.
17. Ibid., 22, 27, 31; Hdt. 3.106; Strab. 5.525.

Irrespective of the uncertainty about the types of Greek horses, there is some information about how cavalry horses were kept, at least in Attica. The main source is Xenophon, whose information may be somewhat idealized but is still useful. As suggested by the lead tablets from the cavalry archive I mentioned above, many—if not most—Athenian cavalry horses were imported from Macedon, Thessaly, Corinth, and Sicyon. No evidence of stud farms in these areas survives, but in the case of Thessaly coinage depicting broodmares and foals is suggestive. Like most things to which the Greeks turned their attention, their stable management was well organized and sophisticated. The scale of operations in Athens was small, however, and each cavalryman was responsible for his own horse. Perhaps as early as the mid-fifth century Athens was contributing to the support of the cavalry, and by the end of the century, according to Xenophon, it was expending "nearly forty talents a year in order to have a cavalry force available for immediate use in the event of war."[18] M. Sage estimates that this amounts to a daily rate of one drachma per rider for grain. The cavalryman bore all other expenses, which could be considerable.[19] Xenophon says that some individuals lost money keeping horses, while others prospered through their sale.[20] Since the rich were obliged to keep cavalry horses, it was in their interest to do so efficiently and economically, as Xenophon recommends. Professionals were at hand to help—for a fee, of course. Trainers were hired to work with young horses, using methods that would not be out of place today: "Colts . . . learn to obey the horsebreaker by getting something they like when they are obedient, and suffering inconvenience when they are disobedient, until they carry out the horsebreaker's intentions."[21] Perhaps more surprising is the fact that Xenophon assigns blame for a vicious horse to the rider, a view that seems to have become more widely accepted only recently.[22]

Perhaps also surprisingly, the Athenian cavalryman kept his mount near his urban residence rather than on his country estate. For the sake of exercise, he would walk to his estate while the horse was led by a servant. After overseeing the farm work, he mounted his horse and practiced exercises useful for mounted military duties. Afterwards, the horse was led back to the

18. *Cav. Cmdr.* 1.19, quoted from Sage (1996) 51–52.
19. Thuc. 6.12.
20. Xen. *Oec.* 3.8–9.
21. Ibid., 13.7. All translations of Greek and Latin authors are taken from the Loeb Classical Library unless stated otherwise. Xen. On Hors. 2.2.
22. Xen. *Oec.* 3.11. See Twelveponies (1982).

city by the servant.²³ More detailed instructions for training cavalry horses are found in Xenophon's *On Horsemanship*.²⁴ Obviously, much of this represents Xenophon's advice for maintaining a high level of cavalry performance that in reality left something to be desired. His humane training methods required time and patience, and in their absence harsher methods must have been used as they have been throughout history. Simple carelessness was also a problem. The Athenian government made provision for this by having the council examine war-horses to insure good condition and withdraw the fodder supplement in cases of negligence.²⁵ A more specific example of carelessness comes from Sparta at the time of the battle of Leuctra in 371. Xenophon reports that "the Spartan cavalry at this period was of the poorest quality. The rich raised the horses. But it was only at call up that the assigned cavalryman appeared. Receiving his horse and whatever arms were available the trooper took to the field immediately. The least physically capable and those without ambition found their way into the cavalry."²⁶ In contrast the Boeotian cavalry were well trained by virtue of their recent campaigns in Orchomenus and Thespiae. In this case poor battlefield performance was determined by lack of preparation beforehand, the very thing Xenophon was trying to prevent at Athens with his equestrian treatises.

Although detailed evidence is lacking, it is clear that in places more suitable for raising horses, breeding was on a much larger scale. A passing reference by Justin in a description of one of Philip's northern campaigns suggests just how large an operation horse breeding in Macedon may have been. In 339 B.C. Philip defeated the Scythians and seized much booty, including twenty thousand well-bred mares that were sent to Macedon for breeding purposes. Unless they were sent on ahead, however, they may not have arrived, as in a clash with the Treballians on the route south he lost much of the booty.²⁷

The only other original source of information on horse care from this period is Aristotle's *History of Animals*. While his comments on horse breeding and the development of the young animals are quite accurate, the brief account of horse diseases is fanciful.²⁸ The former appears to be the kind of

---

23. Xen. *On Hors.* 4.1; Xen. Oec. 11.15–18.
24. Xen. *On Hors*.3.7–8.
25. Arist. *Const.* 49.1; Sage (1996) 52.
26. Xen. *Hell.* 6.4.11. Sage trans. (1996) 139.
27. Justin 9.2. The Latin for *well-bred* here is "nobilis," a term used by Ovid for racehorses. Ov. *Amor.* 3.2.1.
28. Arist. *Hist. An.* 6.22 on breeding, 7.24 on disease.

factual knowledge possessed by professional breeders and is similar to later accounts in Roman agricultural and veterinary writers such as Columella.[29] Given the fact that Aristotle's father was a physician, it seems strange that his comments on horse diseases and treatment are so sketchy and inaccurate. Presumably, much is attributable to his sources, but at least his emphasis on the normal rather than the pathological is consistent with his position as the founder of the natural-history tradition of Western science.

Quite a lot is known about the accoutrements of Greek horses, although in the case of certain articles it is uncertain how consistently they were employed. Most important for the control of the horse and essential for its use in war is the bit, which is held in place by the bridle. If, as Anderson claims, the perforated tongue buckle was unknown in Greek times, the bridle would not have been easily adjustable and would have to have been fitted to each horse.[30] On the other hand, buckles are listed among items of harness on tablets from the Near East during the second millennium, and Connolly shows a buckle on a piece of body armor that is now in the British Museum.[31] Although P. Connolly does not give a date for it, the context of his discussion is Greek.[32] The Pazyryk tombs, containing saddles and bridles preserved by freezing, suggest what was possible. Although the bridles had no buckles, they were capable of adjustment by means of knots, slits in the straps, and loops. Girth straps, on the other hand, did possess buckles made of horn.[33]

The normal bit was the snaffle, of which many varieties are known. In its simple form this consisted of a single bar of metal or two shorter pieces (cannons) joined in the middle by loose rings. To prevent the bit from sliding sideways in the horse's mouth, sidebars or cheekpieces were attached at right angles to the bit. The jointed snaffle is a very common bit today, and in its simple form is also the mildest. For this reason it was seldom used alone in recent times by cavalry, since it was incapable of providing secure control in an emergency situation.[34] A more severe curb bit was joined to the snaffle, and four reins were used. Under most conditions the horse was controlled by the snaffle, while the curb—which if over used could deaden the horse's mouth—was reserved for critical situations. This curb bit, apparently a Celtic innovation, did not appear in Greece until the third century B.C. It adds a

    29. Columela *Agr.* 6.26–36.
    30. *AGH* 43, 57, 59.
    31. Dalley (1984) 162–63.
    32. *GRW* 55.
    33. Rudenko (1970) 120–25, fig. 124; on buckles: 131, pl. 94f.
    34. Hope and Jackson (1973) 42; Clabby (1976) 99.

chain or bar that fits beneath the lower jaw in the chin groove. This gives the rider considerably more leverage, the degree of which can be controlled by the length of the sidebar (in effect, a lever) to which the reins are attached.[35]

In order to improve the effectiveness of the snaffle, the Greeks resorted to two devices used earlier in the Near East. The first of these is the studded cheekpiece, perhaps developed to improve the directional control of chariot horses. The cheekpiece, placed at the outside of the bit on one or both sides as needed, had spikes or bristles facing inward against the cheek, thus influencing the horse's lateral movement. Severity was controlled by the length and sharpness of the protrusions.[36] The second and potentially more severe device, which seems to have been the preferred method of controlling forward motion during the Classical and early Hellenistic periods, included sharp-edged disks and spiked rollers on the mouthpiece itself. Once again, the design of the individual pieces—not to mention the way in which it was used by the rider—determined the severity of the bit. There is no doubt that at times it was used cruelly. Dio Chrysostom, relating an anecdote about the famous painter Apelles, a contemporary of Alexander, describes the difficulty the painter had depicting the bloody froth around the mouth of a war-horse that resulted from a "cruel" bit.[37]

On the other hand, Xenophon advises against such harshness, preferring persuasion to force.[38] Furthermore, since Xenophon recommends a loose rein rather than the light but constant contact with the horse's mouth favored by modern riders, the effect need not have been invariably harsh.[39] Doubtless practices varied from rider to rider. Xenophon's admirably high level of horsemanship may well have been exceptional. It should be noted that the loose rein would have avoided the problem of overcontrol and could have been useful when riding at speed over the abundant rocky terrain in Greece.[40] In combat, however, the average cavalryman probably found the severe bits necessary for control.

Compounding the problem of control for the Greeks is the fact that they probably rode stallions, which are regularly depicted in their art. The precise relationship between the reality and the artistic representation is unknown, however. The flashiness and carriage of stallions lend themselves to display,

35. *AGH* 53, pl. 34d.
36. *AGH* pl. 21, 22.
37. Dio. Chrys. 63.5.
38. Xen. *On Hors.* 10.1; 12.
39. Ibid., 10.3.
40. *HH* 228.

but in combat other qualities are desirable, such as amenability and consistency of behavior. The Scythians also admired stallions, but purportedly rode geldings into battle.[41] Anderson suggests that gelding, which Xenophon approved, was not practiced by the Greeks because of the danger of infection.[42] That may not have been the case, however, since the pathogens that cause postoperative wound infection are not ubiquitous in nature but rather have become common in recent centuries in environments created by human activity such as dissection in hospitals. Group castrations of domestic animals are performed today in the open on a bedding of clean straw without serious risk of infection. Even if by accident a portion of intestine comes out and touches the straw, it is washed in sterile water, reinserted, and sewn up, normally without complication.[43] The Greek stallions may also have been more manageable if the quantity and quality of food used in more recent times was not available to them.

As I have mentioned, treed saddles and stirrups were unknown in antiquity.[44] In their place ancient riders sometimes used saddle pads or saddlecloths. Aside from any decorative effect, pads would have cushioned the back of a horse with a prominent backbone. Treed saddles are designed to avoid this problem by leaving space above the backbone. Whether this was a serious problem in antiquity is unknown, as the exact conformation of ancient horses is unclear. Xenophon does at least acknowledge the problem and recommends choosing a horse with a "double back" (ῥάχις διπλῆ) for a softer ride.[45] This must refer to a horse with a recessed backbone and enough muscle on either side to keep the human pelvic bone from resting on the horse's spine. In this respect the ancient horse appears to have been easier to ride bareback than today's thoroughbred. The ancient horse was generally smaller and narrower, making it easier for the rider to support himself with his thighs.[46] It also appears to have had less prominent withers and backbone.

Although the Assyrians had used them earlier, there is no clear evidence concerning whether the Greeks preferred to ride with or without saddle pads in spite of their appearance on many works of art. They are thought to be an

---

41. Pliny *HN*. 8.165; Strabo. 7.4.8.
42. *AGH* 38; Xen. *Cyr*. 7.5.62.
43. Personal communication from Peter Fretz, former head of the Department of Veterinary Anesthesiology, Radiology, and Surgery, Western College of Veterinary Medicine, University of Saskatchewan.
44. See the introduction, 00–00.
45. Xen. *On Hors*. 1.11; see also Verg. *G*. 3.87, "duplex agitur per lumbos spina," and Ovid *Met*. 12. 401, "tergum sessile," a back fit for sitting on.
46. Xen. *On Hors*. 7.5.

example of Eastern influence, though the Greeks in Sicily were familiar with saddlecloths by the sixth century at the latest.[47] Xenophon mentions riding bareback as well as with a saddlecloth without stating a clear preference, and he criticizes the Persians for using more coverings on their horses than on their beds, showing a greater care for comfort than for horsemanship.[48] Nevertheless, when he is writing about protecting horses with armor, he implies that a saddlecloth will be used.[49] The fact that the Greeks wore no trousers may have been an advantage, for "the human skin, provided it was hardened by practice, gives a good grip on the horse's sides, particularly when both are slightly sweaty."[50] It seems safe to say that whether or not cavalry horses were ridden with saddlecloths was of little practical importance; it is impossible to say whether the horse's back or the rider's stability would have benefited more from their use. In general a rider's control over the horse had higher priority than his comfort, an example of good sense which would perhaps have less appeal today.

As true horseshoes were not invented until the time of the Roman Empire, apparently by the Celts, they can be ignored.[51] Although excessive use of unshod horses, especially on rocky terrain, would lead to lameness (as happened to Athenian cavalry horses in 413 when the horsemen were constantly in action warding off Spartan raids from Deceleia), the hot, dry summer climate of the Mediterranean region would condition the hooves naturally, and it is obvious that the lack of horseshoes did not unduly limit the use of the horse in war.[52]

Armor for both man and horse did exist, its use going back at least to the ninth century B.C. in the Near East. As is frequently the case, it is a matter of determining how regularly and at what period it was employed. Bronze armor for the horse was quite limited, consisting primarily of the chamfron (a face piece), the poitrel (that is to say, pectoral or breast armor), and, occasionally, sidepieces used to protect the horse's flanks and the lower legs of the rider. The sidepieces may have been padded cloth rather than bronze, however. It appears doubtful that these sidepieces saw much use in spite of Xenophon's recommendation, as they appear only on a few monuments from

---

47. Szeliga (1983) 545–47.
48. Xen. *Cyr.* 8.8.19.
49. Xen. *On Hors.* 12.8.
50. *HH* 78.
51. Junkelmann (1990–92) 3: 96; Dixon and Southern (1992) 232–33.
52. *HH* 300; Thuc. 7.27.5.

the fourth century.[53] The Greek cavalryman was normally equipped with a helmet and breastplate and probably high boots but usually no shield.[54] Because it offers the greatest protection without interfering with vision, Xenophon recommends the Boeotian helmet. The breastplate should be shaped to allow sitting and have flaps along the lower edge. The left or rein hand is to be protected by what later would be called a gauntlet, a piece of armor extending from the shoulder to the fingers. Little evidence in art or in other literature exists that this piece was actually used.[55]

The principal offensive weapon was the spear, either the lance for thrusting or one or two javelins for throwing. During the fifth and early fourth centuries the javelin seems to have been the weapon preferred by cavalry. A sword was usually worn at the waist. Xenophon's favorite type was the Persian cutting sabre, whose stroke he preferred to that of the sword.[56] It should be remembered, however, that Xenophon had had much experience among the Persians, and his open-mindedness and willingness to adopt foreign weapons was not typical.

In general Xenophon preferred the javelin to the spear and suggested that it be thrown from the farthest effective range. He recommends carrying two of the shorter Persian javelins of cornel wood, one to be hurled from a distance and the other kept for close combat.[57] Since the Persian weapon is shorter and stronger than the Greek spear, it can be used effectively in close fighting to front, back, and both sides. It too does not seem to have been adopted by the Greeks, however, as Greek cavalry spears of the early fourth century continued to be longer than Persian javelins.

Although no verbal description of Greek cavalry fighting exists prior to the *Histories* of Herodotus, the depiction of mounted warriors in art coupled with our knowledge of weapons and accoutrements allows us to suggest what the cavalryman was capable of doing in battle. The figured evidence, supported later by the testimony of Xenophon, implies that firm control of the horse was of the utmost importance. This is not as obvious as it might appear

---

53. Xen. *On Hors.* 12.8; *AGH* 149, pl. 13a; *GRW* 73; *CCG* 64–65.
54. *CCG* 60–65.
55. Xen. *On Hors.* 12.3–5.
56. Ibid., 12.11. The Persian κοπίς (apparently the same as the Greek μάχαιρα) and the Greek ξίφος. Greek weapons terminology is admittedly confusing. Here, since the Greek two-edged sword could be used for slashing as well as thrusting, Xenophon's preference is presumably based on the greater effectiveness of the curved, single-edged sabre. It is difficult for a cavalryman to stab with his sword and then withdraw it from his victim's body. For swords and sabres, see *GRW* 63, 98.
57. Xen. *On Hors.* 12.12–13.

at first glance. For example, the mounted archer of the steppe, who required both hands for shooting the bow, rode at an extended gallop on a loose rein with little directional control of the horse except for that which he could achieve with his legs. A horse moving at a gallop with his body extended is not well prepared for a sudden change of direction. In the case of the Greeks, however, the figured evidence consistently shows the horses in a "collected" state—that is, well under the rider's control, with the hocks (hind legs) under the body and the forehand (front legs) lightened. Furthermore, the horses are often shown with the head held high, a position that discourages rapid forward movement, which requires extension of the head and neck. Xenophon favors a horse that holds its head high, as it will thus be least able to run away and will also protect the rider with its neck.[58] That riders practiced collection was certain. Xenophon's testimony aside, it is too realistic to have been invented by the artist, unlike the "flying gallop" that is found as early as the Late Bronze Age in Egypt and was common in European art until the last century, when slow-motion photography showed it to be an impossibility.[59] It is possible, however, that collection is somewhat exaggerated in Greek art as an ideal of equine beauty. The collected prancing horses portrayed by the Greeks are clearly on display, and it is probable that they represent a refined, ideal example of what was practiced in combat.[60]

A well-controlled, collected horse is useful for most functions of cavalry. The horse can stop and start quickly, reverse itself, back up, change direction, stand still, and charge at a controlled canter. Charging at a controlled pace is essential if cohesion in the formation is to be maintained. Charging at an all-out gallop may be a spectacular sight, but it quickly becomes a horse race.[61] The rocky terrain of Greece also placed a premium on collection and control, whereas the open plains of the Near East and Asia proved more suitable for galloping and archery. Greek horses, of course, did gallop. Horse races were popular, and the bronze horse with its jockey that was found early in the twentieth century off Cape Artemisium clearly shows the extended position necessary for racing at speed.[62] Military horses would certainly have been capable of galloping when circumstances required, and collection could then

---

58. Ibid., 1.8.
59. Collection existed prior to the Greeks among the Egyptians, where it is found in paintings of chariot horses. See Hansen (1992) 173–79.
60. Xen. *On Hors.* 11.1, 8, 10–12.
61. Keegan (1977) 147–50. Keegan's analysis of the role of cavalry is a necessary corrective to many romantic fictions associated with this arm.
62. Ling (1984) *CAH* pl. to vol. 7, part 1; pl 189. The horse exhibits the "flying gallop."

have been abandoned. Yet, according to Xenophon, even under these conditions control is essential: "It is likewise necessary to know whether, when going at full speed he can be pulled up sharp, and whether he turns readily."[63]

This type of management of the ridden horse accords well with what we have learned of Greek cavalry fighting from later literary sources. Cavalry action generally followed one of two scenarios. The riders could move at a controlled pace against the enemy infantry or cavalry, then halt, launch their javelins, wheel, and gallop away.[64] Or, instead of retiring after hurling one javelin, they could close with the enemy, using the second javelin for over- or underhand thrusting and ultimately resorting to the sword if necessary. The spear was also very useful in pursuit of a fleeing enemy.

---

63. Xen. *On Hors.* 3.5.

64. This tactical method is identical to the caracole of European armies of the sixteenth and seventeenth centuries, with the pistol substituted for the javelin. In the 1630s, furthermore, Gustavus Adolphus demonstrated the superiority of shock tactics when he reintroduced the charge by cavalry carrying lance and sword. Although Gustavus Adolphus took the idea from Polish cavalry, he was in effect duplicating the Macedonian tactics, which took advantage of the inherent moral superiority of close combat over fighting at a distance. As a psychological principle it still applies, but in recent centuries weapons technology in the form of rapid-fire weapons made the horseman too vulnerable to permit these tactics.

Chapter 2

Horse-Drawn Chariots in the Near East and Greece during the Late Bronze Age: Circa 1550 to 1200 B.C.

ON THE BASIS OF EVIDENCE that will likely remain incomplete, it appears that the horse was domesticated at least as early as the late fifth and early fourth millennium B.C. on the Ukrainian steppe. Presumably, it was initially raised for food by humans who had already domesticated cattle, sheep, and pigs for that purpose. Indeed, at the Sredni Stog site of Dereivka it has been estimated that over half of the meat consumed came from horses.[1] Recent examination of the osteological evidence from this site also suggests that the practice of riding occurred there around 4000 B.C., which is earlier than hitherto realized. Although this claim rests upon clear proof only that a bit was used on a seven- or eight-year-old stallion, it is a valid conclusion, since the wheel does not appear until after 3500 B.C. It thus seems reasonable to suggest that on open grasslands the horses were tended by riders rather than herders on foot, for it has been observed that whenever boys have been entrusted with the care of horse herds they have always shown a skill at riding their charges bareback as though it were second nature to them. Furthermore, changes in the Sredni Stog society that occurred after this time find a "unified explanation" in riding. Anthony describes these changes as "increased household size, individual-centered mortuary rituals, increased social differentiation, intensified warfare, territorial expansion, and increased exchange in exotic prestige goods."[2] Given the dearth of information from this early period, nothing can be said about the military use of the horse. The earliest infor-

---

1. Anthony (1991), in Meadow and Uerpmann 2: 261, 263; Piggott (1983) 87; Moorey (1986) 197–98.
2. Anthony (1991) 2: 265, 267–69.

mation of that sort comes from the Near East after 2500 B.C., since it was only then that the horse first appeared in Mesopotamia.[3]

A particularly interesting piece of evidence appears on a Proto-Elamite tablet of the early third millennium that was found near Kashan, Iran (ca. two hundred kilometers south of Teheran). This tablet, found among a collection of accounts, contains depictions of horse heads and numerical symbols. Different classes of horses are identified by various treatments of the mane. V. Scheit, in the original publication, suggested that a horse head with an upright mane represents a stallion, one with a pendant mane a mare, and one without a mane a foal.[4] In spite of W. Amschler's efforts to interpret this document as a breeding pedigree, with the three types of horse heads representing respectively wild stallions, domestic stallions, and mares,[5] the exclusively economic context of the find as a whole and the difficulty of interpreting the symbols argue against this.[6] One other tablet in the collection (#124) contains a single horse head in the midst of much else, while several tablets contain lists of goats, sheep, and cattle.

Clear evidence for the presence of the domestic horse in Mesopotamia was discovered in 1992 north of Damascus in the form of a small, highly detailed clay figurine. Although only five by three inches, it was skillfully modeled, especially with respect to the mane, which lies upon the neck. A hole bored through the muzzle shows that it was equipped with bit and bridle. It was probably a chariot horse, since it was found with models of chariots.[7]

Although earlier scholars were convinced that Indo-Europeans introduced the horse into the Near East, recent evidence from a number of sites throughout the region offers little evidence for assigning priority to any single ethnic or linguistic group in this regard. The Proto-Elamite tablets cited above do not represent an Indo-European language. By the early second millennium, as S. Dalley has pointed pointed out, "there is no longer any doubt that horses were bred, trained, traded and used for a variety of purposes."[8] Her evidence comes from tablets found at Mari, Karana, and Chagar Bazar, to which may now be added Tell Atchana (Alalakh).[9] The peoples associated with the horse in this setting are Amorites and Assyrians. It is clear that the

---

3. Moorey (1986) 198; Zarins (1986), in Meadow and Uerpmann 1: 164, 189.
4. Scheit (1973) 17: 15, tab. 105.
5. Amschler (1935) 233–38.
6. Edwards, Gadd, and Hammond (1971) 1, part 2: 676.
7. *Biblical Archaeology Review* 19, no. 4 (July/August 1993) 16.
8. Dalley (1984) 159.
9. Moorey (1986) 198.

horses were harnessed as teams and possibly ridden, as well as that they performed a variety of tasks including the rapid delivery of small items and the drawing of small wheeled vehicles in religious processions. Mention is also made in the tablets of trainers, grooms, stables, fodder, and harness, including reins and blinkers, evincing an already highly developed stage of equine management. The colors red and white are mentioned for horses' coats. The earliest method of controlling harnessed horses was by means of a nose ring, to which a pair of reins was attached. Figured evidence of riding also shows the nose ring, as well as a seat that is too far back over the loins to be very effective. Notable in these texts is the mention of "pairs of buckles."[10] It would be helpful to know precisely what is meant by this term, as perforated tongue buckles have not been thought to exist until much later.[11] Without buckles it would have been necessary to use knots to adjust halters and bridles intended for more than one horse.

None of this evidence from the early second millennium gives unambiguous proof of the use of horse-drawn war chariots. This particular *argumentum ex silentio* is weak, because it is clear that the Sumerians employed war chariots drawn by wild asses, or onagers, from at least the middle part of the third millennium. These chariots were heavy four-wheeled vehicles that carried two men—a driver and a javelin thrower—and were equipped with a quiver containing additional javelins. They appear prominently on the "Standard of Ur," apparently a display piece from circa 2550 B.C.[12]

The evidence of the texts also suggests that horses were imported into Mesopotamia from the west, from Syria and Anatolia, rather than from the east. In any case the introduction of the horse and subsequently of the war chariot were not sudden events that may be attributed to an intrusive people. The development of the light horse-drawn war chariot occurred during the early centuries of the second millennium. The unanswered question is whether it developed within the confines of the Near East through the efforts of the resident peoples or was introduced from the north and east, the land of the steppe nomads, who had a longer familiarity with the horse. In past discussions of this subject, M. A. Littauer and Crouwel favored internal development, while S. Piggott argued that the chariot was introduced from the north.[13] In an article that reviews the evidence used to support these two

---

10. Dalley (1984) 162–63.
11. Anderson (1961) 43, 57, 59.
12. Groenewegen-Frankfort and Ashmole (1972) 82, pl. 11.
13. Littauer and Crouwel (1979) 70, 99–100; Piggott (1983) 241–42.

hypotheses, P. R. S. Moorey suggests that the information to be gleaned from archaeological finds, artistic representations, and the texts is inconclusive. He does, however, hint at a third possibility that represents a synthesis of the other two. Piggott suggested that the bent-wood technology necessary for making the light fellies of the chariot wheels was invented on the steppe, but it does not inevitably follow that the chariot was also developed there. Perhaps only the new technology was brought south into Mesopotamia and Anatolia. Nonetheless, the latest finds from Russia suggest that a two-horse chariot was in use among Scythians in the North Caucasus around 2026 B.C.[14] Even if the chariot was developed in the north, however, its function there is uncertain, and a recent appraisal by Littauer and Crouwel suggests that it was a prestige vehicle insufficiently maneuverable for either war or racing.[15] Thus it seems likely that the refined tactical use of the war chariot appeared first in the Near East.[16] At the least it is clear that light carts and chariots made their appearance at approximately the same time (ca. 2000 B.C.) over wide stretches of Europe, Western Asia, and the Near East.

It is to the Near East, however, that we must direct our attention in order to understand the historical role played by the war chariot. By the sixteenth century B.C. at the latest it was being employed throughout the eastern Mediterranean. It was known to the Hittites by the late eighteenth century,[17] appeared in Egypt with the Hyksos about the same time,[18] and is portrayed on a limestone stele from Shaft Grave V at Mycenae dated to the sixteenth century.[19]

Although the chariot was employed in war during the Middle Bronze Age, it is not until the Late Bronze Age that one finds clear evidence showing how it was used. This evidence appears on the monumental reliefs set up in Egyptian temples by the great pharaohs of the New Kingdom, especially Rameses II, who was able, by means of this artistic stratagem, to snatch victory from the jaws of defeat at the battle of Kadesh, circa 1286 B.C. In Egyptian chariot tactics, missile weapons seem to have been used exclusively, the principal weapon being the composite bow, with some use of javelins as well.[20] The war chariot was in effect a fast and maneuverable firing platform

---

14. Petrenko (1995), in Davis-Kimball, Bashilov, and Yablonsky, 22.
15. Littauer and Crouwel (1996) 939.
16. Moorey (1986) 203.
17. Wiesner (1968) 80.
18. Gardiner (1969) 171. Besides the horse and chariot, the Hyksos also seem to have introduced the composite bow that is so often found on Egyptian monuments.
19. Wace and Stubbings (1962) pl. 33.
20. Littauer and Crouwel (1979) 91. Shaw (1991) 39–42.

that could be used for a variety of purposes, provided that the terrain was suitable—that is, level and unencumbered. Aside from the noncombat roles of carrying messages and small numbers of important persons, when used in some numbers the war chariot could intimidate and upset infantry, deal with other chariot forces, pursue retreating enemies, protect and serve as scouts for armies on the march, and likely perform other duties that we are no longer able to appreciate. Battle scenes from the monuments show light two-man chariots equipped with bow cases and one or more quivers. One scene on a painted box shows Tutankhamen shooting his bow from a moving chariot, supplied with arrows from three quivers.[21] In any lengthy battle the supply of arrows would have been critical, especially if—as has been claimed—the Egyptians knew the principles of firing in volleys.[22] Recent excavations at Rameses II's capital of Pi-Ramses in northern Egypt have brought to light a huge stone stable capable of housing four hundred horses, further evidence of the importance of chariotry at this time.[23]

Egypt's most powerful enemy in the thirteenth century B.C. was the Hittite Empire of central and eastern Anatolia. The war chariot was no less important among the Hittites there, but our understanding of their tactics is much less clear. The two-horse chariot of the Hittites appears to have been essentially the same as that of the Egyptians, although—holding three men instead of two—it may have been of sturdier construction. In addition to the normal Egyptian complement of driver and fighter, the Hittite chariot also carried a shield bearer whose task apparently was to protect the fighter. Difficulty arises when one attempts to identify the weapons used by the fighter. The bow, the lance, and the javelin have all been suggested, either to the exclusion of the other two or in combination with one of them.[24] The problem in identification arises because the large numbers of Hittite chariot fighters depicted on Egyptian monuments (virtually the sole source of figured evidence for the Hittites) are rarely shown carrying weapons. Spears are found in upright positions in several instances, but whether they were intended for thrusting or throwing is not clear. Some figures have their arms raised above

21. Desroches-Noblecourt (1963) pl. xvii-b, 81.
22. Breasted (1912) 234.
23. News release, Agence France-Presse, Cairo, October 14, 1999.
24. The following are in favor of the thrusting lance: Greenhalgh (1973) 10, Macqueen (1986) 58; the lance and bow: Gurney (1954) 106; and the javelin: Littauer (1972) 147. Beal (1992) 149, who sensibly acknowledges the uncertainty in the sources, writes: "Some of these three man Hittite chariots are shown with one of the crew carrying spears/lances/javelins that appear from the reliefs to have been some seven or eight feet long."

their heads as if they are about to hurl a javelin, but the weapon is missing. The absence of Hittite weapons may reflect Egyptian propaganda, showing an enemy who has abandoned its weapons in flight before the victorious pharaoh. Perhaps even stranger is the lack of any receptacles for weapons on the Hittite chariots, whereas bow cases and quivers are standard on the Egyptian vehicles. On the Kadesh relief of Rameses II on Pylon I at Luxor, some Hittite chariots do indeed have bow cases. Careful examination of the relief, however, shows that the scene containing Hittite chariots had originally portrayed Egyptian chariots but that when it was recut only the human figures, not the chariots, were altered to fit the Hittite type.[25]

On the other hand, Egyptian textual accounts of the battle of Kadesh do suggest that the Hittite forces used missile weapons, as the following quotation from *The Poem* demonstrates: "all their [that is, the Hittites'] arms were weak, and they were unable to shoot. They found not their hearts to seize their javelins. . . . they [the Hittites] were three men in a chariot and they were equipped with all weapons of war."[26] Elsewhere in *The Poem* there are references to the use of bows against the pharaoh, but whether by chariotry or infantry is not clear. For reasons to be discussed below, it seems unlikely that a thrusting lance can be wielded successfully from a moving chariot, thus making it probable that the Hittite chariots carried javelin throwers and archers.

In spite of the difficulties in identifying Hittite weapons and tactics, there is no doubt that chariotry was an important military arm. Implicit in this statement is the fact that chariot forces require a great deal of preparation and training. The archaeologists and philologists have provided us with a document that demonstrates an unexpectedly high level of sophistication in the management and training of chariot horses. This text is attributed to a certain Kikkuli, a horse trainer from the land of Mitanni. It is not an original work but stands, rather, at the end of a period of development and seems to be the product of several Hurrian compilers. The Kikkuli Text, dated to the fourteenth century,[27] is an interesting document, not only because of what it tells us about horse training at this early date but also because it is evidence of a mentality that developed a lengthy, well-thought-out procedure (presumably based on experience) for achieving a specific goal—well-trained and

---

25. Wreszinski (1935) 2: pl. 84.
26. Gardiner (1975) 10, 11, 135–39.
27. Kammenhuber (1961) 6–7.

well-conditioned chariot horses. In this respect it is reminiscent of the later military treatises of the Greeks and Romans, with their emphasis on a comprehensive, calculated preparation for war.

The tablets contain details of a 184-day program that embraces all aspects of the care and training of chariot horses, including instructions for exercising the horses over varying distances at the trot and at the gallop, with chariot and without. Grooming and bathing are mentioned, cures and purges are prescribed, and the type and amount of fodder is indicated. Conditioning fodder consisted of barley and wheat, oats being conspicuously absent, and even in modern times oats are not found in Anatolia.[28] In classical Greece and Rome, too, barley rather than oats was the grain commonly fed to horses.[29] Some would see this as an oversight on the part of the ancients because of the common belief that oats have superior nutritive qualities, as implied in the phrase "to feel one's oats," which is expressed in the following statement: "With the riding horse, the amount should also relate to temperament, and the capabilities of its rider, as oats can have an alarmingly exhilarating effect on some horses. For this reason children's ponies should be fed no oats, or fed them very judiciously."[30] Recent research into the nutrition of the horse, however, shows that there is no appreciable difference among the various feed grains with respect to the type or amount of energy they provide when the comparison is based on weight. In practice, however, some differences might be noticed, since horses are often given grain portions based on volume. When that is the case, horses receiving oats would actually get less energy from the grain, because oats is lighter by volume than corn, for example, which is twice as dense and unlike oats, has no chaff.[31] Among the other procedures described in the *Kikkuli Text* are some that seem to have been intended to inure the animals to contrasts of heat and cold within short periods of time, thus lessening the horses' need for the care and grooming that would be more difficult to provide while they were on campaign.

When one turns to the use of the chariot in Greece and the Aegean during the Late Bronze Age (ca. 1600–1100 B.C.), significant differences are

---

28. Ibid., 308–12.
29. Anderson (1961) 93–94; Veg., *Mulo.* 1.56.10.
30. Edwards (1977) 181.
31. Lewis (1995) 70–77. This is consistent with my personal experience and the observations of equine veterinarians with whom I have talked. Nonetheless, feeding excessive amounts of any grain may have unwanted effects on horse behavior.

immediately obvious. The reason for this, long recognized by scholars, is the difficulty presented by the rough terrain to all users of wheeled vehicles on mainland Greece as well as on the islands.[32] In fact, until the introduction of the automobile in modern times the transport of goods in Greece was largely carried out by men on foot and pack animals, usually the ass and the mule. Thus it would have come as no surprise if little use had been made of chariots by the Mycenaean Greeks. Yet this is simply not the case, for records of several hundred chariots have been found on the Linear B tablets, and frequent representations of them on wall paintings and elsewhere leave no doubt of their importance. Only actual finds of the chariots themselves, such as have turned up in Egypt, are missing.

Had it not been for the great amount of information available on the military use of chariots in the Near East, the evidence from Greece would perhaps have been allowed to speak for itself. Instead, in spite of Homer's description of chariots as vehicles for transporting armed foot soldiers to and from the battlefield, their obvious importance has suggested the idea that they had a notable military use. This is the argument of P. A. L. Greenhalgh, who believes it is "a sound conjecture" (admittedly unsupported by direct evidence) that the "Mycenaeans used massed chariots in the manner of the Hittites" (that is, armed with "long thrusting-spears, apparently about seven feet long").[33]

Greenhalgh supplemented this position in an article published in 1980 in which he attempts to identify the function of a bronze panoply found in Chamber Tomb 12 at Dendra, dating from the late fifteenth century B.C.[34] This widely published find from 1960 consists of bronze plates that would have covered a warrior from his neck to his lower body. Linear B texts from Knossos show this or a similar type of armor on tablets that also contain chariot signs. Because of this, A. M. Snodgrass suggests that the armor may have been made for chariot warriors.[35] Greenhalgh develops his thesis as a support for his idea that the Mycenaean warriors fought from their chariots. Because of the protection that the Dendra panoply afforded the whole body, he believes that it was intended for use without a

---

32. Crouwel (1981) 147–48; Palmer (1965) 194. See Hom., *Od.* 4.601–608, where Telemachus declines a gift of horses from Menelaus because Ithaca is unfit for driving horses.
33. Greenhalgh (1973) 10.
34. Greenhalgh (1980), 201–205. For typical criticism of Homer see Garlan (1975) 118; Keegan and Holmes (1986) 77. For a description of this armor see Snodgrass (1967) 24–25.
35. Ibid., 25.

shield. And since chariot-borne warriors in Mycenaean art appear without shields, full armor would be useful. Greenhalgh further argues that the panoply is too heavy to be used on foot. Nevertheless, this argument remains weak. There is no way of knowing how common such armor was, and it does not turn up on Mycenaean art—the dendra specimen is unique. Even its weight offers inconclusive evidence regarding its use. In the Middle Ages, for example, men-at-arms in full armor (ca. sixty pounds) frequently fought on foot, as they did on both sides at Agincourt in 1415.[36] Comparison with the Hittites is also of little use, since no firm evidence for their chariot tactics exists.

In recent years vigorous criticism has been directed against Greenhalgh's views and even earlier some scholars questioned the analogy with the use of chariots in the Near East.[37] A primary reason for questioning the military value of chariots in Greece, as I have already mentioned, is the terrain. Greece and Crete simply do not possess the open spaces necessary for chariot driving.[38] Now that clear evidence of Mycenaean roads has come to light, it is obvious that the Mycenaeans themselves addressed the problem. There is little doubt that their roads were built for wheeled vehicles. The slight gradient up and down hills and the broad curves that the roads exhibit are unnecessary for pack animals. As wide as 3.5 meters, these highways were supported in places by retaining walls up to 4 meters high and corbeled culverts and bridges, all in Cyclopean masonry. A network of them radiated out from Mycenae. Crouwel suggests that the roads had the primarily military function of moving warriors and equipment at speed in mountainous country.[39]

Crouwel's reminder that the comparison of ancient chariots and modern tanks is a false analogy is relevant here.[40] The tank is an all-terrain vehicle capable of overrunning objects in its path with little or no damage to itself. The chariot, on the other hand, requires level, open country if it or the team of horses drawing it is not to be disabled by striking even slight objects. One should also be careful about using the term *shock tactics*. Neither chariotry nor cavalry was capable of striking a steadfast enemy without suffering irreparable damage to themselves. In all likelihood the shock

---

36. Keegan (1977) 88–95.
37. Wiesner (1968) 95–96. Wiesner accepts the Homeric version as essentially correct.
38. Palmer (1965) 194; Chadwick (1976) 164; Snodgrass (1967) 20.
39. Crouwel (1981) 30–31.
40. Ibid., 145.

they directed against an enemy was psychological or moral rather than physical.[41]

Since there is no evidence that the bow was used from chariots in Greece, the sword was too short to be effective, and head-to-head physical shock was too destructive and wasteful, what tactics remain? There is little evidence that the javelin was used as a missile in Greece, as it was in the Near East. That leaves the thrusting spear suggested by Greenhalgh. It is difficult, however, to understand how this weapon (estimated to have been seven to ten feet in length)[42] could have been used effectively from a moving chariot either against other chariots or against infantry. When two enemy chariots passed each other in opposite directions there would have been opportunity only for a glancing blow, as allowance must be made for the width of the chariot axle (approximately six feet), resulting in a wide angle between the forward direction of the chariot and the line of the thrust, and the effective shortening of the spear by as much of its length as was needed for the grip. Should one succeed in lodging the spear point in the body of an enemy, withdrawing it would appear to have been impossible, as the shaft would have been either broken off or torn out of the hands by the momentum of the passing chariots.[43] This assumes that a chariot-borne spearman could maintain his position in the chariot box at the moment of impact, which is highly unlikely as he would have had no support, short of grabbing the front of the box, to prevent himself from being thrust backward.

The Mycenaean vehicles also lacked some refinements normally found on Near Eastern chariots that would have contributed to battle worthiness. For example, the Egyptian chariot teams were controlled by reins passing through rings (terrets) fastened to the harness on the horses' backs. This apparently gave the driver more leverage and consequently more control. On Mycenaean chariots, however, the reins are portrayed as passing directly from the bridle to the hands of the driver. The Mycenaeans also failed to adopt the stronger six-spoked wheel, remaining content with the earlier four-spoked

---

41. Keegan (1977) 94–97, 146–61. At both Agincourt and Waterloo, Keegan found no evidence of collisions of cavalry against either other cavalry or infantry. Cavalry engagements usually devolved into hand-to-hand combat. The statement of General George S. Patton, Jr., comes to mind: "Very few people have ever been killed with the bayonet or the sabre, but the fear of having their guts explored with cold steel in the hands of battle-maddened men has won many a fight." Blumenson (1985) 153.

42. For arguments on its length as seven feet, see Greenhalgh (1973) 10; as ten feet, see Snodgrass (1967) 16–17.

43. Littauer and Crouwel (1983) 188–89. See also Anderson (1975) 175–87; Littauer (1972) 145–57; Crouwel (1981) 145, 147–49; Kilian (1982) 205–206.

variety. Finally, the Mycenaeans seem never to have adopted the rearward axle position of the eastern chariots, which provided more stability on turns when they were moving rapidly. In Greece the axle was placed beneath the center of the chariot box or only sightly to the rear. According to Crouwel, this axle position was suitable for smooth, level roads but would have allowed the chariot to pivot on its axle when used on rougher, unprepared natural terrain. The result would have been instability for the passengers and annoyance to the horses. Experiments by J. Spruytte using full-sized working replicas of ancient chariots suggest, however, that this is not necessarily the case. All seems to depend on the type of harness that was used by the Mycenaeans. If it was of the Egyptian type, with a neck yoke and no girth, the central axle position would have caused difficulties, because there would then have been no weight on the neck yoke to hold it in place. If, on the other hand, Mycenaean chariots had a dorsal yoke that was kept on the horses' backs by a girth, no problem existed. This was the method in use by the sixth century in Greece, and Spruytte's experiments demonstrate its effectiveness. Unfortunately, the figured evidence of the Late Bronze Age is ambiguous, giving no clear indication of the position of the yoke, whether in front of or behind the withers of the horse. On most examples the forward position seems likely, but the overall accuracy of the portrayals of horses and chariots does not inspire confidence. This may be why Spruytte ignored Mycenaean chariots in his study. In any case the centrally positioned axle is normal for slow-moving carts carrying seated passengers and heavier loads.[44]

The weight of evidence thus seems to be against the possibility that chariots in Late Bronze Age Greece were used as combat vehicles on the battlefield. Homer's description of events seems to be correct after all. The aristocratic warrior was an *apobates*; he rode to battle in a chariot, but leapt down to fight on foot with spear and, perhaps, sword. It is tempting to see a continuation of this practice in the games at the Panathenaia of the Classical period, part of which consisted of an armed warrior who jumped off a speeding chariot and continued the race on foot.[45] It should be noted that in the Middle Ages there was a direct analogy to this practice. Knights usually rode palfreys on the march because they had comfortable traveling gaits—the pace or rack, for example. The destrier, or charger, was led by a squire and not mounted until the man-at-arms was armed and ready to enter battle.

44. Crouwel (1981) 79; Spruytte (1983) 14, 40–49, 52–61.
45. Burkert (1985) 233.

Even if they played little role in battle, the importance of chariots to the aristocratic warrior cannot be doubted. In a hierarchical society they were symbols of his prestige and position, literally placing him above his inferiors—something that applied to cavalry to an even greater extent. The role of chariots in religious ceremonial in Greece was also important. Many centuries later among the Romans, though never appearing on the battlefield, the chariot bore the victorious general in triumph to the Temple of Jupiter on the Capitoline.

Chapter 3

Riding in the Near East and Greece: Late Bronze Age to 500 B.C.

ALTHOUGH THERE IS GOOD reason to believe that horseback riding was practiced in the Near East as early as the fifteenth century B.C., efficient use of armed riders is not attested to before the seventh century, when the Assyrians supplemented the war chariot with cavalry. Evidence of riding in Egypt during the fifteenth century has been found in the tomb of Sen Mut at Thebes, where a single horse burial appeared. Preserved along with the bones of the horse was what appeared to be a saddle cloth made of linen and sheepskin, complete with neck strap and girth.[1] The horse itself stood about fourteen hands high at the withers (56 inches, 140–145 cm.) and was of slender build. Similar horse remains from approximately the same time period have been found in Anatolia in a Hittite context.[2]

Some figured evidence also provides information about riding in this period, but its interpretation is difficult. Most representations of riders from the eastern Mediterranean dating from the Late Bronze Age and Early Iron Age show the rider using what is an awkward and comparatively inefficient seat on the horse. The rider's position, back over the loins of the horse, is the traditional donkey seat. This works very well for the donkey, which is smaller than the horse, has a different conformation, and travels at a much slower speed. It also alleviates the rider's fear of falling off over the head of the donkey. Quite the opposite is true for the larger, faster, higher stepping horse.[3] In this case balance is best achieved by a more forward position, and the

---

1. *WVRA* 97.
2. Powell (1971) 11-12. This height (fourteen hands) is common for riding horses.
3. *CLT* 47.

greater the speed the more forward the seat should be. There seems to be no way of showing whether this use of the donkey seat by eastern Mediterranean riders of horses reflects actual practice or artistic idiosyncrasy. Written descriptions of riding in the region do not turn up until many centuries later. It is unlikely that artists had personal knowledge of riding horses, so the adoption of the donkey seat in art may arise from a mental image of the way in which donkeys were in fact ridden. These smaller equids were a common sight in the ancient Near East, as they still are. Horses—at least ridden horses—were not, since they were most commonly used by the aristocracy to draw chariots.

On the other hand some of this early art work does show riders with what would today be considered an acceptable seat. There is, for example, a relief from Egyptian Thebes of the late fourteenth century that depicts two unarmed Hittite riders fleeing before Seti I.[4] These riders are clearly not using the donkey seat; their seat is more forward, though not as much so as would later become common. There is also an Egyptian wooden statuette now in the Metropolitan Museum of Art. In this piece the rider is in the middle of the horse's back, with his legs well forward.[5] If the neck of the horse were carved more accurately—that is, wider—this horseman's seat would be unexceptionable. Thus, it seems at least possible that the appearance of the donkey seat on the figured evidence results from artistic misconception. As late as the fifth century B.C., a Clazomenian sarcophagus depicts Scythian mounted warriors with a noticeably rearward seat, which at this date is obviously inaccurate.[6] As long as this artistic evidence remains open to a variety of interpretations, it seems a bit rash to attribute the slow development of cavalry in the Late Bronze Age to a lack of riding skills, as has been claimed.[7] In the absence of unambiguous data, uncertainty about early riding skills will remain.[8] It should be borne in mind, however, that at different places and times a variety of riding styles has been found acceptable, some inherently superior to others but all practiced with great skill among equestrian peoples in lands where riding began at an early age. Even today, in parts of the world where pack horses are used, a rider may be seen at the rear of the horse behind the pack. This nevertheless does little to help solve the problem of

---

4. Azzaroli (1985) 43.
5. Zeuner (1963) 320.
6. Rolle (1980) 80–91. See also 107 for an accurate portrayal of a Scythian rider.
7. *CLT* 50; *AGH* 12–13.
8. See Moorey (1970) 38–39, for some problems presented to a rider using the rearward seat.

the ancient practice, for pack animals move slowly and the rider stays in position easily by holding on to the load in front of him. The natural contours of the horse's back and the action of his hind quarters at faster gaits would make the rearward seat a hindrance to serious riding.

Although the Egyptian material is interesting, it is not until the early ninth century B.C. in Assyria that true mounted warriors make an appearance. The pictorial and documentary evidence of this allows a comparatively complete reconstruction of the development of military riding between the ninth and the seventh centuries.[9]

Before proceeding, however, a caveat is in order. We must not overestimate the importance of either cavalry or chariotry during the Assyrian period or earlier during the Late Bronze Age. Sieges rather than battles in the open were both more common and on average more significant simply because the capture of cities, which were usually fortified, was the key to political control.[10] Even when the Assyrians were victorious in field battles, a stubborn enemy might still have to be besieged. For rebels fighting the superior forces of the Assyrian government, taking refuge behind walls was a sensible strategy, since the longer the siege was protracted, the more likely it was that the Assyrians would have to divert troops to other trouble spots. Pitched battles occurred when there was war between major powers and coalitions and each side was sufficiently confident to risk a battle. At such times chariotry and cavalry, fighting alongside the infantry, could play a significant role. The equestrian arms were also of great use in mounting swift raids against less-powerful but troublesome neighbors such as the various nomads, among whom the Arabs appeared in the Near East outside of the Arabian peninsula for the first time.[11]

Although the evidence is incomplete and references to tactical details are lacking, a reasonably clear picture of the decline of chariotry and the rise of mounted warriors is possible. By the ninth century B.C. the appearance of mounted warriors (not simply mounted infantry) was commonly depicted on the monuments, although there is no evidence that mounted warriors were supplanting chariots. The technique of these early riders seems to have been adopted directly from the familiar method of chariot driving. Integrated teams of two men, a warrior and a squire, are depicted riding side by side, the squire holding the reins of both animals, which he apparently controls

---

9. My debt is primarily to *WVRA* 134–39, 142–43.
10. Ep'hal (1984), in Tadmor and Weinfeld, 88–106, esp. 92, 94, 97.
11. Ibid., 95.

even in battle. The warrior alone is armed with a bow, although the squire carries a small round shield in his left hand, holding the reins in his right hand. The warrior of necessity always rides the horse on the right, since that allows him room in which to wield a weapon with his right hand.[12]

This arrangement may appear rather awkward when one looks back from a period of more advanced horsemanship, but the sculptured evidence is clear. Indeed, it is not so strange when one recalls how well horses work together in teams. Assuming much practice and a high level of skill, horses trained side by side could be guided by one hand without particular difficulty. By training a team of horses and riders in this fashion, the archer would have been able to use both hands for shooting.

The bits and bridles of the ridden horses are identical to those of the chariot horses. The rearward seat over the horse's loins is still shown, and saddlecloths secured by girth and breastband occasionally appear. The saddlecloth would prevent the rider's clothing from being soiled by the horse's perspiration (about which the ancient horseman was perhaps less fastidious than modern riders), would provide a more comfortable ride on animals with prominent backbones, and would help prevent sores on the horse's back. However, it might not add much to the rider's stability since—unlike the rigid treed saddle of later times, which is kept in place by the horse's withers—the saddle cloth is apt to slip. At a later date Xenophon the Athenian criticized the Persians for "putting more coverlets on their horses than on their beds, for they think of sitting softly rather than securely."[13]

By the mid-eighth century B.C. the relief sculptures show riders with a more secure forward seat, and the textual evidence provides a glimpse of how these horsemen were employed. In addition to their role in pitched battles, whatever that may have been, they proved their worth in swift surprise attacks on Assyria's nomadic neighbors. In such cases the goal was to reach the enemy's camp before he could elude the attacking force. The sculptures of Tiglath-Pileser III (745–727) from the royal palace at Nimrud depict just such a campaign against the Arabs. Two mounted warriors are shown pursuing an Arab who is riding a camel, their spears poised overhead for a downward thrust. One of the warriors carries a sword at his waist. The seat of the two is well forward and a pad is used. Each rider controls his own horse, the practice of employing teams of horses and riders having been abandoned,

---

12. *AGH* pl. 36, from the Bronze Gates of Shalmaneser III (859–824 B.C.).
13. Xen. *Cyr.* 8.8.19.

which presumably reflects an improvement in horsemanship. The king himself, accompanied by two companions, shoots arrows from a chariot. Other reliefs from the same period portray Assyrian lancers overtaking Urartian (?) horsemen.[14]

Horses also proved to be most useful for surprise attacks in the mountains, where chariots could not travel. Sargon II claimed in a royal inscription that in 714, during his eighth campaign, he took only a single chariot but "1,000 fierce horsemen, bearers of bow, shield and lance" into the mountains against Musasir, southeast of Lake Van.[15] The chariot was for Sargon's personal use, apparently necessary to maintain his royal prestige. It was obviously an impractical hindrance; while it was being transported across the mountains on the backs of men, the king was leading his troops on horseback.

By the seventh century B.C. the supplanting of the chariot by military horsemen is quite evident from the reliefs. The light, maneuverable two-man chariot disappears, its function taken over by riders. A larger chariot, carrying as many as four men, appears on the reliefs. Its function is obviously different from that of the horsemen, who are regularly shown operating in terrain where the heavy vehicles could not go. Some riders carry bows, while others have spears. Both types of warriors are found on a relief of Ashurbanipal (668–627) in a battle against camel-riding Arabs. Infantry, chariotry, and cavalry are intermixed with the enemy on the relief, allowing no interpretation of tactics.[16] Another relief of Ashurbanipal suggests that the spear could be used as a missile weapon from horseback as well as a weapon for thrusting. In this relief some of the riders, all of whom sit on standing horses, are shooting arrows while others hold spears poised in their right hands, ready to be thrown.[17] There is nothing inherently improbable in this. Javelins had been used from chariots at an earlier date, and certainly in later times a multipurpose cavalry spear/javelin was common, its use depending upon the opportunities of the moment. There is no doubt that the Assyrians had

14. Barnett and Falkner (1962) pl. xiii–xvi, lxiv–lxviia.
15. Luckenbill ([1927] 1975) 93.
16. Burnett (1976) pl. XV.
17. Roux (1966) pl. facing 241. Conceivably, the spear held aloft has been raised in preparation for a downward thrust, as elsewhere it is seen being used in this way as well as with an underarm thrust. The weighted object hanging from the reins immediately in front of the horse's breast should also be noted on this and many other reliefs. It appears to be a device to keep the reins in place while the rider uses both hands to work the bow. Anderson considers this "tassel" a "remarkable anticipation of the martingale" used "to provide a certain check on the horse's mouth when the rider drops the reins." *AGH* 12. Strictly speaking, however, the martingale's function is to prevent the horse from pulling up his head when the reins are in the rider's hands.

reached a high level of military proficiency by the seventh century B.C., certainly higher than their Greek contemporaries, who probably had no true mounted warriors at the time.

As a result of the splendid visual evidence supplemented by texts, a serious attempt to describe the tactical role of horsemen during the Assyrian Empire is feasible. When speed and surprise were essential, the benefits of employing horsemen were obvious. This occurred especially on the periphery of the empire, against the nomads of the Near Eastern steppe and the mountain tribesmen to the north. Arrows were shot from horseback, both at the gallop and standing still, on the open plain and in the wooded hills. Mounted spearmen are portrayed striking the fleeing enemy at close range, which at least hints at the possibility of hand-to-hand combat on horseback. It is also probable that the spear was thrown overhand as a javelin.

There is no figured evidence of Assyrian horsemen fighting in formation, as a consequence of which Littauer and Crouwel do not consider them true cavalry.[18] Nevertheless, the level of military sophistication is so high in most other respects that the lack of direct evidence carries less weight in this case.[19] It is, for example, unlikely that the mounted archers fought as individuals, since it is concentrated fire that would make them effective in offensive operations.

The frequency with which horsemen are shown in pursuit obviously reflects the success of the Assyrian army, but no doubt it also owes something to the desire to portray the king's victories graphically by showing the cowardice and destruction of the enemy. In open battle the horsemen presumably had the task of occupying the enemy cavalry, should there be any, and—if they could drive them off—of unsettling the opposing infantry with their missile weapons. Harassment of the enemy flanks also likely occurred. As remained the case throughout the history of cavalry, it is most unlikely that they made frontal assaults on well-formed-up infantry.

The horses of the Assyrians are generally similar to those of peoples to the west (Egypt and Greece, for example) and appear to be unrelated to the Persian type. This is most clear from the shape of the head, the straight or concave profile being common from Assyria westward and the Roman nose characteristic of Persian horses. The heavier body on Assyrian horses is an

---

18. WVRA 143.
19. A brief but excellent appreciation of the Assyrian achievement is found in McNeill (1982) 13–14. See also Malbran-Labal (1982) 59–75. For an essentially similar appraisal of the change from chariotry to cavalry see Noble (1990) 61–68.

apparent rather than a real difference, resulting from an artistic convention of the Assyrians that also distorts human figures.

In short it seems likely that the Assyrian horsemen achieved the highest level of military equitation known in history to their time, which runs counter to the more common view of historians that cavalry originated on the steppe among the nomads of Eurasia. However, a distinction must be made between fine horsemanship and fighting power. Even if the steppe nomads were the first people to acquire a high level of riding skill, there is little evidence to support their claim as the originators of cavalry. The findings of recent scholars tend to support the Assyrian side of the debate, based on both the material finds from archaeological excavation in the Near East and southwestern Asia and a comparison of the military sophistication of the several peoples under consideration. Regarding military sophistication, a comparison of the fighting skills of the peoples later called "barbarian" by the Greeks and the more civilized nations of the Mediterranean and Near East reveals differences that usually favor the more civilized soldiers. Some of these differences persisted even after prolonged contacts between the two groups, largely because of a difference in environments. Higher population density and the hydraulic technology required for agriculture in river valleys necessitated a greater degree of organization and group discipline than was needed on the Eurasian steppes, where fodder for horses was free for the taking and hunting provided much of the food. The nomadic peoples of the steppe did not become truly formidable in a military sense until Genghis Khan instituted new levels of organization and discipline in the Mongol army in the thirteenth century A.D. W. H. McNeill sums it up nicely: "Altogether, a radical rationality seems to have pervaded Assyrian military administration, making their armies the most formidable and best disciplined that the world had yet seen."[20]

In spite of the fragmentary and uneven nature of the evidence, we are able to glimpse intercultural relations as they affected the use of horsemen in the Near East in the seventh century B.C. The peoples involved were the barbarian Scythians, the seminomadic Medes and Persians, and the Assyrians, the latter being representatives of the traditional high civilization of the Near East. The Scythians, Medes, and Persians—who appear to have been related ethnically, linguistically, and culturally—began to pressure the Assyrians from the north and the east in the first half of the seventh century, although it is

---

20. McNeill (1982) 14.

probable that their first appearance in the region occurred earlier. The fact that these related peoples made their presence felt at approximately the same time seems to have been fortuitous, as there is no evidence of collusion. In any event the Scythians disappeared from the scene by the early decades of the sixth century B.C., whereas the Medes and Persians, who seem to have found civilized life more attractive, proved most adept at assuming the mantle of empire when the Assyrians lost their power at the end of the seventh century.

Irrespective of where and under what conditions the horse was first domesticated and ridden, there is good reason to believe that skillful, disciplined military use of horse and rider developed first in the Near East, probably among the Assyrians. It seems clear that during the first four centuries of the first millennium elements of Assyrian culture spread outward to the less civilized lands to the east, north, and west of Mesopotamia. The Scythians in particular were remarkably open to foreign artistic influence from their neighbors on all sides, including the Assyrians.[21]

Occupying Urartu, north of Assyria, by 660, the Scythians later helped the Assyrians defeat the Medes under Phraortes (ca. 625) and, after invading Syria and Judea (ca. 611), were bought off by the Egyptian king Psammetichus.[22] Following the Median conquest of Assyria in 612, the Scythians were driven north to their more traditional home on the steppe. Although they were certainly at home on horseback and owed their military success primarily to their use of the horse and bow, it is not clear that they taught the Assyrians anything about the use of the horse in war. Indeed, there is evidence that the Scythians themselves borrowed the idea for a burr device attached to the bit ends to improve directional control of their horses. Although bits with spiked cheekpieces and burrs had long been common in the Near East and in Mycenae, they do not appear on the steppe until after the Scythian incursion into the Near East. Furthermore, archaeological finds suggest that bronze bits and cheekpieces were in use in the Near East when the steppe peoples were still using bone cheekpieces and soft (rope? leather?) bits, which, to quote Littauer, "implies a far less exacting use of the horse" among the latter.[23]

Indeed, if we look past their hit-and-run tactics, which were based on their remarkable mobility, the Scythians, according to Herodotus, were unable

21. Rice (1957) 75, 151, 153, 167, 195.
22. Ghirshman (1964) 98; Rice (1957) 45; Hdt. 1.103, 105.
23. Littauer (1969) 290, 298–300; Dalley (1984) 159, 164.

to withstand the Persian army under Darius in 513/512. They dared to attack Persian cavalry only when it scattered to forage, retreating when the Persian horsemen took refuge with their infantry, which the Scythians feared.[24] The failure of the Persian invasion of European Scythia was not due to military inferiority but rather to the Scythians' way of life. Having few fixed settlements, their homes were wagons that simply moved away from the Persian threat, while the warriors, refusing set battles, fought only on their own terms. The Persians were frustrated, not defeated. This Scythian lack of confidence does not encourage us to assign to them the premier rank among the world's horsemen at the time. The first horsemen they may have been—the best cavalry they were not.

Another indication of the differences between the Scythians and their more civilized neighbors to the southeast is their attitude toward horse breeding. The majority of the Scythians apparently rode the small, hardy Mongolian pony. Two distinct sources provide evidence for this: the Greco-Scythian goldwork, dated to the fourth century, that has been found in the southern Ukraine; and the frozen horse carcasses discovered in the Pazyryk tombs in the Altai Mountains of central Asia. Obviously, the artwork in gold is much less definitive evidence than the frozen horse remains themselves. The goldwork shows strong Greek influence, perhaps even having been done by Greek artists, and the fact that one of the horse types displayed is very similar to Greek horses may be due to this influence. The geographical proximity of these western Scythians to the eastern Mediterranean, and thus to the horses of the region, is a second possible reason for the similarity. The other horse type on the goldwork seems to be of a coarser variety, with a slightly heavier head, an erect mane (possibly due to cropping), and heavier overall bone structure. This latter type seems to be similar to the great majority of the seven to fourteen horses found in each tomb at Pazyryk at the eastern end of the Scythian's cultural realm. Among the remains found in each of the Pazyryk tombs, however, at least one horse was of a noticeably different, more highly bred variety. These horses seem to have been better cared for, and the splendid trappings found with them suggest that they were more useful for bolstering a warrior's prestige than for warfare. The taller horses (fifteen hands high) were from two to eighteen or twenty years old when they were killed by a blow to the head. All were geldings, and preferred colors were solid browns and chestnuts. Among modern breeds they most resemble the Akhal-

24. Hdt. 4.102, 128; Cook (1983) 59.

Teke, an ancient breed of Turkmenistan. It appears that these fine horses were imported by the Scythians largely for display and were not used to upgrade the local stock. Judging by the condition of the horses in the tombs, S. I. Rudenko, the excavator, felt that the finer, taller type had been stalled during the preceding winter and fed on concentrated feeds, whereas the more common ponies showed signs of having been left out to forage. It is possible, of course, that because upgraded horses had more demanding feeding requirements there was little incentive to upgrade the ponies, which could survive the winters in the open. More settled agricultural peoples would be in a better position to improve the breed in this regard. Almost all modern breeds are artificial creations, tending to degenerate if they are able to survive in the feral state.[25] In the Near East, however, selective breeding had produced fine chariot and riding horses some centuries earlier.

With the overthrow of the Assyrians, military supremacy in the Near East passed to the Medes and Persians. In spite of their own equestrian traditions of some antiquity, these two closely related peoples apparently adopted and carried on the Assyrian military practices. Unfortunately, battle scenes do not appear on the Persian reliefs to provide the kind of vivid evidence that is helpful in studying the Assyrians. Military horses are indeed depicted, but never in action, and several different varieties can be discerned.[26] For a glimpse of early Persian tactics there is Herodotus, who reports that the Median King Kyaxares (625–585) organized the army into companies and segregated the different arms—spearmen, archers, and horsemen.[27] For over 250 years the Median/Persian cavalry remained formidable, not to be outclassed until the time of Alexander. Even then it took a leader of genius and the best-organized, most highly trained army of the day to defeat them.

During the sixth century and probably later, the greatest weakness of the Persian cavalry seems to have been a reluctance to engage in hand-to-hand combat—something that early Greek cavalry also found distasteful. Instead, they preferred to strike at the enemy from a distance with javelins and arrows. This seems clear from the account in Herodotus of the battles between Cyrus, the Persian king, and Croesus of Lydia in 547 or 546. The first battle, an all-day affair, ended in a draw in spite of the fact (if the historian is correct), that the army of Croesus was much the smaller. Thinking that Cyrus

---

25. Rice (1957) 71; Rolle (1980) 117; Rudenko (1970) 28; Spruytte (1983) 111; Bokovenko (1995), in Davis-Kimball, Bashilov, and Yablonsky, 290.
26. Afshar and Lerner (1979) 44–47.
27. Hdt. 1.103.

was reluctant to risk further fighting that year, Croesus returned to Sardis and disbanded some of his troops. Cyrus, however, decided instead to move quickly against the Lydian capital, hoping to find Croesus unprepared. At the arrival of the Persians, Croesus reluctantly led out his troops. Herodotus states specifically that the Lydian strength lay in their cavalry, for they were skilled horsemen armed with long spears (δόρατα μεγάλα). Cyrus feared these horsemen, probably because he had seen their effectiveness in the earlier battle, and he accordingly adopted a stratagem to deal with them. On the advice of Harpagus, a Mede, he placed men dressed for riding on baggage camels in his front line. Next came his infantry and finally his own cavalry. The camels frightened the Lydian horses, which became uncontrollable, and the Lydian spearmen were compelled to dismount in order to carry on the fight. This description of events is convincing, as horses are easily put off by strange sights and smells. Cyrus' horses would have been familiar with these odd beasts. The Lydians were consequently defeated and took refuge behind the walls of Sardis, which fell two weeks later.[28]

Although the length of the Lydian spear is unknown, it would have been longer than the Persian javelin if the account is to make any sense. It is difficult to judge the size of ancient weapons merely from reliefs and art objects. The scale may not be accurate, and the height of the human models is not known. What the figured evidence does show is that the spears of the palace guards on the reliefs at Persepolis (sixth to fifth century) extend from the ground to about a foot above the heads of the guards, while a standing figure, probably a horseman, on a gold plaque from the Oxus Treasure in Bactria (seventh to sixth century) carries a weapon that matches his height.[29] The shorter weapon for the horsemen is understandable, as Persian cavalry often carried two javelins, which would be unwieldy on horseback if they were too long. The Lydian lancers, wielding only one weapon intended for thrusting rather than throwing, would ideally have the longer spear. Later, the Macedonians demonstrated the effectiveness of fighting at close quarters with the lance. By the time of the Persian Wars at the latest, we know that Persian cavalry were sufficiently well organized to be able to charge by squadrons.[30]

Although it derives from a slightly later date (421), when Darius II was mustering troops at Uruk, a cuneiform document offers an authoritative

---

28. Hdt. 1.76–84; see Cook (1983) 28 for the date of this battle. The camels were probably of the Bactrian variety.
29. Ghirshman (1964) pl. 14, 236.
30. Hdt. 9.20.

description of a Persian cavalryman's equipment. He was to report for duty with a horse and its tack, including a saddle, 1 *suhattu* cloth (heavy cloth used as horse armor), 1 coat of iron scale armor, a matching helmet, a neck protector, 1 bow-and-arrow case, 120 mounted arrows, 10 unmounted (?) arrows, 1 *ṭeru* weapon of iron with case, and 2 iron lances.[31] From battle descriptions it is clear that the Persian cavalrymen frequently also carried a sabre (in Greek, μάχαιρα). It is obvious from this information that the Persian cavalryman was—potentially, at least—a formidable opponent.

With the collapse of the Mycenaean civilization in Greece at the end of the Bronze Age, literacy and the Linear B script on which it was based disappeared. For the period until alphabetical writing came into use in Greece in the second half of the eighth century B.C., the primary source of information about riding that we have is archaeological, with vase paintings, sculpture, and coins providing virtually all our knowledge. At this time Homer alone provides some verbal descriptions of the use of horses. With the collapse of the palace economy and the concomitant weakening of the aristocracy, the importance of the horse may have declined. Nonetheless, this animal continued to be associated with the wealthy, and it seems justified to assume that it was used for war, racing, and religious processions. The chariot survived, too, but its relative importance declined as riding became more common. Since throughout Greek antiquity the horse was not considered a work animal except in emergencies, there is no reason to look for a change in its status at this time. Cattle were used for plowing, donkeys and mules as pack animals, and mules for general draft purposes and riding. The degree to which the horse was used for riding outside the military setting is not known. It is clear that some Greeks were skilled riders by the eighth century, however. It is true that Homer refers to riding quite rarely, but when he does so it is obvious that riding is no novelty and the level of ability is high.

Besides a passing mention of riding in a simile in the *Odyssey*, the *Iliad* contains two lengthier descriptions implying that riding was a skill associated with the keeping of chariot horses. In one, Odysseus and Diomedes steal into the camp of the Thracians, slaughter thirteen warriors in their sleep, and seize the white chariot horses of the Thracian king Rhesus. For a moment Diomedes debates with himself whether to take the richly decorated chariot or to slay more Thracians, but, prompted by Athene, he and Odysseus

---

31. Rahe (1980) 96. This translation of the Akkadian, which differs from the text in Rahe, is an updated version kindly provided by Richard Beal. See Gelb et al. (1984) 15 (S): 346b; (1981) 17, part I (Š): 271b.

unhesitatingly mount the horses and ride off.[32] Elsewhere, Ajax is likened to a skilled horseman leaping from back to back of four horses that are harnessed together as they are brought from the plain to the city.[33]

Such skill is not completely unexpected, as riding had been known in Greece for several hundred years and the high level of equitation evidenced in the writings of Xenophon in the first half of the fourth century presupposes considerable experience with horses prior to that time. An Attic Geometric vase of the eighth century bearing a rider on a rearing horse lends further support. There is no reason to believe that the helmeted rider on the vase is not in control of the horse—he is certainly not a timid novice.[34] Today, in the Spanish Riding School in Vienna, the "airs above the ground," including the Pesade (controlled rearing), are performed without stirrups.

Late in this period the poet Anacreon shows the kind of awareness of horse behavior that one would expect in a society where horses had long been familiar animals, comparing a haughty woman to a frisky Thracian filly.[35] Aristotle, referring back to this period in several passages in his *Politics*, makes some interesting comments on early cavalry. He specifically associates the raising of horses and the use of cavalry with oligarchy and the wealthy upper classes, who could afford the considerable expense of maintaining these animals. He even goes so far as to suggest that where the terrain was suitable for horses, oligarchy was likely to arise.[36] Whether these statements are based on knowledge or conjecture on Aristotle's part is impossible to say, but they contain nothing inherently unreasonable. Horses were indeed associated with the wealthy in ancient Greece and, outside of war, do not seem to have been kept for practical purposes as were other equids. The high value that the aristocracy placed on horses is not open to question, being well documented in the literary and artistic remains. Their extreme appreciation of the horse even led to the practice of selective breeding to produce desired types, something that seems to have been done with no other domestic animal in ancient Greece.[37]

Included among Aristotle's remarks is the statement that after the fall of the monarchy cavalry was the most important military arm, because the infantry was useless without a system of tactics—a defect that was remedied

32. Hom. *Od.* 5.371; Hom. *Il.* 10.465–579.
33. Hom. *Il.* 15.679–84. For discussions of riding during this period, see Wiesner (1968) 110–36; *EGW* chap. 6–7; *AGH* 10–11.
34. *EGW* 48 fig. 32.
35. Campbell (1988) 95, frag. 417.
36. Arist. *Pol.* 1289b 33–40; 1297b 16–22; 1321a 5–11.
37. *Kleine Pauly* 4.683, see *Pferd.* W. Richter (1968) 72–73.

by the introduction of phalanx tactics.[38] This, too, has a certain plausibility, as on an individual basis horsemen are more effective than infantrymen. As soon as regular infantry formations came into existence—the fully developed form being the phalanx—this changed. At no time in the history of warfare is there clear evidence that cavalry were able, in frontal attack, to charge and defeat a well-trained body of infantry that preserved its formation. That fact, as well as the rough terrain, the existence of walled cities, and the expense of keeping horses, are some of the reasons why infantry was so important in Greece by the end of this period. Nonetheless, L. J. Worley has argued that Archaic heavy cavalry could have used shock against both cavalry and infantry.[39] Here the key word is *shock*, which refers to cavalry's closing with the enemy and using spears and perhaps swords to inflict damage. But there is no written evidence to support the cavalry's use of shock before the end of the fifth century in Greece, and the information that does survive regarding the earlier period makes it unlikely. Pausanias, for example, says that the Peloponnesians were not good horsemen at the time of the First Messenian War (ca. 735–715), and Aristotle's comment, mentioned above, about the absence of a system of tactics for infantry should also apply to cavalry even if, as he claims, "the strength of armies lay in their cavalry."[40] Thus the horsemen of this period may have had neither the requisite riding skills nor the organization and experience that would have made possible the shock tactics Worley claims. Indeed, K. S. Raaflaub states flatly that "with a few exceptions, such as Thessaly and Macedonia, Greece never witnessed a stage of true cavalry supremacy.[41] Any superiority that cavalry may have had over infantry at this time can be explained more simply by the inherent advantage horsemen have over infantry at low levels of organization, a superiority that is probably due to psychological dominance and mobility. In the north, however, as Raaflaub points out, a greater level of equestrian skill and mounted military ability existed. There, in Thessaly and Macedon in particular, where greater areas of natural pasturage were found, the horse was more common and cavalry traditionally played a more prominent role. Thus it is fitting that the first recorded victory in horse racing at the Olympic Games was achieved by a Thessalian, Crauxidas from Crannon, in 648.[42]

38. Arist. *Pol.* 1297b 19–22.
39. *HCAG* 48, 58.
40. Paus. 8.2; Arist. *Pol.* 1297b 20–22 (trans. Barker [1962] 188).
41. Raaflaub (1999), in Raaflaub and Rosenstein, 132.
42. Glubok and Tamarin (1976) 41.

In the final analysis the evidence from vase paintings provides the only contemporary evidence for military use of the horse during this time. Since the pottery from the early part of the period is devoid of military scenes, all the evidence comes from after 700 and is effectively limited to pottery manufactured in Corinth and Athens, city-states that were traditionally weak in cavalry. Nevertheless, the number of vases containing scenes with military horsemen is sufficient for a rudimentary understanding of the development of Greek cavalry. Greenhalgh's findings can generally be accepted, as long as one bears in mind that they are based on, in Hanson's words, "the shaky evidence of vase painting."[43]

In the seventh century, both at Corinth and at Athens, there is little evidence for cavalry proper, the mounted soldiers most likely being aristocratic hoplites who rode their horses to battle. Depictions of these figures regularly have a full panoply and are accompanied by mounted squires. By the sixth century in both city-states, it is reasonably clear that more lightly armored soldiers, fighting from horseback, existed alongside the mounted hoplites, who fought on foot. The extent to which mounted soldiers fought in a true cavalry formation is unknown. The amount of body armor shown on the horsemen varies, some having only a helmet while others also wear corselet and greaves. The presence or absence of a shield and the type of helmet worn may serve as a criterion. The hoplite is always seen carrying a shield, whereas the cavalryman regularly does without, preferring to rely on a corselet, as this had the advantage of keeping his hands free for holding the reins and a weapon. If the helmet is of the Corinthian type, the rider is certainly a mounted hoplite (assuming the artist's depiction is accurate). This helmet, which—except for eyeholes and space for breathing—completely surrounded the head, severely restricted sight and hearing. It was designed for the hoplite phalanx and, according to V. D. Hanson, "dueling, skirmishing, and hit and run tactics were out of the question with such headgear."[44] Since these activities were an essential part of the cavalry's repertoire, the Corinthian helmet could not have been worn. The principal weapon of the cavalryman is seen to be the spear or javelin, sometimes carried in pairs. The length varies, but this means little because the degree of accuracy sought by the artist is unknown. Some, presumably javelins, are depicted as poised for throwing. Others, used as lances,

---

43. Hanson (1991), in Hanson, 76.
44. Hanson (1989) 71. Even infantry abandoned this helmet in the fifth century for types that left the face more open. The fact that the Corinthian helmet is regularly portrayed in art as pushed back on the head, away from the face, may be due in part to the discomfort it produced.

are held either in an over- or underhand grip, with hoplites frequently shown as the objects of the spear thrust. Occasionally, a sword appears in a scabbard at the waist. There is even an occasional archer in Greek armor appearing on Chalcidian vases of unknown origin, but these are too rare to have much significance. Greenhalgh suggests that they may show Etruscan cavalry.[45]

Since no descriptions of Greek battles of this period exist, it is impossible to interpret the material from the vases with any degree of confidence. All depends on the degree of latitude the artists allowed themselves in portraying these mounted warriors. It is possible that they show no more relation to everyday reality than do the photographs of cowboys on American cigarette advertisements. That comparison is likely too extreme, yet it remains an open question whether Athens had a formally organized cavalry force around 500 B.C. Nevertheless, in spite of the difficulty of interpreting the scenes on the vases, there are reasons for accepting them as valid evidence as long as one does not read too much into what is presented. It is unlikely that the artists invented either physical objects or military ways of doing things that are compatible with what is known to have existed not too much later. Furthermore, the vase paintings record an evolution from mounted infantry to true cavalry that carries historical conviction even if they do not offer chronological or geographical certainty. The evolution that is portrayed on the vases occurred in some parts of Greece, although perhaps not everywhere at the same time. It is perhaps unlikely that by 500 cavalry played an important military role anywhere south of Thessaly, where cavalry traditionally dominated, but there can be little doubt that there were aristocratic cavalrymen on the battlefields in some states, if not in Athens.

To return for a moment to the development of true cavalry as portrayed on the vases, it is noteworthy that the evidence from Corinth and Athens is generally consistent regarding the change from mounted infantry to cavalry. Indeed, in works of the the sixth century battle scenes showing cavalry in action are fairly common. Cavalry, both light and armored, are seen to engage hoplites as well as each other. Though some of the scenes represent mythological battles, the general accuracy of the events depicted seems likely.[46] The various duties of these cavalry can also be surmised: to serve as scouts and messengers, protect the flanks of one's own phalanx, drive off enemy cavalry, harass the flanks and rear of the enemy, attempt to work their way into the

---

45. *EGW* 141–42.
46. For additional commentary on early Greek cavalry see Evans (1987) 97–106.

ranks of a broken enemy formation, intercept supplies, attack foragers and stragglers, and pursue an enemy once he had been routed.[47]

As I have mentioned, the nearest approach to a narrative of a battle is Herodotus' account of the struggle between Cyrus and Croesus in 547/546. In this account the Lydian cavalry are described as carrying a long lance. If this was, indeed, their primary weapon, it sets them apart both from their Greek neighbors to the west, who preferred a shorter spear for either throwing or thrusting, and the Persians to the east, who placed their trust in the bow.

---

47. Vase scenes showing several of these activities may be found in *EGW*, figs. 58, 64, 65, 67, 68, 70.

PART 2

The Greek Cavalry: 500 to 360 B.C.

Chapter 4

The Persian Wars: 500 to 479 B.C.

THE ROLE OF TRADITIONAL aristocratic luxury that is assigned by some historians to cavalry in Greek warfare prior to the rise of Macedon under King Philip II in the middle of the fourth century is one of those misleading truisms.[1] It ignores two important facts that obscure our awareness of what was a steady—one might say, organic—evolution of military practices and attitudes that makes the military success of Philip and Alexander more understandable, though no less spectacular. The first of these is the Greeks' awareness—at least from the time of the Persian Wars—of the general usefulness of cavalry and, especially, the threat that it could pose to a hoplite army when it was well handled. As early as 494, Herodotus states that a Greek army of Aeolians and Ionians under the command of Histiaeus was defeated by a charge of Persian cavalry after the infantry on both sides had fought for a long while. Unless the Greeks became disorganized, it is probable that the Persian cavalry attacked from the flank or the rear. The site of this battle was Malene, in the district of the coastal city Atarneus, which lies west of Pergamum in Asia Minor.[2]

Also obscuring our awareness of the evolving Greek military is the actual assistance, sometimes decisive, that cavalry rendered long before their full integration into offensive tactics, which was the great legacy of Philip. These

---

1. Ellis (1976) 56; *HMND* 5: "All it came to, in most cities, was that a few wealthy men rode on horses; they were useful for scouting or raiding supplies, but they rarely played any serious part in battle; there is no case of Greek cavalry in Greece, putting Thessaly aside, either employing shock tactics or turning the enemy's flank."

2. Hdt. 6.28–29.

journeyman achievements pale by comparison with the spectacular accomplishments of the Macedonians, and this fact has tended to obscure their real importance. For on occasion—as we shall see—they did tip the scales decisively for one side or the other. No matter what the relative difference in ability of armies might be in any individual battle, one must be superior to one's opponent only on that given day. When cavalry forces were small and poorly trained, a slight and—by later standards—insignificant force could change history, as the Syracusan cavalry in 415 appear to have done.

Looking back at the fifth century from the heady, never to be equaled, days of Macedonian triumphs, it is hindsight—demanding of cavalry what we know it could do—that blinds us to what it did, in fact, accomplish. Another incident of events before the Persian Wars that was recorded by Herodotus offers a hint of why Greek infantry had reason to respect—if not to fear—enemy cavalry. In 511 a Spartan army of unknown size, but obviously not large, made a landing from ships at Phalerum, near Athens. The government of Sparta, ever pious, had finally been persuaded by the Pythian priestess to attempt to drive the sons of Pisistratus out of Athens. The Pisistratids, however, had received advance warning and had laid waste the plain of Phalerum to make it suitable for use by their Thessalian allies—one thousand cavalry under the command of their king, Cineas of Conium. These cavalry charged and routed the Spartans, killing—among many others—the commander, Anchimolius. The survivors fled to the ships.[3] Because of this incident, H. Delbrück felt that the Greeks were made aware of the vulnerability of hoplites faced by cavalry.[4] Had this passage of Herodotus survived without the following chapter, we would have an impressive example of Thessalian cavalry defeating Spartan infantry. Fortunately, however, Herodotus tells the full story. Sometime after their defeat, the Spartans sent out a larger army (size not given) under King Cleomenes to attack Athens again. This force entered Attica by land, meeting first with the Thessalian cavalry. On this occasion events turned out quite differently—the Thessalian cavalry were routed, with a loss of forty men.[5] Subsequently, in 510, the Pisistratids were driven into exile. Herodotus identifies no specific reason for the different outcomes of these two battles, but we can hazard a guess. The relative size of the forces was critical. One thousand horsemen was a substantial number, and there is no evidence—indeed, it is unlikely—that the Spartans were allowed the time to

---

3. Hdt. 5.63.
4. *HAW* 109, 116.
5. Hdt. 5.64.

form ranks properly after disembarking. Furthermore, the Spartan commander may have been less than competent. On the second occasion the Spartans took the matter more seriously, sending a noticeably larger army by land under the command of one of their kings. The routing of cavalry by infantry was perhaps the more typical outcome. Nevertheless, Delbrück has a point, assuming that some of the Greeks in attendance at the events were perceptive enough to see the potential of cavalry.

In any case these two battles clearly show the importance of the immediate circumstances on the outcome of any military action. Obviously, victory is independent of what should happen based on past experience, and either cavalry or infantry could defeat the other on any given occasion. As I have stated, if both arms were up to muster the advantage usually lay with the infantry, provided they could protect their flanks and rear. But just as in most human activities, in military matters mistakes and blunders are part of the normal state of affairs, except that in battle results of mistakes manifest themselves immediately and often disastrously.

One striking fact highlighted by Herodotus in his narrative is the need of cavalry for suitable terrain, which was an especially serious problem in Greece. For their greatest effect, cavalry require open country unencumbered by obstacles. In spite of the fact that the first battle was fought on the plain of Phalerum, the area had to be cleared—in this case, according to the Greek (κείρω), by cutting down crops and possibly fruit trees. Obviously, horses could be used in less than ideal terrain and the phalanx itself required a level battlefield, but over the course of time infantry proved themselves to be a bit more adaptable than cavalry. This can be seen in the effectiveness of Greek light infantry and the Roman legion in rough country.

It is not necessary to venture too far into the debate over the origin of hoplite infantry tactics, but it is necessary to summarize the valuable recent discussions, which have clarified this subject immeasurably, in order to understand the role of cavalry prior to the Peloponnesian War. For some time prior to 1985 the debate centered on the date, subsequent to Homer, by which hoplite infantry tactics were in place in Greece, as well as the causes that brought about the transformation from an earlier type of fighting. It was argued, for example, that military advances led both to political change and to the redesign of armor and weapons, resulting in recognizable hoplite tactics by 650.[6] By comparison with this new style of fighting, Homeric warfare

---

6. Snodgrass (1965) 110–12; Detienne (1968), in Vernant, 119–42; Murray (1983) 120–31; Snodgrass (1980) 101–107, 151–52; *GSW* 4 chap. 1.

seemed much less organized and more individual—that is, more heroic, with an emphasis on personal glory. But that was not the whole story, and by the mid-1980s some of these claims were being questioned.

For example, W. K. Pritchett challenged the commonly held view that Homeric warfare was less organized and more individual than warfare from the Late Archaic period on, observing that there was considerable evidence of mass fighting in Homer. Outside the Greek world precedents also existed, since massed formations that the Greeks would have called phalanxes had already appeared in the Near East during the Late Bronze Age. Much of the evidence for the traditional view is archaeological and artistic, showing changes in helmet, shield, and body armor during the eighth and seventh centuries and portrayals of infantry formations of hoplites in the new armor beginning around the mid-seventh century. On the basis of this material, for example, O. Murray believed that the hoplite formation developed between 700 and 650.[7]

Pritchett did well to challenge the older view, and his references to massed formations in Homer are now accepted for what they are, although—since Homer was composing in the eighth century—his descriptions could perhaps be interpreted as anachronisms.[8] But Pritchett continued to accept duels between champions as a historical part of Late Bronze Age warfare, again citing evidence from the Near East.[9] Clearly, these no longer existed as part of later Greek warfare; some significant change had obviously occurred. Homer's descriptions of duels may represent the aristocratic ethos of personal glory, which gradually yielded to subordination to the group during the period following the collapse of Bronze Age society. On the other hand Homer's descriptions could be a poetic device for highlighting the heroes. In any case middle-class infantry became more important, and patriotism—in which glory accrued to the state—developed. It is perhaps the degree of subordination of the individual to group discipline that distinguishes the later from the earlier phalanx, but it is nonetheless a critical difference that could be militarily decisive. Such a high degree of group discipline and training lies at the heart of the success of the Spartans and, later, the Romans. For hundreds of years it is this quality that distinguished Greek and Roman armies from their barbarian adversaries.

Additional insight into the origin of hoplite warfare and its nature was introduced in 1989 by Hanson and recently summarized by S. Mitchell.[10]

---

7. Murray (1983) 123–26. Regarding the visual evidence see also Osborne (1996) 164.
8. *GSW* 4 11–16.
9. Ibid., 16.
10. Hanson (1989); Hanson (1991); Mitchell (1996), in Lloyd, 87–105.

Hanson drew attention to the face-to-face nature of Greek hoplite battle, in which little or no use was made of reserves, flank attacks, and rear guards and scorn was heaped on those enemies who fought with missile weapons from a distance.[11] Apparently by "mutual agreement,"[12] the Greeks strove for a decisive outcome through a few hours of intense fighting. Each side accepted the outcome of battle, whereby they avoided longer wars, civilian casualties, and major destruction of property. This was a form of consciously limited warfare, originating, according to Hanson, in the need felt by land-holding farmers to defend their property as free members of a city-state. More recently, Hanson has argued strongly that this self-limitation arose specifically out of the agricultural setting. He states bluntly: "Greek fighting of the *polis should never be discussed outside the context of farming.*"[13]

As these ideas found greater acceptance, other scholars contributed interpretations and refinements of what is now seen to be a military change of historic significance. As a result, a clear and convincing account of this change can now be read in recent work by Raaflaub. Thus it now seems clear that Hanson's view is essentially correct; as the style of fighting changed, the technological transformation of weapons and armor followed to fit the massed-phalanx combat of the citizen farmers. The change seems to have been underway by the mid-eighth century, and Homer's description of massed armies may be the first record of this activity. The accompanying social, political, and technological changes produced the recognizable classical phalanx within a hundred years. The number of combatants required for phalanx fighting is strong evidence against the theory of dominance of the aristocracy after the mid-eighth century, since their numbers would not have sufficed to fill the ranks. The city-state army became more egalitarian of necessity, while the aristocracy lost political ground to the demos—the men under arms.[14]

These ideas about the development and nature of hoplite warfare are of more than passing interest in a study of Greek cavalry. If we accept Hanson's thesis—as I am inclined to do—that the Greeks reached a tacit agreement to limit warfare, the result has great bearing on any attempt to understand the battlefield deployment of arms other than heavy infantry in phalanx formation. In an environment where no one felt the need for strategic and tactical

---

11. Hanson (1989) 24–25.
12. Ibid., 16.
13. Hanson (1995) 222. The full discussion is contained in chap. 6, 221–89.
14. Raaflaub (1997), in Mitchell and Rhodes, 49–53; Raaflaub (1999), in Raaflaub and Rosenstein, 132–34. Hanson's most recent description of these events is found in Hanson (1999) 56–58.

thought beyond what was useful in the narrow context of hoplite battle, it is no wonder if—prior to the Peloponnesian War—little effort was made to find employment for the other types of troops, including cavalry. As long as the hoplite battle satisfied the needs of the city-state, which was concerned more with the survival of its way of life than with projecting power far beyond its borders, there was a studied indifference to the use of other arms.[15] Even the Spartans, with their military culture, showed little interest in the acquisition of territory beyond what they needed to sustain themselves and had no imperial ambitions until after the defeat of Athens. With the change of outlook in the direction of a broader application of war that arose during the Peloponnesian conflict, creative thought was stimulated; it became important to exploit weaknesses in the enemy rather than to treat them as unimportant or nonexistent. The comparative absence of cavalry from Greek battlefields circa 650–430 was caused less by bias against the horsey aristocrats and the expense of keeping horses than by the realization that they could not contribute much to the desired outcome of hoplite battle. In the latter, asymmetry traditionally took the form of disparity in number and different degrees of discipline and training rather than in types of arms, weapons, and tactics. This was the secret of Spartan success, and when the Athenian leader Pericles kept his hoplites within the walls of Athens and refused to fight decisive land battles, he blunted the Spartan advantage. Relying on his naval strength, Pericles adopted a strategy of attrition.[16] Thus began the great change in military practice that had such profound influence on the following century. In his history of the Peloponnesian War, Thucydides "charted the birth and development of a new kind of warfare, without limits, without rules."[17]

A closer look at the military events of the fifth century shows that traditional hoplite battles were fought in the open on flat ground and were usually short and sharp, with the defeated hoplites throwing down their weapons in order to facilitate their quick departure. Pursuit—if any—was brief, as it was no easy matter to run while carrying weapons and wearing armor in spite of the fact that a hoplite race on the agenda of the Olympic Games since the late sixth century might suggest otherwise. Sieges would naturally result when one side doubted its ability to stand against an adversary in the field.

---

15. Hanson (1995) 232: "in Greece proper, until the Peloponnesian War, landed infantrymen developed a 'system' that deliberately made missiles and mounted warriors incidental to success in battle."
16. Thuc. 2.20–23. Mitchell (1996), in Lloyd, 97.
17. Mitchell (1996), in Lloyd, 101.

South of the plains of Thessaly, where a semifeudal system seems to have survived, large-scale raising of horses was impossible. Not only was there insufficient pasture on which to feed them, but a landscape of cities, villages, and homestead farms was inherently unsuited for a horsey way of life. There was no time, except perhaps for the wealthy, to acquire the high level of skill needed to ride well. Hoplite infantry fighting, on the other hand, was ideal for the citizen soldier who had little time to train, because it relied more on the cohesiveness of the unit than on highly developed individual fighting skills. Where more time was spent on training, as it was in Sparta, it produced military superiority that bore no relationship to other factors such as quality of weapons, tactics, or strategy. Nevertheless, cavalry—although little used—had a legitimate place in war and were not merely a sop to aristocratic vanity. If we wish to understand fully the astounding success attained by Philip and Alexander with cavalry integrated into their forces, then we must ascertain both the fifth-century Greek view of the horseman's military role and the uses to which cavalry were put in the military operations of this period.

The century opened with the Persian attempt to reduce the independent Greek city-states to submission. Collectively known as the Persian Wars (490–478), the struggle really began in 499 with the Ionian Revolt in Asia Minor and lasted until the winter of 479/478, when the Athenians captured Sestos. As far as one can tell from reading Herodotus, cavalry were not used by the allied Greeks at any time during this conflict. On the other hand some of those Greeks who fought on the side of the Persians—the Boeotians, for example—did have cavalry.[18] In light of this as well as the frequent appearance of cavalry in Greek art of the preceding century, it is unlikely that the loyal Greek states were completely bereft of cavalry. One can only assume that they played no important role on the Greek side during the conflict with the Persians. Horsemen were used by the Greeks as messengers at Plataea, so we can be sure that they existed. Probably they were too few to be used as an effective cavalry force against an enemy whose strength in this arm appeared overwhelming.

Although the Greeks may not have employed cavalry at any of the battles of which we have knowledge, their preliminary choice of ground at Marathon, Thermopylae, and Plataea betrays an awareness of the limitations of the phalanx when facing cavalry. Most notable was the absolute need to protect the flanks and rear. The phalanx was incomparable for direct frontal

---

18. Hdt. 9.8–69.

attack, but it lacked versatility and was not self-sufficient when facing an enemy with a strong cavalry arm and an advantage in numbers, as was usually the case during the Persian Wars.[19]

One ancient and universal practice used to protect one's flanks is to take advantage of the topography so that natural obstacles block access to one or both sides. This remains a fundamental principle of tactics, and it matters not at all whether one employs steep hillsides, woods, rivers, ravines, or even man-made structures. This practice obviously restricts freedom of movement, and it fails utterly when one's enemy is able to dictate the choice of battlefield. Ideally, protection for the flanks should be incorporated into an army, which is what eventually happened in Greek warfare. For the moment, however, it is necessary to look at the way the Greeks addressed the problem presented by the invading Persians, whose army not only included substantial numbers of cavalry but was also significantly larger.

Herodotus clearly states that Hippias, the exiled Athenian tyrant and son of Pisistratus, led the Persians to the small plain of Marathon in 490 because it was both suitable for the operation of cavalry and close to Eretria, on the island of Euboea, both of which they had just subdued.[20] After the landing of the Persians, the Athenians arrived and camped on a height that cannot be identified with certainty but that lay at the southwestern end of the plain.[21] With neither cavalry nor archers, the Athenians and their Plataean allies relied on their higher position and, perhaps, some sort of perimeter defense structures to keep the more numerous Persians and their cavalry away.[22]

There are many irremediable gaps in our knowledge of events on the battlefield of Marathon, the first battle in European history for which we possess anything like a description. Of immediate concern is the fact that Herodotus makes no mention of Persian cavalry in his narrative. This is decidedly strange, not only because cavalry were traditionally so important in their armies but, even more, because the historian has already informed us in the chronicle of

---

19. When two Greek hoplite armies fought—whether some cavalry were present or not—level, open ground was chosen by tacit agreement on both sides. Trust in one's phalanx and the desire to give it optimum conditions for success overrode other concerns. No Greek army of the period possessed a separate tactical unit whose function was to outflank the enemy, although outflanking did occur because of the tendency of the phalanx to creep toward the right, that is to say, the unshielded side.

20. Hdt. 6.102.

21. The position of the Athenians was in an otherwise unknown precinct of Heracles (Hdt. 6.108). That the Athenians were camped at the southwestern end of the plain seems likely because of the location there of the *soros*, the mound raised to cover the remains of their dead. At least the fighting occurred there.

22. Hdt. 6.112. The surprise, attributed to the Persians by Herodotus, that the Greeks would charge unsupported by archers and cavalry implies that the Persians had both.

events leading up to Marathon that cavalry, with horses shipped in horse-transports, formed an important part of the expedition. These cavalry were disembarked for the attack on the Eretrians, but no mention is made of their participation during the six days of fighting at the walls of the city, which was betrayed from inside.[23] Because of their rapidity of movement, cavalry are an excellent counter to parties of foragers and soldiers making sallies from a city under attack, and it is likely that the Persian cavalry saw similar service at Eretria.

Debate continues regarding the presence or absence of cavalry at Marathon and the question as to whether they were disembarked from the ships.[24] Later writers do mention Persian cavalry at the battle, Nepos, for example, reporting ten thousand, but the physical problems arising from the transport of ten thousand horses by sea make his figure highly unlikely.[25] Furthermore, a skeptical view of all accounts of Marathon later than Herodotus seems to prevail among historians.[26] Another late source, Pausanias, reports that chance visitors to the plain of Marathon can still hear the neighing of horses and the sound of fighting men—spirits of those who fought in the great battle.[27] Elsewhere, however, in his description of the famous wall painting of the battle in the Painted Stoa at Athens (a fifth-century work by Polygnotus) Pausanias makes no mention of cavalry.[28] An extremely late source, the tenth-century Byzantine lexicon the *Suda*, attributes Miltiades' decision to charge to a message sent to him by the Ionians who had been pressed into Persian service. These unexpected allies from across the Aegean are said to have climbed trees to send the Greeks the message that the cavalry were absent. This, in any case, is the explanation for the lexicon entry "χωρὶς ἱππεῖς—the cavalry are away." J. A. S. Evans interprets this to mean that the cavalry had, indeed, been disembarked, but that they were away on a mission of their own—that is, to occupy the road to Athens—and consequently missed the battle.[29] Snodgrass believes that the Persian cavalry were present but ineffective against the surprisingly rapid charge of the Greeks.[30] R. Sealey agrees with Snodgrass, I think rightly questioning the ability of the Ionians to send an intelligible message

---

23. Hdt. 6.95, 101.
24. Evans (1987) 97–106.
25. Nep. *Milt.* 5.4.
26. See, for example, *XIG* 7–25.
27. Paus. 1.32.4.
28. Ibid., 1.15.3.
29. Evans (1987) 97, 105.
30. *AAG* 102–103.

over a distance of at least a mile.[31] By rights the Persians should have disembarked their cavalry, which was always an essential part of their armies. They had probably planned to march on Athens, but the arrival of the Athenian forces forestalled them. Days of indecision followed. With time to evaluate the site, the Persians may have judged it unfit for cavalry and decided to trust in their superior numbers. On the other hand since the Greeks, before charging, had extended their line to equal that of the Persians, the cavalry may not have had an opportunity to outflank the Greeks in the plain between the sea and the hills. Surprise is always an advantage in war, and the unexpected and rapid charge may have unsettled the Persians. If the Persian horsemen were on the battlefield that day, they must have been on the wings, for the Greeks had weakened their center in order to strengthen the outsides of their line. As Persian cavalry at this period were primarily archers and javelin throwers whose effectiveness would have been severely reduced by the rapid charge of the Greeks, it would come as no surprise if they played no further role in the battle, being neither experienced nor armed for hand-to-hand combat.[32] C. Hignett estimates their numbers at no more than eight hundred, because of the difficulty of transporting horses in ships.[33] All in all it seems a reasonable assumption that Persian cavalry were present on the battlefield but that they had no effect upon the battle's outcome.[34]

Possible evidence of this comes from the identification by E. Vanderpool and E. B. Harrison of the subject of two relief sculptures.[35] The scenes on both of these—a fragment of a sarcophagus in Brescia and the South Frieze of the Nike Temple—are thought to depict the battle of Marathon, as derived from the painting of Polygnotus in the Painted Stoa. Prominent in these scenes are Persian cavalry fighting Greek infantry.[36] If these attributions are correct—and they certainly have merit—then they are solid evidence for a fifth-century tradition that Persian cavalry were present at the battle. This implies that the phalanx of the Greeks was quite capable of rendering ineffective a modest force of enemy cavalry on a battlefield where hills to the northwest and the sea to the southeast may have restricted movement on the flanks.

---

31. Sealey (1976) 190–91.
32. Hdt. 9.48. It should be noted from the later battle at Plataea (479), however, that the description of them shooting arrows and javelins is the important point.
33. *XIG* 69.
34. Cf. Ferrill (1985) 108–10. Hodge (1975) 172 raises another possibility, among several, to explain the absence of cavalry, namely that they may have gone ahead with part of the fleet to Phaleron.
35. Vanderpool (1966) 93–106; Harrison (1972) 353–78; *HA* 8–13.
36. Vanderpool (1966) 105 n. 26, pl. 35; Harrison (1972) pl. 75, fig. 7–9.

After a hiatus of ten years the Persians returned in 480 led by King Xerxes, who personally commanded the great expedition that came both by land and by sea. After bridging the Hellespont at Abydos, the army proceeded through Thrace along the coastal road while the fleet sailed offshore. The advance of fleet and army was closely coordinated, as it was risky for them to be out of touch with each other for too many days. South of Thrace and Macedonia, which were subject to Persia, the army would insure that the fleet had a safe shore on which to land when it was necessary to obtain water and rest the crews. The fleet carried supplies for the land forces and prevented the Greeks from landing behind the army and cutting communications with the bases in the rear. Since it was impossible, both for topographical and logistical reasons, for the Persian army to use an inland route, the Greek decision to block the coastal pass at Thermopylae and engage the enemy fleet off Cape Artemisium in the channel between the mainland and the island of Euboea was strategically sound.

The choice of the narrow pass at Thermopylae absolutely precluded the use of cavalry by the Persians. Their advantage in numbers also proved to be of no use, until they outflanked the Greek position with the aid of a local guide who showed them a path, the Anopaia, which led over the heights to the rear of the sea-level pass. Although Thermopylae was a defeat for the Greeks, it demonstrated the superiority of the Greek infantry as well as the difficulties that the terrain of Greece imposed upon cavalry. The Persians never did overcome the fundamental disparity between their infantry and that of the Greeks. Their only serious attempt to correct the deficiency was to hire Greek mercenaries. In the hands of an able leader, an army comprising Greek infantry and Persian cavalry was a superior instrument, as Cyrus the Younger showed at Cunaxa in 401. Unfortunately for the Persians, however, it was not equal to the test posed by Alexander and the Macedonian army created by his father Philip, in which native Macedonians supplied both infantry and cavalry of the highest quality.

One event mentioned by Herodotus that occurred prior to the battle is of some interest. After arriving in Thessaly, Xerxes held a race for his own horses and—aware that the Thessalian horses were reputed to be the best in Greece—included some of them in the contest. In the event the local horses were left far behind.[37] It is not clear whether this was intended to test "race" horses or cavalry horses, since the Greek collective noun (ἡ ἵππος) can mean

---

37. Hdt. 7.196.

either horses or cavalry. Whether this proves that Persian horses were, on average, faster than Greek ones is also open to question, but there is no doubt that Herodotus takes for granted the existence of different varieties of horses at this time, which agrees with the artistic evidence.

At Plataea in 479 the unfolding of events is more complex, but since it is reported in greater detail by Herodotus, we are able to obtain a better idea of the value of the Persian cavalry and the Greek response to them. Once again cavalry were not present on the Greek side, although both the Peloponnesians and the Athenians used mounted messengers to communicate with each other.[38]

After sacking the evacuated city of Athens for a second time, Mardonius withdrew from Attica. The reasons given by Herodotus for Mardonius' decision to retire into Boeotia are strategically sound and have been accepted by modern historians. The advantage Mardonius had in cavalry, estimated at 10,000 horsemen, would have been lost in Attica, whereas in the plain of Boeotia, in the neighborhood of his ally Thebes, he would have the advantage on ground well fitted for horsemen. In addition, should he be defeated in Attica, the only hope of retreat for an army of such a size would be over the narrow pass of Cithaeron.[39] Thus at the very start of the campaign it is evident that Persian operations were dictated in large measure by the need to make effective use of their advantage in cavalry. The number of combatants on each side cannot be precisely known. The numbers given by Herodotus are atypically low and may be approximately correct, at least for the Greeks, who, he says, fielded 38,700 hoplites. His figure of 69,500 for the Greek light armed seems high. Greek tradition is insistent that the Persians outnumbered the Greeks at Plataea, but it is unlikely that Herodotus' figure of 300,000 for the troops left behind by Xerxes in 480 B.C. is correct.[40] Modern estimates vary, but a reasonable estimate would be about 50,000 infantry and 10,000 cavalry. Since the quality of the troops was more important than the numbers, even accurate figures would have meant little. Aside from the units supplied by their Greek allies, only the native Persian infantry and cavalry had a chance of standing up to the hoplites.[41]

The Greeks followed the Persians into Boeotia, where both armies took up defensive positions immediately to the northeast of the town of Plataea.

---

38. Ibid., 9.54, 60.
39. Ibid., 9.13.
40. Ibid., 8.113.
41. Ferrill (1985) 119; *XIG* 354–55, 438; How and Wells ([1912] 1968) 2: append. 19.

Cavalry dominated the thinking of both commanders. For Mardonius, the Persian, the purpose of his subsequent actions was to entice the Greeks out into the open, north of the river Asopus, which flowed east and west, where cavalry would have the advantage. On the other hand Pausanias, who had occupied the ridges leading northward into the plain, was using the uneven ground of the ridges to keep the Persian cavalry at bay and hoped to decide the issue against the infantry alone. He was also in a better position than Mardonius to play the waiting game. Now that the Persian fleet had been disposed of at Salamis, there was no longer any fear of the Greeks' being outflanked by sea. They could merely wait for the frustrated Persians to depart, whereas Mardonius must have known that the Greek fleet was sailing for the eastern Aegean and Ionia and his need for a decisive victory was essential if the subject Greeks of Anatolia were to be kept from rebellion. Strategically, the Greeks would have been better off defending the fortifications at the Isthmus of Corinth, where any Persian advantage in numbers and cavalry would have been meaningless, but political concerns overruled purely strategic principles. The Athenians were loathe to abandon their homeland indefinitely until Mardonius should give up. The Spartan commander Pausanias—regent and cousin of the minor son of slain Spartan king Leonidas—prompted by the overtures made by Mardonius to the Athenians (who hoped to come to terms and thus secure their fleet), eventually led the Peloponnesian contingent northward.[42] Thus Mardonius obtained the strategic advantage of a battlefield of his choosing. Or, rather, he almost did—for the Greeks refused to come down onto the plain.

Perhaps out of frustration, Mardonius sent cavalry against the Greek position. These concentrated their attacks on the Megarians, who had been stationed at a point in the line where the nature of the ground permitted easy access for the horsemen. Led by the cavalry commander Masistius, they rode against the Greeks by squadrons, discharged their weapons, and rode away. Hard pressed, the Megarians sent a herald to the Greek generals announcing that they would abandon their post if help were not sent. Three hundred picked Athenian troops under the command of Olympiodorus, together with the archers, were sent. There ensued a battle of some duration between the Greek infantry and the Persian cavalry, until Masistius' horse was wounded by an arrow. The animal reared and shook off Masistius, who was immediately attacked by the Athenians. The protection afforded by the scale cuirass

---

42. Hdt. 9.4–11.

he was wearing was so effective that he could only be killed by a blow to the eye. The Persian cavalry now charged en masse in an effort to recover their leader's body. The three hundred Athenians were about to be overwhelmed when other infantry arrived and helped drive off the cavalry.[43]

Clearly, the number of combatants on each side was critical. Before the Athenians were reinforced the cavalry had the advantage, which they then lost to the infantry. If Herodotus is correct, large numbers of troops were engaged on both sides, and the result was a clear victory for the Greek infantry.[44] Up to a point the Persian cavalry tactics are clear. Squadrons of horses charged to a place where they could launch their missile weapons, whether arrow or javelin, after which they wheeled about and retired.[45] The succession of charging squadrons presumably produced an alternation of a flight of missiles followed by a pause, a sort of rhythmic sequence as squadron followed squadron. There is also the likelihood of closer combat, first when Masistius fell and was immediately surrounded and shortly thereafter when the Persian cavalry tried to recover his body, losing more men in the process.

It is less clear what the Greek heavy infantry were doing. Since the Greek hoplite was armed with a thrusting spear and a short sword at this time, it is difficult to see how he could harm a Persian cavalryman shooting from a distance. Archers, of course, could return fire, as happened in the case of Masistius, but the battle was won by the heavy infantry. Their defensive armor, helmet, cuirass, and shield would blunt the effectiveness of the missiles, but their spears would be useful only at close range, and such an opportunity was offered only after the death of Masistius in the fight over his body. Is it possible that hoplites were prepared to throw the spear when such action was dictated by necessity? Of course lighter armed javelin men may have come up as part of the relief force, but that remains only a guess, and understanding of the events is far from clear.

It appears as if at first the Megarians were unable to respond to the repeated charges of the Persian horse, whose mobility and missiles gave them a decided advantage. With the arrival of the Athenians, however, Herodotus reports that a battle of some length was fought, which should have meant give-and-take on both sides. In the struggle over Masistius' body, which must

---

43. Hdt. 9.20–23. Pritchett's comment on the three hundred picked troops—"the context indicates that they were cavalry"—creates a problem where none exists, since the Persian cavalry could not withstand good infantry in sufficient numbers, especially if they were supported by archers. *GSW* 2 224.

44. Hdt. 9.20, 23. Mardonius sent "all the cavalry" (πᾶσαν τὴν ἵππον), while "all the foot" aided the Athenians (ὁ πεζὸς ἅπας ἐβοήθεε). This is perhaps not literally true, but it suggests large numbers.

45. Hdt. 9.18, 22.

have involved close combat, the Athenians had much the worst of it until they were reinforced by other Greek infantry. Then, if not before, the Greeks did inflict casualties on the enemy cavalry.[46] Incidentally, the armor worn by Masistius in the form of a gilded scale cuirass was undoubtedly a luxury item; it remains uncertain whether body armor was worn by ordinary Persian cavalry of this period.

While the Persians lamented the death of Masistius in their camp north of the river Asopus, the Greeks rejoiced in the rout of the enemy horsemen. With the Persians temporarily distracted, the Greeks moved their camp westward to a more suitable site near Plataea where the Gargaphian spring offered a good supply of water.[47] This new position was more exposed than the previous one, and it has been suggested that Pausanias was trying to tempt Mardonius to make an attack.[48] The Persians also moved their camp but made no effort to cross the river, and stalemate resulted. After a delay of eight days, during which each side was content to remain in its secure defensive position, the Persians made a bold and successful move. On the advice of a Theban, Timagenides, on the night of the eighth day Mardonius sent cavalry to intercept Greek reinforcements using a pass over Cithaeron. At the outlet of the pass the Persians captured five hundred draft (or pack) animals and the men attending them, who were bringing grain to the Greek army from the Peloponnese.[49] The failure of the Greeks to protect their supply lines is the type of operational lapse that typically occurs in Greek warfare of this period.

From this point on, apparently, the Persian cavalry continually harassed the Greek lines, shooting arrows and javelins and frustrating Greek attempts to close with them by riding away. During these attacks the Persians succeeded in reaching and rendering unfit the Gargaphian spring, from which the Greeks drew much of their water.[50] Meeting in council, the Greek leaders decided to withdraw even closer to Plataea, where they could occupy a better defensive position and be closer to water. They were also suffering from a lack of food, as the supplies from the south had been cut off.[51]

    46. Ibid., 9.23.
    47. Ibid., 9.24–25.
    48. *XIG* 310.
    49. Hdt. 9.39. The Greek is ambiguous. The five hundred ὑποζύγια could be draft or baggage animals of any type, and sometimes the word is a synonym for donkey. The men attend ζεύγεσι, which usually means a team of animals; thus it seems likely that the grain was transported in wheeled vehicles.
    50. Hdt. 9.40, 49.
    51. Ibid., 9.50, 51.

Through his patience and a judicious use of cavalry, Mardonius had demonstrated the soundness of choosing the Boeotian plain as a battle site. The Greeks now had little choice but to retreat, yet as long as they could avoid a decisive defeat their position was superior to that of Mardonius, who would soon require a victory in order to insure his own security and that of his Greek allies as well as to allay fear of a rebellion in Ionia.

It is impossible to reconstruct the Greek plan of retreat from the pages of Herodotus, in part because it was not completed as intended. In addition to their need for water and desire to reach higher, more defensible ground on Mount Cithaeron, the Greeks probably also hoped to restore their communications with the Peloponnese. Their retreat began under cover of darkness early on the thirteenth day. The Greek center, perhaps confused by an overly complex plan and certainly glad to get out of the way of the Persian cavalry, retired far to the rear and halted at the temple of Hera just outside Plataea, taking no part in the coming battle. That left the Athenians on the left and the Spartans on the right separated and out of sight of each other as they began the withdrawal. The Spartans were somewhat delayed under obscure circumstances; the explanation given by Herodotus has not found favor with modern historians.[52] In any event the Spartans were overtaken by the Persian cavalry making their morning rounds. Having crossed the Asopus and found the ground formerly occupied by the Greeks abandoned, the Persians had continued on in pursuit. The Spartans had not reached cover on higher ground and were forced to halt, at which time they were attacked by the cavalry. Although relatively safe so long as they did not break ranks, the Spartans could not take casualties from the Persian missiles indefinitely, so they sent off a message to the Athenians asking them to come to their aid or—if they were engaged themselves—at least to send the archers.

Meanwhile Mardonius, perhaps thinking that the Greeks were in full flight and afraid to lose an opportunity for victory, sent his Persian infantry across the Asopus. Unable to close with the disciplined Spartans, the Persian cavalry apparently made way for the foot archers, who set up their shields as a defensive barrier and showered the Greek ranks with arrows. Although he had been outgeneraled by Mardonius, it appears that Pausanias was the better tactician. Waiting until it was clear that the enemy infantry were fully committed, all the while suffering casualties from arrows, Pausanias finally ordered

---

52. *XIG* 322–32. Supposedly a Spartan captain, Amompharetus, refused to leave his position because retreating in the face of the enemy would bring shame on Sparta. Perhaps the Spartans were holding back in order to cover the retreat of the rest of the army.

the charge. As the Greeks closed, the Persian archers threw down their bows. The low wall of wickerwork shields offered little resistance to the Greek phalanx, and the final struggle took place hand to hand. The Greeks had a decided advantage in weapons, armor, discipline, and skill, nevertheless, it was only when Mardonius and his guards were killed that Persian resistance collapsed and victory for the Greeks was assured.[53]

On the left the Athenians eventually routed the Greek allies of the Persians. According to Herodotus only the Boeotians had much heart for the fight, their cavalry doing good service in protecting the fleeing foot soldiers.[54] The Theban horsemen, in particular, demonstrated how dangerous cavalry could be to infantry under certain conditions; when word reached the Greek center at the temple of Hera that the Persians were on the run, the Corinthians, Megarians, and Phliasians set out in haste to catch up. The Corinthians were a bit more circumspect and kept to the rough country, but the Megarians and Phliasians ventured out onto the plain. Caught in the open by the Theban cavalry led by Asopodorus as they hurried along in disorder, they were savagely attacked and driven back to higher ground, losing six hundred men.[55] The final event of the campaign was the capture of the fort in which the surviving Persians had taken refuge.

The Greeks had reason to rejoice. Over a period of twenty years, against the seemingly overwhelming numbers of the greatest power of which they had knowledge, they had won victories that literally changed European history and prevented Greece from being reduced to the status of a province. Certainly, it is understandable if even today we read Herodotus' splendid account of these events with more than a touch of emotion. Even allowing for obvious Greek superiority in many areas, one still has the distinct feeling that they beat the odds. Indeed, on two occasions in his narrative Thucydides places in the mouths of speakers the claim that the Greek victory was due to Persian mistakes and fortune.[56] The difference, when it mattered, apparently lay in "fighting power"—the intangible qualities of group character resulting from social, religious, and political cohesion, among other things, that enable an army to fight well over a period of time and under virtually any conditions.[57]

53. Hdt. 9.52–63.
54. Ibid., 9.67–68.
55. Ibid., 9.69.
56. Thuc. 1.69.5, 6.33.5. These speeches, intended to encourage Athens' enemies, were influenced by rhetorical needs but do reflect some current opinion. Cawkwell (1997) 11; *CT* 1 114. Herodotus, 7.139, gives much more credit to the Athenians.
57. For a fascinating study of fighting power in World War II consult van Creveld (1982).

The Persians, in their long conflict with the Greeks, were never able to field an army that lacked ethnic diversity and its attendant dissimilarity of arms and tactics, not to mention the latent hostility of the subject peoples who were required to supply troops.

It is important to state that the performance of the Persian and Boeotian cavalry during the conflict was exemplary. Their presence throughout the campaign had a decisive influence on all aspects of operations. The inability of the Greeks to neutralize them on level ground prevented them from using the phalanx to advantage. The cavalry successfully harassed the Greek front lines, interrupted the flow of supplies, drove the Greeks from water, brought the Spartans to bay in the final battle, protected the line of retreat of their defeated infantry, and destroyed disorganized infantry foolish enough to get in their way. Their major weakness was an inability or reluctance to fight at close quarters against a formation of disciplined infantry. No other cavalry in the Mediterranean basin and the Near East at this time were their betters. For the mounted arm in general, more than a century was required to overcome fully its reluctance to engage in hand-to-hand combat and thus to realize its potential as an integral part of the battle line.

Chapter 5

From City-State to Empire: 479 to 432 B.C.

SINCE GREEK HISTORY AS it has come to be written is largely the story of Athens and Sparta, the fact that the two were traditionally weak in cavalry has encouraged the assumption that the same was true of all the Greek city-states. This is most unfortunate, because it is perfectly clear that some of the others had successfully maintained their equestrian traditions through the Archaic period and were able to field cavalry forces recognizable as such in the sixth and fifth centuries. The performance of the Boeotian cavalry that fought as allies of the Persians stands in stark contrast to the total absence of organized cavalry formations on the allied Greek side. The fact that the Boeotians had cavalry at this time does not mean that they were unaffected by the phalanx mentality of their neighbors to the south but may have been a necessary concession to the Thessalians to the north, among whom cavalry was dominant. A realistic appraisal of local conditions likely encouraged them to add cavalry in meaningful numbers to supplement the infantry. Different local forces were at work among the western Greeks. In the fertile plains of Sicily conditions were right for the raising of horses, and cavalry formed an important part of the armed forces of the large and wealthy Greek city-states on the island.[1] Yet even there, the environmental conditions were probably not sufficient to explain the development of cavalry; the need to campaign against the Carthaginians, based in the western end of the island, more than likely

---

1. For a fine appreciation of cavalry among the western Greeks see Fredericksen (1968) 2: 3–31. Fredericksen 21, 24 traces the origin of Campanian cavalry to Greek colonial influence, specifically to Cumae. This raises the possibility of influence upon Roman military practices, since Rome levied troops from the region at a later date and relied on allied cavalry to make good its own deficiency in this arm.

supplied the catalyst. This situation in Sicily, brought about by the Greeks' having to face enemies with different fighting styles, emphasizes the artificiality of the limited hoplite warfare of central and southern Greece.

By 481, when Xerxes was preparing his expedition against Old Greece, the military reputation of Syracuse under its tyrant Gelon was such that the Greeks sent an embassy to request aid. In the early 490s Gelon had been a member of the guard of Hippocrates, tyrant of Gela. Because of his ability, he soon was promoted to the position of commander of cavalry. In the years immediately following he distinguished himself in the wars that Hippocrates fought against the neighboring towns of Callipolis, Naxos, Zancle, Leontini, and Syracuse. Gelon himself became tyrant of Gela in 491 and gained power in Syracuse in 485.[2] The embassy probably met with him there in the fall of 481. Gelon did, indeed, offer help—and substantial help at that—but the Athenian and Spartan envoys could not grant his demand to be appointed leader of all the allied forces. Of note, however, are the specific forces that he offered to send. These comprised two hundred triremes, twenty thousand hoplites, two thousand cavalry, two thousand archers, two thousand slingers, and a further two thousand whose exact description is unclear because of difficulty in translating the Greek words ἱπποδρόμους ψιλούς. Their dictionary meaning is "light horsemen," but in their commentary W. W. How and J. Wells describe them as light infantry who fought alongside the horsemen, equating them with the Boeotian ἅμιπποι.[3] Even if we err on the side of caution and use the figure of two thousand cavalry, that makes a cavalryman for every ten hoplites and compares favorably with what is found in Greek armies of the next three centuries, during much of which time the value of cavalry was taken for granted. The presence not only of cavalry but of a variety of specialized light armed troops indicates a more advanced level of military thinking than that found at the same time in Old Greece and anticipates the integration of arms that was an essential part of the Macedonian achievement from the mid-fourth century on.

Irrespective of Gelon's wishes—and there was a local tradition in Sicily that he was preparing to send troops in spite of the failure of the embassy—circumstances intervened to prevent him from exercising the option.[4] The Carthaginians, allegedly in concert with the Persians in the west, had landed

---

2. Hdt. 7.154–55.
3. How and Wells ([1912] 1968) 2: 197.
4. Hdt. 7.165.

a large expeditionary force on the north side of Sicily and were besieging the city of Himera.[5] Gelon responded to this by marching out with no fewer than fifty thousand infantry and more than five thousand cavalry. Once again the proportion of cavalry is significant, and in the battle that followed they played a significant, if atypical, role. On his arrival at Himera Gelon fortified a camp, complete with ditch and palisade. Then he sent out all of his cavalry against the enemy, who were foraging widely. With the advantage of surprise the Syracusan cavalry caught ten thousand of the enemy soldiers, who had scattered without formation throughout the countryside.[6]

With due respect for the size and ability of the Carthaginian army, Gelon then employed his cavalry in an unconventional manner to win a great victory. During their scouring of the countryside, his horsemen had captured a courier bearing a message from the Greek city of Selinus, which was allied with the Carthaginians. Its contents were intended to inform Hamilcar, the Carthaginian commander, that the cavalry from Selinus would arrive on the day that he had requested. Using this information, Gelon sent out his own cavalry early on the appointed day to Hamilcar's naval camp. Their boldness carrying its own conviction, they were welcomed into the enemy camp as allies. Once inside, they killed Hamilcar and set fire to the ships while Gelon advanced with his whole army against the camp. A difficult battle ensued, in which the Syracusans came away victorious.[7] It was perhaps patriotism rather than historical judgment that encouraged the Sicilian historian Diodorus to compare the victory at Himera with that at Plataea a year later.[8] Yet he may not have been so far off the mark, for the common practice of viewing Greek history through Athenian eyes tends to obscure the importance of events in the west. The epic battles the Sicilian Greeks waged against the Carthaginians for centuries, until Rome intervened, held an alien people at bay and kept open the route by which Greek culture entered the Italian peninsula, thus decisively affecting European history.

---

5. Collusion with the Persians is reported by Ephorus (fr. 186) in Jacoby (1963) and Diodorus Siculus (11. 1) but is not mentioned by Herodotus. How and Wells think such an arrangement was "highly probable," but Hignett denies it. How and Wells ([1912] 1968) 2: 196; *XIG* 95–96.

6. Diod. 11.21.1–3.

7. Ibid., 11.21.3–22. Since military dress was not uniform, it was difficult to distinguish friend from foe.

8. Ibid., 11.23.1. Tradition held that the battle of Himera was closely associated with the great battles against the Persians in the same year, 480. Diodorus states that it occurred on the same day Leonidas was fighting at Thermopylae (11.24), whereas Herodotus assigns it to the day on which Salamis was fought (7. 166).

The dearth of sources for the period between the end of the Persian Wars and the outbreak of the Peloponnesian War (479–432) is most regrettable. The most lengthy narrative of the events of the mid-fifth century is that of Diodorus Siculus.[9] Unfortunately it lacks detailed descriptions of the many important military actions of the period. Thucydides' *Pentecontaëtia*, which covers these years, is brief and incomplete compared to the *Histories* as a whole, because he sought only to describe the growth of Athenian power.[10]

During this period in the Greek-speaking world, there were two arenas of military activity. In Greece proper the imperial ambitions of Athens dominated relations among the city-states and fostered hostilities on land and sea. To the west in Sicily, once the Carthaginians had been reduced to impotence for the time being, the Greek cities fought among themselves for dominance. In spite of the lack of detail in the spare accounts of Thucydides and Diodorus, they do report the presence of cavalry at many of the battles that occurred. In fact it seems clear that their experiences in the Persian Wars had convinced even the Athenians of the value of the mounted arm; throughout the period they showed increasing interest in cavalry, and by 431 B.C. they had a regular force of one thousand.[11]

The absence of cavalry from most of central and southern Greece in the early fifth century, in contrast to its existence to the north and west—that is, in Thessaly and Sicily—is sometimes attributed to the unsuitability of the country for raising horses.[12] The traditional preference for limited hoplite warfare is the major reason for its absence, however. No doubt the fertile plains of Thessaly and, especially, Sicily would have encouraged stock raising, and—in Thessaly, at least—hoplite warfare never took on the importance it assumed in the city-states to the south.[13] In Thessaly, however, the requisite number of free farmers did not exist since the aristocracy, whose wealth was based on agricultural estates worked by dependent farmers, remained dominant. In the case of Athens democratic antipathy to the aristocracy may also have played a small part. Such an attitude would have had much less influence in Sicily and none at all in Thessaly. A certain amount of inertia may also have been at work, and in Sparta there was clearly no need for cavalry until it was time to fight enemies from outside the Peloponnese who employed this arm.

9. Diod. 11.39–12.28.
10. Thuc. 1.89–118. *HCT* 1 361–65. Hornblower (1987) 133–34.
11. Thuc. 2.3.8. This did not include two hundred mounted archers.
12. *HCT* 1 15.
13. See Diod. 11.72.1, for the fertility of Sicily.

Nonetheless, in the decades that followed the Persian Wars even our few sources provide clear evidence of a growing interest in cavalry on the part of the Athenians. Indeed, in the immediate aftermath of Plataea, Aristides—one of the Athenian generals—reportedly proposed the establishment of a joint Hellenic force comprising ten thousand infantry, one thousand cavalry, and one hundred ships to carry on the war with the Persians.[14] Unfortunately, Plutarch is the only source for this information, and the role that he assigns to Aristides in the assembly of the Hellenes on this occasion has been questioned.[15] On the other hand Plutarch's lack of interest in military affairs makes it unlikely that he added the reference to cavalry on his own. Most likely it came from his source, and it may have gone back to a genuine utterance of Aristides whether he made it at this time or later. Aeschylus, the tragic poet who fought at both Marathon and Salamis, also indicates the importance of the enemy cavalry by his frequent mention of horsemen in his play *Persians*, which was produced in 472.[16] From Megara, west of Athens, comes an inscription that suggests the pride felt by the allies in overcoming cavalry. It seems to refer to graves of Megarians, known to us from a passage in Pausanias, who died fighting Persian horsemen.[17] Nonetheless, there is no evidence that the Athenians attempted to create a native cavalry force until the 450s.

Once the Persians had been forced to evacuate the Balkan peninsula and the immediate threat from the cavalry arm disappeared, there was no reason for the southern Greek city-states to make changes in their hoplite tactics. The first task of the Athenians upon their return to the city was to rebuild its walls as well as to provide the same protection for their port, Peiraeus. This was the work of Themistocles, who earlier had been responsible for building the navy that was victorious at Salamis. Thucydides believed that Themistocles' decision to seek security in walls and ships was due to his observation that the Persian forces had found the sea approach easier than the approach by land.[18] Most of the military actions carried out by Athens in the name of

---

14. Plut. *Arist.* 21.1.
15. Hignett considers Plutarch's statement about Aristides' influence on the reorganization of the Hellenic League to be a fiction, while Hammond seems to accept it at face value. *XIG* 342; Hammond (1959) 250.
16. *Persians*, lines 19, 27, 46, 106, 126, 302, 315, 996. For a discussion of this see Martin (1887) 430. This is a sound work that remains useful. See especially his chap. 4, 427–54 on the military role of Athenian cavalry.
17. *IG* 1051v. 7. Paus. 1.23.1.
18. Thuc. 1.93.7.

the Delian League in the middle of the fifth century occurred away from mainland Greece and were absolutely dependent on its navy.[19]

In the late 460s, however, the strategic picture began to change as concern on the part of Athens' neighbors to the west and south—Thebes, Corinth, and Sparta—manifested itself. The challenge to Athens' growing power and fear of its intentions on the Greek mainland eventually led to what is called the First Peloponnesian War (ca. 460–446). By the end of 462 Athens had concluded alliances with Argos and Thessaly, which unfortunately were to bring more trouble than benefit.[20] Shortly thereafter the Megarians defected from the Peloponnesians and joined Athens.[21] Since Sparta and the Peloponnesian League would be the principal enemies of Athens in any future conflict, the alliances with Argos and Megara are strategically easy to explain. With the aid of Argos, Athens could hope to control the peninsula that forms the northeastern part of the Peloponnese and hinder Spartan access to central Greece. Argos would also be a useful stopping place for ships sailing around the Peloponnese to the Athenian naval base at Naupactus, which was captured about this time from West Locris. Megara offered more direct communications with western Greece, since it lay astride the Isthmus of Corinth with harbors on both sides. The Athenians built long walls from Megara to Nisaea, the eastern harbor on the Saronic Gulf, and manned it with their own troops. Control of the northern part of the isthmus also meant that Athens could prevent an invasion from the south. Corinth's hatred of Athens, which poisoned Greek history until the end of the century, arose at this time because Athens was siding with Megara in a land dispute between it and Corinth. Then too, as Argos was the traditional enemy of Sparta, the whole affair could only lead to a deterioration in relations between Athens and the Peloponnesians. Since little came of these alliances, Athens reaped only ill will from its efforts at strategic diplomacy.

Because Athens had little to fear from the north, the alliance with Thessaly could have been undertaken only to secure cavalry, the principal military arm found in the region. Events in 458/457, however, showed that Athenian control of the Megarid did not present an insuperable barrier to a Peloponnesian invasion after all, as some 11,500 troops marched into Boeotia.

19. The Delian League was conceived as an alliance of city–states around the Aegean, formed to keep the Persians out of the region. It came into existence in 478 or 477 and gradually transformed itself into what was virtually an Athenian empire. Thuc. 1.96.
20. Thuc. 1.102.4.
21. Ibid., 1.103.4.

The Athenians and their allies, numbering 14,000, together with some Thessalian cavalry, met them at Tanagra. During the course of this hard-fought battle the desertion of the Thessalians to the Peloponnesian side may have decided the issue.[22] Thus the Athenian attempt to make up for their deficiency in cavalry by using allied horsemen ended in a fiasco.

There is a possibility that some Athenian horsemen were present at this battle. In his description of Attica, while enumerating the graves that lay outside the city, Pausanias mentions a stele containing a portrayal of two fighting horsemen who died fighting Lacedaemonians and Boeotians in the vicinity of Eleon and Tanagra.[23] Furthermore, there is a fragmentary funerary inscription that lends additional support.[24] Unfortunately, neither piece of evidence can be precisely dated, although the inscription is probably from the third quarter of the fifth century. Given the fragmentary state of our knowledge of this period, there may well have been other battles fought by Athenians at Tanagra of which there is no record.

Be that as it may, in the following year there is strong evidence that Athens did not have a cavalry force as such. At that time an exiled Thessalian king's son, Orestes, enlisted Athenian aid in his effort to return home in style. The Athenians (perhaps hoping to avenge Thessalian treachery at Tanagra), together with some Boeotian and Phocian allies, made an expedition against the Thessalian town of Pharsalus. Although the invader's phalanx marched unopposed and could have reduced Pharsalus by siege, it was the Thessalian cavalry that proved to be the decisive force. Taking advantage of the phalanx's principal weakness of having to operate as a single cumbersome unit, the cavalry simply kept the invaders cooped up in camp until a shortage of supplies compelled them to retire.[25] Nothing better shows the danger of excessive reliance upon a single type of military force than this instance. Out of its environment and lacking auxiliary forces that could contribute tactical versatility, the phalanx proved itself a liability. And so, without a battle, the Thessalian cavalry thwarted the Athenian design. Thus Athenian military involvement in areas outside the region where the limited warfare of hoplite tactics was practicable, coupled with the realization that allied cavalry would not suffice, compelled Athens to face reality and create its own cavalry arm.

---

22. Ibid., 1.107.7, 108.1; D. S. 11.80. *GSW* 2 205, credits the Spartan victory to the Thessalian defection. See also *HA*; *CCG* 12, 13.

23. Paus. 1.29.6.

24. *IG* I^2 946; Wade-Gery (1933)78–79; *HCT* 1 316.

25. Thuc. 1.111.1; Diod. 11.83.34. *HA* 50–52.

As Bugh suggests, this probably occurred in the aftermath of Tanagra.[26] At first the horsemen numbered only three hundred, yet sometime before the outbreak of the Peloponnesian War in 431 the number had been increased to one thousand. It was then commanded by two hipparchs and ten phylarchs.[27] The likelihood that this time is correct is bolstered by the fact that Athens was militarily active in Boeotia in the 450s and 440s; regular cavalry forces seem to have existed there since before the Persian Wars, as we have seen. Since even Thucydides had no interest in providing details of these actions in central Greece, the fact that cavalry are not mentioned means little. A. W. Gomme suggests that the establishment of cavalry in the middle of the century was partially a recognition of the status or wealth of the aristocracy, which is reasonable as far as it goes, and Bugh adds the possibility that it was an effort "to reconcile the aristocracy to the new democratic political order after 461."[28] On the other hand the experiences of the Athenians in central and northern Greece during the preceding two decades should have convinced them of the necessity of having their own cavalry arm. Military necessity would seem to be the principal reason for the change.

The Spartans, on the other hand, were not yet convinced. This is not surprising given the nature of the terrain in the Peloponnese, the fighting practices of their neighbors there, and the Spartans' lack of interest in the outside world. Under these circumstances they did not require cavalry. In spite of their reputation, the Spartans were neither unduly militaristic nor aggressive. When they fought, it was as a result of the self-imposed necessity of keeping their slaves, subjects, and allies in line, not for glory. It was only when they entered upon a prolonged conflict with Athens in 431 that their lack of cavalry revealed itself as a weakness. This is not to say that the Spartans were unaware of the potential value of cavalry before that time, however.

In 432, for example—probably in July—Sparta's allies were asked to present their grievances against Athens to the Apella, the Spartan assembly.[29] Since it was at this meeting that the decision was made to go to war with Athens, Thucydides saw fit to present four of the speeches made on the occasion in his *Histories*. These, of course, are not verbatim accounts, but there is reason to believe that they are faithful to the arguments that

26. *HA* 52.
27. For discussion see *HCT* 1 328; and *HA* 52–74.
28. *HA* 74. Around 461 there seems to have been some change in the structure of the Athenian government that favored the democratic element at the expense of the aristocracy.
29. *HCT* 1 421.

were spoken.[30] The first of these was an attack by the Corinthians upon Athens and the second a reply by the Athenians, who happened to have an embassy in Sparta on other business and were granted permission to speak. Subsequently, the Spartans went into closed session, and from their debate Thucydides included the speeches of Archidamus, (one of the kings) and Sthenelaidas (an Ephor). Of particular interest is the mention made by both speakers of the differences in military power between Athens and Sparta, notably the possession of horses by the Athenians.[31] To be sure, the greatest single advantage that Athens possessed was its navy, yet the mention of horses is noteworthy. The Spartan decision to go to war was not made lightly and, if Thucydides is to be trusted, they had a clear conception of the military problem that they faced. Nevertheless, it was not until the summer of 424 that the Spartans felt desperate enough to establish a cavalry corps. Thucydides draws attention to the fact that this was contrary to their usual custom, and it does not seem to have resulted from any radical change in their view of the way in which land battles should be fought.[32] Indeed, its creation at this time seems to have been prompted by the Spartans' need to add mobility to their coastal forces in the Peloponnese, which were being frustrated by seaborne Athenian raiders.

Thus in spite of a growing—if at times reluctant—awareness of cavalry's usefulness, there was no dramatic change in military practice in central and southern Greece during the first two-thirds of the fifth century. However, the conflict that occupied the Greeks for the remainder of the century produced a revolution in military practice and brought into firm focus—for those who had eyes to see—the hitherto unrealized potential of the mounted arm. This, together with a professionalism fostered by almost incessant warfare, set the stage for the remarkable military achievements of the fourth century that reached their culmination in Alexander.

---

30. Ibid., 252–55. Thucydides himself (1.22) explains the principles on which he reconstructed the speeches he used in his work.
31. Thuc. 1.80.3, 86.3.
32. Ibid., 2.55–56.

Chapter 6

The Peloponnesian War: 431 to 404 B.C.

A RECORD OF THE FIRST twenty-one years of the Peloponnesian War survives in the incomparable work of Thucydides, the greatest historian of antiquity. Thucydides himself held a command for Athens in 421, and he seems to have had more than the usual interest in military matters, for which the military historian can be grateful. Countering this, however, is his assumption—typical of ancient Greek historians writing for a Greek audience—that the reader knew the inner workings of Greek armies from his own experience as a soldier. As a result there are military activities about which we have only the foggiest notion, comparable, say, to the impression of rugby that an American tourist might obtain from the sports pages of a London newspaper.[1] Nonetheless, the information supplied by Thucydides and his successor Xenophon, a lesser historian but an acknowledged military authority, permits us to recognize and describe important changes in military practice and outlook that took place in the last third of the fifth century.

Gomme, in the introduction to his commentary on Thucydides, describes the routine duties of cavalry at this time: "They were used at home to prevent raiding beyond the enemy's armed camp, in enemy country to make a raid; in pitched battles they were present on the wings, to harry an outflanking movement (especially against the left wing) and to hinder pursuit, seldom for a decisive action."[2] This by no means exhausts the potential uses of cavalry, however, for this arm has proved to be exceptionally versatile. At the same time that cavalry's role in warfare was expanding, so, too, was that of

1. For discussion of this problem, see Grundy (1948) 1: 240–42; HCT 1 10–19.
2. HCT 1 15.

light infantry. In both cases the need to add to the versatility of the phalanx was responsible. In the early fourth century in Greece the most successful light infantry were the peltasts, apparently of Thracian origin.[3] Since they were easier to obtain and less costly to maintain, they could be used in place of cavalry for duties in which the operational skills of the two overlapped. Nevertheless, light infantry were inferior to cavalry in respect to mobility, speed, and the capacity for psychological intimidation,[4] while they had the advantage in broken country.

The principal weapon of cavalry during the Peloponnesian War was a type of spear that could be used either for stabbing or for throwing. The latter seems to have been the more common practice. There can be no comparison between this spear and the medieval lance. Not only was the Greek spear shorter than the lance, it was held only by the hand and not (at least regularly) pressed between the side of the body and the arm, in the "couched" position of the Middle Ages. In close combat the right, spear-holding arm moved freely, either in an over- or underhand position, whichever seemed most appropriate at the moment for stabbing and, perhaps, slashing. Thus the strength of the blow came largely from the muscles of the arm and upper body rather than from the momentum of the horse and rider in motion. Doubt has been cast upon the effectiveness of such blows, which were delivered without the benefit of saddle and stirrups. But this overlooks the fact that experienced bareback riders almost invariably have a better seat and more secure leg contact with the horse than riders using stirrups and saddle. When one is riding with stirrups there is the temptation to place too much weight in them, thereby reducing the desirable contact of legs and seat. The extreme example of this is the style of riding used by professional jockeys, who stand in the stirrups during the race and have no contact with the seat of the saddle. There is no reason to doubt that the Greek cavalryman had a functionally secure seat or that he could wield his weapons effectively. One example should suffice. In 334, during the battle Alexander fought against the Persians at the Granicus, Clitus, with one blow of a slashing sword, cut off the shoulder of the Persian Spithridates, who was about to strike Alexander from the rear.[5] The use of stirrups could hardly add to the effectiveness of this sword stroke.

3. Best (1969).
4. At Delium, for example, the unexpected appearance of enemy cavalry caused the Athenian infantry to panic (Thuc. 4.96.5).
5. Arr. *Anab.* 1.15.8.

Although in general little use was made by Greek cavalry of the bow, Athens did have two hundred horse archers in 431.[6] Their tactical function is not precisely known, but Xenophon reports that in battle these horse archers rode out ahead of the other cavalry. This tantalizing bit of information, put into the mouth of Socrates, shows how little we know about types of cavalry and their operational use in the late fifth and early fourth centuries. If the description is accurate, it suggests the role of skirmishers that was fulfilled by the *prodromoi* of Alexander later in the century.[7] The Athenian speech writer Lysias, in a speech written about 395, suggests that serving with the horse archers is less prestigious than serving with the regular cavalry. He goes on to say that cavalry service itself is less dangerous than service in the infantry, accusing the younger Alcibiades of cowardice for choosing cavalry over infantry service.[8] Mounted archers grew more prominent in the Hellenistic period, but they never became an effective striking force of the type that dominated warfare on the Asiatic steppe for centuries. There, riding and archery were skills acquired from early childhood and had long been an integral part of nomadic life. The open steppe was also essential for the success of the tactics later made famous by the Mongols and other nomadic peoples. This way of life had nothing in common with the agricultural and urban one found in the lower Balkans, where both archery and horse riding were peripheral activities.

By the beginning of the Peloponnesian War, Pericles—perhaps more than most other Athenians—appreciated the value of cavalry. In 431, in his speech to the assembly encouraging the Athenians to have confidence about the coming struggle, Pericles mentioned the twelve hundred cavalry, including mounted archers, which Athens had ready.[9] He himself was largely responsible for the development of these cavalry, in spite of the fact that the strategic plan for the war was to assume the defensive on land while employing Athens' fleet—which was superior both in quality and in numbers—to maintain control of the sea.[10]

This plan, with the simplicity of genius, totally changed the principles of Greek warfare and destroyed the opportunity for an almost certain Spartan victory. As I have mentioned, the need to defend the limited agricultural

---

6. Thuc. 2.13.8; 5.84.1; 6.94.4.
7. Xen. *Mem.* 3.3.1.
8. Lys. 15.6; 14.7–8. See also *HA* 221; *CCG* 56–58.
9. Thuc. 2.13.8.
10. Ibid., 1.143.3–5; 2.62.2–3; 2.65.7.

land of the Greek city-states by citizen soldiers had led to the "tacit agreement" whereby decisive battles were fought by hoplite infantry on open battlefields. But now Athens, abandoning the concept of decisive battle, was to show that any coastal city that could keep its sea-lanes open could deny the enemy an opportunity for decisive victory on land. It was painful to watch the Spartans invade and lay waste the territory of Attica, but it was not critical, because the population was safe behind the great system of walls connecting Athens and the port of Piraeus. In the meantime the long coastline of the Peloponnese was vulnerable to sea-borne raids of the Athenians. If Athenian patience outlasted that of the Spartans, resulting in peace based on the status quo, it would in effect be a victory for Athens, which would retain its empire and its mastery in the Aegean.

Why, then, was Pericles interested in cavalry? Although cavalry may have been created to meet the needs of warfare in central Greece during the preceding twenty years, Pericles soon found a use for them in the limited land actions of the early years of the war. When he led out the fleet in 430 to ravage the Peloponnesian coast, he took three hundred cavalry to accompany the four thousand infantry. The cavalry were carried in horse transports that had been converted from older ships, evidence of effort that makes sense only if horsemen were expected to be useful in raids of this sort. It is even possible that horse transports had been used at Athens before this time; at least, that is one interpretation of Thucydides' statement. Gomme and J. Hornblower, for example, feel that in 430 horse transports were made for the first time *out of old ships*, not that they were made for the first time in Athens or Greece at that time. The Persians had already used them in the early part of the century.[11] In any case the expedition carried out several successful raids on the eastern coast of the Peloponnese and returned home safely.

Unfortunately for Athens, Pericles died in the autumn of 429, a victim of the plague that had ravaged the city since 430.[12] Nevertheless, the practice of sending out cavalry continued. In the summer of 425 an expeditionary force of two thousand Athenian hoplites and two hundred cavalry disembarked on Corinthian territory near Solygeia. Although the numbers on each side were low, a battle developed and was fought stubbornly for some time at close quarters. By landing at night the Athenians had eluded the Corinthians, who were waiting at the isthmus several miles away. Upon the Athenians'

---

11. Thuc. 2.56.2; *HCT* 2 163; *CT* 1 329. Hdt. 6.48.2; 7.97. The Persian ships, which were constructed especially for transporting horses, seem to have been larger than warships.

12. Thuc. 2.47–52, 65.6.

arrival one Corinthian company was sent to guard the unwalled village of Solygeia while the rest attacked the Athenian right. Initially driven back uphill, the Corinthians stopped at a loose stone wall from which they threw stones down at their pursuers. They then charged the Athenian right again but could not dislodge them until they were reinforced by a company of infantry. That tipped the scales, forcing the enemy to withdraw to the beach, where they rallied at their ships. On the other wing, meanwhile, both sides had been continually engaged, and it was only some unspecified action by the Athenian cavalry that decided the issue. Then the Corinthians, who had no cavalry of their own, retired to higher ground.[13]

This narrative by Thucydides contains several points of interest. Troops on both sides were able to withdraw without panicking and then to reform, possibly due to the absence of serious pursuit. Contrary to the normal hoplite practice of using the right wing for the attack, the Corinthians assaulted the Athenian right with their left twice, the second time with the assistance of a company of infantry that functioned as a reserve. Finally, it was cavalry that decided the issue for the one side that possessed them. Hanson rightly emphasizes that this use of an aggressive left wing by the Corinthians anticipates the Thebans at Leuctra in 371.[14] Taken together with the decisive action by cavalry, it shows that changes usually associated with the fourth-century Thebans and Macedonians were part of an evolutionary process that began—or at least was intensified—by the Peloponnesian War. It was in response to raids such as these, as I have mentioned, that the Spartans were prompted to create a force of cavalry in 424. Thucydides gives no details, but it seems likely that cavalry gave the Athenians some tactical advantage. Here the foresight of Pericles stands in contrast to the conservatism of the Corinthians, who had not formed a mounted force.

At least once more during the first ten years of the war, Athens sent out an expeditionary force that included cavalry. On this occasion, in 422, twelve hundred hoplites and three hundred cavalry were sent to Thrace under the command of Cleon. In all three of these cases the proportion of cavalry to infantry is comparable to what was found in regular land forces, so no suspicion arises that these were token numbers.[15] Considering the effort and

---

13. Ibid., 4.42–44.
14. Hanson (1988) 194.
15. For most of Greek history the number of cavalry in Greek armies lies between 10 and 15 percent of the hoplite force. At Chaeronea Philip had two thousand cavalry and thirty thousand infantry, of whom twenty thousand are thought to have comprised the Macedonian phalanx. *HM* 2 599.

expense that Athens underwent in order to provide militarily significant numbers of horsemen on these overseas ventures, it seems fair to assume that their role was considered important.

But this was not the only duty that Pericles had in mind for the Athenian cavalry, in spite of his decision not to engage in land battles with the Spartans. As soon as the Peloponnesian forces entered Attica for the first time in the summer of 431, Pericles began the practice of sending out cavalry to prevent raiding parties from laying waste the fields near the city. On one of these occasions an Athenian unit, accompanied by Thessalian allies, fell in with the Boeotian cavalry. The struggle was indecisive until the arrival of hoplites tipped the scales against the Athenians, who retired after sustaining a few casualties.[16] Several years later, in 428, the Athenian cavalry again did good service, hemming in the enemy's light-armed troops and preventing them from harming the land near the city. Thucydides describes this cavalry action as the usual practice, indicating that such forays were a regular component of the defense of Attica.[17] Spence describes this employment of cavalry as "mobile defense," but that seems too strong a term, as it usually implies more than harassment. Nonetheless, the fact that it was employed over a long period of time suggests its value, probably representing a continuation of Pericles' policy.[18]

During these early years of the war, one of the most strongly contested areas lay in the northern Aegean, in the Thracian Chalcidice. There cavalry played an interesting and not altogether negligible role. Initially, trouble in the region resulted from the rebellion of some members of the Delian League, which by this time had been transformed into an Athenian empire. Potidaea, which had revolted in 432, surrendered in early 429. In the summer of that year Athens attempted to reduce another rebellious city, Spartolus, with two thousand hoplites, two hundred cavalry, and some locally obtained peltasts from Crousis. In the initial battle just outside the walls of Spartolus, the Athenian infantry succeeded in driving the Chalcidian hoplites inside their walls, but their cavalry and light armed troops were defeated by their Chalcidian counterparts. The latter, emboldened by their success and encouraged by the arrival of peltasts from Olynthus, attacked the Athenian infantry, who withdrew in the direction of their baggage train. Whenever the hoplites attempted a counterattack, the more nimble peltasts and cavalry simply got

16. Thuc. 2.22.2.
17. Ibid., 3.1.1; *CT* 1 381.
18. Spence (1990) 91–109; *CCG* 129–33.

out of their way; as soon as the Athenians resumed their retreat, the peltasts rushed after them hurling javelins. The cavalry provided the coup de grace, charging in wherever they could and routing the panic-stricken Athenian infantry. After taking refuge in Potidaea, the Athenians recovered their 430 dead and returned to Athens.[19] It was a major defeat for the Athenians in an area from which they derived revenue and raw materials. The battle is also of interest because, as Gomme pointed out, it was "the first in which an intelligent use was made of light-armed troops (including the peltasts) in combination with cavalry against a hoplite force."[20] Numbers may have been as decisive in this action as novel tactics. Yet Gomme's statement stands, and the action itself is evidence that military innovation could occur away from the main theater of conflict and in small-scale operations.

In the winter of 429/428, a battle in lower Macedonia that was of little importance to the main events of the war offers a hint of cavalry tactics among Greece's northern neighbors. According to Thucydides, Sitalces, king of the Odrysian Thracians, invaded Macedonia with an army numbering 150,000. Of these 50,000 were cavalry, including some Scythian horse archers. In spite of Thucydides' usual accuracy and the fact that he had good contacts in Thrace, these numbers seem unrealistically high. Sitalces' action was motivated in part by a promise to his Athenian allies to help end the war with the Chalcidians in Thrace.[21]

The Macedonians, under King Perdiccas, took refuge in strongholds throughout the countryside, giving no thought to the collection of an infantry force, an arm in which they were notoriously weak. Confident in their cavalry, which was reinforced by contingents from other parts of the country, they attacked the invaders. Wherever the Macedonians charged the Thracians fell back, unable to withstand the skilled horsemen protected by cuirasses. Nevertheless, numbers decided the outcome. When the Macedonians realized they could not overcome the masses of troops that were surrounding them, they desisted and came to terms with Sitalces.[22] Although the account is extremely brief, it leaves the impression that the Macedonian cavalry fought at close quarters, presumably with lances and swords rather than javelins. They were also better trained and had better defensive armor than the Tracians. Their campaign, which had no well-defined goals, was little more than

19. Thuc. 2.79.
20. *HCT* 2 213; *CT* 1 361.
21. *CT* 1 374.
22. Thuc. 2.96–100.

a huge plundering raid that soon ran short of provisions and had to return home. The Athenians' failure to support Sitalces with a fleet as promised contributed to the lack of success, but the choice may have been made for them by Sitalces' decision to move so late in the season, when winter storms made sailing a risky business.[23]

The limitations of the equestrian arm in Greece at this time are clearly shown in an indecisive cavalry action between the Athenians and Boeotians in the Megarid in 424. The Athenians, with about four thousand hoplites and six hundred cavalry, were attempting to reduce Megara when Peloponnesian relief forces of six thousand hoplites and six hundred cavalry arrived. While the infantry forces on both sides played a waiting game, the Boeotian cavalry made an unexpected attack upon the Athenian light-armed troops that were scattered throughout the plain. As these troops were driven down to the sea, the Athenian cavalry, in turn, rode out and engaged the Boeotians at close quarters. There followed a cavalry fight of some duration, which ended without advantage to either side, although the Boeotian commander was killed. This action had absolutely no effect on the infantry forces, and the outnumbered Athenians grew impatient and wisely withdrew.[24] For all practical purposes the cavalry might as well not have been present. It is worth noting, however, that the Athenian cavalry held their own with the highly respected Boeotian horsemen.[25] Perhaps their regular employment since the beginning of the war was manifesting itself in a higher level of performance.

Quite the opposite was the case later in the same year, when a major battle was fought near Delium in eastern Boeotia. Pericles' defensive strategy had been abandoned and a broader offensive plan adopted, which included seizing the Megarid and occupying at least the eastern part of Boeotia. If successful, this would close the land route into Attica and perhaps confine the war to the Peloponnese. Indeed, in the speech attributed to the Athenian general Hippocrates just prior to the battle, the reason given to justify fighting is that victory would deprive the Peloponnesians of the Boeotian cavalry, without which they could not invade Attica.[26] This is a remarkable statement, even if somewhat rhetorical, because it suggests that the best infantry force in Greece was unwilling to invade unless it was supported by cavalry. No doubt, without the Boeotian cavalry to keep the Athenian horsemen at bay,

23. Ibid., 2.101.
24. Thuc. 4.68.5; 70–72.
25. *CT* 2 241; *HCAG* 61.
26. Thuc. 4.95.2.

foraging and damaging the countryside would be difficult. To achieve this plan, an overly complex coordinated attack against two separate areas of Boeotia—Siphae and Delium—was set in motion by the Athenians at the beginning of winter. The plot, which relied on help from inside the towns, was betrayed, so that one of the generals, Demosthenes, was unable to occupy Siphae from the sea. In addition there was a mistake about the dates, and Demosthenes arrived too early.[27] As a result, the Boeotians were not distracted as had been planned, and when the Athenian general Hippocrates marched to Delium and fortified the temple of Apollo there, they responded quickly. Upon arriving, the Theban Boeotarch Pagondas, who was in command, persuaded his troops to attack the Athenians the same day.

Each side had about seven thousand hoplites, but the Boeotians had the advantage in the other arms, their one thousand cavalry apparently outnumbering those of the Athenians (whose numbers are not given), while the latter had nothing to match the ten thousand light-armed troops and five hundred peltasts of the Boeotians, since their own light troops were on their way home. At the approach of the enemy Hippocrates marshalled his troops and detached three hundred cavalry to guard the fort at Delium. The cavalry were instructed to join the battle if a good opportunity should present itself. This last detail is noteworthy, because Greek generals of the period usually committed all their forces at one time, holding nothing back in reserve. Gomme suggests that this force could have been decisive if it had appeared on the battlefield at a critical moment.[28] Just as remarkable was the counter to this by Pagondas, who forestalled them by detaching units of his own. If these were cavalry, the number of Boeotian horsemen at the battle would have to be reduced accordingly. The impressive thing about Pagondas' action is that he obtained information about events in the enemy army that occurred beyond his own line of sight at a time when reconnaissance was almost unheard of in Greek armies.[29]

When the two armies met, the Athenians were drawn up eight deep, giving them a front of about 850 men. On the Boeotian side, the Thebans, who occupied the right wing, lined up in files 25 men deep, providing an advantage in weight on the southern end of the battle line, which seems to have run north and south. The other Boeotians were ranged to the left of the

---

27. Ibid., 4.89.
28. *HCT* 3 563.
29. For a discussion of scouts see *GSW* 1 127–33. His negative verdict on their value may be generally accepted, as long as one keeps exceptions like Pagondas in mind.

Thebans in a northerly direction, in files of unknown depth. If the two battle lines were coequal, which seems likely from the description of the battle, then the files of the allies would have been less than eight deep, since the Thebans had shortened their section of the front by forming 25 men deep. The Thebans probably numbered between 2,000 and 4,000, which would have allowed the allies to line up five, four, or three men deep, in inverse ratio to the number of Thebans.

Only the two lines of hoplites took part in the battle, since ravines to the north and south prevented the troops on the flanks—where the cavalry were posted—from engaging. Soon the whole line was pivoting around its center in a counterclockwise direction as the heavier Theban contingent pushed the Athenian left back, while at the same time the Athenian right had broken up and routed the allied left from the center north and was slaughtering the Thespians, who now paid a price for resisting when their neighbors to the left and right departed. As soon as Pagondas became aware of the disaster on his left, he dispatched two units of cavalry around a ridge to the north out of sight of the enemy. The appearance of these cavalry came as a shock to the victorious Athenians on the right wing, who thought they were part of a relief army. Coupled with the steady advance of the Thebans at the other end of the line, the cavalry's appearance produced a complete rout of the Athenians, who fled in several directions. The slaughter of the fugitives by Boeotian and Locrian cavalry in pursuit ended at sunset, as the battle had been fought late in the day and night allowed most to escape. Among the dead were about 500 Boeotians and just under 1,000 Athenians, including the general Hippocrates. A considerable number of noncombatants was also killed, apparently during the cavalry pursuit.[30] The pursuit by the cavalry is another example of deviation from traditional hoplite fighting.[31]

This was a serious blow to Athenian hopes to enhance their position on land, as they had begun to realize that Pericles' defensive strategy would never provide a decisive victory. Purely from the standpoint of military history, the battle was a remarkable event. Credit for this seems to belong to Pagondas, who showed himself to be a worthy predecessor of the great Theban generals of the fourth century, Epaminondas and Pelopidas. Pagondas' appreciation of the tactical possibilities was exceptional, to which was added a system for obtaining information that allowed him to implement his tactical ideas. First,

---

30. Thuc. 4.90–101. For discussion of the site and battle see *SAGT* 2 24–36.
31. *CT* 2 308; *HCAG* 96.

he found out about the Athenian cavalry at Delium and detached units to isolate them from the battlefield. Then, apparently for the first time in Greek military history, he employed the Thebans in a depth of twenty-five men, an example of tactical asymmetry that provided decisive weight at one point in the battle line. This practice was further developed by the Thebans, and ultimately by the Macedonians, in the following century. During the battle itself Pagondas—unlike most hoplite generals, who usually fought in the ranks—retained an exceptional presence of mind that enabled him to react to the information he received about the disaster on his left. Thereupon, by issuing a direct order to two cavalry units, which would have been impossible if he had been fighting in the ranks, he produced the collapse of the victorious Athenian right wing by means of surprise and gained the victory. His adroit use of two arms in coordination with each other and his control of events during the course of the battle are far in advance of his time. The vigorous pursuit by the cavalry is also noteworthy.

In the summer of 422, while Athens was attempting to preserve its control over the cities of the Thracian Chalcidice, it suffered a severe defeat at Amphipolis, which lay to the east on the Strymon River. Considering the number of troops involved—fewer than two thousand hoplites on each side—it was not a major battle. Nonetheless, because the commanders on both sides, Cleon the Athenian and the Spartan Brasidas, were killed, the battle assumed greater importance, having removed two of the most outspoken leaders in favor of continuing the war. Of more immediate interest, however, is the fact that peltasts and cavalry played a decisive part in the action.

Brasidas was inside Amphipolis when Cleon landed at the mouth of the Strymon and seized Eion as a base. Cleon's plan was to await reinforcements from Macedon and Thrace, but—the impatience of his troops forcing his hand—he moved north to Amphipolis in what can be described as a reconnaissance in force. Cleon stationed his force on a hill to the east of the city, where it was protected by a north-south wall through which access could be gained by at least two gates, the northern one named the Thracian gate. Brasidas, who felt that his soldiers were inferior to the enemy, decided to resort to a stratagem, since he saw that the Athenians were not in good order and were obviously not expecting a fight. Consequently, he divided his forces and prepared to sally forth from both gates and surprise the Athenians. When Cleon learned that the feet of many horses and men were visible beneath the gates, he ordered a withdrawal southward to Eion. When, in his impatience, he turned his right wing to the south—thus exposing the unshielded side to the wall—Brasidas saw his opportunity and ordered the attack from both gates. The left wing, which was out of reach on the way south, fled; the now-outnumbered right was caught and withdrew to the hill where it had been stationed earlier. It repelled several attacks by hoplites but, unable to withstand the javelins of the cavalry and peltasts, the right wing broke ranks and fled.[32]

Cleon's principal mistake was that he did not provide a covering force on his right side. This should have been the assignment of the cavalry that he had brought north with him, but they are not mentioned by Thucydides, and their absence is a real puzzle. Even without them, Cleon can be faulted for not having detailed some of his hoplites to cover the right side as they attempted to depart without a fight. As evidence that this was not a regular battle, Thucydides offers the extreme disproportion of casualties on each side—six hundred Athenians compared to only seven of their opponents. Such a disparity in casualties was not unusual when fleeing troops were vigorously pursued, especially by cavalry. In this debacle the Athenians paid a price for not heeding earlier lessons about the value of cavalry and peltasts. Cleon must take the blame for the Athenians' poor tactical dispositions.

At the battle of Mantinea in 418, when the Athenians joined the Mantineans and Argives against the Spartans, cavalry were posted in their typical position on the wings at the start of the battle. As Thucydides' narrative develops, however, it appears that the horsemen played no important part in the fighting. That is not to say that they must have been inactive, for it is clear from the study of other, later battles that when cavalry were evenly matched they sometimes simply kept each other occupied without any advantage accruing to either side. Under such circumstances it was unusual for any outflanking move to occur, and the fighting was decided solely by the infantry. Such is likely to have been the case at Mantinea, as we know that the Athenian cavalry were still present at the end of the fighting. The battle was won by the courage and discipline of the Spartans under their king, Agis. It is interesting to note that the Athenian cavalry prevented serious losses to their infantry by covering their retreat, thus displaying one of the important but less spectacular duties of the mounted arm.[33]

In the summer of 415 the magnificent expeditionary force that was expected to conquer Sicily sailed forth from Athens' harbor, the Piraeus. The events of the next two years were the stuff of high tragedy, except that the players were not actors on a stage. Born of excessive ambition fostered by

32. Thuc. 5.6–10.
33. Ibid., 5.64–67.

arrogance, the expedition was doomed by petty factional strife, incompetence, and ignorance of the military and economic situation in Sicily. And for any bright young military leaders who were capable of profiting from past mistakes, there were some lessons to be learned about the uses of cavalry.

The Athenians were not totally oblivious to the problems they faced, for during the debate preceding the vote the general Nicias, who opposed the plan, had attempted to persuade his fellow Athenians not to take on such an enormous and foolhardy enterprise. Nicias may have exaggerated the resources of the Syracusans and other Sicilians, but his arguments were based on fact. The two principal advantages that they had over the Athenians were their many horses and the fact that they grew their own grain and did not have to import it.[34] Nicias specifically recommended a large land force of infantry to deal with the cavalry, which might otherwise restrict their movements.[35] He specified archers and slingers to be used against them but did not recommend taking cavalry from Athens, presumably because the transport of horses over such a great distance would be impractical but also due to the hope that cavalry could be obtained from the allies of Athens in Sicily.[36]

After their having established a base at Catana, the Athenians' first attempt to raid Syracusan territory was thwarted by the Syracusan cavalry, who in the process killed some light-armed troops before they could regain the ships.[37] This failure contrasts sharply with the earlier success of the Athenians when they raided the coast of the Peloponnese. Then they had the advantage in cavalry.

After a rather fruitless display of force along the north coast of Sicily that was apparently intended to win over allies, the Athenians decided to attack Syracuse directly. Fear of the Syracusan cavalry, however, caused them to employ a stratagem whereby they induced the entire Syracusan army to march against the Athenian base in Catana, while they themselves sailed around to Syracuse and established a base inside the Great Harbor facing the Olympieum.[38] The Syracusan cavalry, riding on ahead, first recognized the ruse and informed the infantry, which quickly turned back to help the city, reaching it after the Athenians had disembarked. As they prepared for battle, the Athenians' overriding concern was the protection of their flanks from the

34. Ibid., 6.20.4.
35. Ibid., 6.21.1.
36. Ibid., 6.22.
37. Ibid., 6.52.2.
38. Ibid., 6.64–65.

enemy cavalry. Consequently, they chose ground where one flank—probably the right—was covered by walls, houses, trees, and a lake or swamp, while the other was protected by bluffs to the south.[39]

Although the Syracusans placed twelve hundred cavalry on their right flank for the battle that took place the following day, these cavalry played no effective role until their own infantry had been routed. At that time, still undefeated, they were able to stop the Athenian pursuit, thus minimizing the loss of life among their fellow citizens.[40] In spite of their victory the Athenians despaired of accomplishing anything in the face of the Syracusan horsemen. Consequently, after an exchange of dead under truce, the Athenians abandoned their camp and sailed back to Catana, hoping to build up their own cavalry force over the winter with reinforcements from home and help from their allies in Sicily.[41]

K. J. Dover, in his continuation of Gomme's commentary on Thucydides, correctly stresses the importance of these events: "In retrospect it seems fair to say that the achievement of the Syracusan cavalry in preventing the Athenian hoplites from following up their victory and in thus inducing Nikias and Lamachos to put off any further assault of Syracuse until the following spring (71.2) was one of the decisive moments of the whole campaign."[42] Delbrück, on the other hand, underestimates the contribution of cavalry on this occasion when he remarks: "The enemy cavalry accomplished nothing except to slow the pursuit."[43] Delbrück not only ignores the effect that this had on the Athenian leaders but also the fact that the Athenians were constrained to select a battle site offering physical barriers on the flanks as protection against cavalry.

The ineffectiveness of the pitifully small number of the Athenian cavalry (thirty) requires no comment, but Dover does ask a pertinent question about the failure of the archers and slingers, "whose function it was to prevent this fatal domination of the battlefield by cavalry."[44] After all, Nicias himself had specified it as the task of these light troops in his speech before the Athenian assembly.[45] And indeed, a few years later, subsequent to the defeat and death

39. Ibid., 6.66.
40. Ibid., 6.67, 69–70.
41. Ibid., 6.71. The Syracusan dead amounted to 260; those of the Athenians and their allies, about 50.
42. *HCT* 4 346. Following Dover, Kagan also expresses a fine appreciation of cavalry in the Syracusan campaign (1981) 239–41.
43. *HAW* 132.
44. *HCT* 4 346.
45. Thuc. 6.22.1.

of Cyrus at Cunaxa in 401, Xenophon and the Ten Thousand found that archers and slingers could be used effectively to interrupt pursuit by cavalry.[46] In the case at hand, however, it appears that they were too far out of position to be of any use. Under ordinary circumstances these troops, after opening the action, would have retired behind the lines and could not have protected the Athenian hoplites who had run forward in pursuit.

Nonetheless—whatever the explanation—it was a missed opportunity for the Athenians, who had a chance to destroy part of the Syracusan army through a vigorous pursuit. One need not wait until the time of Philip and Alexander to find the effective use of pursuit of a defeated enemy, for it was becoming a normal part of battlefield tactics in the second half of the fifth century, the Athenians, indeed, having acquired a certain reputation in this regard by the beginning of the war.[47] Among the major Greek powers only the Spartans were disinclined to use it, making only brief, short pursuits.[48] This was in accord with the traditional Spartan code of honor, which called for manly face-to-face combat. The Spartan dislike of missile weapons also seems to have resulted from the observation that arrows could not distinguish between the coward and the brave.[49] One should add, however, that this martial ethos—if, indeed, it did exist—was likely to be forgotten when Spartan officers served overseas, away from the conservative restraints of their government. Then an uncharacteristic brilliance and versatility were at times evident, for example in Brasidas, whom I have already mentioned; in Gylippus, who thwarted the Athenians during the Syracusan campaign; and to a lesser degree in Xanthippus, who assisted the Carthaginians during the First Punic War.

By the following summer (414) the Athenians had again landed near Syracuse, now accompanied by 650 cavalry. From Athens had come 250 cavalrymen, for whom horses had been obtained from the Sicilian allies. The latter supplied the remaining horsemen, 300 alone coming from Segesta. These cavalry quickly proved their worth, combining with a force of hoplites to drive off a unit of Syracusan cavalry that was attempting to interrupt the building of a fort at Syce, west of the city.[50]

During the summer of 414 both sides spent much time and energy in building walls, the Athenians trying to isolate the city, the defenders counter-

---

46. Xen. *An.* 3.4.15.
47. Thuc. 1.70.5.
48. Ibid., 5.73.4.
49. Ibid., 4.40.
50. Ibid., 6.94, 98.

ing. One battle that developed from this activity was costly for the Athenians, because Lamachus—one of the original commanders of the expedition—was killed. Initially, the Athenians had caught the Syracusans by surprise and routed them, their right wing fleeing to the city, the left along the river Anapus. Three hundred select Athenian troops attempted to cut off the latter but were routed in turn by the Syracusan cavalry, which chanced to be nearby. The successful cavalry attack carried over against a division of the Athenian right wing, which likewise panicked. Lamachus saw the situation from his position on the left wing and rushed over to retrieve it, accompanied by some archers and the Argives. Unfortunately, he rashly crossed a ditch with only a few followers, found himself trapped, and was killed. The Athenians did not even recover his body, which was carried back to the city by the Syracusans. The cavalry had once again proven their worth. The Athenian forces were left under the sole command of Nicias, who had never been an advocate of the expedition and whose ability—however it might be judged—was now being blunted by a chronic kidney ailment.[51]

The real turning point in the campaign came with the arrival of Gylippus, a Spartan sent out by his government to command the defense of Syracuse. He landed at Himera, put together a force of about three thousand infantry and two hundred cavalry, and marched overland to the city.[52] Gylippus arrived just before the Athenians had time to finish their north-south wall across the peninsula to the west of Syracuse, the completion of which would have sealed off the city. Had that happened, Thucydides thought Syracuse would have been lost.[53] Shortly thereafter, Nicias fortified Plemmyrium, the height across the Great Harbor south of the city, and stationed the ships there. Thucydides believed that this was the beginning of the deterioration of the crews. Not only was there an insufficient supply of fresh water, but a third of the enemy cavalry had been posted nearby, and they killed the Athenian foragers when the latter went out to collect firewood.[54]

The first major battle under the command of Gylippus was a defeat for the Syracusans, partly because they fought with their flanks covered by the walls being built by both sides to gain control of access to the city on the landward side. Within these confines there was no room for their cavalry to

---

51. Ibid., 6.101.4–6; *HCT* 4 481 and facing diagram.
52. These numbers come from Diodorus (13.7.7) and are consonant with the incomplete account of Thucydides (7.1.5).
53. Thuc. 7.2.5.
54. Ibid., 7.4.4–6.

take part in the fight. After the Syracusan dead had been recovered under a truce, Gylippus called the troops together and admitted that his choice of a battlefield that excluded their cavalry and javelin men from the formation had been a mistake.[55] This admission—especially from the mouth of a Spartan—is significant, reflecting the changes that were taking place in Greek military thinking about the use of cavalry and missile-hurling troops.

Gylippus did not make the same mistake again. On the first suitable occasion thereafter he again led his troops out. The Athenians did likewise, for they knew that if they could not clear the Syracusans from the height and finish their wall, they would not be able to surround the city and force its surrender. On this occasion the Syracusan cavalry and javelin men were posted against the left flank of the Athenians. The cavalry attacked their opponents and routed them, resulting in the defeat of the entire Athenian army, which retreated behind its fortifications.[56] The important point is that cavalry charged and routed infantry—presumably hoplites—and, in so doing, decided the battle. Thucydides gives few details and one can only guess at what happened. Perhaps the boldness of the cavalry produced a psychological shock to the Athenians and intimidated them, as it was impossible for cavalry to succeed with a frontal assault on numerically superior, well-prepared infantry who kept their nerve. It is perhaps more likely that the Syracusan cavalry were able to attack the flank of the Athenian infantry.

Incidentally, a minor skirmish in Boeotia in 414 reveals something about the use as well as the limitations of cavalry and javelin men. When the Athenians sent reinforcements to Sicily under Demosthenes in the summer of that year, they intended to include Thracian peltasts, who were traditionally agile, light-armed javelin throwers, although in this instance they are described as carrying curved slashing swords. As it turned out, these troops, thirteen hundred in number, arrived in Athens too late to sail with the fleet. Short of funds, the Athenians dismissed them. While transporting them home, the Athenian ships put into shore in order to make a raid on nearby Mycalessus. The unsuspecting town was easily captured, and the Thracians massacred its inhabitants with barbaric delight. Upon getting word of the raid, the Thebans came to help and overtook the booty-laden Thracians before they had time to reach the ships, which were some distance away on the Euripus channel. Although they lost their booty, the Thracians put up a skillful defence

---

55. Ibid., 7.5.2–3.
56. Ibid., 7.6.2–3.

against the Theban cavalry, which arrived ahead of the hoplites. This they accomplished by using their native tactics, in which small groups of men darted out from the main body, briefly engaged the enemy, and then rejoined the rest. For whatever reason, the Thebans were either unwilling or unable to bring the Thracians to bay. The number of Theban troops is not given, but it is not unlikely that there were too few of them to accomplish a great deal. Some casualties on both sides occurred during the pursuit to the coast, but most of the Thracian losses occurred at the beach, where the ships stood out of range of arrows, causing difficulty for the Thracians as they could not swim.[57] In this situation the speed and mobility of the cavalry allowed the Thebans to overtake the Thracians and force them to abandon their booty. On the other hand the agility and tactics of the peltasts prevented the cavalry from doing them much harm.

The arrival in Sicily of substantial reinforcements from Athens during the summer of 413, under the command of the able general Demosthenes, did not change the outcome.[58] The end of this expedition, the finest and largest ever sent out by a Greek state, came in September 413. The Syracusan cavalry played an essential part to the last. Demosthenes made one last attempt to cut off the city with a night attack on Epipolae, the height west of the city. The Syracusans, though initially caught off their guard, finally beat off the attackers, who suffered heavy losses. When daylight came, their cavalry killed the stragglers. The Athenians themselves had some cavalry left, although these seem to have been too few to have any effect. In addition low morale reduced the effectiveness of all the troops. During one sally from the gates of their fort, seventy Athenian cavalrymen abandoned their mounts in an effort to get back within the walls through the narrow gates.[59]

After a desperate, unsuccessful attempt to break out of the harbor with the ships, Nicias and Demosthenes decided to withdraw by land to Catana. Perhaps as many as forty thousand men began the march.[60] The Syracusan cavalry and missile troops took up their task in earnest, aided by hunger and thirst. During the day the cavalry and javelin men harassed the Athenians from the flanks, causing many casualties and preventing them from foraging. With time now on their side, the Syracusans clearly felt no need to risk casualties

---

57. Ibid., 7.27, 29–30.
58. Ibid., 7.42.1. He brought seventy-three ships carrying five thousand hoplites as well as javelin men, archers, and slingers.
59. Ibid., 7.44.8; 51.1–2.
60. Ibid., 7.70–72, 75.5. The figure has been questioned but may be close to the truth if Thucydides counted noncombatants, including slaves. See *HCT* 4 452; Kagan (1981) 337.

in the hand-to-hand fighting of a formal battle. Demosthenes, his forces suffering attack on all sides, surrendered on the sixth day. Nicias, whose division had gone ahead of that of Demosthenes, experienced two more days of constant attack from the numerous horsemen and light armed troops. When they reached the Assinarus River, the men rushed forward in disorder in the vain hope that safety lay on the other side or in an uncontrollable desire to drink. Many were slaughtered while they were drinking, and the few who reached the other side soon perished at the hands of the cavalry. Only about seven thousand were formally taken prisoner. Some did escape, and many of these were captured by individual soldiers.[61]

All in all, the Syracusan cavalry had acquitted themselves splendidly and out of all proportion to their numbers. They had a major role in the defeat and destruction of the Athenian land forces both directly, in battle, and peripherally, by attack and intimidation that prevented foragers from seizing necessary supplies. Clearly, Athenian mistakes made this easier than it might have been; still, the Syracusan cavalry's accomplishments are there to be read in the pages of Thucydides. In surrounding the Athenian forces in the open and destroying them with missile weapons and cavalry, they remind one of the success that the Parthians later had with these tactics against the Romans at Carrhae in 53. In that instance, however, the Parthians used mounted archers.

The great war lasted for another decade, most of the subsequent action taking place at sea in the eastern and northern Aegean or on land in Asia Minor. These events are described in the *Hellenica* by Xenophon, who picks up the narrative where Thucydides leaves off in 411. This former pupil of Socrates, who also wrote two invaluable treatises on cavalry and horsemanship, was an experienced soldier and an eyewitness to many of the events that he describes.

In spite of the disaster in Sicily, the Athenians took encouragement from the Spartans' inability to force a decision on land in Greece by attempting the recovery of their lost allies in the north. The Spartans became interested in this region once they realized that the sea-lanes into the Black Sea, through which grain reached Athens, constituted their enemy's lifeline.[62] They consequently made an effort to gain control of the towns along the Bosporus. Details of the fighting that ensued from 410 to 406 are lacking, but the constant

---

61. Thuc. 7.78.3, 6–7; 81.2; 82.3; 84.2; 85.1; 87.4.
62. Xen. *Hell.* 1.1.35.

employment of cavalry as an integral part of the forces on all sides, including deployment from ships, demonstrates how much had changed since the time of the Persian Wars. For a while the Athenians had considerable success against both the Spartans and the Persians, who had now become allies. On one occasion at Abydos in 409, for example, Alcibiades defeated the Persian Pharnabazus and his numerous cavalry with Athenian infantry and cavalry and, together with the cavalry and 120 hoplites, pursued the defeated Persians until nightfall.[63]

By the time Athens surrendered in 404, the cumulative military experience of the preceding thirty years had transformed the nature of Greek warfare. A hoplite phalanx manned by citizens was no longer sufficient to guarantee victory. Thousands of men who had become used to fighting were for all practical purposes mercenaries. Cavalry and light-armed troops, especially peltasts, had been used for a variety of functions in widely differing circumstances and had been joined with each other and with heavy infantry to increase the versatility of armies. An appreciation of the ability of cavalry was demonstrated by brilliant tacticians such as Pagondas, Brasidas, and Gylippus, whose adroit use of integrated forces foreshadowed the methods of the great generals of the fourth century. On the Athenian side, Demosthenes proved to be the most professional and open-minded general of the war. As early as 427/426, while fighting in Aetolia, he realized the limitations of hoplites and regularly thereafter included light-armed infantry among his forces.[64] As G. Cawkwell rightly says, "This was an anticipation of the role of specialist arms in the next century."[65] Given the literate nature of Greek society and the great curiosity about military matters that its generals exhibited, there can be little doubt that succeeding generations of Greeks learned much from the historical works of Thucydides and other writers. When this reflective historical influence was combined with the practical experience of uninterrupted military service, all the ingredients were in place for the spectacular military developments of the fourth century.

63. Xen. *Hell.* 1.2.16; Plut. *Alc.* 29. For other examples see Xen. *Hell.* 1.1.1–1.4.21.
64. Thuc. 3.97–98; 4.67.2; 7.31.5 (slingers and javelin throwers), 7.33.4, 35.1, 42.1 (javelin throwers, slingers, and archers).
65. Cawkwell (1997) 50.

Chapter 7

The March of the Ten Thousand: 404 to 399 B.C.

THE EXPERIENCE OF THIRTY years of warfare of all types in different parts of the Greek world clearly manifested itself in the years following the Peloponnesian War as—in typical fashion—the Greeks easily found reasons for fighting among themselves. The most interesting campaign in the aftermath of the war, however, was directed against the Persians. The famous expedition of the Ten Thousand, immortalized by Xenophon in his *Anabasis*, was part of an attempt by Cyrus the Younger to depose his brother Artaxerxes from the throne of Persia. Cyrus had been appointed supreme military commander of the satrapies in western Asia Minor in 408 by his father and had provided invaluable assistance to the Spartans during the Peloponnesian War, perhaps even insuring their victory over Athens. During the time when he was aiding the Spartans, Cyrus learned to value the quality of the heavily armed Greek infantry. Upon the death of his father, Darius II, in 404, Cyrus was disappointed in his hopes of becoming king when his brother Artaxerxes was chosen. Further embittered by his brother's distrust of him, Cyrus resolved to attempt a military coup.

Although he had large forces at his disposal, including high-quality Persian cavalry, Cyrus supplemented these with more than 13,000 Greek mercenaries, 10,600 of which were hoplites.[1] The Athenian Xenophon joined the mercenaries at the personal request of his friend Proxenus, a Boeotian mercenary commander hired by Cyrus.[2] Cyrus concealed his true intentions from

---

1. Xen. *An*. 1. 2. 3–9; 1. 7. 9, where the number of hoplites is given as 10,400.
2. Ibid., 3. 1. 4.

the Greek mercenaries with the pretext that he intended to campaign against the Pisidians of south-central Asia Minor.

Meanwhile Tissaphernes, Cyrus' predecessor in western Asia Minor, whose authority had been reduced by the arrival of Cyrus, rode east with about five hundred cavalry to inform the king of his brother's plans. Forewarned, Artaxerxes gathered his forces and met Cyrus in a decisive battle in the fall of 401 at a site near Cunaxa, which lies north of Babylon in a location not precisely identified. The total number of troops involved in the battle is unknown, since Xenophon, like most Greek historians, exaggerated the Persian numbers. The thirteen thousand Greeks were stationed on the right, with one thousand Paphlagonian horse covering their right flank. In the center was Cyrus himself, with six hundred horsemen. Xenophon's description of the armor and weapons of Cyrus' Persian cavalry is of particular interest. Defensive armor consisted of cuirasses, thigh pieces, and helmets, while there were javelins and Greek slashing swords for offense. Protection for the horses consisted of face- and breastplates.[3]

The battle began on the right with a charge by the Greek hoplites, who shouted the paean and frightened the enemy's horses by clashing spear against shield. The Persian ranks broke before the Greeks came within arrow shot, and a vigorous pursuit followed. Cyrus, however, held back; due to the size of the king's army, he was dangerously outflanked on his left. In fact the king, with six thousand horsemen in the center of the royal line, was already beginning to encircle Cyrus' left. The latter, at the head of his six hundred cavalrymen, charged and routed the king's six thousand. This action and the earlier success of the Greek hoplites show the tremendous advantage well-trained, highly motivated troops have over an inferior enemy. The initial success of Cyrus' smaller body of cavalry may have been due to the willingness of this apparently select group to close for hand-to-hand fighting, a possibility that is suggested by their adoption of the Greek slashing sword. Presumably they unnerved the king's cavalry, which relied on the traditional tactics of javelin throwing. Furthermore, the king's cavalry were halted and less able, either physically or morally, to receive Cyrus' charge. Unfortunately, with victory all but won, Cyrus forgot his duties as a commander and succumbed to the fatal attraction of revenge. Spying his brother, he rushed off in his direction while the majority of his own six hundred men scattered in pursuit. Cyrus' mistake was his too-rapid charge, which destroyed his formation's integrity and left

---

3. Ibid., 1. 8. 3–7.

him fighting unsupported. Just as he reached his brother and struck him a blow on the cuirass, a javelin struck Cyrus beneath the eye. While the king's wound was not serious, that of Cyrus was mortal. His cause as well as employment for the Greek mercenaries died with him.[4]

Such is the version of events given by Xenophon. Other surviving accounts in the works of Diodorus and Plutarch differ to a greater or lesser degree, and no modern reconstruction of events seems entirely satisfactory. Perhaps the best is that of Anderson in his book on Xenophon.[5] Tactically, the battle was anything but a showpiece. Cyrus was taken by surprise at the king's presence, and some of his troops never did come up in time to join battle. Even on the victorious Persian side it was a battle of missed opportunities, as Tissaphernes, with his cavalry, had failed to take the Greek phalanx in the rear after passing through the Greek peltasts along the river. The latter, under the command of Episthenes of Amphipolis, were unable to resist the Persian charge and had opened a gap that allowed the cavalry to pass through them. Although the peltasts did inflict injuries upon the horsemen as they rode past, it was potentially disastrous to allow them access to the Greek rear. Fortunately for the Greeks, Tissaphernes rode on to the Greek camp and the phalanx finished the day unbeaten and in formation, although abandoned by Cyrus' other troops and no longer possessing any reason for its presence in Mesopotamia.[6]

In spite of the fact that the Greek peltasts had suffered no casualties, their inability to resist horsemen demonstrates the incompleteness of even the best Greek infantry without cavalry support. This defect now bedeviled the Greeks as they set out on the long retreat home. Indeed, had the Persians been willing to take the casualties, there is little doubt that they could have destroyed the Ten Thousand. Instead, having failed to destroy Greek resistance through the murder of their leaders at a parley, they were content to harass the enemy with cavalry and light missile troops and drive them out of the empire northwards, where hill tribes and the harsh climate could be expected to finish the job.

Although demoralized by the death of their generals, the Greeks elected replacements, among them Xenophon. The new leaders assembled the soldiers and addressed them in turn. In a well-known passage, Xenophon

---

4. Ibid., 1. 8. 17–29.
5. Diod. 14–23; Plut. *Artax.* 9–13, who cites two authorities, Deinon and Ctesias, whose versions differ. Anderson (1974) 105–12. See also *HAW* 154 and Cawkwell (1972) 38–39.
6. Xen. *An.* 1. 10. 7–8.

attempted to alleviate the men's fears about the threat posed by Persian cavalry and their own deficiency in that arm:

> If any of you feel disheartened because of the fact that we have no cavalry, while the enemy have great numbers of them, you must remember that ten thousand cavalry only amount to ten thousand men. No one has ever died in battle through being bitten or kicked by a horse; it is men who do whatever gets done in battle. And then we are on a much more solid foundation than cavalrymen, who are up in the air on horseback, and afraid not only of us but of falling off their horses: we, on the other hand, with our feet planted on the earth, can give much harder blows to those who attack us and are much more likely to hit what we aim at. There is only one way in which cavalry have an advantage over us, and that is that it is safer for them to run away than it is for us.[7]

These words have been used as evidence of the inherent weakness of Greek cavalry, but once again we must remind ourselves that military effectiveness is relative and has to be judged in context.[8] Furthermore, the psychological element is as important as the material—indeed, more so, other things being equal. The fact that the Greeks feared cavalry speaks for itself; before his death their commander, Clearchus, had specifically mentioned the efficiency and numbers of the Persian horsemen.[9] Xenophon's task in this desperate situation was to raise the morale of the Greeks, whose apprehension in the face of the enemy cavalry was eminently reasonable. Xenophon was undoubtedly an exceptional horseman, but on this occasion, as J. G. P. Best pointed out, "he must have known better."[10] That Xenophon could argue in this manner suggests that the typical hoplite he was addressing had little or no experience with horses. A person who is afraid of falling off will not become a good rider, because the necessary state of relaxation will be absent and his fear and tension will be transmitted to the horse, which will respond more or less noticeably according to its own nature. Indeed, it is easy to get the impression, when studying accounts of cavalry, that the riders are reckless daredevils.

---

7. Ibid., 3. 2. 18–19 (Warner trans.). Xenophon presents the case for cavalry in *Cyrop.* 4. 3. 9–23.
8. Kromayer and Veith ([1928] 1963) 53; Lammert (1913); *RE* 8.2 col. 1700.
9. Xen. *An.* 2. 4. 6.
10. Best (1969) 59. See also Anderson (1974) 124.

It was no long time later that Xenophon found it necessary to take measures against these very cavalry and the missile troops who were harassing the retreating Greeks. By selecting the best of the horses that were being used as baggage animals—some former cavalry mounts among them—and equipping the riders with corselets, a modest but effective cavalry force was created. The corselet was apparently felt to be necessary because cavalrymen did not carry shields until late in the reign of Alexander. In addition two hundred Rhodians who were serving as hoplites were outfitted as slingers, a class of troops for which the island was famous. They possessed a real advantage over their Persian counterparts because their small lead sling bullets far outranged the hand-sized stone bullets of the enemy.[11]

Even these seemingly minor changes proved their worth on the following day, when Mithradates came up with one thousand horsemen and four thousand archers and slingers. As soon as the enemy missiles began to find the range, the Greek cavalry, hoplites, and peltasts detailed for the task charged. The Persians immediately broke into flight, during which many of their infantry were killed and about eighteen cavalrymen were captured.[12] Several days later Tissaphernes arrived with a larger army. This, too, accomplished nothing, as the arrows and bullets of the Greeks could not fail to find targets among the densely packed Persians. Xenophon remarks that the lead bullets of the Rhodians outranged the Persian arrows as well as their stone bullets.[13] Admittedly these successes were due largely to the timidity of the barbarians and the desperation of the Greeks, yet the foundation of the disparity in behavior, on this occasion as on many others in their history, was the superiority of the Greeks in discipline, training, and weapons. Aside from the Persian cavalry, which were of high quality, the troops comprising the barbarian army were usually inferior, at times even having to be forced into battle under the lash.[14] The comparative ease with which these alterations were made in the Greek army suggests not only an admirable adaptability but also an appreciation of the value of the different fighting arms and the need for creating integrated forces.

The weakness of a hoplite army unattended by cavalry and missile troops is again highlighted by events that occurred near the end of the long march home. After passing through the mountains and snows of Armenia,

11. Xen. *An.* 3. 3. 16–20.
12. Ibid., 3. 4. 4–5.
13. Ibid., 3. 4. 13–15.
14. Ibid., 3. 4. 26.

eight thousand survivors reached the Black Sea, whence they went, mostly by sea, to Heraclea. There they split up into three parties, one comprising four thousand Arcadian and Achaean hoplites, another fourteen hundred hoplites and seven hundred peltasts, and, under the command of Xenophon, a third group of seventeen hundred hoplites, three hundred peltasts, and forty horsemen.[15] The first group of hoplites split up into ten companies, each under an elected general, in order to plunder Thracian villages in the countryside. Their plan was at first a success, but some of the Thracians escaped and rallied their comrades. Formed in a body and fighting as cavalry and peltasts, the Thracians overtook two booty-laden hoplite companies. The result was disastrous. Only eight men survived from one company, none from the other. The other Greek companies gathered together on a hill and made camp. The situation was desperate, however, for the Thracians surrounded the hill and constantly increased in number as large groups of horsemen and some peltasts arrived. Emboldened by their initial success, the Thracians repeatedly attacked the Greeks, riding and running up within range, hurling javelins, then hurrying away before the more heavily armed hoplites could close with them. Having no cavalry, javelin men, or archers of their own, the Greeks suffered badly. Had it not been for a successful ruse perpetrated by Xenophon and a relief force, the whole group might have perished.[16] In this case as elsewhere, the weakness of hoplites alone against a quicker, more agile enemy is apparent.

The news of the Greek hoplites' success against the Persians at Cunaxa and the latter's reluctance to engage them in open battle after the death of Cyrus had a lasting effect in Greece, serving as something of a backdrop to events in the later fourth century that culminated in the Macedonian invasion of the Persian Empire.

---

15. Ibid., 6.2.16.
16. Ibid., 6.3.

Chapter 8

The Corinthian War: 395 to 386 B.C.

THE PERIOD IMMEDIATELY FOLLOWING the Spartan victory in the Peloponnesian War in 404 brought disillusionment to many Greeks. Sparta had not fulfilled its promise to restore liberty to the Greeks. Instead, it consciously clothed itself in the mantle of empire that it had stripped from Athens. In many cities of the Aegean political control was achieved through military garrisons and governors (harmosts). In return for Persian gold during the war, Sparta acknowledged the Great King's claims to the Greek cities of Asia Minor. Nevertheless, whether for reasons of state or because of the personalities involved, the Spartans had decided to assist Cyrus the Younger—actively though not openly—in his effort to overthrow his brother Artaxerxes II in 401. Cyrus had replaced Tissaphernes as satrap of western Asia Minor in 408. The two Persians became enemies, and Cyrus developed a close working relationship with Lysander, the Spartan commander who had defeated the Athenians. The result was that when Cyrus marched east in 401 to challenge his brother, most of the Greek cities of coastal Asia Minor were under the control of Lysander, not Tissaphernes.

After the death of Cyrus, Tissaphernes was reappointed military commander of western Asia Minor. On his arrival in 400 he demanded the surrender of the Greek cities but they refused and called upon the Spartans for assistance. As the heirs of the Athenians, who had performed this task for much of the fifth century, the Spartans may have felt some obligation to respond, but a stronger encouragement was probably the fact that they had already broken the spirit of their arrangements with the Persian government when they aided Cyrus. Indeed, its own imperial interests rather than altruism dominated Sparta's foreign relations at this time, a fact of which the mainland Greek powers—that is to say, Athens, Thebes, Argos, and Corinth—were only too well aware. The fact that Thebes and Corinth, Sparta's allies in the war against Athens, now turned against it is proof of Sparta's failure as an imperial power. As a result, by the early fourth century the major Greek city-states were inclined to view Sparta with varying degrees of suspicion or even hostility. The Persians, who had already come to blows with the Spartans in Asia Minor, sent agents armed with gold to stir up trouble for them in their own backyard. Thus the stage was set for what is called the Corinthian War.

The early fighting between Sparta and Persia in the east that was a prelude to the Corinthian War is relevant to an understanding of the growing role of cavalry in Greek warfare. Believing that the Persians were preparing a campaign to drive them from Asia Minor, the Spartans sent out an expeditionary force led by King Agesilaus in 396. The force was augmented by survivors of the body of Greek mercenaries who had fought at Cunaxa with Cyrus, including Xenophon. According to Xenophon, Tissaphernes' strategy in this campaign was dictated by cavalry: "Tissaphernes knew that Agesilaus had no cavalry (and it was difficult for cavalry to operate in Caria); he also believed that Agesilaus was angry with him for deceiving him. He therefore assumed that he was in fact going to move into Caria against his own establishment there; so he brought his whole infantry back across the river into Caria, and led his cavalry round into the plain of the Maeander, imagining that he was strong enough to grind the Greeks into the ground with this arm alone before they ever reached the areas where cavalry could not operate."[1]

Agesilaus, however, marched north into Phrygia, plundering as he went. On one occasion, in the vicinity of Dascylium on the Propontis, an advance scouting party of cavalry topped a rise only to find themselves facing a like-sized body of Persian cavalry about four hundred feet away. These belonged to the satrap Pharnabazus. According to Xenophon, "The Greek cavalry was drawn up four deep in a phalanx formation, and the natives were in a column with a front of not more than twelve but many more deep. Then the natives charged, and when they got to close quarters every Greek who hit his man broke his spear, but the natives with their javelins of cornel wood soon killed twelve men and two horses. At this the Greek cavalry broke and fled, but Agesilaus came up in support with the hoplites, and then the natives retired, with the loss of one man."[2] Of special interest are Xenophon's

---

1. Xen. *Hell.* 3.4.12 (Warner trans.).
2. Ibid., 3.4.13–14 (Warner trans.).

descriptions of the cavalry formations, differences in weapons, and hand-to-hand fighting.

The alignments of both cavalry forces seem to be variations of the typical rectangular formation used by both Greeks and Persians. In contrast the rhomboid and wedge-shaped formations used by the Thessalians and Macedonians in the fourth century offered greater opportunity for penetrating the enemy line and wheeling about.[3] More noteworthy is the contrast in quality between the Persian cornel-wood javelin and the longer Greek spear; the former showed itself to be superior, and Xenophon recommended its adoption by Greek cavalry in his work *On Horsemanship*.[4] In this passage the Greek spear is described as weaker and less manageable than the Persian javelin, which is carried in pairs so that one can be thrown at the outset and the other used for fighting at close quarters. There is no evidence that Greek cavalry took Xenophon's advice and, indeed, it is hard to believe that Greek spears, which could also be used both ways, were always quite so fragile.

After this sobering experience Agesilaus withdrew to his winter quarters in Ephesus, determined to correct the deficiency in cavalry that prevented him from facing the Persians in open country. In lieu of personal service he induced the richest men of the cities to supply horses, arms, and riders. The winter and spring were spent outfitting and training all branches of the army, prizes being offered as incentives to the best divisions, including an award for horsemanship.[5]

Although the overall outcome of Agesilaus' campaigns in Asia Minor was disappointing, the immediate result of the off-season preparations on the fighting in the early summer of 395 was impressive and led directly to the downfall of Tissaphernes. Unfortunately, there is much debate among modern historians about the details of the battle of Sardis, in which the forces of Tissaphernes were decisively defeated. The problem arises because two widely divergent accounts of the battle—both by contemporary writers—survive. In addition to Xenophon's work, significant fragments of an anonymous history covering the years 411–386 were found at Oxyrhynchus in 1906 and published in 1908.[6] Judged on its merits as a work of great importance, it has also lent greater credibility to the corresponding passages of Diodorus, who has

---

3. See Ascl. *Tac.* 6.1–5.
4. Xen. *On Hors.* 12.12.
5. Xen. *Hell.* 3.4.16–17; *Ages.* 1.25. Worley (*HCAG* 136) assumes that Xenophon was Agesilaus' cavalry advisor at this time, which is a distinct possibility.
6. See Grenfell and Hunt (1908) 110–242; Bruce (1967).

clearly derived much of his narrative from the Oxyrhynchus historian by way of Ephorus. Since the publication of this work, the majority of historians has preferred its version of the battle of Sardis to that of Xenophon.[7] For present purposes, however, a neutral position—that of J. R. Hamilton—suffices: "What is clear is that Agesilaus defeated a Persian force of probably considerable proportions, sacked the enemy camp and obtained a great deal of booty, and advanced upon Sardis, where he pillaged the suburbs and outlying areas after failing to take the city."[8] To this can be added the fact that cavalry did play some role in the fighting—in the battle itself according to Xenophon, in the pursuit according to the Oxyrhynchus historian.

Whether Agesilaus, given adequate resources, could have realized his dream of conquering western Asia Minor is an open question, but he did show that it was militarily feasible for a Greek army to do so. With his realistic appraisal of the situation and his "(for a Spartan) unusual originality," he created a combined arms force in which "hoplites and horsemen acted in close co-operation."[9] In retrospect it seems clear that the experiences of Cyrus' Ten Thousand Greeks and the success of Agesilaus east of Greece, preserved in published accounts as well as in the living memory of the participants, formed the conceptual basis of the later conquest of the Persian Empire by the Macedonians.

By late summer of 395 an anti-Spartan alliance had been formed by the representatives of Thebes, Athens, Argos, and Corinth. The allied strategy was to keep the Spartans and their allies out of central and northern Greece by maintaining control of the Isthmus of Corinth. In the opening battle of the conflict, the battle of Haliartus in Boeotia, the Spartan general Lysander lost his life. As a result of this, Agesilaus was recalled from Asia in 394. Since the battle of Sardis he had accomplished little except for widespread plundering of

---

7. Xen. *Hell.* 3.4.23–24; Ox. Hist. 6.4–6. For arguments against Xenophon see, for example, Bruce (1967) app. 1, 150–56; Cartledge (1987) 215–16; Cawkwell (1972) app. 405–406. For a defense of Xenophon see Anderson (1974) 155–58. Arguments against Xenophon are: that he has Agesilaus take a less logical route from Ephesus to Sardis, resulting in a different battle site; that the Oxyrhynchus historian provides more detail, including an ambush; that Xenophon has Tissaphernes in Sardis, not at the battle, and so forth. Nevertheless, the fact that Xenophon was with Agesilaus during this period and may even have been at the battle cannot be dismissed so easily. Furthermore, since Xenophon took every opportunity to glorify Agesilaus, it makes no sense for him to place Tissaphernes in Sardis, thereby somewhat diminishing the glory of the victory. And if he were in Sardis, it is consistent with the incompetence he showed during the campaigns against Sparta, for which Artaxerxes had him removed and executed. Finally, if either writer resorted to fiction, it could just as reasonably have been the Oxyrhynchus historian adding the ambush to explain the Spartan victory over a numerically superior foe.

8. Hamilton (1979) 203.
9. Robinson (1965) 300.

Persian territory, but the booty from this was substantial and would help finance the war against the allies. With a well-outfitted army Agesilaus crossed the Hellespont and followed the same route that had been used by Xerxes a century earlier when he invaded Greece. In spite of the necessity of having well-trained cavalry to deal with the Persians in Asia Minor, the two large battles fought in central Greece in 394 clearly showed that there, at least, hoplite infantry remained dominant. To what extent this was dictated by the physical constraints of terrain and economic conditions rather than tradition and stubborn conservatism is difficult to say. Both factors probably played their part, and indeed the former reasons were legitimate, for the most significant military change at this time was Iphicrates' employment of a force of effective, well-trained peltasts—light infantry who could perform many of the contemporary duties of cavalry but were much less costly to maintain, while at the same time they were more adapted to the rough country of Greece. On the other hand Greek cavalry of this period almost certainly lacked nerve—a fearless, aggressive mentality that was essential if horsemen were to engage in close combat with spear and sword. Such qualities do not seem to have been common among cavalrymen until the rise of Macedon under Philip. Their absence in 394 may reflect a lower level of training and discipline or perhaps an incomplete awareness of the full potential of cavalry. As a general rule the Greeks seem to have preferred to hurl the javelin from a distance, as is recommended by Xenophon.[10] Obviously, during pursuit the fugitives were struck by hand-held weapons.

The first of the major land battles of 394, which took place on the coast between Corinth and Sicyon in the late spring, occurred before Agesilaus arrived in central Greece. Although cavalry were present on both sides, no mention is made of their role in the battle. Their numbers are given, however: 600 on the Spartan side, 1,550 on the allied side, the majority of the latter supplied by Boeotia (about 800) and Athens (about 600). It is possible that this disparity in cavalry forces represents the varying appreciation of horsemen by the states concerned. Throughout its history Sparta generally ignored the mounted arm, whereas Thebes and the Boeotians, as I have noted, had fielded a true cavalry force at least as early as the Persian Wars, in the early part of the preceding century.[11] Since this battle was won by the Spartans, it appears that the allies were unable to take advantage of their superiority in cavalry.

10. Xen. *On Hors.* 12.11–12.
11. Xen. *Hell.* 4.2.16–23.

While Agesilaus was marching south through northern Greece, the use to which he put his cavalry against the Thessalians—who constantly harassed him—makes the inactivity of those cavalry during the battle of Coronea that took place soon thereafter all the more intriguing. Fed up with the attacks on his rear guard, Agesilaus sent most of his cavalry to the rear to challenge the Thessalian horsemen. Due to the proximity of the hoplites, however, the Thessalians chose discretion and, wheeling about, retired in good order. At that point Agesilaus saw an opportunity too good to pass up and ordered his cavalry to attack the Thessalians before they could turn around and offer resistance. The surprise worked. Polycharmus, the Thessalian cavalry commander, together with his companions, did turn to meet the charge, but they were quickly killed in the fighting. The remaining Thessalians simply fled, some being killed or captured by Agesilaus' cavalry in pursuit. The Spartan king was delighted with this victory over a people who prided themselves on being the best horsemen in Greece.[12]

Later in the summer as he marched southward through Boeotia, Agesilaus, with reinforcements from the Peloponnese, met the allies near Coronea in the second major battle of the war. Once again the fighting was decided by the hoplites. The number of combatants is not given, although Xenophon reports that Agesilaus was greatly superior in peltasts and that the cavalry were evenly matched. He makes no mention of the latter in his battle description.[13] Beyond the probability that the tactics were largely dictated by the conditions I have mentioned above, there is also the possibility that the cavalry on each side simply nullified the other. If the cavalry kept each other occupied, there would have been no opportunity for them to engage the infantry from the flank or the rear, which was especially likely to occur when the two sides were evenly matched.

A good example of the tentativeness that chronically infected Greek (in this case Spartan) cavalry, as well as the failure to understand its tactical potential, appears as an addendum to the remarkable success of Iphicrates and his peltasts against a Spartan hoplite company (*mora*) near Lechaeum in 390. The Spartan company of about 600 men was returning to Lechaeum from escort duty when the Athenian commanders in Corinth—Callias and Iphicrates—observed that it was unprotected by either peltasts or cavalry. The Athenians decided to attack the Spartans with peltasts who could hurl javelins

12. Ibid., 4.3.3–9.
13. Ibid., 4.3.16–21.

from a distance and then retire with impunity, since there were no light forces or cavalry to catch them. Callias led out the hoplites and drew them up near the city, while Iphicrates, with his peltasts, attacked the Spartans on their unprotected side. The peltasts advanced within javelin range, hurled their weapons, and quickly retired when the hoplites charged. The slower hoplites soon ceased their fruitless pursuit and returned to their ranks. As they did so the peltasts attacked again, inflicting more casualties without suffering any themselves. Even with the arrival of Spartan cavalry, the situation did not improve, since the Spartans did not take advantage of their speed and mobility to act independently but formed up with the front of the hoplites and advanced and retreated with them. Xenophon criticized this timid use of cavalry and offered the suggestion that they should have pursued the retreating peltasts and killed some of them.[14] Finally the Spartans fled, some escaping by sea in boats sent out from Lechaeum or in the company of the cavalry. About 250 perished.[15]

This victory over Spartan hoplites earned a reputation for Iphicrates that lasted throughout antiquity and beyond. It also resulted in attempts to explain such an anomalous event, about which modern scholars still disagree. Both Diodorus and Nepos attribute a number of reforms to Iphicrates that converted the heavily armed hoplite into the lighter, more versatile peltast, so named for the smaller shield, or pelta. Other changes were the lengthening of the spear by half, the near doubling of the size of the sword, and the introduction of a type of light footwear named *iphicratids* after their inventor.[16] It is odd, however, that Diodorus makes no mention of peltasts in his work prior to this passage, in spite of the fact that they were a common element in Greek armies by the end of the fifth century and appear frequently in Thucydides. It seems reasonable to accept Best's argument that the peltasts of Iphicrates (whatever their place of origin) were not essentially different from the type of soldiers known as Thracian peltasts, who played an increasingly important role in the warfare of the fifth and fourth centuries, especially as mercenaries.[17] Their success under Iphicrates, a leader of ability, was presumably due to their high levels of training, discipline, and morale. Victory on this occasion required daring, yet it is not that surprising given the mistake of the Spartan commander who dismissed his covering force of cavalry.

14. Ibid., 4.5.6.
15. Ibid., 4.5.13–18.
16. Diod. 15.44.2–4; Nep. *Iph.* 1.3–4.
17. Best (1969) 102–10, 134–42.

Thirty years earlier the Athenians had shown how vulnerable a hoplite force could be when it was faced by light-armed missile troops. In that one-sided struggle on Sphacteria, a Spartan company of 420 hoplites took 128 casualties before surrendering.[18]

The fact that the Greeks of this period made more use of peltasts than cavalry to increase the versatility of their armies could be justified on economic grounds as well as by the fact that they were effective. In his description of Spartan preparations for an expedition against Olynthus in the north in 383, Xenophon reports that the allies could substitute a money payment in lieu of troops. Under this arrangement the amount for a cavalryman was to be four times that of a hoplite, a fact that gives an indication of the expense of fielding cavalry.[19] Peltasts would certainly be no more costly than hoplites.

The Corinthian War came to an end in 386 under the terms of a settlement known as the King's Peace. By the early 380s mutual interests had once again brought Persia and Sparta together, and—in circumstances similar to those that brought an end to the Peloponnesian War—a Spartan fleet brought Athens to terms by intercepting its Pontic grain ships. Under the terms dictated by the Persian king Artaxerxes, Sparta retained its position of dominance in the Greek world. In the long run the peace settled nothing, and the overbearing behavior of Sparta in the years immediately following led to more warfare.

---

18. Thuc. 4.33–38. (425 B.C.) Thucydides reports that Athenian casualties were light because it was not a formal, hand-to-hand battle.
19. Xen. *Hell.* 5.2.20–21.

Chapter 9

Interlude—Spartan Decline: 386 to 371 B.C.

FOLLOWING THE KING'S PEACE, Sparta's continued interference in the affairs of city-states far beyond its traditional sphere of influence in the Peloponnese was bound to have unwanted results. For example, in 382—in response to an appeal from Acanthus and Apollonia, two city-states threatened with forcible absorption by an aggressive Chalcidian League under the leadership of Olynthus—the Spartans sent out an army of the Peloponnesian League under the leadership of Agesilaus' stepbrother Teleutias. He marched north with the levy of ten thousand and was joined by other allied forces along the way, including four hundred high-quality cavalry under Derdas of Elimia. When he arrived in the vicinity of Olynthus, Teleutias formed up his army a little more than a mile from the walls. He himself commanded the left wing comprising the Peloponnesian infantry and the cavalry of Derdas. On the right were the allied infantry and the cavalry of Laconia, Thebes, and Macedonia. The Olynthian cavalry initiated the action with a vigorous charge against their Laconian and Theban counterparts. Polycharmus, the Spartan cavalry commander, was unhorsed and repeatedly wounded as he lay on the ground, while his horsemen were completely routed. This unsettled the allied infantry, who also retreated. A psychological stroke by Derdas saved the day, for—ignoring the enemy troops—he and his men rushed for the gates of the city in order to cut off the Olynthians from secure refuge. When the Olynthian cavalry saw this, they broke off their attack, turned back, and raced for the gates. Many of them were killed as they passed Derdas' cavalry, but they and the Olynthian infantry found refuge behind the walls. Although Teleutias and the infantry on the left advanced, they do not seem to have engaged the enemy, and all the fighting seems to have fallen upon the cavalry. Xenophon felt that but for Derdas the whole army would have been in danger of defeat.[1]

In 381, during the second year of the campaign, fighting was limited to cavalry sorties and raids. On one occasion in the spring, about six hundred Olynthian cavalry made a plundering raid into the territory of Apollonia. As it happened, Derdas and his horsemen were breakfasting when they saw the Olynthians riding carelessly up to the walls. Derdas led his men out in good order and routed the enemy, pursuing them more than ten miles back to Olynthus and killing about eighty along the way.[2]

For a while the Olynthians kept close to their own walls, but not too much later poor Spartan leadership gave their cavalry a chance to redeem themselves. Teleutias was approaching the city in order to destroy any remaining trees and cultivated fields when the Olynthian horsemen came out to meet them in an unhurried, orderly manner, even venturing to cross the river that lies to the west of the town. Angered at such boldness, Teleutias ordered the peltasts under Tlemonidas to charge them at the run. At this the Olynthians turned and unhurriedly recrossed the river. When some of the peltasts crossed the river in disorganized pursuit, the Olynthians turned and charged, killing Tlemonidas and about one hundred others. This infuriated Teleutias, who ordered the horsemen and peltasts to pursue the enemy while he brought up the infantry. The Peloponnesians then made the mistake of approaching too close to the walls and allowing themselves to be disrupted by the missiles of the defenders. At this point the Olynthians sent out their cavalry and peltasts, who succeeded in routing the confused enemy. When Teleutias was killed, his troops scattered to the four winds, suffering heavy casualties at the hands of their pursuers.[3] Subsequently, the Spartans sent out a larger army that eventually succeeded in starving the Olynthians into surrender in 379.[4] Nonetheless, the cavalry on both sides had shown themselves to great advantage.

In 378 and 377 substantial Peloponnesian levies under the command of Agesilaus invaded Boeotia. Although Agesilaus failed to entice the Thebans out to fight a major battle in defense of their land and crops, he did cause them considerable distress. During these campaigns cavalry played an important

---

1. Xen. *Hell.* 5.2.40–43.
2. Ibid., 5.3.1–2.
3. Ibid., 5.3.3–6; Diod. 15.21.1–3, who gives a perfunctory description of the battle but adds that the Lacedaemonians lost twelve hundred men.
4. Xen. *Hell.* 5.3.26.

role and were involved in several actions that exhibit the significant role mental attitudes play in warfare. Upon entering Theban territory in 378, Agesilaus found that a trench and palisade had been constructed around the most valuable land. Thus he had to content himself with destroying the countryside on his side of the barrier, while the enemy troops marched parallel to him on the other side. On one occasion the Theban cavalry charged out through an exit in the barricade and caught some of Agesilaus' troops off guard. Many peltasts and some cavalrymen were killed before Agesilaus turned to aid them with the hoplites and the rest of the cavalry. At this the Thebans panicked, behaving "like men who have got drunk in the middle of the day." They threw their spears while they were still out of range, turned, and fled, in spite of which twelve of them were killed.[5]

An even more spectacular change of fortune occurred later that year after Agesilaus had departed for home, leaving Phoebidas behind as harmost in Thespiae. When Phoebidas continued to raid their territory, the Thebans sent out their whole levy against him in the hope of gaining some measure of revenge. At first Phoebidas cleverly used his peltasts to prevent any enemy soldiers from leaving the ranks. The Thebans were vexed at this and began to retire in some haste, soon turning to panic. Then Phoebidas overreached himself by urging an ever bolder pursuit, which led to his peltasts' trapping the Theban cavalry at an impassable ravine. There, with the courage of desperation, the horsemen turned to face their pursuers. The few peltasts leading the pursuit were frightened by this and fled, spreading the contagion, as the Thebans took heart and charged in turn. As it was late in the day, most attained the walls of Thespiae in safety, but Phoebidas and some others were killed.[6]

In the following year, 377, an insignificant action elicits a comment from Xenophon the horseman that shows one of the advantages of cavalry over infantry. Agesilaus had once again entered Boeotia with the Peloponnesian levy, this time reinforced with Olynthian cavalry who were serving under the terms of the recent peace treaty between Sparta and Olynthus. After an indecisive battle Agesilaus was leading his army from Thebes to Thespiae. Along the way mercenary peltasts of the Thebans dogged his heels, "but the Olynthian cavalry . . . wheeled round and, bearing down on the peltasts, chased them up a slope and killed great numbers of them; for men on foot are easily

---

5. Ibid., 5.4.38–40. (Warner trans.).
6. Ibid., 5.4.42–45.

overtaken by cavalry when going uphill where riding conditions are good."[7] This is very much to the point, because horses—with their powerful hindquarters—go uphill with more control and greater ease than they go downhill. It also means that there is no a priori reason why cavalry cannot charge uphill when circumstances require it.

In the year 375 two incidents further demonstrated that cavalry were being used regularly and in a variety of ways in the struggle between Sparta and Thebes. In one case Plutarch makes a bare statement that the Theban Charon (probably as Boeotarch) gained a cavalry victory at Plataea.[8] Of greater importance for our understanding of the evolution of tactics, although minor in terms of the numbers involved, was the second case—a battle fought near Tegyra. Once again Plutarch is the primary source, but on this occasion he provides more detail, since in retrospect this battle was seen as a prelude to the great Theban victory at Leuctra four years later.[9] The battle itself was quite unplanned, for Pelopidas, leading the Sacred Band—an elite infantry force of three hundred—and some cavalry, had marched against Orchomenus, hoping to catch it unprotected by its Spartan garrison, which was away in Locris. The Spartans, however, were not so careless, and had replaced the garrison. Disappointed, Pelopidas began his march home. He was soon brought up short when the two companies of Spartan troops returning to Orchomenus were seen advancing towards him in a narrow pass. In spite of being outnumbered by at least two to one, Pelopidas decided to fight. He ordered the cavalry to move up from the rear and attack the Spartans and placed himself at the head of the Sacred Band, confident that his troops could at least cut their way through to safety. Convinced that the Thebans could not stand against them, the Spartans advanced, but in the Sacred Band they finally met a force of hoplites that was their equal in training, discipline, and spirit. When their leaders were killed in the first clash, the Spartans faltered and opened up a lane by which the Thebans could pass through. By now Pelopidas had bigger things in mind and used the opening for a more vigorous attack, finally routing the entire Spartan force.[10] Two things attract one's attention in this account, the first being the use of cavalry to initiate the attack.

---

7. Ibid., 5.4.54. (Warner trans.). Xenophon gives advice for riding up and down hill in *On Hors.* 8.6–8.

8. Plut. *Pel.* 25.5; see *TH* 41.

9. As reported by Plutarch, *Pel.* 16.1, and Diodorus 15.81.2.

10. Plut. *Pel.* 16–17; Diodorus (15.37) puts the number of Thebans at five hundred, the Spartans at twice that number. The number of Spartans depends on the size of the company (*mora*), for which Plutarch gives three figures from different sources (Ephorus, 500, Callisthenes, 700, Polybius, 900).

Regrettably, no other mention of cavalry is made and Pelopidas' purpose is not mentioned. Although the decisive action was performed by the infantry, the initial cavalry attack may have been intended to catch the Spartans out of formation and disrupt their attempt to change from marching to battle array.[11] Pritchett, in his discussion of the topography of the battle site, suggests that the cavalry led the main charge. This is unlikely, however, as cavalry were incapable of successfully attacking well-prepared hoplites.[12] The second and perhaps more important point is the coordination of cavalry and infantry.[13] On this occasion Pelopidas recognized the opportunities offered by the immediate circumstances, evaluated them, and made quick, valid decisions.

The ubiquitous appearance of cavalry in actions such as these and its regular use in battles of the early decades of the fourth century represent a fundamental change from the almost exclusive role played by infantry prior to the Peloponnesian War. Many individuals from different city-states contributed to this development, thus providing an essential prelude to the military advances of the second half of the century.

11. Buckler (1995) 53.
12. *SAGT* 4 115–16. In a military context the verb used by Plutarch (προεμβάλλω) clearly means "to lead the charge." It is regrettable that he gives no other details of the cavalry's part in the action. In their absence one might suggest that the cavalry "softened up" the Spartan infantry by hurling javelins, as peltasts had done earlier at Lechaeum and Sphacteria.
13. Buckler (1995) 54.

Chapter 10

Theban Ascendancy: 371 to 362 B.C.

PRIOR TO THE MACEDONIAN victory over the Greek states in 338 at Chaeronea, the most important battle of the fourth century was that at Leuctra in 371. This Theban victory over the Spartans was a decisive event in Greek history, for it brought the military dominance of Sparta to an end. Cavalry were present on both sides and played some part in the battle. Xenophon provides an informative comment on the relative quality of the mounted forces of each side: "The Theban cavalry, as a result of the war with Orchomenus and with Thespiae, was in good training, but the Spartan cavalry at that time was in very poor shape. This was because the horses were kept by the very rich, and it was only after an order for mobilization that the appointed cavalryman appeared to get his horse and whatever arms were given him; he then had to take the field at once. Also the men who served in the cavalry were the ones who were in the worst physical condition and the least anxious to win distinction."[1] Such a dismal state of affairs is surprising, given the appreciation for cavalry that King Agesilaus had gained when he campaigned in Asia Minor. Since he was still alive, although not at the battle, one can only assume that the Spartan system was incapable of reform.[2] This statement of Xenophon's also draws attention to the fact that we usually know very little about the quality of troops involved in any battle.

---

1. Xen. *Hell.* 6.4.10–11.
2. In one sense this is incorrect, since Plutarch (*Ages.* 20.1) says that the Spartans had one thousand cavalry at Leuctra, and it is clear that in terms of numbers the Spartans had attempted to rectify their deficiency in this arm. Nothing, however, seems to have been done to improve the quality of the native Spartan horsemen.

Although my primary interest is in the cavalry action that initiated the battle, some mention should be made of the reason for the Theban victory because there is a great deal of controversy regarding the nature of this event. In spite of the claim by P. Cartledge that "the precise details [of this battle] are as ever unrecoverable," a study by Hanson suggests that the primary contemporary source, Xenophon, does give sufficient information to explain what happened.[3] When the two sides faced each other on the plain of Leuctra, probably neither had more than ten thousand troops, and the Thebans may have had no more than seven thousand. Each side seems to have had almost one thousand cavalry. For some reason Cleombrotus, the Spartan king, stationed his cavalry in front of the phalanx, to which Epaminondas responded by placing his own horsemen opposite them. The superior Theban cavalry had no trouble defeating the Spartan horsemen and putting them to flight, an event that in itself is of little moment. More important is the fact that the Thebans drove the Spartan cavalry back into their own infantry lines instead of off to the sides. Consequently, the Spartan hoplites were thrown into some confusion at the very time when the Theban infantry attacked.[4] In addition, in Epaminondas the Spartans faced a military leader of ability, commanding troops who had already shown their skill in dealing with Spartan hoplites. Much of Epaminondas' later fame rests upon the claim that he employed novel or at least uncommon tactics at Leuctra. He arranged his phalanx to a depth of fifty men, against twelve of the Spartans. Contrary to common Greek practice, this striking force was placed on the left of his line, against the Spartans under Cleombrotus, who—as the stronger element—were in the typical position on the right of their line. Furthermore, he supposedly advanced with his line sloping back from left to right in an oblique formation, insuring that the strongest parts of each army met in the decisive encounter. Although Epaminondas decided to pit strength against strength, he nonetheless achieved local superiority by greatly deepening his line and perhaps also by the unexpected matching of strength. When their king was killed, the Spartans lost heart and retired from the battlefield. Although defeated, however, they were able to withdraw in some order and reformed in front of their camp on a slope above the plain. The result changed Greek history.[5]

    3. Cartledge (1987) 238; Hanson (1988) 190–207.
    4. Xen. *Hell.* 6.4.10–13.
    5. Ibid., 6.4.13–15; Diod. 15.51–56; Plut. *Pel.* 20–23. For modern reconstructions see Anderson (1970) 192–220; *HAW* 165–69; *TH* 62–66; *SAGT* 4 116–19; Cartledge (1987) 236–41. There are also some hints that Spartan morale was lower than usual; see Cartledge (1987) 241. In addition not the least of Epaminondas' qualities as a commander was his insistence on high levels of training and discipline. Xen. *Hell.* 7.5.19.

Exactly why the Spartans placed their cavalry in front of their hoplites is not clear. Xenophon attributes it to the fact that the space lying between the two armies was a plain, but unless he meant to imply that the flanks were somehow obstructed, it does not explain the arrangement. Delbrück argued in favor of obstruction on the flanks, but J. Buckler, among others, thought that the cavalry's purpose was to screen the movements of the infantry, thereby gaining time.[6] Pritchett suggests that Epaminondas' placement of his cavalry was not merely a counter to the placement of Cleombrotus' cavalry but was based on Pelopidas' success at Tegyra.[7] Whatever the reason, it seems that this deployment of cavalry was a mistake, as has been suggested by both C. Tuplin and Hanson.[8] In any case the effect is clear—the rout of the Spartan horsemen and the disruption of the enemy line. It seems impossible to avoid the conclusion that the Spartans had to open their ranks to allow the cavalry a way through before the hoplites could fight their battle. Irrespective of the intentions on either side, the Theban cavalry had contributed their share to the victory, having produced some disruption in the enemy line. However, it is difficult to agree with Delbrück, who observes "that it was not first the Macedonians, but Epaminondas, who conceived the tactics of combined arms," for the cavalry action was most likely brought about by a mistake of the Spartans that Epaminondas took advantage of on the spot. It seems to have been a skirmish rather than an integral part of the battle, and thus the point of Pritchett's comment that "the history of Greek cavalry needs to be revised in the light of Tegyra and Leuktra"[9] should be limited to the first of the two battles.

Hanson's conclusion that "Examination of the various 'innovations' in Greek battle tactics that Epameinondas has often been credited with at Leuktra reveals that none can be seen as either revolutionary or even especially novel" is convincing, supporting the idea that military change after the Peloponnesian War was the result of incremental changes by many gifted leaders.[10] His confidence in Xenophon is, I think, well placed, since it is difficult to ignore a contemporary who was an experienced and capable soldier. The victory itself may be seen as a result of a Spartan mistake in using poor cavalry

---

6. *HAW* 168–69; Buckler (1980a) 88–89.
7. *SAGT* 4 118.
8. Tuplin (1993) 135; Hanson (1988) 196.
9. *HAW* 167; *SAGT* 4 119. In regard to combined arms, the use of hoplites, peltasts, and cavalry in combination was not uncommon by the end of the fifth century; Best (1969) 75, 77; Xen. *An.* 7.6.25–30; Hanson (1988) 196.
10. Hanson (1988) 205–207.

improperly, the effect upon morale of the death of Cleombrotus, and the fact that the Spartans met an enemy at least as well prepared as themselves.

After the battle the Spartans took refuge in their camp and sent a messenger home to announce the disaster. The Thebans sent word of the victory to Athens, where the messenger was rebuffed, and to their ally Jason, tyrant of Pherae and commander (*tagus*) of the Thessalian federal league. Jason responded by marching so rapidly through the land of the Phocians, with whom he was at war, that they had no time to gather an army to oppose him—a feat that elicited the fitting comment from Xenophon that this was "a good example of how speed often counts for more than force when it comes to getting things done."[11] Jason, one of the great "might-have-beens" of Greek history, was considered by Xenophon to be the greatest man of his time.[12] He was certainly the most powerful leader in northern Greece in the late 370s, until his premature death at the hands of assassins in 370. He controlled considerable numbers of troops, reckoned by Xenophon at twenty thousand hoplites, eight thousand cavalry, and numerous peltasts. This constituted the largest army in Greece, and it is no wonder if the city-states were suspicious of Jason's ambition. Later in the century the Thessalian cavalry proved their worth as part of the army with which Alexander conquered Persia. Unfortunately for the Thessalians, their unity and influence did not long survive Jason's death. On this occasion Jason argued against the Theban suggestion that they attack the Spartan camp together and succeeded in convincing his allies to allow the Spartans to return home under a truce. In doing so he was probably looking primarily to his own interests, which did not welcome a too-powerful Thebes.[13]

During the winter of 370/369 the Thebans sent a large army into the Peloponnese to aid the Arcadians against the Spartans. The Spartans, in turn, sent to Athens for assistance. Anxious over the rising power of Thebes and desirous of preserving the balance of power on land, the Athenians sent out their full levy under the command of Iphicrates. Unwilling to face Epaminondas' veterans in the open, Iphicrates was content to harry the Thebans as they marched home north across the Isthmus. One event that occurred at this time did give Xenophon an opportunity to criticize Iphicrates' handling of cavalry. He reports that Iphicrates sent out the entire cavalry force of the Athenians and Corinthians to learn whether the Thebans had passed Oneum. His criticism is that

---

11. Xen. Hell. 6.4.21 (Warner trans.).
12. Ibid., 6.4.28.
13. Ibid., 6.4.20–25.

scouting parties should be small, so that if retreat became necessary there would be no problem of congestion when they retired through difficult country. On this occasion that did happen, and twenty horsemen were lost.[14] In theory Xenophon's complaint is sound, but—if Buckler's interpretation of this passage is correct—Xenophon may have misinterpreted Iphicrates' motives. He suggests that the cavalry were detailed to attack the retreating Thebans and do as much harm as they could.[15] Presumably, Epaminondas was able to deal with these attacks just as he was able to do in Thessaly in 368 (for which Diodorus provides details).[16]

In 369 Epaminondas led a second invasion of the Peloponnese, but again no major battles took place. As he passed Corinth on his way home he did make a halfhearted attempt on one of the gates but in general he was content to plunder the countryside. One minor incident mentioned by Xenophon points up the importance of the intangible qualities of morale and confidence in battle. While the Thebans were still camped near Corinth, more than twenty triremes sent by Dionysius of Syracuse to aid the Spartans arrived with Celtic and Iberian infantry and about fifty cavalry. On the following day, according to Xenophon, the Thebans and their allies spread out in detachments to plunder: "The cavalry of the Athenians and the Corinthians, seeing the strength and the numbers of the opposition, kept their distance from the enemy army. But the cavalry sent by Dionysius, in spite of their small numbers, rode along the enemy's line either as individuals or in small detachments and charged down upon them, hurling their javelins. When the enemy moved out against them, they would fall back, and then face about and hurl their javelins again." By repeating this pattern the cavalry made the enemy army advance or retreat at will.[17] It is impossible to say why the western cavalry exhibited such boldness and initiative, but such qualities are invaluable in any army, and later on their possession by the Macedonian army contributed much to the success of Philip and Alexander.

In the early 360s the Thebans were also drawn into the affairs of Thessaly and—to a lesser degree—Macedon. Pelopidas seems to have been the moving force behind this involvement. In 369 he led a Theban force into Thessaly to help the Thessalians against Alexander, the new tyrant of Pherae, who was laying claim to the position of *tagus*. He was modestly successful in

---

14. Ibid., 6.5.51–52.
15. *TH* 295, n. 30.
16. Diod. 15.71.5–6. See page 134 for a description.
17. Xen. *Hell.* 7.1.20–21 (Warner trans.)

containing Alexander and returned the following year on an embassy without troops. Alexander violated his diplomatic status and arrested him. Incensed at this, the Thebans quickly sent out a force of eight thousand hoplites and six hundred cavalry under the command of the Boeotarchs Hypatus and Cleomenes. Epaminondas, not having been reelected, was serving in the ranks. The Boeotarchs apparently did not appreciate the difficulty of fighting in Thessaly against an enemy who was superior in cavalry. When their Thessalian allies abandoned them and a force of Athenians joined Alexander, the Thebans decided to return home. Alexander had no intention of letting them off so easily, however, and when they broke camp and marched away, he followed with a vastly superior body of cavalry. These continuously showered javelins upon the retreating Thebans, killing some and reducing the rest to impotence. Taking things into their own hands, the rank and file called upon Epaminondas to lead them out of trouble. He promptly posted the light-armed troops and cavalry in the rear and repulsed the attackers, thereby providing security for the hoplites. By turning about to offer battle and using skillful formations Epaminondas saved the army, although it represented the first military setback for the Thebans in some years.[18] Once again, as at Pharsalus in 457, Thessalian cavalry rendered a hoplite army ineffective. Furthermore, it seems likely that Alexander's cavalry, by virtue of their numbers, could have done serious damage to the Thebans if they had been willing to take some casualties themselves. Presumably, they were content to be rid of the Thebans.

A number of small-scale actions at Phlius, a loyal Spartan ally, during the years 370–366 demonstrate the value of aggressive behavior by horsemen even when their number is small. Phlius lay southwest of Corinth on the upper reaches of the Asopus River, a location that made it a tempting object of attack for Sparta's enemies. Initially, the Argives attacked Phlius in full force and ravaged the land. The Phliasians, too few in number to meet the Argives in the open, waited until the enemy turned homeward and then sent their sixty cavalry out to attack the cavalry and infantry posted as a rear guard. The Phliasians routed them completely, killing some in the process.[19] Sometime thereafter some Phliasian exiles, with the help of the Argives and Arcadians—six hundred in number—seized the acropolis of Phlius. The citizens rallied and were on the point of clearing the acropolis of the enemy when

18. Diod. 15.71.5–6.
19. Xen. *Hell.* 7.2.4.

the Argives and Arcadians surrounded the city. The fighting continued until the acropolis was clear and the Phliasians sent out their cavalry, which prompted the enemy to retire.[20]

The same enemy returned the following year to destroy the crops and thus bring them to terms. The Phliasian cavalry and some picked troops, aided by Athenian cavalry, caught the enemy at a river crossing, defeated them, and succeeded in keeping them away from the crops.[21] Later the Theban governor at Sicyon led out his garrison troops, the Sicyonians and Pelleneans, and the tyrant Euphron with two thousand mercenaries to lay waste the Phliasian plain. This force approached from the northeast, planning to descend Mount Tricaranum to the plain. On the heights opposite the Corinthian gate, which faced east, the Theban general posted the Sicyonians and Pelleneans to prevent the Phliasians from making a sortie above and behind him. Before he reached the plain, however, the Phliasians sent out their cavalry and picked troops to bar the way. They succeeded in doing so, and the skirmishing lasted most of the day, taking on a regular pattern. Euphron's infantry dared not venture onto the plain, where the cavalry dominated, and the cavalry in turn had to limit their pursuit because of the mountainside's uneven terrain. In this ebb and flow the damage was done by missile weapons, presumably javelins. Finally, the invaders had had enough and retired by a roundabout route over Mount Tricaranum. The Phliasians, seeing the retreat as an opportunity to attack the troops posted at the Corinthian gate, set out in haste along the road that ran parallel to the city wall. The cavalry arrived first and attacked, but the Pelleneans held their ground. A second attack aided by some newly arrived foot soldiers was more successful, and hand-to-hand fighting ensued. The Theban general and his troops could only watch from a distance as many of the Pelleneans and a few Sicyonians were killed.[22]

The final episode in this series of vignettes reported by Xenophon saw the Phliasian cavalry and hoplites, aided by the Athenian general Chares and his mercenaries, thwart a Sicyonian attempt to build a fort on Phliasian territory.[23] As usual, the cavalry played a decisive role and showed how effective they could be in preventing an enemy from achieving his goals. It is also noteworthy that the cavalry and infantry worked closely together.

20. Ibid., 7.2.5–9.
21. Ibid., 7.2.10.
22. Ibid., 7.3.11–15.
23. Ibid., 7.2.20–23. See Tuplin (1993) 145 for an appreciation of these actions at Phlius.

A much more spectacular success for cavalry can be seen in Pelopidas' final Thessalian adventure in 364 at Cynoscephalae. In this year Alexander of Pherae once again threatened the members of the Thessalian League, who called in turn upon Theban support. Pelopidas went north with three hundred good-quality cavalry and was joined by Thessalian infantry at Pharsalus. From there he marched northeast into the valley of the Enipeus River as Alexander marched west. The two armies confronted each other north of the Enipeus, where parallel ridges reach south into the plain. Each side attempted to occupy the heights with infantry, while at the same time Pelopidas sent his cavalry against those of the enemy, driving them southward into the plain. Alexander's infantry reached the heights first, where they withstood the initial attack of the Thessalian hoplites. Seeing that his infantry were stopped, Pelopidas recalled his cavalry from the plain and set them against the southern flank of the enemy. Pelopidas himself grabbed a shield (he presumably had been fighting from horseback) and ran to join his infantry, whom he inspired to make several attacks. The combined infantry/cavalry attack induced Alexander's infantry to make an orderly retreat down from the ridge.

When Pelopidas, from his new vantage point at the top, spied his old enemy Alexander marshaling his mercenaries on the right, he rushed forth to challenge the king personally. Virtually alone, Pelopidas was killed by the spear thrusts of the mercenaries, among whom Alexander had sought refuge. In the meantime the Thessalian infantry, fearing for Pelopidas' safety, had crested the hill and run down to his aid as the cavalry came uphill from the south. At this, Alexander's infantry lost their cohesion and fled for their lives, some three thousand of them being killed in the long, bloody pursuit.[24] Although a tactical victory for the Thessalian League and the Thebans, the effect of this battle was negligible, as Alexander was still at large and in the death of Pelopidas the Thebans had suffered an irreparable loss. Upon hearing of the events, the Thebans sent out a proper army (seven thousand infantry and seven hundred cavalry), defeated Alexander, and reduced him to the status of a subject-ally, thus ending his efforts to unite Thessaly.[25]

Although the battle itself may not have been significant, an appreciation of Pelopidas' tactical flair and qualities of leadership is essential in order to reconstruct the military history of this period. His notable actions on this

---

24. Plut. *Pel.* 31.3, 32. The account in Diodorus gives no useful details. The twenty thousand troops he assigns to Alexander seem to be too many (15.80.4–5).

25. Plut. *Pel.* 35.1–2; Diod. 15.80.6.

occasion included not only his daring attack on a numerically superior foe, his inspiring personal leadership in the ranks, and his masterful improvisation, but also his aggressive use of cavalry, his ability to recall them from pursuit and have them regroup (probably by means of signal horns), and his combined use of infantry and cavalry against hoplites. A generation later, all of these tactics are found in the battles of Alexander the Great.[26]

One other point deserves consideration. In his discussion of the Theban intervention in Thessaly, Buckler suggests that Pelopidas virtually created the well-trained Thessalian infantry that fought at Cynoscephalae.[27] Apparently he took on this task during his first intervention in Thessaly in 369. Such a program, which was obviously undertaken with an eye to the future, represents an astute grasp of the relative merits of both infantry and cavalry—namely, that in an army consisting of both arms, each is indispensable to the other. The question whether cavalry can defeat infantry or vice versa is immaterial; they usually stand or fall together. Even if he did not have a major hand in the development of effective Thessalian infantry, Pelopidas doubtless understood this principle. Overall, his military ability is great—perhaps superior even to that of Epaminondas.

In 362 Epaminondas led the full levy of the Boeotian League into the Peloponnese in what proved to be his final campaign. The Arcadian League—the instrument by which Thebes had controlled the Peloponnesian enemies of Sparta—was rent by dissension that threatened Theban influence. The Arcadian factions found rallying points in two old enemies, the cities of Mantinea (which was oligrchic and anti-Theban) and Tegea (which was democratic and pro-Theban). While the democratic group was summoning the Thebans, the oligarchs requested military assistance from Athens and Sparta. It was possibly Epaminondas' intention on this occasion to stake everything on a pitched battle, which—if successful—would make Thebes dominant in Greece.

When Epaminondas arrived at Tegea he quartered his army within the city to await events, hoping that the Mantineans, now camped around the city, would come out to fight. They were expecting reinforcements from Athens and Sparta, however, and made no move. Upon hearing that Agesilaus was marching north with the main body of the Spartan army, Epaminondas conceived the idea of a night march south in order to intercept them and force

---

26. See the comments of Buckler, *TH* 180, and *SAGT* 2 118–19.
27. *TH* 116–17.

an engagement in the open. Fortunately for Agesilaus, he was still within ten miles of Sparta when a deserter from the army of Epaminondas reached him. In spite of the lack of surprise the Thebans did attack the unwalled city, and for a while there was hard fighting in the very streets of Sparta—an unprecedented and unwelcome experience for the inhabitants. Nevertheless, the defenses held and Epaminondas withdrew northward, having no intention of awaiting the Mantineans, who were coming to help the Spartans. The main body of his army marched back to Tegea, but the cavalry were detailed for a surprise attack on Mantinea in the hope of seizing cattle and those Mantineans who might be outside the walls harvesting grain. As Buckler correctly points out, "Epameinondas chose his cavalry alone for this mission because speed was once again the significant factor in this attack and because only mounted forces enjoyed the mobility to retire easily, should the Spartans and Mantineans return from Sparta more quickly than anticipated."[28]

For the second time in two days Epaminondas' surprise failed, this time due to the timely arrival at Mantinea of Athenian cavalry who had set out from Eleusis. Both groups of horsemen reached the city about the same time, and although the Athenians had not yet taken their morning meal, they were prevailed upon to ride out to protect the cattle, workers, and citizens. In spite of weariness from their respective marches, both sides fought vigorously at close quarters, the Athenians besting the Theban and Thessalian horsemen.[29] Although Xenophon fails to mention it, his son Gryllus was killed fighting on the Athenian side.[30] The intensity of this clash, fought by two travel-weary bodies of cavalry, is remarkable and suggests that the fighting quality of cavalry had greatly improved over the preceding one hundred years.[31]

---

28. Ibid., 212; Xen. *Hell.* 7.5.1–14; Diod. 15.82.5–83.5.

29. Xen. *Hell.* 7.5.15–17.

30. Diog. Laert. 2.54; There is some interesting confusion here in the ancient sources, for Pausanias says that Gryllus killed Epaminondas at Mantinea, citing a claim by the Athenians supported by the Thebans, and describes a painting showing this at Athens by the mid-fourth-century Corinthian artist Euphranor. Paus. 1.3.4.; 8.115–17; 9.15.3.

31. It is difficult to say which side was more travel worn. The Thebans and Thessalians had covered about seventy-five miles in forty-eight hours and had been involved in the attack on Sparta. The Athenians, for their part, had gone about eighty miles and had had some sort of trouble along the way at Corinth, which was neutral. Since they apparently arrived before noon, they may have been on their way for one and one-half to two and one-half days. Customary marching speed for cavalry without changing mounts and excluding rest stops is five to eight miles an hour. Over easy ground that amounts to twenty-five to forty miles a day. The shorter the distance, the greater the degree the horses could be pushed beyond it. See Jankovich (1971) 148. This seems consonant with the capability of Alexander's cavalry (cf. Arr. *Anab.* 3.15.3–5; 21.7–9; 25.6).

Unable to delay any longer because of a time limit that had been placed on the campaign and also because his own men had their fields to harvest, Epaminondas decided to march north from Tegea and engage his enemies near Mantinea. The two armies came to face each other at the narrow point of the plain that lies between Tegea and Mantinea. According to Diodorus (who is not notably reliable in such details), the Thebans and their allies comprised about thirty thousand infantry and three thousand horse, while the enemy had respectively about twenty thousand and two thousand. Agesilaus and his allies had taken up a sound defensive position at the narrowest point in the plain, with their flanks covered by hills. It is unclear whether the cavalry were on the flanks—for which there may not have been sufficient space—or out in front.

Initially, Epaminondas drew up his forces in line facing the enemy to the north, but instead of advancing against them he led his men toward the west and, upon reaching the mountains there, had them ground their arms and act as if they were preparing to encamp. The enemy, convinced there would be no battle that day, relaxed and dismissed their formations. Meanwhile, Epamiondas reinforced his left to a great depth by bringing up companies of infantry from the right. With all of his Boeotian troops now massed on the left, Epaminondas gave the order to take up arms and march to the attack. Xenophon likened this formation to the prow of a ship. The ranks of the weaker allies, holding the center and sloped obliquely to the right rear, were not expected to close with the enemy. In order to keep the Athenians out of action on his right, Epaminondas posted some cavalry and infantry on hills opposite them to prevent them from aiding their own right wing. When—contrary to expectation—the enemy saw the Boeotians advancing, there was a confused rush to rearm, bridle the horses, and reform their line. The psychological advantage, as Xenophon noted, now lay with the Boeotians. The distance that the Boeotians had to cover before reaching the enemy occupied sufficient time to allow the Spartans and their allies to reform the infantry and draw up the cavalry six deep in a phalanxlike line. Epaminondas, on the other hand, placed his cavalry in a deep column and intermixed light infantry (*hamippoi*) with them, thus expecting to rupture the shallow ranks of the opposing cavalry and demoralize the enemy. Events unfolded as Epaminondas had intended, except that he himself fell in the fight against the Spartans. His troops immediately lost all heart for the pursuit of the fleeing enemy, and what should have been a decisive victory became—for all practical purposes—a draw.

The only Boeotian troops that did continue to fight—the light infantry attached to the victorious cavalry—worked their way over to the Athenians on the right, where most of them were killed. The collapse of Boeotian morale at the death of Epaminondas and the abrupt cessation of fighting remain something of an enigma, especially since Pelopidas' men at Cynoscephalae fought even more vigorously to preserve the victory after he fell there. Perhaps the Thebans had come to recognize fully Epaminondas' unique capabilities, which for ten years raised them above themselves to supremacy in Greece. Seldom in history have two individuals had such an enormous effect upon the military and political fortunes of their homeland as did Epaminondas and Pelopidas.[32]

Despite the dearth of details on the combat itself, Xenophon provides one piece of information that is noteworthy. At the point in the battle when the victorious Boeotian cavalry stopped the pursuit and turned back, they were behind the main line of the enemy and had to pass through fleeing soldiers in order to reach their own formation.[33] How the Boeotian cavalry reached that position is not stated. Perhaps around the flank, but possibly they went through the ranks of the Spartan phalanx itself, especially if its files parted to allow their own fleeing cavalry a means of escape. In any event the Boeotian cavalry had achieved a level of tactical skill that was part and parcel of Macedonian success in the following decades.

The *hamippoi*—the light troops serving with the Boeotian cavalry—are a bit of a mystery. When describing the preliminaries to the battle of Mantinea in 418, Thucydides mentions the presence of five hundred Boeotian cavalry and five hundred *hamippoi*, suggesting that there was one of the latter for every cavalryman. In addition to his mentioning them at the second battle of Mantinea in 362, Xenophon describes their role in a passage in *The Cavalry Commander*, where he recommends their use, stating that cavalry is weak without them. He apparently sees their value as one of surprise, as he points out that they may be hidden among and behind the taller mounted men. If they were used, it is clear that they would have affected the tactical options available, as they were slower and less mobile than horsemen. Nonetheless, they do not seem to have played much part in Greek warfare and are noticeably absent from the Macedonian armies.[34]

32. Xen. *Hell.* 7.21–25; Diod. 15.85–87. Although lacking details of the fighting itself, Xenophon's account has been preferred to that of Diodorus, whose source for these events—Ephorus—was already criticized in antiquity by Polybius (12.25f.3–5). See also *TH* 213–19; *SAGT* 2 63–66.

33. Xen. *Hell.* 7.5.25.

34. Thuc. 5.57.2; Xen. *Cav. Cmdr.* 5.13.

Part 3

The Age of Philip and Alexander: 359 to 323 B.C.

Chapter 11

Timoleon and Philip: 359 to 336 B.C.

IT IS REGRETTABLE THAT the ancient sources provide so little information about two of the most intriguing personalities of the mid-fourth century: Philip II, king of Macedon, and Timoleon of Corinth. Not only were they outstanding military leaders, but each was also unique in Greek history. Timoleon's brilliant and highly improbable political and military career was characterized by periods of self-effacing retirement in both its prologue and its postscript that suggest a lack of personal political ambition so un-Greek as to be suspicious. Philip, whose ambition was boundless, created the finest army in the Balkan peninsula and led it from victory to victory with a farsighted and patient strategy that was unequaled even by his son Alexander. Although this chapter primarily concerns the reign of Philip, it is certainly fitting to cast a glance briefly to the west, to Sicily, to observe the career of Timoleon and the important events that were unfolding there, since in two of the military arms—artillery and cavalry—the western Greeks were in advance of those of the homeland and had been so for some time.

I have mentioned the importance of cavalry in Sicily, and we can assume that its relatively open and fertile countryside fostered this arm from an early date. Of equal importance was the fact that from the time of their arrival in Sicily in the mid-eighth century, the Greeks faced military threats from non-Greeks who had different military traditions. In addition to the indigenous peoples—Sicans (central), Sicels (east), and Elymi (west)—the Greeks soon found themselves facing Carthaginians in the west. Thus they were exposed to military challenges, including differences in technology, fighting styles, and combinations of arms, that were not experienced by their mother cities. The latter, due to their geographic isolation, had the luxury of a limited, idiosyncratic type of warfare. A more open-minded and adaptable military mentality soon became evident among the western Greeks. Not only were cavalry more important, but artillery—in the form of catapults—seems to have been invented at Syracuse in 399 under the direction of Dionysius the Elder as part of the preparations for war with Carthage.[1] At first these machines comprised a larger than normal composite bow resting horizontally on a frame that was itself supported by a stand. Later, during the 340s, the much more powerful torsion catapult was employed by Philip II during the sieges of Perinthus and Byzantium, proof that military innovation could and did travel from west to east.[2]

While it cannot be demonstrated that other military innovations passed in this direction, it must not be forgotten that the Greek-speaking world was one large cultural continuum that extended from the shores of the Black Sea and western Anatolia through the lower Balkans to Sicily and southern Italy. Thus it should occasion no surprise if—allowing for the generally free movement of individuals within this area—there was a common fund of military experience and exchange of ideas. While this does not imply that the same practices were employed everywhere, it does help to explain the ability of Greek commanders away from home to exploit local strengths and weaknesses. Three instances of this use of shared knowledge have already been described: the Spartans Gylippus and Agesilaus and the Athenian Xenophon. The Corinthian Timoleon can be added to the list. He and the two Spartans are particularly interesting, because they recognized the value of cavalry when they commanded armies outside of southern Greece in spite of the fact that their native states were comparatively deficient in this arm. This suggests that there was a greater understanding, at least among the better commanders, of the importance of cavalry even in Greece than its use there would indicate and that local conditions rather than military backwardness determined their use.[3]

---

1. Diod. 14.42.1. The modern authority is Marsden (1969) 55.
2. Marsden (1969) 60; Diod. 16.74–75. The torsion catapults possessed two separate bow arms, which were powered by twisted springs of hair or sinew set vertically into a rectangular frame. Although the sources are incomplete, Marsden makes the plausible suggestion that these machines were developed in Macedon under Philip's direction. Given his ambition and resources, he was in a more favorable position than most of the Greek city–states to support technological advances.
3. In any event Philip himself had to defer to the force of circumstances and develop good infantry and artillery before he was able to confront the Greek city-states directly. Incidentally, another Greek soldier abroad is the Spartan Xanthippus, who adroitly combined infantry, cavalry, and elephants to help the Carthaginians defeat the Roman general Regulus during the First Punic War. Polyb. 1.32–36.

Timoleon's greatest victory, during a career that pitted him against the Sicilian tyrants as well as the Carthaginians, occurred in early June 340 at the Crimisus River. In spite of Plutarch's rather brief account, a useful picture of the tactical functions of cavalry in the battle survives. In order to meet the enemy in their own territory, Timoleon had marched almost the entire length of the island westward from Syracuse. Against seventy thousand troops, including chariot and cavalry forces, Timoleon had five thousand infantry and one thousand cavalry. On the day of the battle, as the two armies approached each other, Timoleon's forces crested a hill to find the Carthaginians already crossing the Crimisus below them. It was immediately apparent that the Greeks need fight only as many Carthaginians as had already crossed the river, whose rain-swollen waters produced disorder in the ranks. When the Greeks charged, only the four-horse chariots and ten thousand Carthaginian infantry were preparing to face them. Timoleon ordered the cavalry, under Demaretus, to charge ahead in an effort to prevent the infantry from forming up. This was frustrated, however, by the chariots, which were moving back and forth in front of and parallel to the Carthaginian line. Seeing that the horsemen were unable to interfere with the infantry, Timoleon signaled to them to ride around the ends of the enemy line and attack the flanks while he advanced with the infantry. Timoleon—who was subsequently known for his intimate relationship with *Fortuna*—now benefited from the timely intervention of a fierce thunderstorm and succeeded in completely routing the Carthaginians.[4]

It remains to comment on one of the real gems of this narrative in Plutarch—at last, a use for chariots. Modern historians have been at pains to explain the use of these often splendid vehicles in classical warfare, and in this battle at least they obviously served the defensive function of holding Timoleon's cavalry at bay while the infantry formed up behind them. It is true that the Greeks and Romans themselves scarcely used chariots during the Classical period, but they were still found in eastern armies, where they seem to have been an anachronism. Alexander had no trouble dealing with the Persian chariots at Gaugamela (331), and Antiochus III's attempt to use them against the Romans at Magnesia (190) proved equally abortive. Once, in 395, they did contribute to a minor success against scattered Greek foragers in the army of Agesilaus. On that occasion the Persian Pharnabazus, with two scythe-bearing chariots and four hundred cavalry, caught about seven hundred Greek infantry in the open. Although the Greeks crowded together, they were not

4. Plut. *Tim.* 25–29; Diod. 16.78–80.

in military formation and were incapable of sustaining the Persian charge that was led by the two chariots. Greek complacency and the shock of being caught off guard, rather than the chariots, determined the outcome.[5]

It is of more than passing interest that at the very time Philip of Macedon was creating his integrated army, Timoleon was coordinating cavalry and infantry to good effect in Sicily. No direct contact between the two is suggested, nor is it at all likely. What is probable is that they were individually adapting the legacy of their immediate predecessors to their current needs. Furthermore, the comparison with Philip is not gratuitous, for Timoleon was the greatest Greek general of the age—the only tactician who might have thwarted Philip at Chaeronea in 338—but, as G. T. Griffith put it, "he, unfortunately, at this moment was otherwise engaged."[6] Unlike many successful military leaders, Timoleon was equally adept at the arts of peace. After defeating the Carthaginians and driving the tyrants out of the Greek cities of eastern Sicily, he repopulated the area, set up autonomous democracies, and restored prosperity. His work accomplished and his eyesight failing, he withdrew from public life and spent his remaining years on a country estate provided by the Syracusans.

But now I would like to turn to the principal subject of this chapter, beginning with events in the Balkans at the beginning of the 350s. Of three rulers who departed from the scene at this time, Perdiccas, the king of Macedon (d. 359), was the least important. Artaxerxes II, king of Persia (d. 359/358), was potentially the greatest threat to Greece because of the resources of his empire, while Alexander of Pherae (d. 370) had been more than a nuisance—at least to the Thebans, whose general Pelopidas had died in battle against him. Their successors could be expected to play roughly the same roles. Nevertheless, within a year of his accession, Philip—the successor of Perdiccas—had shown that a change had indeed come to Macedon. The battle against the Illyrians in 359 in which Perdiccas had lost his life had cost the Macedonians four thousand men and shattered the morale of the survivors. Philip may very well have been present. In any event he realized what had to be done to save the kingdom. It is unclear whether Philip was elected king immediately or merely appointed regent to the young Amyntas, the son of his dead brother. There is no doubt, however, that he was in charge, and the de facto beginning of his reign can be dated at the summer of 359.[7]

5. Xen. *Hell.* 4.1.17–19.
6. *HM* 2 396.
7. Diod. 16.2. *HM* 2 208–209, 702–704.

Controversy surrounds the changes that Philip introduced, both regarding the specific acts and their chronology. Obviously, he did not transform a defeated and demoralized army overnight into the superb instrument that defeated the Greeks in 338. Nonetheless, much had been accomplished by the following year when he met and defeated the Illyrians. The passage in Diodorus describing the changes is brief but suggestive:

> bringing together the Macedonians in a series of assemblies and exhorting them with eloquent speeches to be men, he built up their morale, and, having improved the organization of his forces and equipped the men suitably with weapons of war, he held constant manoeuvres of the men under arms and competitive drills. Indeed he devised the compact order and the equipment of the phalanx, imitating the close order fighting with overlapping shields of the warriors at Troy, and was the first to organize the Macedonian phalanx.[8]

The results of these changes are stated by his son Alexander in his speech to his army at Opis in 324, and both Frontinus and Polyaenus cite examples of Philip's training methods and discipline.[9]

The context in which these events transpired was local, for Philip could not yet have had thoughts of fighting the Greek city-states and their hoplite armies. The greatest danger was presented by Bardylis and the Illyrians, and thus it is worth emphasizing that Philip's reforms primarily concerned the infantry. The cavalry were already first rate, but Philip realized that they alone were not sufficient for military success. Up to this time the Macedonian infantry had been negligible, but Philip now transformed them into a superior fighting force according to Greek military principles. Although they were sometimes collectively referred to as a phalanx, the Macedonian infantryman bore a closer resemblance to a peltast than to the more heavily armed hoplite. Both had less body armor and carried a smaller shield, in the case of a peltast, a *pelte*, whence the name. The two essential new ingredients were the adoption of the *sarissa*, a longer thrusting spear, and the unprecedented intensity of training and drill to which the men were subjected. The reorganization of the infantry into efficient tactical units was also significant.[10]

---

8. Diod. 16.3.1–2.
9. Arr. *Anab.* 7.9.2; Frontin *Str.* 4.1.6, 4.2.4; Polyaenus 4.2.10.
10. Discussions of Macedonian infantry can be found in *HM* 2 414–28; Cawkwell (1978) 30–33; *CE* 260–66.

The longer spear and the higher level of training may have gone hand in hand, for a *sarissa* fourteen to eighteen feet long was more difficult to wield than a hoplite spear of seven to ten feet and must have weighed three to four times as much. If handled with strength and discipline, its advantage over the shorter weapon is obvious, and it may also have posed a greater threat to cavalry face on. On the other hand, movements to either flank or to the rear would be correspondingly more difficult.[11] No mention is made of changes in the cavalry, but given Philip's reputation as a drillmaster, it is probable that they were also subject to more intensive training.

Before the end of 359 Philip was in action in Macedonia near Methone, where he defeated the mercenaries of Argaeus, an Athenian-supported pretender to the Macedonian throne. Early the next year he invaded Paeonia to the north and won a victory that brought the Paeonians into some sort of subordinate relationship with Macedon.[12] Encouraged by these successes, Philip next turned his attention to the Illyrians in the west. Just enough detail about the ensuing battle survives in Diodorus to allow us some interpretation.

When the two armies faced each other early in the campaigning season of 358, they were evenly matched in numbers if not in quality. Both fielded about ten thousand infantry, with Philip having a slight advantage in cavalry—six hundred to five hundred. Philip himself led the best of the Macedonian infantry on the right wing, while the cavalry were instructed to ride to the outside and fall on the enemy flanks. The Illyrians, under their king, Bardylis, formed a square and fought vigorously. For some time the battle was even, "but later as the horsemen pressed on from the flank and rear and Philip with the flower of his troops fought with true heroism, the mass of the Illyrians was compelled to take hastily to flight. When the pursuit had been kept up for a considerable distance and many had been slain in their flight, Philip recalled the Macedonians with the trumpet."[13]

G. T. Griffith is absolutely correct when he says that "Philip's performance looks remarkably mature."[14] He overestimates the effect of the mounted arm, however, when he describes this action as "victory by cavalry," for it was the conscious attempt at coordination of infantry and cavalry and their successful cooperation during the battle that was essential.[15] It is also necessary

---

11. Ascl. *Tac.* 5.1.2 and Theophr. *Hist. Pl.* 3.12.2 describe the *sarissa*. See also *HM* 2 421.
12. Diod. 16.3.5–6; 4.2. Dates for Philip's reign are from *HM* 2 722–26.
13. Diod. 16.4.5–7.
14. *HM* 2 213. See also *TS* 58.
15. *HM* 2 214.

to emphasize that Philip led the infantry. Furthermore, coordination itself was not sufficient to insure success, especially when the numbers were so evenly matched. Superior fighting ability was also required, since the infantry had to fight vigorously without losing formation and the cavalry had to defeat their counterparts before they could pay much attention to the Illyrian infantry. Philip's "mature" performance may also have owed more to the general advance of Greek military skill than to his originality. Nevertheless, the Macedonian army functioned henceforth during the reigns of Philip and Alexander as an integrated force. Subsequently it was complemented by the addition of various types of specialized troops—archers, slingers, artillerymen, other varieties of cavalry, and so forth—so that under Alexander the proper combination of troops, adjusted to each occasion, proved victorious again and again.

Two other facets of this victory stand out—the pursuit of the enemy, in which more than seven thousand were supposedly slain, and the recall of the pursuers by trumpet. In a sense none of this was new, and it is difficult to identify Philip's contribution precisely, except—and this cannot be overemphasized—that he brought all the elements together, applying them with an intensity and consistency that raised Greek warfare to new heights. Thus the reorganization and preparation of the Macedonian army reflect a major part of his genius, assuring that his diplomatic and tactical ability would not be wasted for want of the proper instrument.[16]

The suggestion that Philip derived his ideas from his predecessors in no way diminishes his achievement; it is rather the opposite, for he alone had the insight and ability to apply the military legacy successfully to the particular circumstances he faced. Whether it is possible to identify specific direct

---

16. A recent observation by Van Creveld (1991) 97 fits nicely into this discussion: "Where arms and equipment on both sides were approximately the same, as they normally were in encounters between the principal powers, the factor which decided the issue was not technology, but the ability to combine hardware, training, doctrine, and organization into a single decisive whole. The whole had to be perfect, not only in the sense of tailoring the different constituents to match each other, but above all in relation to the specific enemy and circumstances and purpose at hand. So it was during the period 1500–1830; so it has always been, and so it always will be." Two statements by Demosthenes in the *Third Philippic* provide contemporary perspective on the general background to Philip's military career and his own contribution. While commenting on a comparison of Philip and the Lacedaemonians at their peak (47), he states: "While practically all the arts have made a great advance and we are living to-day in a very different world from the old one, I consider that nothing has been more revolutionized and improved than the art of war." Shortly thereafter (49) he attributes Philip's success not to the phalanx of hoplites that he leads, "but because he is accompanied by skirmishers, cavalry, archers, mercenaries, and similar troops." Notwithstanding Demosthenes' hostility to Philip, these statements ring true and are confirmed by other sources, as has been shown. Griffith is certainly correct in concluding (*HM* 2: 428–29) that "well-informed Greeks at this time did see Philip's army as a well-balanced combination of arms, in which not only the cavalry but also the less spectacular auxiliaries were of importance."

influences on Philip's military thinking is another matter. Aside from what he would have learned as a youth in Macedon, the most obvious influence on him during his formative years came from Thebes. It was perhaps Greece's misfortune that Philip was a hostage in that city-state at the very time when it was at the height of its military success under Epaminondas and Pelopidas. In Thebes from circa 369–367, when he was fifteen to seventeen years old, Philip learned to appreciate the value of good infantry of the Greek type as well as the contribution that well-trained cavalry could make to the victory of that infantry.[17] Although he was a hostage, Philip's position was more that of a guest than a prisoner, living as he was at the house of Pammenes, a supporter of Epaminondas. Plutarch mentions the great influence that Epaminondas had upon Philip.[18] No doubt he was also aware of the contributions of the other famous commanders of the first half of the century. His appreciation of discipline and training, for example, may have owed something to Iphicrates, whom he had met in Macedon in 368.[19] Xenophon's influence on Philip would have been twofold, arising both from his personal accomplishments, which became part of the living tradition, and also from his extensive literary production. Such literary influences on Philip are hard to demonstrate but must have been important and would have included works not only of Xenophon but also of Thucydides, not to mention lost works exemplified by the extant fragments of the Oxyrhynchus historian and one book on the defense of fortified positions by Aeneas Tacticus. Direct Persian influence is also possible, as has been suggested by D. Kienast.[20]

We next hear something of Philip's military activity in 353, when he became involved in the Third Sacred War. This conflict was precipitated by Phocian resistance to a judgment issued by the Amphictyonic Council, which controlled the Delphic sanctuary in central Greece. Following the death of Philomelus, the Phocians elected Onomarchus to succeed him as general. Events conspired to draw both Onomarchus and Philip into Thessaly at this time. Philip accepted an invitation to assist the Thessalians against Lycophron, tyrant of Pherae, while Onomarchus decided to help the latter, as his earlier

17. *HM* 2 204–205, 425; *HAW* 175; Cawkwell (1978) 151.
18. Plut. *Pel.* 26.5. Markle (1975) 141 believes that "in coordinating cavalry with infantry as a striking force Philip was only copying what Epaminondas had done at Mantinea." Nevertheless, it seems unlikely from the evidence cited above that Epaminondas originated the idea, which by this date seems to have been appreciated by a number of military leaders.
19. Nepos, in his *Iphicrates* (2.1), notes this Athenian general's emphasis on drill and obedience. See also *GSW* 2, chap. 11, 208–31.
20. Kienast (1973) 269–73.

efforts to bribe the Thessalians into neutrality had failed. Philip got more than he bargained for; Diodorus mentions that he experienced two defeats at the hands of the Phocians. Although cavalry are not mentioned, Polyaenus preserves some interesting details of what is thought to be the second of these battles. His account follows:

> Onomarchus preparing to give battle to the Macedonians chose a position in front of a crescent-shaped mountain. On the high ground on each flank he concealed stone-throwing catapults and the ammunition for them. Then he advanced on to the level ground below. When the Macedonians came to meet them and opened fire with their missiles, the Phocians made a show of fleeing towards the recess of the mountain. The Macedonians charged in pursuit, but the men posted on the hilltops opened fire with the artillery and began to punish the Macedonian phalanx. And then Onomarchus gave the trumpet-call to the Phocians to turn and charge. With this charge at their backs as they tried to withdraw, and with the stones from up above still coming down on them, the Macedonians had all they could do to escape and make their retreat.[21]

The effectiveness of artillery on this occasion resulted from their protected position on the mountain. Their lack of mobility made them vulnerable on an open battlefield, where they could easily be overrun, as a result of which they played no part in the pitched battles of this period. The clever trap clearly caught Philip by surprise. His troops were thoroughly shaken and came close to mutiny. Nevertheless, he restored the situation and returned the following year with new resolve, meeting Onomarchus on ground more to his liking on a coastal plain in southeastern Thessaly. Each side mustered about twenty thousand infantry, but Philip's three thousand horsemen, including those of his Thessalian allies, outnumbered the five hundred of Onomarchus. Diodorus states merely that "a severe battle took place and since the Thessalian cavalry were superior in numbers and valour, Philip won."[22] If Diodorus is correct, the mercenaries of Onomarchus fought well despite their deficiency in cavalry. This seems reasonable, since none of Philip's victories—including Chaeronea—came easily, and it is a mistake, I

---

21. Polyaenus 2.38.2. (Griffith trans., *HM* 2 269); Diod. 16.35.
22. Diod. 16.35.5; *HM* 2 274.

think, to view cavalry as some sort of magic tool with which to pry apart the ranks of the phalanx. The Macedonian victories of the period resulted as much from hard fighting as from superior generalship. On this occasion a slaughter ensued when the Phocians broke ranks and fled. Over six thousand Phocians and their mercenaries perished, among them Onomarchus. In this battle on the Crocus Plain, Philip avenged the only serious defeats of his career.[23]

In 349 Philip invaded the Chalcidic peninsula in order to deal with Olynthus and its allies. The little that is known of the fighting that occurred around Olynthus until its fall in the late summer of the following year attracts attention because of the part—albeit an unusual one—assumed by the Chalcidian cavalry. Diodorus reports that Philip won two victories in the open against the Olynthians, then invested the city (losing many men in the process), and finally captured it through treachery.[24] The opposition of the Chalcidians was not negligible, for they could field 10,000 infantry and 1,000 cavalry.[25] G. T. Griffith's remark that "they were unusually strong in cavalry" is unnecessary, as cavalry were always more numerous and important in northeastern Greece, which has more open, fertile land and, like Sicily, was inhabited by non-Greeks with different military traditions.[26] The Athenians felt sufficiently threatened by Philip's aggression to send three relief expeditions north, the last of these apparently arriving too late. The forces in the first two groups totaled 6,000 peltasts and 150 cavalry. The last expedition comprised 2,000 hoplites and 300 cavalry, the latter being sent in horse transports.[27] Their sending cavalry amounting to 15 percent of the hoplite force indicates the Athenians' appreciation of their value. The fact that fewer cavalry were sent out with the peltasts may have been due to a degree of overlap in the function of those two arms due to their having greater mobility than the hoplites. Although, as I have stated, we have no details of the fighting, the behavior of the Olynthian cavalry made a major contribution to the eventual capture of the city. In an action that according to Demosthenes, was without precedent, Philip won over 500 Olynthian cavalrymen—arms and all—through the treachery of their officers.[28] Precisely when this occurred during the campaign is unknown, but it doubtless did much to undermine the morale of the rest of the citizens.

23. For a fuller discussion of these events see Buckler (1989) 66–77.
24. Diod. 16.53.1–2.
25. Dem. *Emb.* 266.
26. *HM 2* 322. A ratio of infantry (hoplites) to cavalry of 10:1 is not unusual in Greek armies.
27. Philoch. *Fr. Gr. H.* 328.
28. Dem. *Emb.* 267; *HM 2* 322–24.

The next event in Philip's career that sheds some light on his use of cavalry took place in 339 during his punitive campaign against the Scythians. Their king, Atheas, had just renounced his alliance with Philip and was refusing to pay tribute. No details of the fighting survive, but Justin records a complete victory in which Atheas died in battle.[29] It is likely that Scythian strength on this occasion, as usual, lay in their horse archers; indeed, they are depicted on the coins of Atheas. When fighting on their own terms, that is to say, shooting volleys of arrows from a distance and retiring when charged, setting ambushes, and so forth, the Scythians were formidable enemies. In order to defeat them soundly it was necessary to bring them to bay, depriving them of their superiority in archery by means of hand-to-hand fighting. Failure to do so had earlier wrecked Darius' trans-Danubian campaign, and even Alexander had only partial success against them.[30] It seems likely that Philip was able to force them to stand and fight, perhaps aided by the topography. His well-disciplined, integrated army of infantry and cavalry seems to have been ideal for the purpose, judging by later Byzantine advice for campaigning against nomadic peoples of the Scythian type. Although the Scythians ceased to be a recognizable political force by the end of the first millenium B.C., their name survived for centuries as a collective term for the nomadic peoples who lived on the steppes northeast of the Mediterranean.

The *Strategicon*, a military treatise transmitted under the name of Maurice and dating from the period A.D. 590–610, contains information that seems applicable to Philip's victory, for in spite of the passage of almost a thousand years, the weapons and tactics of the horse archers of the steppe had not significantly altered. This remarkable Byzantine work is finally receiving some of the attention it deserves, as the recent appearance of a new text edition and translations into English and German attest.[31] In its description of the Byzantines' "Scythian" enemies, the *Strategikon* states that they do not like close fighting, they are very adept at archery from horseback, they delight in fighting from a distance, and infantry formations give them trouble.[32] To

---

29. Justin. 9.2–3.
30. Hdt. 4.128; Arr. *Anab.* 4.4.4–8. See also Arr. *Anab.* 4.5.4–9 for Scythian tactics.
31. Dennis and Gamillscheg (1981); Dennis (1984).
32. Maurice *Strat.* 11.2.21, 29, 52, 67. It is extremely tempting to correlate another recommendation made in the *Strategikon* with an earlier mention of Philip's fight with the Scythians found in Frontinus' *Stratagems*, 2.8.14. There Frontinus claims that Philip placed his most loyal cavalry in the rear with orders to kill any soldiers who tried to desert. Since this appears to be inconsistent with Philip's relationship with his men, it seems permissible to suggest that this was a tactical disposition, especially as the recommended battle formation for a mixed force of infantry and cavalry against the "Scythians" in the *Strategikon* has the cavalry posted behind the infantry. 11.2.85–89.

deal with them, according to the treatise, "Level, unobstructed ground should be chosen, and a cavalry force should advance against them in a dense, unbroken mass to engage them in hand-to-hand fighting."[33] Philip's army was well suited to deal with this type of enemy, provided that they could be induced to stand and fight, for the Scythian advantage in archery was nullified at close quarters. It is precisely their willingness to fight at close quarters that distinguishes mid-fourth-century Greek cavalry from their predecessors, and Philip enhanced this tactical development through better organization and increased discipline and training. Justin attributes Philip's victory to cunning, since the Scythians were superior in courage and spirit. Although this seems to slight the valor of the Macedonian soldiers, it may reflect Philip's ability to force a battle under conditions unfavorable to the Scythians, as I have suggested.[34]

The only other battle fought by Philip about which some information survives is that of Chaeronea in 338. Unfortunately, his employment of cavalry on this occasion is anything but clear. This battle was Philip's crowning military achievement, although it represented a diplomatic failure insofar as he had hoped—perhaps naively—to settle matters with the Greek city-states without a fight.

The battle must be reconstructed from a brief, undetailed account in Diodorus and scattered references in several other writers.[35] According to Diodorus, Philip had more than thirty thousand infantry and no fewer than two thousand cavalry. No numbers are given for the Greek allies, but modern estimates give them a slight advantage over Philip in spite of Diodorus' statement to the contrary.[36] It would be caviling, however, to question his statement that Philip was the best general on the field, to which must be added the superior quality of his cavalry and the higher level of training and discipline—not to mention experience—of his infantry. The advantage also lay with the Macedonians in respect to unity of command. Furthermore, the long *sarissa* of the Macedonian phalangite gave him an advantage over the spear of the hoplite, at least while he was in formation on the battlefield.[37]

The battlefield lay to the east of Chaeronea between rising ground on the south and southwest and the river Cephissus, which flows to the south-

---

33. Dennis (1984) 118.
34. Justin 9.2.14.
35. Diod. 16.5–86; Justin 9.3.9.; Frontin. *Str.* 2.1.9; Polyaenus 4.2.2, 7; Plut. *Alex.* 9.2, *Pel.* 18.5, *Dem.* 20.2. The best recent reconstructions are *HM* 2 596–603; *TS* 60–63.
36. *HM* 2 599, n. 4; Diod. 16.85.6.
37. It has, however, been argued that the phalangite was not armed with the *sarissa* until sometime after Chaeronea. See Markle(1977) 323–39; Markle (1978) 483–97.

east. Thus two natural barriers afforded protection to the flanks of the allied Greek line, especially on the right, where the Theban Sacred Band was posted alongside the river. Philip commanded one wing facing the Athenians, apparently on the Macedonian right, while Alexander—assisted by Philip's most notable generals—opposed the Boeotians on the left. Since there was no place for cavalry on the flanks and no mention of them is made in the admittedly brief battle descriptions, their role is unknown and must consequently be conjectured or omitted.

At some point Philip is described as having conducted a sham retreat (not mentioned by Diodorus) intended to draw out the Athenians. Both Frontinus and Polyaenus suggest that this was intended to tire the keen but less well trained and seasoned Athenians. Frontinus pointedly contrasts the great experience of the Macedonians with the untrained impetuosity of the Athenians, and Justin describes the battle as a victory of battle-honed Macedonian valor over Athenian numerical superiority.[38] Philip may also have hoped to disrupt the articulation of the allied line. The Macedonian right halted, apparently at the river Haemon (a tributary of the Cephissus flowing northeast behind the Macedonians) and then charged and routed the enemy. It was probably at this point that Demosthenes, fighting as a hoplite, threw away his arms and fled.[39] On the other wing Alexander is said to have been first to attack the Sacred Band and to break through the continuity of the enemy formation.[40] The three hundred men of the Sacred Band fought and died on the spot. After the battle Philip saw them lying where they had faced the *sarissas* of the Macedonians and admired their courage.[41] These events on the allied right seem to be confirmed by the modern excavation of the Macedonian burial mound containing *sarissas* in a location consistent with mention of it by Plutarch.[42]

A more fundamental question about Chaeronea is whether Alexander was commanding cavalry or infantry. In spite of the absence of clear evidence from the ancient sources, the majority of modern historians is convinced that Alexander was leading cavalry during the battle, apparently basing their judgment on

---

38. Frontin *Str.* 2.1.9; Polyaenus 4.2.2., 2.7; Justin 9.3.9. Diodorus, however, says that Philip had the advantage in numbers, 16.85.6.
39. Plut. *Dem.* 20.2.
40. Plut. *Alex.* 9.2; Diod. 16.86.3.
41. Plut. *Pel.* 18.5.
42. Plut. *Alex.* 9.2. This reconstruction owes most to Griffith. *HM* 2 596–603. The mound was excavated by Soteriades (1903) 301–30.

his later use of the mounted arm in Asia.[43] A satisfactory argument against cavalry, however, is provided by P. A. Rahe, who points out that "the inability of ordinary Greek cavalry to charge through the phalanx had nothing to do with any deficiency in equipment and tactics. The problem lay with the horse. A horseman can charge into a mob, but only if those in his path give way before him. If those in the crowd link arms and stand their ground, the horse will shy," and goes on to day that "the effect of shock cavalry is psychological and not physical."[44] Buckler, apparently independently, reached the same conclusion, emphasizing the fact that no ancient source mentions cavalry at the battle.[45] Perhaps most telling is Plutarch's statement that the Sacred Band faced Macedonian *sarissas*, a weapon that the ancient sources never associate with the Macedonian regular cavalry.

These arguments should be sufficient to cast serious doubt on the claim that cavalry broke into the Sacred Band at Chaeronea. Indeed, precisely because this elite Theban unit of heavy infantry fought and died where it was posted in the battle line, it is more likely to have faced infantry rather than cavalry.[46] The *sarissa*-bearing Macedonian phalanx would have presented a dense array of spearpoints that was essentially impenetrable, and when individuals fell wounded, others moved up from behind. The much looser formation of cavalry would have made it easier for the steadfast Thebans to parry lance thrusts as well as to injure horses but more difficult for that cavalry to inflict intense slaughter in a confined space. When cavalry kill large numbers of infantry, it is usually done against men in flight. In 326, even against Mallian infantry in India, Alexander was unwilling to bring his cavalry to close quarters until his own foot had arrived, at the sight of which the Mallians turned and fled.[47]

43. *AG* 16 is typical: "Alexander had led the cavalry charge at Chaeronea." See also Markle (1978) 490–91. Bosworth, on the other hand, states that "in the plain of Chaeronea the Macedonian phalanx proved its superiority over traditional hoplite forces." *CE* 16.

44. Rahe (1981) 84–87, quote from 85–86. Rahe's argument rests largely on Keegan (1977) 153–59, whose sound observations have, I think, rescued the cavalry charge from the excesses of Hollywood film makers. Any horse that is not in an uncontrollable frenzy will respond to the instinct for self-preservation when it faces a barrier. If one or more horses could be forced to strike unyielding infantry, others might follow under the influence of the herd instinct, but the net destruction to one's cavalry force would be unacceptable.

45. Buckler (1990) 75–80. In spite of the evidence the story of Alexander's cavalry charge at Chaeronea has taken on a life of its own, appearing in most general histories of Greece and most recently in the *National Geographic*. Alexander (2000) 48.

46. Plut. *Pel.* 18.5.

47. Arr. *Anab.* 6.8.6.

There is also reason to believe that when Philip entered central Greece in 338 he was prepared to settle the issue with infantry rather than cavalry. Whereas in 352 Philip brought twenty thousand infantry and three thousand cavalry into southeastern Thessaly against Onomarchus, the army that he led into Boeotia had thirty thousand infantry and no fewer than two thousand horsemen. The difference was not accidental, as on the plains of Thessaly he could count on an opportunity to employ his superior cavalry. In Boeotia, on the other hand, he was meeting an allied army comprising the best infantry in Greece, and because of the nature of the terrain he could expect fewer chances to use cavalry. His preparations proved to be sound, for he accepted battle on the plain of Chaeronea, where the allies protected their flanks with natural obstacles. Given the tactical possibilities and the meager evidence of the surviving sources, it is most likely that Alexander was in command of the infantry on the left wing and that the struggle was primarily one of infantry with cavalry in some subordinate but unknown role. In a sense it was Philip's battle to lose, for even if he faced the best hoplites in Greece, his Macedonians were for all practical purposes professionals who had the advantage in experience, training, and technology.

When Philip was assassinated in 336, his son Alexander, though only twenty years old, quickly showed that he was worthy of his father's legacy. Philip's lifework presented him with a unified, soundly administered kingdom; an army without equal, and plans for the invasion of the Persian Empire.[48] In creating the Macedonian army it is clear, in spite of the scanty sources, that Philip left his mark on virtually every aspect of the military arts. He imposed new levels of efficiency and intensity through his use of organization, training, drill, and discipline. The army was equipped with new weapons, principally the *sarissa* and torsion catapults. He achieved complete integration of infantry and cavalry, supported the efforts of the two major arms with specialized light troops, and confirmed the victory of these forces with relentless pursuit. His logistical innovations enabled his army to travel faster and farther than any contemporary army.[49] Foresight and a concern for support functions may be seen in his efforts to send twenty thousand mares to Macedon after his victory over the Scythians. Presumably these would have been used as broodmares to provide remounts.[50] Regarding cavalry in particular, he certainly

48. Philip's general Parmenio had already crossed over to Asia Minor in the spring of 336 to prepare for the crossing of the main army by freeing the Greek cities there. Diod. 19.91.2.

49. For a broad treatment of Philip's army see *HM* 2, chap. 12.

50. Justin 9.2.16; 9.3.1–3. These horses were apparently captured by the Triballians as Philip was returning home.

improved discipline and training; he may have altered the cavalry lance; and he is credited with the introduction of the wedge-shaped formation, which increased maneuverability and better enabled the cavalrymen to work their way into the enemy ranks when a suitable opportunity presented itself.[51] Thus, in retrospect, it seems clear that Philip and his immediate predecessors permanently altered the nature of Greek warfare. The immediate—although temporary—result was a noticeable asymmetry of opposing forces on the battlefield. For over two hundred years, while organizational and technological symmetry prevailed among Greek armies, Spartan superiority in training and discipline had insured victory. This situation came to an end with the appearance of the *sarissa*, with cavalry more willing to fight at close quarters, and with the combination of arms.[52]

None of this is understandable, however, without the acknowledgment of Philip's tremendous accomplishments in the administration of his kingdom. During his reign agriculture largely replaced pastoralism, with an attendant growth in town population. The territory of the kingdom was increased, adding greatly to the agricultural and mineral wealth. Evidence of the economic significance of his accomplishments is found in the widespread discovery of Philip's gold and silver coinage from France to the Near East.[53] Macedon was not merely a military upstart created by ephemeral military genius but rather a large, wealthy, well-managed state that was a major economic and political force until it was dismantled by Rome after the battle of Pydna in 168.

---

51. Ael. *Tac.* 18.4 says the wedge-shaped formation was borrowed from the Scythians and Thracians.

52. The growing emphasis on cavalry, based on a greater willingness for hand-to-hand combat, can be viewed as an adaptation by horsemen to the traditional Greek preference for the decisive, bloody battle of the phalanx, which as early as the Persian Wars had shown its superiority to missile tactics. Hanson (1989) 10.

53. *HM* 2 650–71. Some impression of this can also be gained from a visit to the Macedonian capitals, Dion, Aegeae, and Pella.

Chapter 12

Alexander: 336 to 323 B.C.

THE PRECEDING CHAPTERS WILL have made clear the matchless legacy bequeathed to Alexander by his Greek and Macedonian predecessors and in particular by his father, Philip.[1] The use to which Alexander put this inheritance, together with his personal alterations and additions to it, represent the pinnacle of purely military achievement in Greek history.

Though this book is primarily a military assessment, the vexing problem of Alexander's personality and character should not be overlooked. This hoary question has produced answers that virtually run the gamut from saint to sinner, and it is incumbent upon anyone who studies Alexander—even from a limited perspective—to identify his own view of the matter. The military historian is even more obliged to respond, since Alexander's fame rests squarely on his military achievements. This has become more obvious now that earlier views representing him as an apostle of Hellenism or an advocate of the brotherhood of man have been overturned by recent scholarship. A. B. Bosworth in particular presents a convincing, unsentimental, and sobering account of Alexander's military behavior that should put to rest any tendency to view him as an enlightened romantic.[2] Thus it now seems clear that the

---

[1]. For a brief account of Alexander's military qualities see Burn (1965) 140–42. More detail is given in *CE* 5–19. The most complete study of Alexander as military leader, and in many ways still useful, is Fuller (1958).

[2]. See his recent work, *CE*. An earlier excellent account of the historical interpretation of Alexander's personality can be found in Green (1974) 478–88. The most influential liberal view of Alexander is that of Tarn (1948). The most recent generally positive view is found in Hammond (1989) 224–26. Another recent appraisal that is compatible with my views can be found in *ACHS* 3–6. For a harsh appraisal of Alexander as "monster," see Hanson (1999) 188–91.

glory derived from his phenomenal military success has at times obscured the fact that he was at heart a military adventurer on a grand scale whose character was influenced far more by Homer's Achilles than by the instruction of Aristotle. Throughout his short, active life Alexander refused to allow any constraints—whether physical or moral—to stand in the way of his ambition. Everything was subordinated to military necessity.[3]

Such an acknowledgment of Alexander's single-minded pursuit of military success is essential to any understanding of the military history of his time. Although in the strict sense he was inferior to his father as "king of the Macedonians" and his role in the spread of Greek culture was incidental to his desire for conquest, the application of his genius to military matters was as complete as is humanly possible. His unparalleled success in combining an appropriate blend of different arms to meet a great variety of enemies on all types of terrain makes it inevitable, I think, that we accept Alexander's tactics as definitive in practicable, human terms in their own time and place. This implies that he pushed the cavalry arm to the limits of its potential—subject, of course, to the constraints of contemporary technological and economic circumstances and the type and number of horses available. That is to say, he employed cavalry of several types wherever it was beneficial, and when the mounted arm was conspicuously absent, we must assume that it would not have been effective.

Because of the intensity with which he conducted military operations as well as the force of his personality, Alexander seems to have stretched human ability to its limits, and it is partly for this reason that none of the Successors was his equal. He was in essence inimitable, and whereas the benefits of organization, training, and discipline could be transmitted to succeeding generations, his incredible success was too idiosyncratic for emulation.[4]

The meager sources for Philip's reign provide little information about the composition and numbers of the army that he bequeathed to his son. Reasonably precise figures first become available for the invasion of Asia Minor in 334, when—according to Arrian and Diodorus—Alexander had slightly more than 30,000 infantry and 5,000 cavalry.[5] Only Diodorus provides a

---

3. Green (1974) 487–78; *CE* 28, 30, 33, 137–39, 250. For a review of Bosworth, see Walbank (1990) 254–55, who is favorable and comments: "This book has the merit of not trying to prove any thesis." A more critical review appears in Devine (1991) 61–66 .

4. Another reason Alexander was seldom imitated is the fact that his "heroic" battlefield behavior was anachronistic even in his day. Alexander succeeded because he was unusually lucky at surviving enemy inflicted wounds. See Wheeler (1991), in Hanson, 125.

5. Arr. *Anab.* 1.11.3; Diod. 17.17.3–5. For the discussion about numbers see *AA* 1 lxixf; *HM* 2 411; *AG* 26; *CE* 61.

breakdown of these forces, listing the cavalry at 1,800 each for the Macedonians and Thessalians, 600 supplied by the Greek allies, and 900 identified as Thracians, *prodromoi*, and Paeonians. Since the Macedonians comprised eight squadrons and the latter group of 900 comprised five squadrons, it seems that the squadron varied from 180 to 225 men. The squadron was not merely an administrative subdivision but served as the normal tactical unit, whether stationed in the battle line or assigned to a special detail. Unlike the Persian cavalry, who preferred to fight at a distance with javelin and bow,[6] Alexander's cavalry were trained to fight at close quarters with lance and sword. Presumably they were also skilled in the use of the javelin.

The Macedonian cavalry wore only a modest amount of defensive armor, apparently differing in no essential way from their Greek counterparts. This comprised a metal cuirass and helmet but apparently no shield.[7] Cavalry that fought outside the formal battle line may have had no metal defensive armor at all, but the meager evidence is hardly suggestive, much less conclusive.[8]

The major modern controversy regarding arms and armor centers on the cavalry lance, the physical nature of which must be known before a proper understanding of the fighting technique and tactics of Macedonian cavalry can be gained. Unfortunately, no unambiguous archaeological or figured evidence survives to provide an easy answer to this question. Consequently, I will cull any pertinent descriptions of cavalry combat in which the use of the lance is indicated from the narrative accounts of Alexander's battles. I will then examine the archaeological and figured evidence and compare it with the literary sources.

The only informative accounts of the employment of the lance at this time are found in the battle narratives of the four major sources—Arrian, Diodorus, Curtius, and Plutarch.[9] Even among them there are virtually no descriptions of the lance itself, except for a comment by Arrian that Alexander had the advantage at the Granicus in 334 because his horsemen used cornel-

---

6. Arr. *Anab.* 2.11.3; cf. Quint. Curt. 3.11.14. The more heavily armed Persians were at a disadvantage against the more mobile Thessalians. Atkinson (1980) 238 observes that this suggests the Persian cavalry was not suited to close combat.

7. *HM* 2 413; *CE* 262; *AG* 30–31; *AAG* 119–20; *GRW* 58–59, 65, 72–73. This information is drawn largely from physical evidence that is difficult to interpret—the Alexander Mosaic, the Alexander Sarcophagus, finds from tombs, and coins.

8. Paeonian coins of the reign of Patraus (ca. 340–315), for example.

9. In this section as well as the one following on tactics, I am concerned with the internal and external consistency of these four major sources. The battles under discussion are Granicus 334; Issus 333; Gaugamela 331.

wood lances against javelins.¹⁰ Since javelins were designed for throwing, they were shorter and had lighter, thinner shafts. Consequently, the Persians were at a disadvantage in the hand-to- hand fighting preferred by the Macedonians. In principle, they might have been able to get inside the point of the lance and then use their shorter javelins to good effect, but the Macedonians were too forceful and experienced to permit it.¹¹

The two words used to identify this lance, *xyston* and *dory*, were applied rather indifferently by the historians and were commonly used for the infantry spear as well.¹² *Xyston*, however, appears to have been more frequently used in reference to the cavalry lance, and both are usually distinguished from the javelin, *akon*, and *palton*.¹³

Although Alexander employed mounted archers and javelin men at various times in a number of ways, the decisive combat in cavalry fights always resulted from close fighting with hand-held weapons, either lance or sword.¹⁴ Fortunately, there exist several vivid descriptions of this type of fighting that offer a good idea of the use to which these weapons were put once the charge had brought the Macedonians to close quarters. From the battle at the Granicus:

> Though the fighting was on horseback, it was more like an infantry battle, horse entangled with horse, man with man in the struggle. (Arr. *Anab.* 1.15.4)

> For the enemy pressed upon them with loud shouts, and matching horse with horse, plied their lances, and their swords when their lances were shattered. (Plut. *Alex.* 16.4)

From the battle of Gaugamela:

---

10. Arr. *Anab.* 1.15.5. For discussion see *AHA* 122; Lane Fox (1975) 76.
11. Arr. *Anab.* 1.15.5. By the time Darius met Alexander at Issus, he had outfitted some of his cavalry with lances (ξυστά) and swords (ξίφη) in order to offset the Macedonian advantage at the Granicus. (Diod. 17.53.1. Diodorus does not mention cavalry specifically here, but the context requires it.) Darius' attempt failed, however, probably since his cavalry could not match that of the Macedonians in skill, discipline, and experience.
12. *Xyston*, Arr. *Anab.* 1.16.1; Diod. 17.20.3. *Dory*, Arr. *Anab.* 1.15.2,6; Plut. *Alex.* 16.4.
13. *Xyston* as cavalry lance; Xen. *Cyr.* 4.5–58. cf. *xystophoros* used of cavalry: Xen. *Cyr.* 7.5.41, 8.3.16; Polyb. 5.53.2; Diod. 19.27; Ascl. *Tac.* 2.12; Arr. *Tac.* 4.4; Plut. *Flam.* 17. For the sake of consistency I shall use *lance* to refer to the cavalry weapon and reserve *spear* for infantry.
14. Archers and javelin men were used as skirmishers to initiate action, during attacks on fortified places, in rough terrain, and so forth.

The cavalry with Alexander, and Alexander himself, pressed vigorously, shoving the Persians and striking their faces with their spears. (Arr. *Anab.* 3.14.3)

The barbarians, who were drawn up in depth, since they were in squadrons, rallied, and clashed with Alexander's troops front to front: there was no more javelin-throwing and no maneuvering of horses, as usual in a cavalry engagement, but each strove hard to break his own way through; they kept on giving and taking blows unsparingly. (Arr. *Anab.* 3.15.12)[15]

In a battle with the rebel satrap Satibarzanes in 330:

The Persians did not give way till in single combat with Erigyius Satibarzanes was struck in the face and killed. (Arr. *Anab.* 3.28.3.)

From these passages it seems clear that the Macedonian cavalrymen, sitting atop milling and pushing horses, stabbed and thrust with their lances in an effort to injure the chests and faces of the enemy. When the shaft of the lance broke, either the stump was used—most likely reversed in order to bring the metal butt spike or rear spearhead into play—or the broken shaft was dropped and the sword was drawn. In either case we have clear evidence for the "intimacy" of this style of fighting.

The sword, referred to as a *machaera* or *kopis*, seems to have been a very effective weapon.[16] It was about twenty-five inches long, yet—because it was heavier toward the point and curved—it could be used for a murderous downward cut. Thus even from the comparatively unstable position on a horse's back, this sword was capable of severing a man's arm at the shoulder, as Cleitus demonstrated when he saved Alexander's life at the Granicus.[17] Alexander himself was wounded by a Persian sword at the Issus, an occasion on which the zone of combat seems to have been especially crowded.[18] None-

---

15. This comment seems to refer to the tactics of javelin-throwing cavalry and may serve as a contrast to hand-to-hand combat here. There is no evidence that Macedonian cavalry of the line fought with javelins.

16. *Kopis*: Arr. *Anab.* 1.15.8. *Machaera*: Xen. *On Hors.* 12.11; Xen *Cyr.* 1.12.13. Illustrated in *CAH* pl. to vol. 7, part 1, 83, no. 102.

17. Arr. *Anab.* 1.15.8; Diod. 17.20.6; Quint. Curt. 8.1.20. Because the sword could be used with great precision at close quarters, it may have caused more mortal wounds than spears or missile weapons. See Grmek (1989) 28 for a discussion of wounds in Homer.

18. Arr. *Anab.* 2.12.1; Plut. *Alex.* 20.5; Diod. 17.33.7; Quint. Curt. 3.11.4.

theless, the lance was probably the preferred weapon of the Macedonians, apparently retained on any given occasion as long as it was serviceable. Curtius reports, for example, that at Gaugamela Alexander killed several opponents in succession with the same spear (*hasta*).[19]

The lance, at a minimum, must have been somewhat longer and heavier than a javelin, as suggested by Arrian. On the other hand it will have been short and light enough to have been manipulated easily in one hand and thus suitable for use in the close combat described by the sources, where the sword was also an alternative.[20] This suggests a weapon of seven to ten feet in length that could be thrust in several directions with some ease. The figured evidence, (which I will discuss further) shows two basic grips, overhand and underhand. There is no reason to question this, as it accords well with physical principles and is identical to the technique used by Greek hoplites, who carried a spear of about the same length. It is noteworthy, however, that when the Macedonian infantry adopted the *sarissa*, which measured approximately sixteen to eighteen feet at this time, they also had to adopt a two-handed grip.[21] Apparently either the over- or underhand grip was suitable for use against both cavalry and infantry. In the case of the former, thrusting blows were aimed at the rider's head and upper body, seeking the vulnerable face and neck and possibly intending to apply leverage to a higher part of the victim's body, thereby unseating him more easily.

Xenophon complements this picture of close fighting when he describes the secondary use of the javelin by cavalry as a stabbing weapon, recommending that it be used to the front, sides, and rear.[22] Comparison with the fighting technique of eighteenth- and nineteenth-century cavalry is quite helpful on this point. At that time, for example, there existed drills for lance thrusts in virtually every direction around the rider. In a particularly useful treatment on French lancers during the Napoleonic era, N. de Lee describes the techniques of employing the cavalry lance. He identifies three basic offensive movements: thrusts, parries, and cuts.[23] With the hand gripping the lance at its point of balance, thrusts were made along the longitudinal line of the

---

19. Quint. Curt. 4.16.23. Lane Fox (1975) 75–76 argues that most close fighting was done with the sword because all of Alexander's wounds were inflicted with a sword or dagger. That may hold true of Persian cavalry, who often discharged javelins and were found to use swords at close quarters, but it does not automatically apply to the Macedonian cavalry, who were trained to use a lance in close fighting.
20. See note 36 below.
21. *HM* 2 421; *GRW* 69; *TS* 53–54.
22. Xen. *On Hors.* 12,12.
23. Lawford (1976) 22–23; de Lee (1976) 9–10.

lance in all directions around the rider. The thrust, which allowed blows to be struck at the greatest distance from the rider, was most effective to the front. When approaching other cavalry, the lance was held in the "guard" position, which required the shaft to "pass over the horse's head, with the point at the level of the horse's ears." This technique had been recommended by Xenophon for cavalry in formation as a means of keeping the lances from crossing each other.[24] Such similarities between ancient and modern practice, of which many are found in Xenophon's work on equitation, are probably due partly to tradition and partly to basic physical and behavioral traits of both horse and rider.[25] When the effectiveness of the thrust was reduced by closeness and crowding, the parry—a horizontal sweep of the lance—was recommended. The hand grip was retained, and leverage was achieved by pressing the rear of the shaft between the elbow and the side of the body. Although there is no clear evidence for the parry in the ancient sources, it would seem to be a natural position in close fighting. Cuts were parries delivered, with an appropriate change of angle, against infantry. If nothing else, this description of the fighting technique with the Napoleonic lance shows what was possible with a weapon that was nine feet long and weighed about four pounds. It was clearly a versatile weapon at close quarters. De Lee's account of the use of the sabre is also interesting. Although the French were trained to thrust with this weapon, the British favored the cut, and in practice this may have been more common because of the difficulty of delivering thrusts in the excitement and movement of battle and also because "it was easier to deliver cuts than thrusts to the sides and rear."[26]

The type of close mounted combat that the written sources depict is entirely consistent with the riding skills that result from sitting a horse without saddle and stirrups as well as with the collected style of riding recommended by Xenophon and commonly depicted in the figured evidence. All else being equal, the bareback rider will be more skilled than one using a saddle. He will have a deeper seat with a lower center of gravity; he will of necessity develop a better sense of balance, since no security will be offered by the shape of the saddle or the lateral support from stirrups; and he will have better control by virtue of the close contact between his legs and the sides of the horse.[27] It

24. de Lee (1976) 9; Xen. Cav. Cmdr. 3. 3. δόρατα. . . . ὡς ἥκιστα ἂν ἀλλήοις ἐπαλλάττοιτο.
25. When the "art" of riding was revived in the sixteenth century by Frederigo Grisone, it was based on Xenophon's work. Podhajsky (1980) 10.
26. de Lee (1976) 8.
27. The Plains Indians, although they possessed saddles and stirrups, preferred to ride bareback when in combat.

is worthwhile to repeat Xenophon's observation that the Persians put so many covers on their horses' backs that they traded riding skill for comfort.[28]

As important as the rider's skill is, it represents only a part of riding. Aside from the obvious fact that horses could not be ridden if they were not amenable to human control, they possess certain physical and behavioral characteristics that lend themselves to exploitation for the purposes of riding. Among these qualities are size, speed, a strong back, social behavior, and a timid character that allows a 150 pound human to control a 1,000-pound animal. In addition I should like to draw attention to two other traits that can be enhanced through training and are compatible with close fighting with hand-held weapons: collection and shoulder barging. Collection can be described as bringing the hind legs (hocks) under the body, whereby the horse brings up and arches the neck and bends the head downward from the poll, producing a shortening of the body.[29] Although the term *prancing* is not completely synonymous, it conveys the essence of collection. A collected horse is under control, balanced between the hand (bit) and leg aids, has stability, and is capable of moving quickly in any direction because the hind legs are positioned for maximum effort. Whenever ground has to be covered at speed, the stride can be extended by means of the appropriate aids. Collection is found frequently in Greek art, as in the Parthenon frieze, as well as in contemporary dressage exhibitions such as those performed at the Spanish Riding School in Vienna. On the other hand the ancient bronze racehorse found in the sea off Cape Artemisium (ca. 200) and now in the National Museum, Athens, exhibits an extended gallop. Collection clearly offers advantages to a rider in a melee, where he must stop, start, change directions, and wheel about in order to bring his weapon to bear on the enemy and to avoid the latter's attack.

Xenophon recognized that horses sometimes exhibit collection naturally, especially when stallions show off in front of mares, and he recommended the development of this behavior through training.[30] He even suggested selecting

---

28. Xen. *Cyr.* 8.8.19.
29. Podhajsky (1980) 43. On collection, see Xen. *Cav. Cmdr.* 3.14; Xen. *On Hors.* 1.12, 8.5, 10.15–16, 11.2, 11.8. A remark by Xenophon (*On Hors.* 11.8) implies that artists may have emphasized collection to enhance the image of the horse, but the existence of collection is not in doubt. The appearance of stirrups in the early Middle Ages introduced the potential for fundamental changes in riding, cavalry tactics, and even the training of cavalry recruits. It then became easier to ride with less skill, providing hitherto unknown lateral stability and making it easier to produce usable cavalry or dragoons in a comparatively short time from recruits with little or no experience with horses. This last point was especially valid in respect to the rise of urban life in Europe and the recruitment of cavalrymen from the ranks.
30. Xen. *On Hors.* 10.3–17. Contemporary equine ethologists confirm Xenophon's observations. "Even advanced training, such as dressage, mimics the horse's natural actions. These include the

horses whose conformation indicated a natural proclivity for collection.[31] Even without formal schooling, it is probable that a horse would gain some collection as a result of the experience gained in sham fights. This type of military exercise, which Xenophon seems to take for granted, must have been employed by the highly trained Macedonians.[32]

The other natural behavior that would have been useful to cavalrymen who fought at close quarters is shoulder barging. This is an aggressive action by one horse against another whereby the threatening animal bumps its rival with its shoulder.[33] In modern horse racing and polo, riders exploit the behavior to bump a rival. On the racetrack it often results in a foul, but in polo it is an intentional, if controlled, part of the sport and is referred to as *riding-off*. To accomplish the desired result, the rider approaches an opponent from the side, riding in the same direction, and guides his mount so that it pushes or bumps the other horse and rider out of the way. In polo the action is governed by strict rules in order to prevent injury. For example, the angle of approach may not exceed forty-five degrees, since the danger of injury resulting from a collision increases the closer the angle is to ninety degrees. When horse and rider are practicing this maneuver, they begin at a walk against a stationary opponent and, with increasing skill and confidence, proceed to the canter and gallop.[34] Since Arrian mentions that there was much pushing of cavalry at the battle of the Granicus, apparently initiated by the attacking Macedonians, it is probable that their horses were trained in some form of shoulder barging.[35] The action may have contributed to the superiority of the Macedonian cavalry, whose training for combat at close quarters better prepared them for physical contact of man and horse than did the javelin tactics of the Persians.

---

passage—a high, floating trot in which the horse appears to dance from one diagonal to another, and piaffe—the same, performed in place. These movements simulate the stallion's approach in his attraction towards a mare" Fraser (1992) 246. Fraser observes that such behavior is inherent in the neural circuits even in mares, although in the absence of human interference it is expressed only rarely, as in the case of an ovarian tumor, which causes abnormally high levels of serum testosterone (41).

31. Xen. *On Hors.* 1.12. "The broader and shorter the loins the more easily will the horse lift his forehand and collect his hind quarter." Anderson's trans. (*AGH* 158). This is another indication of the level of Xenophon's knowledge of equitation. Judging a horse's behavioral potential on the basis of its conformation is simply (although not simple to do) a matter of evaluating the physical qualities that are the basis of the behavior.

32. Xen. *Cav. Cmdr.* 1.20; 3.11, 5.4, Xen. *On Hors.* 8.10–11.

33. Morris (1988) 28–29.

34. Price and Kauffman (1989) 60–62. See also Disston (1973) 149, who emphasizes the importance of training.

35. Arr. *Anab.*1.15.2; 15.4.

Taken together, all the evidence supports the conclusions that the Macedonian cavalry were trained primarily for close combat with lance and sword and that the lance was approximately seven to ten feet in length—that is, longer than the javelin and Greek infantry spear but shorter than the Macedonian *sarissa*. This conclusion is quite different from that of M. M. Markle, who believes that Alexander's Companion Cavalry employed the *sarissa* when making a direct assault upon the enemy.[36] Since his arguments are based primarily on the archaeological and figured evidence, it seems appropriate to evaluate this material within the context of his remarks.

Initially, Markle proposed that the cavalry *sarissa* was identical to the infantry weapon of the Macedonians, that is to say, a spear 15–16 feet long and weighing as much as 14 pounds.[37] In a subsequent article he reduced these figures to 14.5 feet and 6.6 pounds.[38] This down sizing seems to have resulted from a growing awareness of the difficulty of manipulating such a long, heavy spear with one hand from the back of a horse.[39] An awareness of the difficulty is very much to the point, because the physical properties of the weapon determine the manner in which it can be used. Since momentum is a product of mass and velocity, a light lance thrust quickly downward or forward by arm power, excluding the motion of the horse, would be easier to bring into play and would have as much or more striking power as a heavy *sarissa*, whose greater inertia would be difficult for arm and shoulder muscles to overcome. The *sarissa* would be efficient only in a straight-ahead charge, with the momentum provided by the motion of the horse. Once embedded in an enemy or his horse, it would have to be dropped in favor of the sword, as Markle acknowledges.[40] Obviously, it would have been useless

---

36. Markle (1977) 323–39; Markle (1978) 483–97; *MAT* 87–111. Markle's arguments have met mixed reactions. Connolly (*GRW* 71) accepts them without qualification, as does Devine (1989a), in Hackett, 105–106. On the other hand Bosworth (*CE* 262–63) believes they fought in dense formation with a "shorter thrusting lance." Manti, in a detailed discussion, suggests a nine-foot lance weighting 4.2 pounds, which he calls a *sarissa* (1983) 78. Although Manti's conclusions are correct, I believe he has misinterpreted some of the evidence. For example, he cites Ael. *Tac.* 12 for the statement that the cavalry *sarissa* is eight cubits long (at 13.5 inches a cubit), but Aelian is only discussing infantry weapons at that point, and 8 cubits is the lower limit on length. Furthermore, Manti (77), argues for a cubit of 13.5 inches rather than the 18-inch Attic cubit used by others when estimating the length of the *sarissa* (see *AAG* 118). Hammond, who earlier had favored the longer lance, *TS* 63, now follows Manti (Hammond [1989] 106).

37. Markle (1977) 333–34.

38. *MAT* 88–92.

39. It was extremely cumbersome and difficult to handle (*MAT* 90), and "in battle the lance could not be shifted from the lower to the upper position without the use of both hands" (106). The left hand, holding the reins, would not ordinarily be used.

40. *MAT* 106.

in a melee of the kind described in the literary sources above. Furthermore, the advantage in length of the *sarissa* is not as significant as at first appears, for the lighter lance, requiring less strength to manipulate, can be held behind the midpoint of the shaft. Thus the lance offers greater reach relative to its total length than the *sarissa*, which—as Markle suggests—was held in the middle.[41] In the hands of the infantry, however, the *sarissa* was a two-handed weapon, gripped well to the rear in order to allow most of the shaft to project ahead of the first row of men. Indeed, its great length relative to the depth of each row of men permitted four or five rows of *sarissa* points to project in front of the first line of footmen.[42] Because of the size of the horses and their more open formation, cavalry carrying *sarissas* could match this neither in compactness nor in number.

Two monuments are of particular importance to Markle's claims: the *Alexander Mosaic* and the *Alexander Sarcophagus*. The former is a Pompeian mosaic copy of an earlier Hellenistic wall painting of part of the battle of Issus.[43] Alexander's weapon in this scene is an extremely long lance held in his right hand. Markle estimates its length at four and a half meters (14.6 feet), using the figures of men and horses in the mosaic for comparison.[44] My own calculations, using the head of Alexander's horse for comparison, suggest a lance between twelve and one-half and fifteen feet in length, and are thus essentially in agreement with Markle.[45] This does not solve the problem, however, for directly behind Alexander is the figure of a Macedonian cavalryman wielding a much shorter lance in an overhand grip. Although damage to the mosaic obscures the extension of this lance behind the rider, the after portion of the shaft would have been no longer than the forward part and may have been shorter. A calculation of its length, again using the horse head for comparison, suggests a figure between seven and eight feet—too long for a javelin but within the limits of a useful cavalry lance. Actually, all that has been determined by this exercise is that Alexander and the cavalry-

---

41. This rearward grip is shown in the painting from Kinch's tomb near Naoussa in Macedonia. Hatzopoulos and Loukopoulos (1984) 70. Miller (1982), 152–69.

42. *TS* 53; *GRW* 78.

43. The mosaic is in the National Museum, Naples, the sarcophagus in the Archaeological Museum, Istanbul (ca. 310). See Groenewegen-Frankfort and Ashmole (1972) color pl. 42, 76; fig. 487, 350.

44. *MAT* 105.

45. Whereas Markle used a human figure estimated to be between 170 and 180 cm. tall, I used the head of Alexander's horse with an estimate of 21 to 24 inches for its length. Since ancient horses were smaller on average than modern riding breeds, the lower figure may be closer to the original. It is, of course, an unverifiable assumption that the artist was using accurate proportions of man and horse.

man behind him carry different weapons, the length of each consistent with its type. From the mosaic alone, it is impossible to determine which type of weapon was normally carried by Macedonian cavalry into battle. It is certainly possible that the scene on the mosaic that shows Alexander's *sarissa* piercing a Persian cavalryman represents an attempt to glorify Alexander rather than to portray historical reality.

The *Alexander Sarcophagus* also shows Alexander holding a long lance that can be called a *sarissa*. Although the bronze weapons on this high relief in marble are missing, holes in the stone indicate the original position of the fittings for attaching them. I agree with Markle that the forward portion of Alexander's weapon was a little over seven feet long, which would indicate that it was a *sarissa*, assuming that the rear portion, not originally shown on the relief, was the same length.[46]

Of equal significance, however, is the wall painting from Kinch's Tomb, near Naoussa in Macedonia.[47] It portrays a cavalryman attacking an infantryman who is carrying a shield. The rider's lance is certainly not a *sarissa*, for—using the same principle of comparison as above—its size may be estimated at between 8.1 and 9.2 feet. The horseman's grip on the shaft is at a point about two-thirds of the way back from the forward spearhead, not in the middle, as Markle suggests would be the case with a *sarissa*. Nevertheless, although he gives no estimate of its length, Markle identifies this weapon as a *sarissa*. He explains the position of the gripping hand by suggesting that the rider is no longer concerned with the weapon's balance, since its point is supported by the shield in which it seems to be embedded.[48] It is noteworthy that the lance has a second spearhead on the rear of the shaft. To judge by the descriptions of fighting as well as the figured evidence, this or a butt spike may well have been normal.[49] This tomb painting is also of interest because it may have represented a type of commemorative scene that had currency in the Balkans during the fourth and third centuries, which is suggested by its similarity to a series of coins minted by the Paeonian king Patraus, who ruled from about 340 to 315. Not only did Patraus' reign coincide with those of Philip and Alexander, but some of his cavalry played a prominent role in Alexander's Asiatic campaigns. In spite of differences in dress, the scene on

46. *MAT* 106.
47. Dated by Markle (1982) 91 to circa 300; by Miller (1982) 168 n. 35 to circa 200. See also Miller (1993) pl. 8a, who describes the painting as a combat scene of the deceased against a barbarian. It now survives only in a colored drawing.
48. *MAT* 90.
49. Manti (1983) 79; *MAT* 90, fig. 6.

the wall painting is remarkably similar to that on the coins. A lancer is charging to the right against an infantryman holding a shield, which in both cases is described as "Macedonian."[50] This attribution should not be pressed too hard, however, since it seems more likely that the shields belong to a common Balkan type.[51] Another similarity is the position of the horse's legs in the wall painting and coins. The lance shown on the coins also seems to be less than ten feet in length, although it is perhaps best not to emphasize it, as scenes on coins are regularly adapted to fit a round field. Nevertheless, long lances were at times shown on coins, as can be seen in an issue of Eucratides of Bactria from 156.[52]

The figured evidence is clearly inconsistent. It is also inherently unreliable, because it is impossible to determine when and to what end artistic license may be present. In the case of the *Alexander Mosaic* two different weapons appear in the same scene. Given the crowded portrayal of fighting, Alexander's *sarissa* would seem to be out of place. Perhaps the *sarissa* on both the scenes was a means of linking the figure of Alexander to his victim while showing them in full rather than allowing one to obscure the other. This may very well have been a symbolic rather then a literal linking, intended to show that the Persian Empire was "spear-won land."[53] In the scene the cavalryman receiving the spear thrust represents Persia.

Markle also adduces purely archaeological evidence in the form of spearheads found in and around Macedonian tombs of the Hellenistic period, including the so-called Tomb of Philip.[54] Without a doubt these represent real evidence, but the archaeological context alone offers no hint regarding the use of these weapons or whether they should be considered cavalry or infantry spears. In addition to the ambiguous nature of the finds, there are difficulties with Markle's interpretation of them. A case in point concerns butt spikes, which were found only in association with large, heavy spearpoints, presumably the heads of *sarissas*. Contrary to accepted opinion, Markle believes that infantry used light *sarissas* without butt spikes, which—he feels—

---

50. Hammond (1989) 105; Forrer (1975) pl. 86; Mørkholm (1991) 83 pl. 12, nos. 185–87.
51. *HM* 2 669.
52. *MAT* 90–91. These lances also exhibit an after spearpoint.
53. See Junkelman (1990–92) 1: 180, who sees the *Alexander Mosaic* as a mix of the real and the symbolic, depicting the decisive moment during the battle of Issus when Darius turned to flee, with the Persian rider, transfixed by Alexander's lance, representing the enemy army. For discussion of such symbols referring to "spear-won land," see Billows (1995) 25–27. For ancient use of the term, see Polyb. 5.67.
54. *MAT* 88–92; *CAH* pl. to vol. 7, part I, 83, no. 101.

could injure men in the rear ranks: "For cavalry, however, which charged in less dense formations, the butt spike, besides being a counter weight, had two other functions. It served both as a support by which the lance could be implanted against the ground so that a charging horse could be transfixed by falling upon the point without the rider holding the lance being unseated and as a spare point in the event that the sarissa-head should be broken off."[55] No doubt exists regarding the use of the butt spike as a counterweight and as a spare point,[56] but it is another matter to suggest that a rider can implant the butt end of his lance in the ground and use it against a charging horseman. Simple calculation shows that a fifteen-foot *sarissa* held in the middle with the butt resting on the ground would have its point about ten feet off the ground at an angle of about forty-two degrees. There is no way a *sarissa* can be used effectively in this position. Even if it could, one of the cavalryman's principal advantages—mobility—would be lost.

In short I find no convincing archaeological or figured evidence that the principal weapon of the Companion Cavalry was a long *sarissa*. Furthermore, the absence of the word *sarissa* as a designation of the cavalry spear in the ancient sources is striking, especially since it is used in contexts where it lends clarity to the narrative. In Polybius, for example, in the description of the battle of Raphia in 217, there is an account of the action between elephants with men fighting from the towers mounted on their backs. These men struck each other with *sarissas* at close quarters. Given the extra distance between the fighting men caused by the bodies of the elephants, the use of the longer *sarissa* makes sense.[57] Thus all of the evidence taken together strongly supports the conclusion reached earlier that the cavalry weapon was an easily manipulated lance seven to ten feet in length.

One point that I should address before turning to a discussion of tactics is the role of a mixed formation of cavalry squadrons comprising units identified as Paeonians and *prodromoi*, with the occasional addition of Greek mercenary cavalry.[58] The *prodromoi* represent something of an enigma, because

---

55. Markle (1982) 90, followed by Devine (1989a) 106.
56. See Polyb. 19.29.3, for rear weight on infantry *sarissa*; Arr. *Anab.* 1.15.6; Polyb. 11.18.4, for the use of broken spears. See also Manti (1983) 76, who suggests that the rear point was heavier than the front one to counterbalance the weight of the longer forward part of the shaft. As mentioned above, although he calls the cavalry spear a *sarissa*, Manti judges its length to be nine feet despite the fact that his claim for this measure is based on a misreading of Ael. *Tac.* 12, which refers to an infantry spear.
57. Polyb. 5.84.2.
58. Excluding the mercenary cavalry, the number of squadrons was either four (*AHA* 1 110; *CE* 262) or five (*AA* 1 lxxiii; Hammond [1989] 126).

they are also referred to as *sarissophoroi* (*sarissa* bearers).⁵⁹ Furthermore, since these units are usually considered to be light cavalry, there is the apparent paradox that the light cavalry carry a longer, heavier spear than the heavy cavalry of the line. Interpretations of this vary from simple acceptance to the conclusion that the term had lost its literal meaning. A compromise suggestion is that the *sarissa* was used for battle, while other, lighter weapons were carried when the men were scouting and on patrol.⁶⁰ Compounding the problem is the use by contemporary historians of the terms *heavy* and *light* cavalry, which may well be anachronistic. In recent centuries these terms had specific meanings both in respect to physical characteristics and to tactics. Light cavalry, with lighter armor and smaller horses, exhibited quickness and agility to carry out their duties. They threatened and enveloped the enemy flanks and rear, participated in pursuits, covered retreats, served as a rear guard, and saw service as scouts. The more formidable heavy cavalry, on the other hand, charged at the trot or canter, with united ranks, and brought heavy masses to bear against the enemy line.⁶¹ Although a variety of firearms was employed by both, the characteristic weapon in close combat was the lance for the light cavalry, the saber for the heavy. Little of this applies to Greek and Macedonian armies of the fourth century. Even the heavily armored horsemen of the later Hellenistic period and Roman times do not match up with heavy cavalry, because their principal weapon was a long, heavy spear wielded with both hands rather than a sword.

These rather clear-cut distinctions that are characteristic of modern cavalry do not seem to have existed among the cavalry forces of the various peoples who lived in the Balkan peninsula in the fourth century B.C. Of course the obvious exceptions were the missile troops, mounted archers, and javelin throwers. But among the cavalrymen who fought with lance and sword, it is virtually impossible to identify significant differences in arms, armor, and horses. To some degree real differences may be obscured by inadequate information from the ancient sources, but enough literary and figured evidence survives to suggest that notable changes did not occur until after the time of Alexander. Other types of cavalry existed in western Asia and the Near East,

---

59. Arr. *Anab.* 1.14.1, 6; 3.12.2; Quint. Curt. 4.15.13. In *AHA* 1 110 the equation "is clear and unchallenged."

60. *AA* 1 lxxx; *HM* 2 413; *CE* 262.

61. de Lee (1976) 23; Scott ([1861] 1968) 154–55. Hammond also seems to have some reservations about the appropriateness of the modern terms. Writing about the regular Macedonian cavalry, he says: "All these were 'heavy' cavalry in the sense that the horsemen wore armour, moved in a tight formation, and fought with spear or lance at close quarters." *HM* 3 541.

but—except for his addition of mounted archers—Alexander does not seem to have been overly impressed with them. Late in his career, when he incorporated eastern troops into his Companion Cavalry, he armed them with Macedonian lances.[62] In Alexander's army the distinction among the various groups of cavalry seems to have been based on tactical assignment and ethnic origin. This, of course, might reflect real differences in training and skill, not to mention loyalty and reliability. All in all, it may be more accurate to think in terms of "cavalry of the line" rather than "heavy cavalry" and mounted "skirmishers" (or *prodromoi*) in place of "light cavalry."

As was true of all the units in Alexander's army, the mounted skirmishers (Paeonians and *prodromoi*) performed a variety of tasks, but they seem to receive the least credit for their role in the major battles. Apparently any cavalry unit was potentially subject to scouting duties, as when the four squadrons of *prodromoi* were sent ahead during the approach to the Granicus River in 331, they were joined by the Apollonian squadron of Companions.[63] The skirmishers also joined various other units of cavalry and infantry on special assignments as elite troops, the most important example of which was the pursuit of Darius after the battle of Gaugamela in 330.[64] It is their participation in more formal combat that deserves greater attention, however. In the battle at the Granicus, the attack was initiated by the *prodromoi* and Paeonians in the company of a battalion of infantry and Socrates' squadron of Companion Cavalry.[65] Bosworth correctly describes the task of the advance forces as that of absorbing the momentum of the Persian charge and allowing Alexander to countercharge with fresher troops.[66] These forces also drew volleys of javelins upon themselves, presumably giving Alexander a better chance to force the issue with the hand-to-hand fighting that was vital to Macedonian success.[67] The fact that the advance force included infantry and Companion Cavalry shows that their common function was more important than identity by type. At the battle of Issus, although no details are given about

---

62. Arr. *Anab.* 7.66.5; *CE* 272. Cf. Quint. Curt. 3.11.14,15, where the mobility of the Thessalian cavalry at Issus gave them an advantage over heavily armored Persian horse and rider. Atkinson suggests that their heavily armored cavalry (possibly cataphracts) were not suited to close combat (1980) 238. Plut. *Luc.* 28.2–3.

63. Arr. *Anab.* 1.12.7. *AHA* 1 110.

64. Arr. *Anab.* 3.18.1; 1.21.2. *CE* 95. See also Arr. *Anab.* 3.8.2.

65. Arr. *Anab.* 1.14.6. *AHA* 1 121. Infantry sometimes joined cavalry in an attack and on this occasion were part of the skirmishers.

66. *CE* 42.

67. Arr. *Anab.* 1.15.1–5.

their part in the battle, the Paeonians and *prodromoi* were again posted in front of the cavalry of the line.[68]

Arrian's description of events before and during the battle of Gaugamela offers more detailed evidence for the importance of the skirmishers. After crossing the Tigris River some days before the battle, *prodromoi*, scouting ahead, reported seeing an indeterminate number of Persian cavalry. With the apparent intention of capturing prisoners for interrogation, Alexander led the Royal Squadron, a squadron of Companion Cavalry, and the Paeonian *prodromoi* out against them. The Persians, no more than one thousand in number, fled, but several were captured when their horses tired.[69]

On the day of the battle the several groups of cavalry and infantry comprising the skirmishers were again posted on the right, but apparently more around to the flank than was usual in order to counter the length of the Persian line, which extended beyond that of the Macedonians both to right and left. Menidas and the mercenary cavalry were in front at the apex of a delta (wedge). Behind them from left to right were the *prodromoi* and the Paeonians. At the base of the delta were infantry consisting of half the Agranian javelin men, the Macedonian archers, and the so-called old mercenaries.[70] The base of the delta was not parallel to the rest of the line, which ran obliquely to the left rear, but at an angle to it. It is not clear whether the delta was directly facing the opposing cavalry or also at an angle to them.[71]

The formation on the right flank was important, because Alexander's forces were badly outnumbered and in serious danger of being outflanked.[72] To diminish this possibility Alexander gradually moved to the right, drawing the Persians with him. The Persians gained nothing by merely keeping up with the Macedonians and were being drawn away from their prepared positions. To put an end to Alexander's lateral motion, Darius ordered his cavalry to ride around his enemy's right. Alexander responded by sending Menidas and the mercenary cavalry against them, but the greater numbers of Scythians and Bactrians drove them back. Alexander then ordered the Paeonians and *prodromoi* forward to counter the Persians, who also sent in additional

68. Ibid., 2.9.2.
69. Ibid., 3.7.7–8.2; Quint. Curt. 4.9.24–25.
70. Arr. *Anab.* 3.12.2–3.
71. Devine (1975) 375 believes it was drawn back to the right. Marsden (1964) 48–51 believes it was parallel. *AA* 1 510, doubts the evidence allows a conclusion to be drawn. *AHA* 1 302 agrees with Devine. Arr. *Anab.* 3.12.2; Diod. 17.57.5; Quint. Curt. 4.13.30.
72. With regard to numbers on the Persian side, the ancient sources are too fantastic to be trusted, with totals reaching over a million (Arr. *Anab.* 3.8.6; Diod. 17.53.3; Quint. Curt. 4.11.13). For discussion see *AHA* 1 293.

reinforcements. In spite of being outnumbered and suffering numerous casualties, the Macedonian skirmishers continued to attack by squadron. As Darius kept feeding cavalry units into this fight against the skirmishers, a gap developed in the Persian line that Alexander—leading the Companions and part of the adjacent phalanx—exploited decisively at the critical moment.[73]

The great contribution of the skirmishers on this occasion is beyond doubt. In addition to absorbing the initial impetus of the enemy, they kept the numerically superior enemy cavalry occupied and thereby helped to cause the mistake, in the form of a gap in the enemy line, that was necessary for Alexander's success. As a result Alexander was able to lead fresh, well-formed cavalry and infantry against a weak point in the Persian line.[74]

The following year (330) the *prodromoi* and mercenary cavalry joined the Companion Cavalry and Macedonian phalanx for the final pursuit of Darius.[75] This last mention of *prodromoi* by Arrian creates something of a problem. The alternate name for them, *sarissophoroi*, appears for the last time in the events of 329. On this latter occasion their four squadrons and a hipparchy of mercenary cavalry initiated an attack on a Scythian cavalry force. The highly mobile Scythians, riding in circles and shooting arrows, thwarted them. Next Alexander sent a second attack comprising three hipparchies of Companions and the mounted javelin men and then followed with the rest of the cavalry, forcing the Scythians to flee.[76]

The mounted javelin men were a new formation, appearing for the first time in 330 but regularly thereafter. They were included in many of the expeditions led or sent by Alexander to subdue the local dynasts in the northeast regions of the former Persian Empire between the years 330 and 327/326. On one occasion forty of them were assigned as an escort for a local ruler, and twice they led an attack against the enemy ahead of the main Macedonian forces.[77] The function of the javelin men, whose ethnic identity is not given, seems to have been essentially the same as that of the skirmishers. It is impos-

73. Arr. *Anab.* 3.13–14.2. Marsden (1964) 47–53; *AHA* 1 305–306; *CE* 82–83.
74. Marsden (1964) 50. Devine (1975) 383 considers Menidas' initial charge "an error of carelessness" on Alexander's part because they were so heavily outnumbered, although he feels that the tactical plan for drawing the enemy was sound. This criticism seems unnecessary. Alexander's forces were outnumbered everywhere on the battlefield and he was certainly willing to take losses in exchange for a chance to defeat Darius once and for all. Furthermore, Alexander was always compelled to trust in the qualitative superiority of his forces, because he was constantly inferior in number.
75. Arr. *Anab.* 3.20.1.
76. Ibid., 4.4.7; *AHA* 2 30.
77. Arr. *Anab.* 3.24.1, 25.2, 25.6, 29.7; 4.17.3, 23.1, 25.6, 26.4; 4.4.7, 26.4.

sible to say whether they are a reintroduction of traditional Greek javelin-carrying cavalry or eastern in origin.[78]

In the year 327/326 just prior to the last mention in Arrian of the mounted javelin men, a new unit of mounted archers appeared, playing a prominent role in the fighting in the East until 325. These mounted archers joined detachments of infantry and other cavalry in mopping-up operations by the army as it moved into India. Against King Porus at the Hydaspes, they appeared prominently both in the preliminary actions and in the battle itself. Then, when Alexander marshalled his forces after crossing the river, he stationed the mounted archers in front of the cavalry of the line. Shortly thereafter, at a time when Alexander thought he was facing the entire Indian army, they led the attack against the cavalry of Porus' son. Finally, in the battle one thousand of them began the attack against Porus' left wing in order to cause confusion by their volleys of arrows and the charge itself, thus allowing Alexander to charge with the Companions while the enemy was disorganized and not fully deployed. When giving the list of casualties after the battle, Arrian mentions that the mounted archers were the first to engage. On one occasion in the aftermath of the Hydaspes, they served as a screen in the opening action against an enemy who had taken refuge behind a palisade of wagons. By riding along in front of the wagons and shooting arrows, they kept the Indians from making sallies before Alexander was ready and forced them to take casualties prior to the beginning of his attack.[79]

In all of these events the common theme is the initiation of the attack on the right in order to unsettle the enemy there and allow Alexander to follow with fresh cavalry of the line who had a physical and psychological advantage. From 334 until 330, lancers comprising *prodromoi* and Paeonians were used. Mounted javelin men replaced them for the period 330–327/326, when they in turn gave way to the mounted archers, who saw service from 327/326 until 325.[80] Although the ethnic origin of the latter two groups is unknown, they obviously enjoyed Alexander's complete confidence and trust or they would not have been given such a critical assignment. The change of arms from lances to javelins to bows presumably represents a response to the

---

78. Macedonian according to *AHA* 1 352; Oriental, *AA* 1 lxxiv. See also *AHA* 2 119 (Arr. *Anab.* 4.17.3).

79. Arr. *Anab.* 4.24.1, 29.8; 6.6.1, 21.3, 22.1; Quint. Curt. 5.4.14. Curtius is perhaps in error here, because the date is too early (331) and Arrian does not mention mounted archers. At the Hydaspes, 5.12.2, 13.4, 15.1, 16.4, 18.3. As a screen, Sangala, 5.22.5.

80. According to Bosworth these were Sacae and Dahae, *AHA* 2 291; Quint. Curt. 8.14.5.

type of troops the Macedonians faced as they moved east as well as the ease of recruiting them from the local populations. Such changes on his part were to be expected, as one of Alexander's greatest qualities was adaptability.

Although Alexander obviously made excellent use of these troops as skirmishers, the idea may not have originated with him. Already in fifth-century Athens there existed a unit of horse archers who had the privilege of charging the enemy first.[81] They were replaced in the 390s by cavalry known as *prodromoi*, which was not a change in name only since the *prodromoi* were armed with the javelin, as were the regular Athenian cavalry (*hippeis*). Yet whereas the *hippeis* had some social standing, the *prodromoi* seem to have been recruited from the Thetes, the lowest socio-economic census class.[82] Unfortunately, the absence of literary evidence on these cavalry units prevents a clear understanding of their tactical employment.

Nevertheless, it is reasonable to suggest that the term *prodromoi* could be used for a generic type of cavalry whose function was consonant with its etymology—running or going in advance.[83] This might apply to scouting as well as to leading the attack on the right wing, and—given the tactical importance of this latter role in the major battles of Alexander—it should at least be included, if not emphasized, in a definition of its meaning. Accordingly, Bosworth's translation of *prodromoi* as "scouts" is incomplete and diverts attention away from their more important duties. Furthermore, his description of them as lightly equipped also seems to be incorrect.[84] Although perhaps wearing relatively less body armor, they likely carried the same weapons as the cavalry of the line—lances and swords and perhaps even the heavier *sarissa*, as their alternate name implies. Bosworth suggests that the *sarissa* was used only in battle against other cavalry, but if that is true it would mean that they fought differently from the line cavalry, for which there is no evidence.[85]

It is true that Arrian usually distinguishes between Paeonians and *prodromoi*, but that could be no more than an effort to distinguish ethnic from Macedonian *prodromoi*, since the *prodromoi/sarissophoroi* are generally considered to be Macedonian.[86] If that is the case, then two references—one in

81. Xen. *Mem.* 3.3.1; *HA* 221–24; *CCG* 58.
82. Xen. *Cav. Cmdr.* 1.25; *RE* 23 (1957) cols. 102–104.
83. *CE* 262, n. 17, allows for the possibility that *prodromoi* was used as "a generic term for light cavalry." I would substitute *skirmishers* for *light*.
84. *CE* 81, 265, 327.
85. *CE* 262–63. He points out that the *sarissa*'s length made it impossible to use in close formation, suggesting that the *prodromoi/sarissophoroi* attacked in an open order either widely spread out or massed in single, extended lines.
86. *CE* 262, n. 17.

Diodorus, the other in Arrian himself—become more intelligible. When detailing the forces with which Alexander crossed into Asia Minor in 334/333, Diodorus identifies nine hundred Thracian and Paeonian *prodromoi*.[87] Then in 331, when Alexander—just prior to Gaugamela—led a detail of cavalry in pursuit of some Persian cavalry, Arrian mentions that he took the Royal Squadron, one squadron of Companions, and "of the *prodromoi* the Paeonians."[88] In view of this it seems best to accept the possibility that the term was subject to more than one use in antiquity rather than to insist that a lack of absolute consistency indicates error in the ancient sources.

This discussion of the various types of skirmishers may seem to place undue emphasis on troops that did not form part of the battle line, who were often not Macedonians, and whose formations and arms changed with some regularity. Nevertheless, their true importance is discernible in their common and essential function of preparing the enemy for Alexander's main attack in his major battles. By causing disorder in the enemy ranks and blunting the energy of the enemy's initial contact (including a reduction in the number of available missiles), the skirmishers both psychologically and physically prepared the way for the attack of Alexander's fresh troops. The value of their task assumes greater significance because Alexander's forces were usually outnumbered and thus had to depend upon superior leadership, fighting quality, and tactics. An essential part of this superiority was the employment of mounted skirmishers to set the enemy up.[89]

Since Alexander was usually the aggressor, a good starting point for a discussion of battle tactics is the charge. Traditionally, the charge has been viewed as the principal function of cavalry on the battlefield. Yet painted scenes from the eighteenth and nineteenth centuries and movies in the twentieth offer images of cavalry charges that often have little in common with reality and are not helpful to our efforts to understand what was meant by a charge in the battles fought by Alexander. In his battles the tactical goal was to engage the enemy in hand-to-hand conflict with the cavalry of the line at a critical spot in their formation. Once physical contact was made, Alexander relied on the superiority of his forces to break into and then rout the enemy at the point of contact. Except rarely and incidentally, the charge itself was not sufficient

---

87. Diod. 17.17.4.
88. Arr. *Anab.* 3.8.1, καὶ τῶν προδρόμων τοὺς Παίονας. See also *AHA* 1 110.
89. Devine, discussing the battle of the Granicus, calls these tactics a feint (1988) 17. I disagree. A feint is an attack made at one point to divert attention from the main attack at another point. For Alexander the attack of the skirmishers was part of the main attack, directed in the same general area.

to accomplish this. Rather, enemy resistance was broken by the relentless pressure of hand-to-hand combat, for which the Macedonian cavalry were better prepared than their counterparts, who preferred the comparative security of loosing missiles from a distance. It was precisely this mental edge—a sort of fierceness—that permitted Alexander to strike directly, quickly, and decisively at the enemy battle line.[90] Whatever the origin of his "bloody-minded" outlook, it was supported by exceptional weapons skill, training, and discipline.

Although the rate of advance of the charge might vary from battle to battle, no evidence suggests that speed in itself was essential. Indeed, J. Keegan observes that "for some reason, a firm and unhurried tread is far more intimidating in an attacker than a trot or run."[91] On three occasions—at the Granicus (334), at Gaugamela (331), and against the Scythians (329)—infantry advanced with the cavalry, either mixed or adjacent to them, and in general the advancing cavalry of the right wing were articulated with the infantry phalanx to their left. Failure to maintain close contact would open up a dangerous gap in the battle line, as happened at Issus. Clearly, the participation of infantry in the main attack precluded a rapid charge. To emphasize and perhaps belabor a point, the Companion Cavalry on the right and the Thessalians on the left were cavalry of the line and did not normally act independently of the formation until enemy resistance was broken at the point of attack, at which time they would carry the fight in any suitable direction and eventually take part in the pursuit. Where speed was a factor it had a specific purpose, as at Issus, where it helped avoid missiles and may also have been

---

90. The importance of mental attitude may be observed in the French revolutionary cavalry of the 1790s, whose "murderous spirit" was something that was not to be found in any other cavalry force in Europe. Johnson (1989) 29.

91. Keegan (1987) 157–58. Here Keegan is discussing the advance of infantry during the Napoleonic Wars, but the psychological principle should be universal. The most commonly used word to express the idea of attacking or charging was ἐβάλλω, used intransitively: Arr. *Anab.* 1.15.3, 2.10.3, with δρόμῳ added when speed was needed to avoid missiles, 2.11.2, 3.13.3 (twice), 3.14.1, 3.14.3 (twice), 3.14.6, 3.15.1, 4.4.7, 5.15.2, 5.16.4. Other verbs used occasionally are: ἐπίκειραι, Arr. *Anab.* 2.11.3; ἐλαύνω, Arr. *Anab.* 4.4.7; ἐπιτίθημι, Arr. *Anab.* 5.16.2, 17.2; ἐπιλαύνω, Arr. *Anab.* 5.17.4; προσπίπτω, Arr. *Anab.* 3.13.4. The substantive form (ἐμβολή, προβολή) is rare and is coupled with δέχομαι in the sense of receiving the charge, Arr. *Anab.* 3.13.4, 5.17.2. The frequent use of ἐμβάλλω for charge is consistent with the use of the wedge by Macedonian cavalry, since one of its primary meanings is to insert something into a specific spot, leading to the idea of breaking into with a point, whence the nouns ἔμβολος and ἔμβολον, wedge. Speed can actually be a disadvantage, as the following observation by a Napoleonic cavalryman shows: "When a regiment or a squadron of cavalry charges in line in column, it cannot long maintain the order in which it sets out; the horses animate one another, their eagerness progressively increases, and the best mounted horsemen generally find themselves far before the others which breaks the order of battle" de Rocca (1990) 76.

intended for intimidation (as claimed by Arrian).[92] Whether or not Alexander intended to cause panic with the charge, it seldom happened. One apparent exception occurred in 335 when the Getae—shocked that Alexander had crossed the Danube so easily—did not even withstand the first charge of his cavalry but fled to their city.[93] Even on this occasion the effect may have owed more to the surprise of seeing the Macedonians on their side of the river than to the charge itself.

For Alexander, then, the charge of his Companion Cavalry was intended to close the distance between the combatants in order to bring hand-held weapons into play. As a result it was of less tactical significance than the typical charge of European cavalry in recent centuries. The latter, which regularly operated as discrete units independent of the infantry lines, could attack with surprise and speed from any conceivable direction, subject only to such constraints as the nature of the terrain and the dispositions of the enemy.[94]

The tactical unit in the Greek and Macedonian cavalry was the squadron (ἴλη).[95] Among the Greeks and the Persians the traditional formation for squadrons was the square, which—because of the length of horses—had two or three times as many riders across the front in ranks as in the files from front to rear.[96] The Thessalians preferred a diamond (or rhomboid) formation, allegedly invented by Jason, Tyrant of Pherae (ca. 385–370).[97] In Macedon the wedge formation was favored, apparently having been borrowed from the neighboring Thracians and Scythians.[98]

Depending upon circumstances, each formation had its strengths and weaknesses. The pointed leading edge of the diamond and wedge formations permitted easier change of direction and penetration of gaps in the enemy line.

92. Arr. *Anab.* 2.10.3–4.
93. Ibid., 1.4.3.
94. Charges of this sort could be carried out on no higher authority than that of their immediate commander, as was the case at Marengo in 1800, where Kellerman's charge against the flank of an advancing column of Austrian grenadiers apparently saved the day for Napoleon. Johnson (1989) 50–51.
95. Sometime around 330 there was a change in the formal organization of the Companion Cavalry. Hitherto the squadron had been the basic unit, but at this time the hipparchy, a unit that comprised at least two *ilai*, appears. Arr. *Anab.* 3.29.7; 4.24.1; 5.11.3, 16.3, 22.6; 6.6.4, 7.2, 21.3–4, 27.6; 7.6.4. These references cover the years 329–324. Precise information about the number of hipparchies and the complement of each is lacking, although there appear to have been between four and eight in addition to the Royal Agema (formerly the Royal Ile). There is no evidence that this change influenced the tactical use of cavalry. Squadrons continued to exist and could easily be detached from their hipparchy. Arr. *Anab.* 6.21.3. Cf. *CE* 268–70; *AA* 2 485–86.
96. Ascl. *Tac.* 7.4.
97. Ael. *Tac.* 18.2; Ascl. *Tac.* 7.2.
98. Ael. *Tac.* 18.4; Ascl. *Tac.* 7.3. The long recension of Aelian (40.2–6) credits Philip with the invention of the wedge. Devine (1989b) 61.

The wider front of the square presented more of a barrier to an enemy and brought more riders into action at the same moment. As long as the principal weapon of Greek and Persian cavalry remained the javelin, the square offered the best opportunity for launching a number of missiles simultaneously.[99]

Although the later tactical writers are consistent regarding the types of cavalry formations used by these various peoples, there is little evidence in the historical sources to support them. In any event the formations must have been temporary for cavalry armed with lance and sword. Once contact was made, the formation often dissolved and, unlike his counterpart in the phalanx, the cavalryman then fought as an individual. The only mention of a wedge-shaped attack made by Alexander appears in Arrian's account of the decisive moment during the battle of Gaugamela, but it referred to a large formation comprising several squadrons of Companion Cavalry and part of the phalanx.[100] If A. M. Devine's interpretation is correct, this was a large, hollow wedge (∧) in which each of the several units maintained its usual tactical formation, no description of which is given.[101] Arrian makes reference to a wedge of Persian cavalry at the Granicus, but there is no way of telling whether it is an exception to the normal Persian square or a contradiction of the tactical writers.[102]

Although the principal goal of Alexander's attack was to cause a collapse of the enemy line at a crucial point, that was not the end of it. Whenever conditions permitted, there followed a vigorous pursuit and the destruction of the enemy forces. Because of their mobility and speed, cavalry were ideal for this task. They were also more effective when fighting out of formation, unlike hoplites.[103] Pursuits figured prominently in all of Alexander's major actions from 335, when three thousand Getae perished in a pursuit that ended only with nightfall,[104] to 326, at the Hydaspes, when fresh troops under Craterus joined the slaughter.[105] At the battles of Issus and Gaugamela the effort to seize Darius himself lent greater urgency to the pursuit, since Alexander realized that without their king Persian resistance would be much reduced if not eliminated. Thus these pursuits had strategic significance as

99. Cf. Devine (1983) 201–17.
100. Arr. *Anab.* 3.14.1–2.
101. Devine (1983) 214–16; *AHA* 1 307. See Arr. *Anab.* 1.6.3 for mention of a wedge-shaped phalanx formation.
102. Arr. *Anab.* 1.15.7.
103. Lazenby (1991), in Hanson (1991) 101.
104. Arr. *Anab.* 1.2.7.
105. Ibid., 5.18.1.

well.[106] Only at the Granicus was the normal pursuit not carried out, for Alexander turned aside in order to destroy the twenty thousand Greek mercenary infantry, who for some reason had been stationed behind the Persian battle line.[107]

Although I have discussed several facets of Macedonian tactics and fighting technique, a brief description of Alexander's battles will be useful before summarizing the principles of his cavalry tactics. The earliest battle of note was fought in 335 against the Triballians, a Thracian or Illyrian people whose kingdom lay south of the Danube and north to northwest of Macedon. In spite of being accounted more backward than their neighbors to the south, the Triballians had been able to inflict a defeat and a serious thigh wound on Philip as he returned from his Scythian campaign in 339.[108] Their restlessness in the year following Philip's death in 336 prompted Alexander to march against them with a substantial Macedonian force.[109] Alexander caught the Triballians in a glen by a river and put his army in battle order. He sent unprotected bowmen and slingers out ahead of his line to draw the enemy out into the open—a tactic analogous to his later use of mounted skirmishers. When this was successful, Alexander ordered an attack by those cavalry on the left and right flanks while he led the remaining cavalry and the infantry phalanx against the enemy's center. The Triballians held their position as long as the fighting was done with missiles from some distance, but they collapsed and fled once physical contact was made.[110] In spite of the brevity of Arrian's narrative, several things stand out. The attack was made by all elements of the Macedonian force; Alexander led cavalry and infantry together against the enemy center; and the Macedonian superiority at close quarters was decisive.[111]

In the following year, 334, Alexander faced his first test against a Persian army in northwestern Asia Minor at the river Granicus. Although the Persian commanders and satraps in the area had Greek mercenary infantry, only cavalry faced Alexander's forces during the crucial phases of the battle. In the most widely accepted view of the battle, the Persian cavalry awaited the Macedonians on the far (eastern) side of the river. The Thessalian, Greek,

---

106. Ibid., 2.11.3, 6; 3.14.4, 15.3–6. Actually, any destructive pursuit following a decisive victory had strategic value if it ended the war. For an interesting discussion see Weigley (1991) xiv–xv.
107. Arr. *Anab.* 1.16.2. See *AHA* 1 124–25 for a discussion of Alexander's motives. Devine questions this number of Greek mercenaries. See his review of Bosworth (1991) 61–62.
108. Justin, 9.3.1–3.
109. Estimated by Bosworth at fifteen thousand, *CE* 29.
110. Arr. *Anab.* 1.2.4–7.
111. Ibid., 1.2.4–6; *CE* 29; *AG* 47; *GA* 222.

and Thracian cavalry were on the left of the Macedonian phalanx. Archers and the Agrianian javelin men were on the extreme right, supporting the Companion Cavalry. To their left were the skirmishers, comprising *prodromoi*, Paeonians, a squadron of Companions, and a battalion of infantry, which collectively initiated the action. Alexander followed with the rest of the right wing, moving obliquely to the left and forward as he crossed the stream. This oblique crossing, perhaps aided by the northward flow of the current, was adopted so that the Persians could not attack Alexander's flank, the horses and riders apparently facing the enemy as they moved diagonally in the direction of the horses' left shoulder. In equitation today this would be called a leg yield or—at a higher level of training—a half pass. The initial attack by the skirmishers was driven back, but they had forced the Persians to expend some of their javelins and had blunted their initial response before Alexander arrived. At that time the struggle for the riverbank was fought at extremely close quarters, with the cornel-wood lances of the Macedonians proving superior to the Persian javelins. The Persians were also bothered by the light infantry mixed in with the Macedonian cavalry, their resistance collapsing first at the point where Alexander was leading the attack against the center. Instead of pursuing the fleeing Persians, Alexander attacked the Greek mercenaries, who had not taken part in the battle.[112]

Objections have been raised to locating the battle at the riverbank, and Diodorus does describe the crossing as unopposed, but it is difficult to disregard the detailed account of Arrian, who is rightly considered to be the most reliable of the Alexander historians. If the battle did take place at the riverbank, then it is obvious that the topographical conditions were not prohibitive. Furthermore, crossing the river to attack the Persians on the opposite bank is consistent with Alexander's approach to the enemy on other occasions. The momentum produced by a rapid charge had little to recommend itself to the Macedonian cavalry, who relied on superior skill in close combat, whereas the Persians, armed with javelins, may have judged the height of the riverbank to be a fair trade-off for their usual practice of riding up and throwing javelins. They were not as sanguine about close combat as the Mace-

---

112. Arr. *Anab.* 1.14.6; Diod. 17.19–21; Plut. *Alex.* 16; *AHA* 1 114–25; *CE* 40–44; Hammond (1980a) 73–76; *GA* 147–54; Hammond (1980b) 75. Arrian claims twenty thousand Greek mercenaries were present, a figure rejected by many scholars, for example, Badian (1977) 284. Devine suggests four thousand to five thousand as a reasonable number (1986) 271–72. For the topography see Foss (1977) 501–502, who finds no topographical impediments to a battle at the riverbank. *AG* 70–72 locates the ancient riverbed one kilometer to the east of the modern stream and thus closer to the foothills.

donians, and even a slight advantage in height would have lent impetus to their missiles. In addition horses—thanks to their powerful hindquarters, as already noted—move upslope with great confidence and control, even increasing their speed without encouragement from the rider if they are given their head. That such an attack was not logical means nothing, for Alexander's leadership was largely intuitive, and he certainly knew the value of the daring and unexpected.

At Issus in 333 Alexander again faced a Persian army that had taken up a defensive position on the far side of a stream bed. Here the battle lines ran roughly east and west along the river Pinarus, with the flanks bordered by the sea on the west and by mountains on the east (Alexander's right). Darius placed his infantry, including thirty thousand Greek mercenaries, in the center, while most of his cavalry were on his right, the seaward side, as he saw more room for his horsemen to maneuver there. Darius himself seems to have been in the center or somewhere to the left of center, with more cavalry and infantry on his left. There was some initial skirmishing in the foothills to the east, where the Macedonians were successful at preventing a Persian outflanking movement. A major cavalry fight developed on the other wing, where Parmenio and the Thessalians were extremely hard pressed, but it was mainly a holding action. The main attack was carried out by the right wing, with the Paeonians and *prodromoi* leading the way in front of the Companions. This advance, which was directed at Darius, somewhat to the left, developed into a rapid charge in order to avoid a heavy discharge of Persian missiles. Once again Macedonian superiority at hand-to-hand fighting proved decisive, as the Persian troops around Darius broke and fled. Yet Alexander's unusually rapid charge had opened a gap on his left between the cavalry and infantry, and Darius' Greek mercenaries exploited it. A fierce but indecisive infantry fight developed, but since Darius and those around him were already in flight, it was wasted effort by the mercenaries and their Persian comrades. News of Darius' flight and a flank attack by the Macedonian right broke their spirit, and the general Persian collapse forced the Persian cavalry on their right to disengage from the Thessalians and flee.[113]

113. Arr. *Anab.* 2.8–11; Diod. 17.33–34; Plut. *Alex.* 20; Quint. Curt. 3.9.11; *AHA* 1 206–17; *CE* 60–62; *AG* 100–106; *GA* 170–80. Plutarch's very brief mention of the battle describes a flank attack by Alexander as the only tactical operation, giving no other details. This is likely to be a misplaced emphasis on the flanking move that Arrian describes as occurring after the rout of Darius. Given the physical obstacles on the flanks and numerical superiority of the Persians, there is no reason to believe that Alexander planned a flanking movement as the decisive stroke. The evidence of the other three sources suggests that Darius and his entourage were the principal focus of attack from the beginning. Polybius, citing

These cavalry, encumbered by heavier armor, suffered severely during the pursuit.[114]

Once again, Alexander's decision to strike at the critical spot was decisive, as Darius' flight took the fight out of his infantry in the center and the cavalry on his right, who had been holding their own against the phalanx and the Thessalians. Alexander's grasp of the psychological aspect of battle was an essential part of his success, but it rested on the confidence he had in his cavalry's ability to penetrate the enemy line with hand-to-hand fighting.

The final large battle against the Persians in Mesopotamia at Gaugamela in 330 led to Darius' death and the dissolution of the Persian Empire. The terrain, generally unencumbered but in places prepared by the Persians, favored their cavalry and chariots, which greatly outnumbered Alexander's forces. The primary concern of the Macedonians was to avoid being outflanked on both wings. Fuller correctly describes Alexander's task as "to defeat an attack of double-envelopment by an attack of penetration."[115]

Cavalry occupied the flanks of both battle lines. Alexander's infantry were stationed in the center in two lines, the Macedonian phalanx facing the Persians and a second line—apparently Greek allies and mercenaries—with orders to face to the rear in the event of an encirclement. The Persian center, where Darius took his usual place, appears to have been a mix of infantry and cavalry, with elephants (not referred to again and ignored in modern reconstructions) and chariots in front. Darius had also stationed cavalry and chariots in front of each wing. As a precaution against the danger of being outflanked by the more numerous Persians, Alexander placed several cavalry units on each flank angled to the rear of the main line. On the right these comprised the Paeonians, the *prodromoi*, and the mercenary cavalry. Directly in front of the Companion Cavalry on the right were the Agrianians, the archers, and the javelin men.

As the two battle lines approached each other, Alexander moved obliquely toward his right as a further counter against a Persian flanking movement with the intention of reaching uneven ground beyond the area that had been prepared by the Persians for their chariots and cavalry. In response Darius

---

Callisthenes, also notes Alexander's desire to face Darius (12.22.1). See Fuller, *GA* 59–60; Bosworth, *CE* 61, which represents a change from an earlier position that depended on Plutarch, *AHA* 1 213. Favoring a flank attack are Hammond, *AG* 105 and Green (1974) 231.

114. The fact that at least some Persian cavalry were more heavily armored than the Macedonians helps explain the latter's superiority in close combat where unencumbered mobility was essential. See Atkinson (1980) 238; Bosworth, *AHA* 1 215.

115. *GA* 168.

ordered the cavalry on his left to put a stop to Alexander's lateral movement. As a result a cavalry fight developed with the Macedonian skirmishers (the Paeonians, *prodromoi*, and so forth), becoming a major clash as each side fed more cavalry units into the struggle. The Macedonian horsemen were initially forced back by enemy numbers, but—supported by reinforcements—they regrouped and charged, squadron by squadron, until they disrupted the Persian cavalry formation. In the meantime a gap had opened in the Persian line due to the departure of cavalry units to the flank, and Alexander was close enough to take advantage of the mistake. Forming a wedge of Companion Cavalry and part of the phalanx, he charged into the breach, heading straight for Darius. Once again the fierce hand-to-hand combat of the Macedonians broke the Persian resistance and a rout ensued. At some point during this struggle on the Macedonian right the Persian chariots charged Alexander's position, but they did no substantial harm, either being disabled by arrows and javelins or allowed to pass harmlessly through the ranks, which had been trained to receive them. The pursuit lasted until nightfall, but Darius escaped.[116]

Evidence of Alexander's concern to bring his enemies to bay so that he could shatter their resistance with a direct attack is also apparent in the Macedonians' battle against the Scythians on the northeast frontier of the Persian Empire in 329. The highly mobile mounted Scythian archers practiced hit-and-run, in-and-out tactics that allowed them to avoid the more static hand-to-hand fighting preferred by the Macedonians. This episode is of particular military interest, because it shows Alexander at his best, effectively employing various arms and technologies.

Alexander had just put down a rebellion in the satrapy of Bactria and felt it was necessary to intimidate the Scythians, whose cavalry had been drawn south to the border formed by the river Jaxartes (modern Syr-Darya) in the hope of finding the Macedonians vulnerable to attack.[117] His first problem was to discover a way to cross the river in the face of an enemy who occupied the opposite bank. The means of crossing was conventional: swimming, straw-stuffed skin floats, ships, and rafts. The clearing of the opposite bank was more novel, as Alexander ordered the arrow-shooting catapults to fire upon the Scythians. Impressed by the unexpected range and penetrating power of the missiles, the Scythians withdrew some distance

---

116. Arr. *Anab.* 3.11–15; Diod. 17.57–61; Quint. Curt. 4.13–16; Plut. *Alex.* 33. *AHA* 1 297–312; *CE* 80–85; *AG* 139–48; *GA* 153–80.
117. Arr. *Anab.* 4.3.6.

from the river.[118] That was all Alexander needed to effect a crossing. He first landed foot archers and slingers, who kept the Scythians at a distance while the infantry and cavalry crossed.[119] Once his forces were across, Alexander launched his attack with a hipparchy of mercenary cavalry and four squadrons of lancers (*sarissophoroi*). The nimble Scythians declined to receive this attack and, confident in their numbers, rode around the troops, shooting their arrows with little risk to themselves. Alexander then combined archers and the Agrianian javelin men with his cavalry and led them against the Scythians. When they were close enough, he sent three hipparchies of Companions and the mounted javelin men ahead and followed with a charge of the remaining cavalry squadrons in column formation. This disrupted the ring of encircling riders and—although details are not given—with the aid of the light infantry, seems to have brought some of them to bay. The Scythians broke off the fight and fled, suffering 1,000 casualties and 150 captured.[120] Whatever the details of how it was done, Alexander was able to thwart the traditional Scythian tactics and this (as Fuller suggests), rather than the casualties, seems to have brought them to terms.[121]

Alexander's last major battle was fought on the banks of the Hydaspes River in 326 against the Indian prince, Porus.[122] On this occasion enemy numbers did not present a serious problem, since Porus had only his local troops, not an imperial levy. Porus had earlier refused to offer even token submission to Alexander and apparently felt confident that he could prevent a Macedonian crossing of the Hydaspes. In the event he was proved wrong, and Alexander succeeded in secretly and quickly bringing over 6,000 infantry and 5,000 cavalry. The remaining forces were left in camp at the ford to the south where the two armies had originally faced each other.[123] The numbers for Porus' army, as given by Arrian, were 4,000 cavalry, 300 chariots, 200 ele-

---

118. This was not a true use of catapults as field artillery, since the machines were protected from the enemy by the river. Until the Romans of the empire mounted catapults on animal-drawn carts (*carroballistae*), stationary catapults were too vulnerable to be useful on the battlefield. Trajan's column contains representations of *carroballistae*. Bosworth *AHA* 2 28/9 prefers the version of Curtius (7.9.2–9), who says that ship-borne catapults cleared the riverbank immediately prior to landing.

119. Contributing to the effectiveness of this were the greater accuracy of foot over mounted archers; in addition to injury, the unsettling effect that lead sling bullets had on the Scythian horses; and the unwillingness of the Scythians to close with the unarmored archers and slingers and sweep them away as lance-bearing cavalry could have done. For the effect of slingers on horses, see *GSW* 5 60.

120. Arr. *Anab.* 4.4.4–9; Quint. Curt 7.9.1–16; *GA* 237–41; *CE* 110–11; *AHA* 2 30.
121. *GA* 239.
122. Arr. *Anab.* 5.8.4–18.3; *AHA* 2 262–311.
123. Arr. *Anab.* 5.11.3–4, 14.1.

phants, and about 30,000 infantry, the latter apparently quite poor by Macedonian standards.[124] It was the elephants that made a direct crossing impossible and consequently forced Alexander to make some tactical changes. In spite of his having captured some elephants earlier in 326, it was clear that the Macedonian horses had not adjusted to their presence sufficiently that they could be trusted to cross a river when opposed by these great beasts.[125]

After the successful crossing Alexander led his 5,000 cavalry on ahead, confident of his superiority in this arm and determined to make an attack on Porus as soon as he found him. He was met by an advance party of 2,000 cavalry and 120 chariots commanded by Porus' son. Thinking initially that this was the main Indian army, he sent the mounted archers ahead (Sacae and Dahae, according to Curtius) in order to blunt their attack and then followed with the cavalry by squadron rather than in line. It proved to be an easy victory, and Porus' son was among the 400 killed. The chariots were immobilized by river mud and captured.[126]

When Porus learned of these events, he moved his main army north to meet Alexander, leaving a small force—including some elephants—to prevent the rest of the Macedonians from crossing in his rear. Finding suitable ground for his cavalry, he stopped and formed his battle line. Porus placed his elephants in a line across his front, where they would deter the Macedonian cavalry and deal appropriately with the infantry. The Indian infantry were behind the elephants, while the cavalry covered the flanks. Chariots were posted in front of the cavalry. When Alexander came up and saw the Indian dispositions, he realized that the line of elephants in front would prevent him from charging Porus' center. Consequently, he decided to attack Porus' left with his superior cavalry. Making initial contact once again were the mounted archers, whose task as skirmishers was to throw the enemy into disorder by means of their missiles and the charge itself. This occurred while the Indian cavalry were moving to their left in order to keep pace with Alexander's attack in that direction, the purpose of which was to strike the

---

124. Some scholars have suggested that more Macedonian troops must have filtered across before the battle, but there is no evidence of this in the sources. Bosworth's account seems closest to the sources, *CE* 127. Bosworth also points out that neither side could remove all forces from the riverbank without betraying their intentions. Different figures for Porus' army are found in the other sources. Curtius (8.13.6) omits the cavalry and lists only 85 elephants; Diodorus has 50,000 infantry, 3,000 cavalry, 1,000 chariots, and 130 elephants (17.87.2); and Plutarch mentions only 20,000 infantry and 2,000 cavalry (*Alex.* 62.1). Noteworthy is the fact that Alexander was superior in cavalry both in number and—as events showed—in fighting quality.

125. Arr. *Anab.* 4.30.7–9, 5.11.4.

126. Ibid., 5.15.1–2. Quint. Curt. 8.14.5.

Indian flank before there was time to deploy from column to line. To compound matters for the Indians, two hipparchies under the command of Coenus appeared in their rear, probably passing behind the Indian infantry.[127] The Indian horsemen, not wanting to receive Alexander's charge, retired to the elephants, which in turn were led against the cavalry. The Macedonian infantry engaged the elephants about the same time. Encouraged by the elephants' initial success, the reformed Indian cavalry charged Alexander but were driven back. The Indians were then forced together into a confused mass, attacked by the phalanx from the front and by cavalry on the flanks and rear. The killing lasted until a gap appeared in the Macedonian cavalry and the survivors fled. The elephants had been dealt with by shooting their drivers and disabling the animals themselves with spears, swords, and axes. Meanwhile, Craterus had crossed the Hydaspes in Porus' rear and appeared in time to add fresh troops to the ruthless pursuit.[128]

In spite of the imperfect nature of the sources, a consistent residue of information from the six battles just described remains, permitting a reasonably accurate picture of Alexander's cavalry tactics. Although it seems clear that Alexander made a great personal contribution to the practices and principles that had evolved in Greek and Macedonian warfare up to the time of his accession, it is not obvious that the tactics characterizing his battles were the natural outgrowth of his inheritance. Perhaps the most important reason for this is the fact that he was a realist. Thus his tactics were strongly influenced by the fighting style of his Persian opponents. With their numerous fine missile-hurling cavalry, poorly supported by weak infantry, they encouraged Alexander to place more emphasis upon mounted troops than would have been the case had he fought his battles against typical Greek armies, whose strength lay in the phalanx. A second influence was his "heroic" view of battle—one might almost say, his "Achilles complex"—at a time in Greek warfare when the typical general was gradually becoming less a hoplite and

---

127. There is a question regarding where these cavalry under Coenus came from. Arrian (5.16.3) says that Coenus' force was sent to the right (Porus' right, to judge from the context), with orders to attack from the rear when the Indians were occupied with the mass of cavalry over against them. Curtius (8.14.17) says merely that Coenus charged the left (presumably in the rear). If these hipparchies rode around Porus' right and eventually attacked his left rear, either the battle line was short or Alexander's attack on Porus' left took considerable time to develop. Fuller, *GA* 196–97 suggests that Alexander sent Coenus to Porus' right, concealed by a dip in the ground, with orders to return (in front of Porus' battle line) when Porus' cavalry were engaged with Alexander's and strike their flank and rear. Bosworth suggests that they came around behind the Indian infantry, *AHA* 2 296.

128. Arr. *Anab.* 5.16.1–18.3; Quint. Curt 8.14.17–30; Diod. 17.87–88; Plut. *Alex.* 60.1–6; *CE* 128–29; *AG* 206–10; *GA* 190–99.

more a battle manager.[129] A third point is that—except for numbers—Alexander always had superior fighting ability at his disposal, so that a significant military asymmetry existed between his forces and those of his enemies. Most of this superiority resulted from the inherent qualities of the Macedonian army and was based on discipline, training, arms skill, professionalism, and cultural outlook, all of which had been enhanced by experience.

Added to this was the intangible effect of Alexander's personal genius. Though this is impossible to analyze and quantify, it is nevertheless essential not to underestimate its role, as exemplified in his intuitive response to battlefield conditions; in the emotional, charismatic, and virtually unmatched personal effect that he had on his soldiers; and in the intimidating intensity with which he applied military force. For these reasons Alexander cannot be judged purely within the context of Greek military history, nor should his successors be overly criticized for not matching his success. Comparison is difficult, if only because they fought against a different kind of army. Although Alexander's success was largely sui generis, a description of the tactical principles upon which it rested will help to explain that success.

Under ideal circumstances Alexander preferred to achieve his aim of conquest by a quick, decisive victory in open battle—a continuation of Greek practice. Nevertheless, he was prepared to employ any type of military activity necessary to defeat the immediate enemy he faced, whether this required relentless siege operations, the seizing of mountain strongholds, small-scale campaigns of some variety, or large battles in the open. In his major battles, our present subject of concern, he usually hoped to achieve victory by direct frontal attack on the enemy line in order to penetrate it and bring about its collapse—a result not to be expected had he ever fought a good Greek army.

When Alexander formed his battle line prior to an engagement in the open, it is clear that there was a standard disposition. Following Greek and Macedonian practice in general, the cavalry were stationed on both wings, with the infantry phalanx stretching in a long line of eight or more ranks in between. The Macedonian cavalry always took their place on the right, tactically the more aggressive wing under Alexander's direct command. Allied cavalry, except for several specific units, were placed on the left.[130] The Thessalian cavalry, second only to the Macedonians in prestige and probably their equal in fighting ability, were usually found on the left. This was not de rigueur, however, for at Issus they were transferred to the left from an original position on

---

129. See Wheeler (1991), in Hanson, 121–70.
130. Arr. *Anab.* 1.2.5, 14.1–3, 2.8.9, 3.11.8, 5.13.4; Diod. 17.19.6, 32.1, 57.1; Quint. Curt. 3.9.8.

the right.[131] Two qualities set the Macedonian army apart from any Greek army that had sufficient cavalry to cover its flanks in this way: fighting ability and the way in which Alexander employed the various units during the course of the battle.

Based on this formation, Alexander's tactical plan was conceptually straightforward and simple. The left and center were to provide resistance, whereby the enemy would be held and occupied. This was dangerous and very exhausting work, often demanding more continuous effort than that of the more mobile right wing, as Parmenio—who commanded the left until his execution in 330—well knew. The function of the infantry and cavalry of the right wing was to move against the enemy at a decisive point and cause a collapse that permitted penetration. They could then attack the newly created interior flanks and the rear in the hope of inducing panic that would lead to flight. The specifics always seem to have been based on the environment of each battle, for Alexander always exhibited a great appreciation of the enemy dispositions that faced him.

The attack was initiated by the mounted skirmishers on the right wing and carried through by the cavalry of the line, sometimes in conjunction with infantry units. The skirmishers had the unenviable task of drawing first blood against numerically superior opponents. This task was an integral part of Alexander's tactics, for it initiated the disruption of the enemy units (usually cavalry), forced them to use up some of their missiles, and took the edge off their fighting spirit before the Macedonian cavalry—fresh, well-formed, and under Alexander's direct leadership—closed for hand-to-hand combat. Skirmishers had indeed been part of Greek armies for centuries, but Alexander assigned them a truly critical role that required more vigorous fighting and staying power than they had previously exhibited. The attack of the cavalry of the line and the accompanying infantry of the right wing was directed at the Persian center or left center, where the commanders were usually found. At Issus and Gaugamela this was Darius himself, and at these battles there were strategic as well as tactical reasons for the particular point of attack.[132]

The subsequent penetration of the Persian line depended on successful close combat with hand-held weapons, a type of fighting in which the Macedonians were clearly superior. This "shock" action was as much psychological as physical against enemies not well prepared for it, having the advantage

---

131. Arr. *Anab.* 1.14.3, 2.8.9, 9.1, 3.11.8; Diod. 17.19.6, 32.1, 57.1; Quint. Curt. 3.9.8.

132. Arr. *Anab.* 2.8.11; 3.11.5. Note Keegan's comparison of Alexander and Wellington, whose method in this regard was "to make the elite their target and break it by ferocious attack" (1987) 148.

of producing quicker and more decisive results. Deviation from this tactical plan at the Hydaspes resulted from a decision Alexander made on the spot upon seeing the line of elephants across the Indian front and shows his grasp of reality and ability to adapt quickly to local circumstances.[133] On this occasion the advantage in fighting ability and the opportunity to attack the Indians simultaneously from the flank and rear were decisive. The infantry phalanx bore more than its usual responsibility in the battle since it faced the full fury of the elephants.

Once disruption of the opposing line was achieved, Alexander made every effort to destroy the fleeing army by means of a vigorous pursuit, often for a considerable distance. Achieving this was not as simple as it sounds, since a great deal of energy was expended in the battle itself. Genuinely effective pursuits have been relatively rare in military history, and Alexander's success in this respect testifies to the degree of discipline and conditioning of the Macedonians.[134]

When Alexander crossed from Europe to Asia Minor in 334, intent upon destroying the Persian Empire by a war of annihilation, there is every reason to believe that he was aware of the advantage his army possessed in respect to fighting ability. For generations the Greeks had believed in their military superiority over the Persians, and a detailed description of Greek success against Persians could be read in Xenophon's *Anabasis*. As early as 380 the Athenian orator Isocrates began to advocate a great crusade against the Persians as a means of uniting the fractious Greek states. This was based largely on an awareness of Persian military weakness. Eventually, in 346, Isocrates addressed his appeal directly to Philip, Alexander's father.[135] Consequently, the best explanation of Alexander's tactics of direct attack and penetration lies in his conscious awareness of this differential in fighting power and his correct assessment of how to take advantage of it. The frequency and success of his pursuits is circumstantial evidence in support of this, insofar as comparatively quick, decisive victories on the battlefield meant that there was proportionately more energy remaining for pursuit.[136] Also contributing to Alexander's success was a command structure that permitted orders and instructions to be issued prior to battle, including options that were contingent upon what

---

133. Arr. *Anab.* 5.16.2.
134. Weigley (1991) xv.
135. Isoc. *Paneg.* 3, 66–68, 138–39, *Phil.* 16, 83–105, 127–55.
136. For an example of a victorious army "too much fatigued to follow the enemy," see de Rocca (1990) 68.

the enemy did during the course of the battle.[137] Thus there was nothing derelict—except for the danger to his own person and the royal house—about his determination to be in the thick of the fighting. His presence, leading the attacking right wing contributed more to eventual victory than any orders he might have been able to give from some vantage point away from the fighting.

Because this book is a study of cavalry operations, I should point out that there is no evidence that Alexander favored cavalry over the other arms when he chose the forces with which to confront the enemy on any given occasion. Two incidents in India show this very clearly. After victory on the Hydaspes he marched against the Cathaeans, an autonomous people living south of the kingdom of Porus. He found them in a defensive position on a hill behind three lines of wagons. When he led the cavalry of the right wing against the wagons, the Indians refused to come out and simply shot volleys of arrows against the horsemen. Realizing the futility of using cavalry, he dismounted and successfully led the phalanx against the wagons. Shortly thereafter, against the Malli, he went ahead with the cavalry, leaving the infantry to catch up as soon as they could. When the large number of Mallian infantry realized that only the cavalry were present, they formed up and prepared to offer resistance. Alexander, seeing that the formation was solid, decided to wait for his infantry, content for the time being to have his horsemen circle and advance but not come to close quarters.[138]

Yet this appreciation of each arm is nowhere more apparent than in the composition of the many ad hoc smaller formations of several arms that were detailed for a variety of special assignments. Indeed, during the long periods between the major battles Alexander was usually busy addressing countless problems that required the use of military force. At least two dozen of these special details are mentioned by Arrian, unfortunately without much description of the fighting in which they engaged. What is of interest, however, is that no matter what the task—these details—with few exceptions, comprised both infantry and cavalry, often more than one type of each.[139]

Excluding reconnaissance missions, Arrian makes reference to twenty-seven of these expeditions that were sent out or led by Alexander during the years from 335 to 324.[140] When he was assembling the special forces, Alexan-

---

137. Arr. *Anab.* 1.14.1; 2.8.4, 9.1; 3.12.1, 12.4, 13.6; 5.16.3. This instructing one's subordinates in what is now called a "common tactical doctrine" was also essential to Admiral Nelson's success during the Napoleonic Wars. See Weigley (1991) 327.
138. Arr. *Anab.* 5.22.5–23.3; 6.8.5–7.
139. Green (1974) 134 dubs these "commando brigades."
140. Arr. *Anab.* 1.5.10, 6.9, 19.8, 20.5; 2.4.3, 4.6, 5.1, 5.6, 20.4; 3.8.2, 18.2, 18.5, 21.2–7, 24.1, 25.6, 29, 7; 4.3.7, 22.1, 22.7, 23.1, 25.6; 5.2.5; 6.6.1, 16.1, 21.3, 22.1, 29.1.

der chose from five different types of troops: two mounted (line cavalry and skirmishers) and three infantry (phalangites, javelin men [the Agranians], and archers). On seven of these twenty-seven occasions he used all five types of troops; details of four and three types were used six times each, while he limited himself to two types eight times. The only time infantry was excluded occurred just prior to Gaugamela, when a Persian cavalry force of about one thousand appeared ahead of the Macedonians and Alexander led the Royal Squadron, one squadron of Companions, and the Paeonian *prodromoi* against them. Since his intent was to capture some of the Persian riders, who fled at his approach, the slower infantry would have been of no use in the pursuit.[141] As for cavalry, they were left out only three times: in 335 during a night attack on an unguarded camp of Illyrians in the Balkans; in 333 in a night march on the Cilician Gates; and shortly thereafter on a short campaign into the Cilician highlands.[142] In all three instances rough terrain was presumably the reason for not using cavalry. The fact that two of these events took place at night should have no bearing, since horses see well in the dark.

Perhaps the clearest indication of the value that Alexander placed on a mixed force comes from the final pursuit of Darius in 330. With his troops already weary from several days of forced marches, Alexander decided upon a nighttime dash across fifty miles of desert. As it was obvious that the infantry would not be able to keep up, he dismounted five hundred cavalrymen and replaced them with infantry carrying their usual arms. They were clearly intended to fight on foot once they arrived at their destination.[143]

Of the infantry types the phalangites were used most frequently (nineteen times).[144] The Agranians and the archers were usually used together (fifteen times), whereas each appeared only once on its own. The total number of troops used on any occasion also varied considerably, ranging from approximately twenty-five hundred to more than ten thousand.[145] Sometimes all the available troops of one type were chosen, at other times only a portion. For

141. Arr. *Anab.* 3.8.2.
142. Ibid., 1.6.9; 2.4.3, 5.6; *AHA* 1 189–90, 195.
143. Arr. *Anab.* 3.21.2–7; Quint. Curt. 5.13.8, who gives their number as three hundred and calls them *dimachae*, a term used to refer to mounted infantry. Obviously the infantry chosen knew how to ride, but one may ask how, if they had not been riding enough to keep their leg muscles in condition, they survived a fifty-mile ride well enough to walk, much less able to fight.
144. This includes regular phalangites and hypaspists. The hypaspists were an elite infantry force usually stationed on the center right between the phalanx and the cavalry and perhaps acting as some sort of link between them. *CE* 259–60.
145. Arr. *Anab.* 4.3.7; 1.20.5. These figures are not precise, since Arrian often names the units rather than the number.

example, six hundred—or one half—or all the Companion Cavalry might be used.[146] The number of infantry from the Macedonian phalanx that were used varied from fifteen hundred (one *taxis*) to six thousand (four *taxeis*).[147]

This consistent practice of employing military formations comprising a mixture of arms under a great variety of circumstances was a fundamental principle of Alexander's tactics. Although not uncommon among their Greek predecessors, this coordination of arms reached a new level of application under Philip and Alexander that rested upon noticeably enhanced fighting ability. With respect to the line cavalry, their relationship to the adjacent infantry can best be described as articulation—a more physically interdependent relationship than coordination. Implicit in this was an understanding of the fighting qualities of the several types of troops and an ability to deploy them in a way whereby the whole was, indeed, greater than the sum of the parts.

Without any doubt Alexander was a military genius, and—as I have said—precisely because of that he defied successful emulation. Moreover, it remains difficult to offer a definitive judgment of his tactical ability, because his army never faced a comparable Greek formation in open battle. If we knew more about his part in the battle of Chaeronea as well as his handling of the Greek mercenaries in the Persian armies, a better answer might be forthcoming. Granted his tactical open-mindedness and exceptional adaptability, no doubt his tactics against a unified Greek army under the command of the likes of a Timoleon would have been instructive, but it is unlikely that he could have matched the decisiveness of his victories over the Persians. It is even possible that the ferocity and intensity of his fighting style would have been counterproductive against the Greeks, with whom a lasting political relationship was desirable. Historically, of course, such hypothetical reflections are meaningless, since one must defeat only the enemy of the moment. This Alexander never failed to do.

---

146. Ibid., 1.20.5, 4.22.1, 22.7.
147. Ibid., 3.29.7; 4.22.1.

Part 4

The Aftermath: 323 to 150 B.C.

Chapter 13

The Successors from the Death of Alexander to the Battle of Ipsus: 323 to 301 B.C.

R. WEIGLEY REMARKS OF THE great French commander that "Napoleon Bonaparte was scarcely the model type of the professional soldier . . . his place in the intellectual evolution of military leadership is not that of an outstanding professional but that of a genius, whose mental and intuitive powers reached far beyond any understanding that schooling alone might have supplied."[1] The same comment can be applied to Alexander, a fact that helps explain the difficulty of comparing the deeds of the Successors with the spectacular military career of the young Macedonian king. Although individually they could not match his military genius, the generals who fought each other for pieces of his empire were by and large first-rate professionals who had learned well from the thirteen years of almost constant campaigning that comprised his reign. Unlike their king, several of the Successors lived long enough to consolidate their military victories by means of statesmanship, administrative and organizational skills, and a bit of luck, with the result that they created kingdoms that became the focal points of the Hellenistic Age.[2]

Their collective military performance is perhaps unsurpassed in history. The only comparable groups that come to mind are the generals of Genghis Khan in the thirteenth century and those of the Wehrmacht in the twentieth. In fairness to the Successors it must be admitted that Alexander—as is evident from the preceding chapter—was in many ways an anomaly, and whereas his great success called forth generations of emulators, none was his equal. In

---

1. Weigley (1991) 307.
2. For a sound, readable narrative of the Hellenistic period and its culture see Green (1990).

reality it was Philip who set the standard by which the Successors should be judged. Although a lesser genius than his son, Philip transformed the Macedonian army, created the Macedonian state, and practiced the highest level of statecraft of his age. Unfortunately, this comparison, at least from the military perspective, is impossible because of the meager sources for Philip's reign.

That is not to say that Alexander had no influence on the age following him. Quite the contrary, for even the memory of him in the decades following his death was at times almost palpable.[3] What is difficult is the evaluation of his military influence, for even if some individuals among the Successors appreciated all the various facets of his success, none of them had sufficient opportunity to apply them effectively to the military problems that presented themselves. Complicating matters for the Successors was the simple fact that they knew each other well from the years during which they had shared campaigns under Alexander. Knowing each other's personal strengths and weaknesses both helped and hurt them all, probably most limiting their opportunity to do the unexpected.[4] Furthermore, it can be doubted whether anyone completely understood the reasons for Alexander's astonishing career. Even his officers, who obviously discussed tactics and other military matters both before and after his death among themselves, would not have had complete insight. An accurate perception of what is transpiring in one's very presence is a rare gift. The Successors, who had been his generals, must have had a better understanding of these matters than outsiders, but those who heard of his victories at second or third hand may have been overly impressed by the apparent rather than the real cause of success. It would have been most difficult to grasp the point at which his genius took over, going beyond the skilled application of military principles.

One of the obvious contributing causes of Alexander's success was cavalry. Consequently, the uses to which the mounted arm was put after his death should tell us much about how well his methods were understood and might even offer a hint of the fate his tactics would have had if they had been brought

---

3. According to Plutarch (*Alex.* 74.4), when Cassander was king of Macedon the mere sight of an image of Alexander at Delphi produced shuddering, trembling, and a near faint.

4. In his memoirs of the American Civil War, U. S. Grant draws special attention to the fact that he benefited from personal knowledge of many of the leading generals of the Confederacy that he gained at West Point and during the Mexican war. "A large part of the National Army, for instance, and most of the press of the country, clothed General Lee with just such [almost superhuman] abilities, but I had known him personally, and knew that he was mortal; and it was just as well that I felt this." Grant (1989) 96. See also 151, where it is clear that knowledge of General Pillow's inclination not to send out scouts enabled Grant to make a personal reconnaissance of his lines without danger.

into play against contemporary Greek and Macedonian armies. Complicating the comparison with Alexander is the fact that the Successors employed elephants on a regular basis, whereas Alexander never used them in battle, perhaps because elephant behavior was too unpredictable to fit well with his tactics. Irrespective of how useful these beasts proved to be in the following decades, their presence would have influenced the tactical planning and operations of commanders in the field.

Alexander's premature death exposed the regions of the eastern Mediterranean to decades of political confusion, disruption of everyday life, and almost incessant warfare as the Successors worked out among themselves the political dynamics of an empire that had been held together by the forceful character and constant campaigning of one man rather than the less personal bond of political institutions. The commanding presence that had taken a comparatively small Macedonian army to what must have seemed to his soldiers like the ends of the earth was at no time more noticeable than in its absence. Dynastic forces had never been very strong in Macedon, and Alexander's half-brother Arrhidaeus and posthumous son Alexander IV proved to be nonentities who were doomed from the start.[5] As a result, at the same time that disputes arose in the army in Asia, the subject states in Greece began to contemplate casting off the Macedonian yoke.

If, at the mere rumor of his demise in 335, Thebes had rebelled and several other states in Greece had wavered, it was small wonder that many of them were eager to make a serious try for freedom in 323.[6] Adding to Greek hopes was the realization that many good Macedonian troops were still away in the East. Two other circumstances had a stimulating effect on these events. The Athenians were already considering war in 324 in order to avoid implementing Alexander's decree regarding the restoration of exiles, which would have required them to return the island of Samos to its former occupants. Furthermore, Antipater, the vice-regent in Macedon, was slow to respond to events in Greece, thus encouraging those who might be wavering. In 335 Alexander had marched rapidly into Greece at the first hint of trouble, and his unexpected presence south of Thermopylae put a premature end to debate in

---

5. For discussion of problems of the Succession, see *HM* 3 98–107; Carney (1994) 357–80. See also *CAH* 7 I for the general history of the period.

6. *HM* 3 107–16; Diod. 18.11–17 (for the Lamian War). Since Diodorus provides the only reasonably full account of the events after Alexander, it is fortunate that his primary source for books 18–20 seems to have been Hieronymus of Cardia, an eyewitness to many of the events from Alexander's death to the 270s. See Hornblower (1981). Other references to the Lamian War occur in Justin 14, 5–6; Arr. *Fr. Gr. H.* 156,1.9–12. For a recent translation of Arrian's *Events after Alexander*, see Goralski (1989) 81–108.

the Athenian assembly and effectively isolated Thebes. Admittedly, Antipater did not have an army the equal of Alexander's, but his subsequent behavior in the war that followed suggests that he achieved less with the forces at his disposal than Alexander might have done. This should not be taken as criticism, however, for Antipater was politically wiser than Alexander and used his political skills effectively both in Greece as well as in Asia until his death in 319.[7]

The revolt in Greece proved to be a serious matter, involving a number of military actions on land and sea. It was called the Lamian War after the city in north-central Greece where the initial land action occurred. The majority of the Greeks signed on, including virtually all the Thessalians—a surprising fact given the essential part they had played in Alexander's eastern campaigns and unthinkable were he still alive.

The allies were led by Leosthenes, an Athenian soldier of fortune who had brought eight thousand of Alexander's mercenaries from Asia. Together with the levies of the Greek states, his forces numbered well over twenty thousand. Antipater marched against him with thirteen thousand Macedonian infantry and only six hundred horsemen, the two thousand Thessalian cavalry having gone over to the Greeks. This forced Antipater onto the defensive, as he was now outnumbered in cavalry as well as infantry. Not too surprisingly, the Macedonians were defeated. Nevertheless, their losses were not great and—thanks to their discipline—they retired in good order to Lamia, where they withstood a siege while awaiting reinforcements. Diodorus states that the defection of the Thessalian cavalry gave the Greek allies the advantage in numbers, which led to their victory.[8] This change of sides also explains why Antipater brought so few cavalry with him, for he had counted on the Thessalians. The victory itself did not mean much, for although the allied cavalry controlled the battlefield, they were incapable of harming the well-disciplined Macedonian infantry. In spite of the absence of details about this battle, subsequent events suggest that the Thessalians fought exceptionally well. During the winter of 323/322 Leosthenes was killed during a Macedonian sortie from Lamia and was accorded heroic honors.

In 322 reinforcements for Antipater arrived from Asia Minor under the command of Leonnatus, satrap of Hellespontine Phrygia. Before he could join the Macedonians in Lamia, however, he was intercepted by the Greeks and brought to battle. His twenty thousand infantry and fifteen hundred cavalry

---

7. Baynham (1994) 331–56.
8. Diod. 18.12.3–4.

faced twenty-two thousand foot and thirty-five hundred horse. The allies placed their hopes of victory in the Thessalian cavalry, under the command of Memnon, apparently due to the effective part played by the Thessalians in the first battle as well as fear of the Macedonian phalanx. Nevertheless, it is strange that in both this and the final battle the Greeks should place so much trust in cavalry when historically their strength lay in their infantry. In any event only the cavalry were seriously engaged.

Diodorus says that the battle lasted for a long time. If that is true the Macedonians must have fought well, as they were outnumbered more than two to one. Possibly their only serious mounted opponents were the two thousand Thessalians, "exceptional for their courage," since the Greek cavalry may not have been physically and psychologically prepared for the close combat favored by the Macedonians.[9] After fighting brilliantly, Leonnatus was killed and his body was carried back to the baggage train. The intact phalanx withdrew to rougher terrain to avoid cavalry attacks to the flanks and rear by the victorious Greeks and Thessalians, who occupied the field of battle and erected a trophy. Nevertheless, there had been no rout, and the training and discipline of the Macedonians once again proved their value. In effect the battle was a draw and meant nothing. Antipater arrived the next day bringing the two armies together into one camp under his command. Unwilling to commit his troops to battle while they were inferior in cavalry, which were necessary to protect the flanks, he then withdrew to Macedon.

While stalemate existed on land in the spring of 322, the Macedonians achieved more decisive results in a number of naval encounters in the Aegean Sea. Details are extremely sparse, but it is clear that the Greeks were defeated in several battles between late spring and midsummer. In the third and final encounter the Macedonian fleet commander, Cleitus, a former hipparch of Alexander, defeated the Athenian admiral, Euetion, off Amorgos and ended Athens' role as a naval power forever.[10]

In spite of this the Greeks remained confident on land because of their recent victories. The odds were substantially altered, however, when Craterus, one of Alexander's great generals, brought more reinforcements from Cilicia in Asia Minor. According to Diodorus, the Macedonian army that now reentered Thessaly numbered forty thousand heavy infantry, three thousand archers and slingers, and five thousand cavalry. In August of 322 the final battle took place

9. Ibid., 18.15.2.
10. *HM* 3 113.

in central Thessaly near Crannon, south of the Peneus River. The Greek allies were at a numerical disadvantage, having only twenty-five thousand infantry and thirty-five hundred cavalry. With their infantry inferior both in number and quality, their tactical decision to risk all on a cavalry fight was predictable. Their hopes once again rested upon the Thessalians, and as far as the cavalry fight went, they were justified. So determined were the allies to make this a cavalry battle, they initially stationed the cavalry in front of the infantry line. Whether he was prepared for this disposition or merely took advantage of what presented itself, Antipater wisely ignored the cavalry fight, even though it was going badly for the Macedonians, and led his phalanx against the enemy infantry. The way that he avoided the fighting horsemen is not mentioned. Perhaps the cavalry had moved out of the way. The Greeks were no match for the Macedonian phalanx and withdrew to rough ground, followed shortly by their cavalry, who broke off their fight with the Macedonian horse. Neither side had inflicted much loss on the other, with the dead reported to be 500 for the Greeks and 150 for the Macedonians. Diodorus' claim that the allied cavalry were successful may be doubted, as the Macedonian horse were not routed and, in fact, by keeping the enemy horsemen engaged they gave Antipater the chance to use his infantry without interference.

This rather mild defeat coupled with the more decisive losses at sea broke the will of the allies, although at first they collectively insisted upon peace terms. After further nudging by Antipater, who began a systematic reduction of the cities of Thessaly, they settled with him individually, their alliance destroyed. The terms were lenient, which was politically wise, and it may be that Antipater's desire for political conciliation explains the lack of vigor with which he prosecuted the war. This desire is also understandable given the fact that neither Antipater nor most of his troops had served with Alexander. Nevertheless, considering the size of his army at Crannon, the modest result is militarily disappointing and exhibits little evidence of Alexander's influence.[11]

In spite of the brevity of the battle descriptions, the actions of the Lamian War are of considerable tactical interest. The Greeks quickly recognized the value of the Thessalian cavalry and were so confident in their superior fighting ability that they made no effort to coordinate its role with that of the infantry. That was a mistake, for although it was successful in the first two battles, it was not decisive, and on both occasions the Macedonian phalanx

---

11. Diod. 18.6.4–17.5. *HM* 3 113–14. Perhaps this was partially intentional, as Alexander's harshness would have been politically unwise.

retired intact, well able to fight again another day. In the end the Greeks pushed the odds too far. At Crannon the cavalry were so busy with each other that Antipater was able to attack the enemy infantry with his phalanx virtually at his leisure.

Neither army fought as well as it had in 338 at Chaeronea, and this Greek bid for freedom seems a rather halfhearted affair. The Greek failure to coordinate the two arms seems inexplicable in light of the fact that it had been seen previously in Greek armies and was a hallmark of the Macedonians. Fear of the Macedonian phalanx from the days of Chaeronea may have played a part, and the success of the Thessalians in the first battle may have increased the Greeks' overestimation of cavalry's contribution to success, which returned to Greece with Alexander's discharged mercenaries. Uncritical accounts of Alexander's victories over Persian armies, which were inferior to the Greeks and Macedonians in fighting power, may have suggested to the Greeks that cavalry was the answer to their needs. In this they were obviously mistaken. We cannot ask of them or of the Successors that they be as successful as Alexander, and we must make allowances for the human error that is normal under the chaotic and dangerous conditions of warfare. Nor should we forget von Moltke's comment that "In war with its enormous friction even the mediocre is quite an achievement."[12] Nevertheless, it is worth asking why such poor use was made of cavalry and infantry in combination, given the fact that some thousands of veterans from Asia were present on the Greek side and that Leosthenes, their leader until his death, had also been in Asia. The quality of the troops that Alexander faced in the east has already been mentioned. Some indication of the meaning of qualitative superiority vis-à-vis peoples whom the Greeks considered barbarians can be seen in the Thracian campaigns of Lysimachus following Alexander's death. When Lysimachus was assigned Thrace as his province, he promptly invaded the region in order to bring the rebellious Odrysian king, Seuthes III, to heel. His small force of four thousand infantry and two thousand cavalry was met by twenty thousand and eight thousand respectively. Confident in his troops, he risked battle with characteristic boldness. The result was essentially a draw, but Lysimachus had inflicted many more casualties on the Thracians than his own men had suffered. The immediate sequel to this event is not recorded, although at some point Seuthes again became a Macedonian dependent. Ten years later, in 313, Seuthes was decisively defeated by Lysimachus when he attempted to regain

---

12. Quoted in Van Creveld (1985) 13.

his freedom. The clear advantage of the well-trained and highly disciplined Macedonian troops was recognized by Diodorus.[13]

The next events that shed light on the employment of cavalry occurred in Asia Minor. There, in the growing divisions among the Macedonian leaders, the military skill of Eumenes of Cardia began to manifest itself. A Greek among Macedonians, Eumenes was the only outsider to achieve high military distinction after Alexander's death. He had been secretary to both Philip and Alexander and was commander of a hipparchy of Companions at the end of Alexander's life. In spite of limited military experience during those years, he proved an able and loyal supporter of the legal heirs to the throne of Macedon and the empire—more loyal, in fact, than any of the leading Macedonians except the regent, Perdiccas. When he was assigned to the satrapy of Cappadocia and Paphlagonia in 322, his instructions were to insure the obedience of Armenia, which had been allotted to Neoptolemus, the former companion of Alexander. When Eumenes found that he was unable to work with Neoptolemus and had difficulty with the Macedonian infantry as well, he strengthened his position by creating a body of cavalry from the local population. Plutarch describes these events in some detail, indicating that Eumenes accomplished his task "by offering the natives of the country who were able to serve as horse-men immunity from contributions and tributes, and by distributing horses that he had bought among those of his followers in whom he placed most confidence; the spirits of these men, too, he incited by honours and gifts, and developed their bodies by exercise and discipline; so that a part of the Macedonians were amazed, and a part emboldened, when they saw that in a short time he had assembled about him no fewer than sixty-three hundred horsemen."[14] This rather remarkable accomplishment presupposes a certain level of riding skill among the inhabitants of the region. In light of the subsequent military success of these troops, it also draws attention to the reason for the perennial success of Greco-Roman armies against the barbarians—namely, superiority in organization, training, discipline, and tactics. Alexander's willingness to incorporate eastern troops into his army after suitable training and outfitting also confirms this, and contemporary opposition on the part of the Macedonians was due largely to ethnic bias.

---

13. Diod. 18.14.2–4; 19.78.3. See also *HM* 3 111, 157, where it is said of Lysimachus that he "alone of Alexander's generals came close to him in generalship." His daring and rapidity of movement were especially noteworthy.

14. Plut. *Eum.* 4.2–3. See also Diod. 18.29.3–30.1.

In midsummer 321, while Eumenes was thus occupied with cavalry recruitment, Neoptolemus had come to terms with Craterus to betray him. The plot was uncovered, however, and when Neoptolemus refused an order from Eumenes to submit, both sides prepared to fight. In the resulting battle the Macedonian phalanx, quickly proving itself superior to Eumenes' infantry, routed them. That should have settled the matter, but the victors broke ranks to pursue the fleeing enemy and Eumenes—who had already routed Neoptolemus and his cavalry with his own newly trained horsemen—charged the scattered infantry, forcing them to surrender. Had Neoptolemus' phalanx retained its formation, it is unlikely that Eumenes could have gained much more than a draw. Thus he reaped the benefits of his foresight and gave more than a hint of his military ability.[15]

According to Plutarch, Eumenes then rejected an offer from Craterus and Antipater to abandon Perdiccas and, upon learning that Craterus and Neoptolemus had been sent out against him, he prepared for battle. Each side mustered twenty thousand infantry, but in this arm the advantage clearly lay with Craterus, whose troops were almost all Macedonians, while those of Eumenes were a mixed lot. Eumenes' hopes rested on his cavalry, who had already proved themselves against Neoptolemus and outnumbered those of Craterus five thousand to something over two thousand. This disparity in number and quality reveals something of the problem of recruitment after Alexander's death. During his lifetime there were only two Macedonian armies competing for limited resources of infantry and cavalry, the home army under Antipater and the expeditionary force led by Alexander. After 323, however, as many as five generals in various parts of the empire were trying to raise and maintain armies. Of necessity the problem was met by employing local levies, a practice begun by Alexander himself sometime after 330 when replacements from Macedon declined.[16] The disparity in quality between Macedonian troops and the local levies was most obvious in the case of infantry, because horsemanship was more common in the areas east of Greece and cavalry was traditionally the dominant arm. Thus Eumenes' success is understandable and could not be matched in respect to infantry.

In the battle between Eumenes and Craterus that now took place, the cavalry were stationed on the flanks with the commanders leading their respective

---

15. Plut. *Eum.* 5.3; Diod. 18.29.5–6.
16. *CE* 271–73. *HM* 3 188–89, for estimates of Macedonian troops in various locations, and 125 for information on Asiatics trained in Macedonian weapons and tactics. See also Billows (1995) 183–220.

right wings. In each case they led some of their cavalry out ahead of the infantry. Since Eumenes did not entirely trust the loyalty of his own Macedonian troops in a fight against the well-respected Craterus, he sent two hipparchies (four squadrons?) of foreign cavalry against him while he himself led a picked body of three hundred Macedonians against Neoptolemus. Although the accounts of this battle by Plutarch and Diodorus are similar or complimentary, to a remarkable degree, they differ markedly regarding the fate of Craterus. Both agree that he attacked vigorously and acquitted himself well, but Diodorus describes him as falling from his mount and perishing unrecognized under the hooves of the horses. Plutarch, on the other hand, says that he fell from his horse after a blow to the side by a Thracian and that his body was recognized by one of Eumenes' officers, who guarded him as he lay dying.[17]

Plutarch's rather more detailed description of the cavalry fight portrays exactly what one would expect from officers who had attended Alexander. At the first clash the spears were broken and they then fought with swords, demonstrating a continuation of the hand-to-hand combat favored by Alexander. After Craterus fell, his right wing apparently collapsed and took refuge with the phalanx. The cavalry action on the other wing was more even and longer lasting, having a decisive duel between Eumenes and Neoptolemus as its centerpiece. Two clashes had occurred before they caught sight of each other, at which point they closed with drawn swords. Dropping the reins, they grabbed each other and fell to the ground as their horses rode out from under them. Eumenes rose first and disabled Neoptolemus with a sword stroke behind the knee. Nonetheless, Neoptolemus fought back from his knees and inflicted some annoying but negligible wounds on Eumenes before he was killed by a blow to the neck.[18] Neoptolemus' death and news of the rout on the other wing decided the cavalry fight in Eumenes' favor. The infantry were hardly—if at all—engaged, and the leaderless phalanx of Macedonians came to terms with Eumenes, although subsequently they broke their word and escaped to join Antigonus. The infantry in particular in this fight seem to have been poorly motivated. Nepos reports that Eumenes gave Craterus—an old friend from his days with Alexander—a notable funeral and sent the bones to his wife and sons in Macedonia.[19]

Except for a boost to his prestige, Eumenes had accomplished little either militarily or politically by these victories, and it must be emphasized that he

17. Diod. 18.30.5; Plut. *Eum.* 7.3–4.
18. Diod. 18.31; Plut. *Eum.* 7.4–7. These two accounts are similar in content but not in language.
19. For the entire battle see Diod. 18.30.5–32; Plut. *Eum.* 7; Nep., *Eum.* 4.

was unable to defeat Macedonian infantry as long as they remained in formation. To add to Eumenes' problems, his patron, Perdiccas—the effective regent for Alexander's children—was killed in a mutiny of his Macedonians in Egypt, where he was attacking Ptolemy.[20]

Antipater, the new regent, gave command of the royal army to Antigonus along with instructions to deal with Eumenes. This contemporary of Philip, born about 382, had been serving as satrap of Phrygia since 333 and now began a twenty-year career that brought him closer than any other of the Successors to recreating Alexander's empire until he was killed at the battle of Ipsus in 301. His actions "recall on the one hand the tireless energy of Alexander and on the other the political realism and cunning of Philip II,"[21] and he typically wasted no time in going after Eumenes.

At this point in his narrative Plutarch offers us a glimpse of the perennial problem of supplying remounts for cavalry, one of those essential support functions for ancient armies about which we know little. When Eumenes was preparing for the coming struggle with Antigonus, he "fell in with the royal herds of horse that were pasturing about Mt. Ida, took as many horses as he wanted and sent a written statement of the number to the overseers."[22] Apparently the confusion caused by the struggle for power among the Successors had not disrupted the imperial administration that Alexander had simply taken over from the Persians.

The first battle between Antigonus and Eumenes was decided by treachery—a characteristic of the period that bedevils one's efforts to judge events from a strictly tactical perspective. On paper Eumenes, with twenty thousand infantry and five thousand cavalry against ten thousand infantry (half good Macedonians), two thousand cavalry, and thirty elephants, had the advantage. Unknown to Eumenes, however, his cavalry commander, Apollonides, had been won over by Antigonus and deserted with his men during the battle. The only point of tactical interest is that the site of the battle at Orcynii in Cappadocia was suitable for cavalry.[23]

With his forces reduced to about six hundred, Eumenes sought refuge over the winter of 320/319 in a well-provisioned fortress in the northern Taurus between Cappadocia and Lycaonia called Nora. Some welcome insight

20. Sorting out the changing alliances of Alexander's Macedonian officers after his death is a subject unto itself. A good, succinct account can be found in Errington (1990) 114–61.
21. *CAH* 7, part I, 40 (by E. Will).
22. Plut. *Eum.* 8.3. Presumably these horses would have required training.
23. Diod. 18.40; Plut. *Eum.* 9. 2. *ACHS* 75–76.

into contemporary military preparation is offered by a story reported by Diodorus, Plutarch, and Nepos. The fortress was too small to permit normal conditioning exercises, forcing Eumenes to improvise. Diodorus reports:

> Seeing that the horses, unable to exercise themselves because of the rough and confined space, would become unfit for use in mounted battle, Eumenes devised a certain strange and extraordinary exercise for them. Attaching their heads by ropes to beams or pegs and lifting them two or three double palms (one double palm equals six inches), he forced them to rest their weight upon their hind feet with their forefeet just clearing the ground. At once each horse, in an effort to find footing for its forefeet, began to struggle with its whole body and with its legs, all its members sharing in the exertion. At such activity sweat poured freely from the body and thus kept the animals in top condition through their excessive labours.[24]

The professional attitude toward proper preparation was an essential component of Greek and Macedonian military success and seems to have been surpassed only by that of the Romans in intensity.[25]

With Eumenes cooped up in Nora and Perdiccas dead, the latter's brother, Alcetas, appeared to be the only remaining threat to Antigonus and the central power. Antigonus wasted no time and, by means of forced marches into Pisidia, caught Alcetas napping.[26] He was consequently able to occupy some strategically important heights. In response Alcetas quickly formed his phalanx and personally led the cavalry against Antigonus' troops on the heights, where a serious engagement took place. Although Antigonus had clearly outgeneraled Alcetas, the latter's defeat was already assured by the disparity in numbers, for his sixteen thousand infantry and nine hundred cavalry were no match for Antigonus' forty thousand and seven thousand respectively, not to mention some elephants. Antigonus, recognizing the importance of Alcetas' person, led six thousand cavalry against the phalanx in order to prevent him

---

24. Diod. 18.42.3–4; Plut. *Eum.* 11.3–5; Nep. *Eum.* 5.4–6.
25. For more on this subject see *GSW* 2 chap. 6, 11, 12.
26. Twenty-five hundred stades (ca. 287 miles) in seven days, according to Diodorus 18.442. Billows (*ACHS* 78) doubts Diodorus' statement that this march was undertaken by Antigonus' entire force, but thinks it was done, rather, by a "mobile elite force." In either case forty miles a day for seven days would have been a remarkable feat.

from returning to it. When the attack on the heights was repulsed, Alcetas abandoned his troops there and, with difficulty, escaped to his phalanx. Numbers then decided the issue, with the elephants attacking in front, cavalry on all sides, and infantry occupying a superior position above them. Rout followed panic and confusion. Alcetas did manage to escape with his Pisidian allies but was later betrayed by them under pressure from Antigonus and committed suicide.[27]

The superiority in numbers that Antigonus enjoyed on this occasion allowed him to split his forces and detach cavalry to isolate Alcetas' phalanx. Alcetas' division of his forces seems less justifiable, but he was in an untenable position and the attempt to seize the heights may have been worth the gamble. Perhaps there was a race for the heights that Diodorus fails to record. In any event the lack of coordination between infantry and cavalry is noteworthy.

In their quest for decisive victory against each other, the Successors sought at times to gain an advantage by employing war elephants. Alexander had had some experience with these animals before he reached India and had prepared his troops accordingly for the battle against Porus. Yet he himself, as noted above, never employed them, and there is no evidence that he intended to do so. Nevertheless, between 321 and 217 they were used at least seven times in important battles. The appearance of this expensive arm in major conflicts during this period is something of an enigma. Alexander's decision not to use them seems to have been militarily correct for him, although they could be effective against unprepared troops and horses naturally shied in their presence. It is clear, however, that well-prepared, disciplined troops were able to deal with them.[28]

A vivid example of the hazards of placing too much faith in elephants is provided by Polyperchon's attack on the city of Megalopolis in the Peloponnesus in 318. When Antipater died in 319, the regency passed as planned to Polyperchon, one of Philip's old officers. Antipater's son Cassander, deemed too young by his father, refused to accept this setback to his hopes for power and, with the support of Antigonus—himself now a rebel against the central regency—engaged in open war with Polyperchon. The Greek cities were held largely by supporters of Antipater, and they now inclined toward his son. Polyperchon took the initiative by issuing a decree promising the restoration

---

27. Diod. 18.44.2–46. Polybius (4.6.7) says that peltasts rather than cavalry charged the ridge. Billows's suggestion that it was a mixed force is attractive (*ACHS* 79).

28. For discussion of their military value see *HMND* 92–100; Seibert (1973) 348–62; Scullard (1974) 245–50.

of democracy if Antipater's adherents were driven out. In the Peloponnese only Megalopolis held out for Cassander. Just prior to Polyperchon's advance against this city, his forces in Attica had amounted to twenty thousand Macedonian infantry, four thousand allied infantry, one thousand cavalry, and sixty-five elephants.[29] The force that attacked Megalopolis was somewhat smaller than this, because a portion was left behind with Polyperchon's son Alexander.

The Megalopolitans wasted little time preparing for the expected siege. They dug a moat around the city, prepared a palisade, repaired the walls, and made weapons—catapults included. The attackers brought up towers and, by digging mines, caused the collapse of part of the city wall. The defenders fought stoutly, preventing the Macedonians from breaking in, while workers hastily built a second wall inside the breach. The following day Polyperchon cleared rubble from the area of the breach so he could use his elephants to break into the city. Diodorus continues:

> The Megalopolitans, however, under the leadership of Damis, who had been in Asia with Alexander and knew by experience the nature and the use of these animals, got the better of him completely. Indeed, by putting his native wit against the brute force of the elephants, Damis rendered their physical strength useless. He studded many great frames with sharp nails and buried them in shallow trenches, concealing the projecting points; over them he left a way into the city, placing none of the troops directly in the face of it, but posting on the flanks a great many javelin throwers, bowmen, and catapults. As Polyperchon was clearing the debris from the whole extent of the breach and making an attack through it with all the elephants in a body, a most unexpected thing befell them. There being no resistance in front, the Indian mahouts did their part in urging them to rush into the city all together; but the animals, as they charged violently, encountered the spike-studded frames. Wounded in their feet by the spikes, their own weight causing the points to penetrate, they could neither go forward any farther nor turn back, because it hurt them to move. At the same time some of the mahouts were killed by the missiles of all kinds that poured upon them from the flanks, and others were disabled by

---

29. Diod. 18.68.3. The ratio of cavalry is low, typical of armies operating in central and southern Greece where the terrain is less than ideal for mounted operations.

wounds and so lost such use of the elephants as the situation permitted. The elephants, suffering great pain because of the cloud of missiles and the nature of the wounds caused by the spikes, wheeled about through their friends and trod down many of them. Finally the elephant that was the most valiant and formidable collapsed; of the rest, some became completely useless, and others brought death to many of their own side.[30]

Unwilling to incur further losses and facing problems elsewhere, Polyperchon departed with most of his army.

The defection of Antigonus from the regency had been prompted by a desire to seize supreme power for himself. Under these circumstances he decided to make terms with Eumenes, whose help he hoped to enlist. In this he was deceived, for when Eumenes was released from Nora under oath, he was concealing his true feelings of loyalty to the regency under Polyperchon.[31] Once free, Eumenes quickly gathered 2,000 infantry and between 500 and 1,000 cavalry and departed Cappadocia for Cilicia, where he took command of the Silver Shields, who had been instructed by Polyperchon to place themselves at his disposal. In fact it appears as if Polyperchon was attempting to replace Antigonus with Eumenes as general of Asia.[32] Eumenes continued to recruit successfully as he moved east into Persia, where the satraps were loyal to the regency. They met him at Susiane with 18,700 infantry, 4,600 horse, and 120 elephants. Antigonus was not too far behind, however, and was able through a stratagem to bring Eumenes to bay. Antigonus realized that even with forced marches he was unlikely to catch Eumenes, so he left the infantry behind with Pithon and personally led the cavalry in pursuit. He overtook the rear guard at daybreak, his appearance convincing Eumenes that Antigonus' entire army was on the scene and that he had no option but to prepare for battle.[33]

Thus a major battle came about in Paraetacene on the border between Persia and Media in the autumn 317. The two armies were reasonably well matched. Antigonus mustered 28,000 heavy infantry, perhaps 5000–6,000 light infantry, 8,500 cavalry, and 65 elephants. Eumenes, in turn, had 17,000

30. Ibid., 18.70–71. Quotation from Ibid., 18.71.2–6.
31. Ibid., 18.53.5; Plut. *Eum.* 12.1–2.
32. *ACHS* 83–84.; Diod. 18.58.1–2; Plut. *Eum.* 12.3. The Silver Shields were an elite unit of three thousand heavy Macedonian infantry from Alexander's army. Diod. 18.59 3; Plut. *Eum.* 12.2–3.
33. Diod. 19.26.6–7.

heavy infantry, 18,000 light infantry, 6,000 cavalry, and 125 elephants.[34] Both generals placed their heavy infantry in the center with cavalry to right and left on the wings. The elephants were stationed in single lines in front of each main battle line with light-armed infantry interspersed among them. Eumenes' left wing, under Eudamus, enjoyed the defensive advantage of being at the base of a hill covering the outside flank, and this may also have been the case for Antigonus' right, which faced it. The offensive wing in each army was the right where the respective commanders led units of cavalry. Both Eumenes and Antigonus had small advance guards of their own slaves, but these seem to have played little part in the battle and are not directly comparable to Alexander's *prodromoi*. The description of the battle, as is often the case in Diodorus, is unsatisfactory, but it appears that most of the serious fighting involved the phalanxes, which engaged each other for some time. In the meantime Antigonus' mounted archers on the left wing, under the leadership of Pithon, took advantage of their superior numbers and mobility and outflanked Eumenes' elephants. Their arrows proved so effective against the elephants that the attack was stopped and Eumenes was forced to transfer mounted reinforcements from his other wing. With their aid Eumenes restored the situation and drove Pithon's forces—who were not supported by regular cavalry—back to the foothills.

When the battle between the phalanxes ended with a rout of Antigonus' troops by the veteran Silver Shields, victory seemed assured for Eumenes. But the Silver Shields, who drove their opponents back to the nearby hills, lost contact with their own battle line. Ever quick to grasp an opportunity, Antigonus led cavalry from his right wing into the gap that opened in the enemy line. Up to this point there was apparently little action on this wing, where Antigonus had kept his cavalry in formation and in place in spite of the rout of the infantry to his left. Eudamus' cavalry, facing Antigonus, must also have been biding their time, perhaps lulled into false security by the success of the Silver Shields, for they were caught by surprise when Antigonus charged through the gap and struck their exposed inside flank. When they were driven off with considerable loss, Eumenes recalled his victorious center and right with a signal horn and led them to the aid of Eudamus and the fleeing cavalry. This gave Antigonus time to send some of his quickest horsemen to his own fleeing troops with instructions to reform at the foothills. Eumenes did likewise, and for a while it appeared as if they might renew the

---

34. Ibid., 19.27–28. For a discussion of the numerical inconsistencies in the account of Diodorus, see Kromayer and Kahnes (1924–31), in Kromayer and Veith 4: 391–413. For the battle itself see 413–24.

struggle by the light of a full moon, but exhaustion and hunger precluded it. To judge by the casualties Eumenes had the better of the fighting, yet the battle was essentially a draw, as neither side was able to destroy the fighting power of the other.[35]

It should be noted that once the gap in Eumenes' line opened, Antigonus did not direct his cavalry attack against the infantry. Even more important in the sequel was Eumenes' decision to recall his victorious forces when he might have been able to inflict irreparable damage on Antigonus' phalanx. Diodorus specifically credits Antigonus' attack with saving those who were fleeing, and this proved to be decisive in the long run as it allowed him to fight again another day.

It is not immediately clear why Eumenes felt it necessary to recall his victorious troops in order to bring relief to Eudamus. R. A. Billows's suggestion that Antigonus' attack made it necessary for the "victorious phalanx to halt and about-face" (perhaps to assume the defensive) is not an obvious conclusion, since two-thirds or more of Eumenes' army was victorious and Antigonus' advisors had recommended escape.[36] Devine's conclusion is no more compelling. He proposes that Antigonus' advantage of terrain prevented Eumenes from destroying his army, but that is not stated by Diodorus.[37] The cavalry attack by Antigonus may well have been a gamble. This accords well with his actions over the years, which suggest that compromise was not in his nature and that he was willing to risk everything for a chance to restore Alexander's empire.[38] Eumenes may simply have made a mistake. He and Eudamus had both served under Alexander, and a strong bond of friendship may have led Eumenes to make a personal rather than a professional decision. Antigonus himself did exactly that on occasion with respect to his son Demetrius, as we will see, and it may have cost him his chance of success. Had Eumenes left Eudamus to his fate, Antigonus might have found himself the leader of a cavalry detachment and little more.

There are several other logical objections to the battle narrative reported by Diodorus, which Delbrück raised years ago. Where were the elephants, for example, while the phalanxes were engaged? Why was Antigonus' right wing so inactive until late in the action, especially since it was initially intended to

---

35. Diod. 19.30–31. Diodorus' casualty report lists Antigonus' losses at 3,700 infantry and 54 cavalry killed and over 4,000 wounded but for Eumenes only 540 and a few cavalry killed and 900 wounded. See *ACHS* 92 n. 20, 98 n. 23; Devine (1985c) 75–86.
36. *ACHS* 98, apparently following *HMND* 63. Diod. 19.30.7, 10.
37. Devine (1985c) 75.
38. As Polyaenus suggests, 4.6.5.

lead the attack? How did a small portion of an army that was mostly in flight stabilize the battlefield and turn defeat into a draw?[39] There are, unfortunately, no good answers to these questions, but it must be observed that Delbrück's dismissal of Diodorus' account rests on excessive rationalism and rigid logic. Battles, once set in motion, are chaotic events, subject to a great variety of physical and psychological forces and incapable of being captured even on sound film in the twentieth century.

What seems to be plausible and historically important in this narrative is the impression that cavalry and infantry each fought primarily against their counterparts rather than as part of an articulated or coordinated force that struck a key point in the enemy line, as was the case with Alexander.[40] The explanation for this seems to lie in the nature of the enemy; whereas the armies of the Successors were usually well matched and the level of generalship was high, Alexander faced notably inferior enemies in spite of their number, and no leader who could match him personally. Quite simply, he was able to employ tactical options that were unavailable to the Successors. M. Cary noted the symmetry between Antigonus and Eumenes years ago: "The actions of Paraetacene and Gabiene, in which the two best generals of the age were pitted against each other, are almost unique in ancient warfare."[41]

With this indecisive outcome it is no surprise that the struggle between Antigonus and Eumenes continued. Following the battle, both armies withdrew into winter quarters. In midwinter 317/316, Antigonus broke camp early and moved against Eumenes in an attempt to surprise his troops while they were widely scattered in the area of Gabiene. This attempt failed, however, as Antigonus was unable to keep his approach secret, thus giving Eumenes time to collect most of his forces into a fortified camp. When Antigonus learned that the elephants were slow to come into camp, he conceived a plan to intercept them. To accomplish this he sent out cavalry comprising two thousand Median lancers and two hundred Tarentines, together with all of his light infantry. When Eumenes learned of the danger to his elephants, he dispatched fifteen hundred of his strongest cavalry and three thousand light infantry. Although Antigonus' party reached the elephants first, their four hundred escort troops

---

39. *HAW* 238–40.

40. It is almost as if there were three separate battles. See Kromayer and Veith (1924–31) 4. 421. Tarn rightly points out that good defense limited the use of cavalry in the Hellenistic Age but attributes it to an awareness of the risk of outflanking rather than to the similarity of opposing armies and the presence of elephants, *HMND* 66.

41. Cary (1978) 239.

resisted until Eumenes' relief force arrived and rescued them.[42] The sending of a mixed force of cavalry and infantry by both commanders follows the practice of Alexander. The apparent vulnerability of elephants alone further highlights the value of combining arms.

The final battle between these two antagonists occurred a few days afterward in the Gabiene region of Persis on a dry salt plain. Once again both placed cavalry on the wings, infantry in between, and elephants across the entire front. The number of combatants was sufficiently even to allow quality and generalship a chance to decide the issue. The figures Diodorus gives for Antigonus are 22,000 heavy infantry, 5000–6,000 light infantry, 9,000 cavalry, and 65 elephants, and for Eumenes, 17,000 heavy infantry, 19,700 light infantry, 6,000 cavalry, and 114 elephants. A major difference between this and the last battle was the decision by Eumenes to pit strength against strength. Accordingly, he placed his best troops and elephants on his left against the opposing right wing commanded by Antigonus and his son Demetrius. Eumenes instructed the cavalry on his own right, under Philip, to avoid battle and await the turn of events elsewhere. The fighting began with an advance of elephants followed by cavalry, which soon produced a dust cloud that obscured vision. Antigonus took advantage of this, sending the Median cavalry and a body of Tarentines from his left wing around behind Eumenes' line to seize his camp, which contained the families and baggage of the Silver Shields. Meanwhile, Antigonus led his cavalry on the right against Eumenes' horsemen. This panicked Peucestes, and he fled with his cavalry (apparently the 150 he led at Paraetacene), drawing 1,500 more with him. Eumenes then rallied the remaining cavalry and, with the help of his elephants, directed an attack at Antigonus himself. Bitter fighting ensued, continuing until Eumenes' best elephant fell. He then retired to his right wing with his remaining cavalry and took command there. Once again, Eumenes' infantry, following the example set by the Silver Shields, were victorious.

When Eumenes learned that his camp had been captured, he attempted to rally his cavalry for an attack, but Peucestes refused to obey and—with night approaching—he had little choice but to desist. In the meantime, after Eumenes had abandoned the fight against Antigonus, the latter divided his cavalry, sending one part with Pithon against the Silver Shields while keeping the rest with himself to await Eumenes' next move. Pithon's attack was frustrated

---

42. Diod. 19.39.2–6. Diodorus attributes Antigonus' attack on the elephants to an attempt to deprive the enemy of the strongest element of his forces. It may just as well have been due to his desire to give his cavalry more options in the coming battle.

by the disciplined and experienced Macedonian infantry, who formed a square and withdrew safely to a river behind the lines. Eumenes joined them at dusk. In the war council that followed he was unable to convince his commanders to renew the battle. Self-interest dominated, the satraps proposing a withdrawal to the upper satrapies while the Macedonians could think of little else but their families and possessions now in the hands of Antigonus. Eumenes' plea to renew the battle against an enemy whose infantry was crushed and cavalry were no better than equal fell on deaf ears. In any event, the possession of the camp decided the day, as the Macedonians seized Eumenes, handed him over to Antigonus in exchange for their families and belongings, and entered Antigonus' service.[43]

For all his military skill and qualities of leadership, the Greek Eumenes was an outsider in Macedonian eyes. He knew that his hold on the Macedonian troops was tenuous, and he went to great lengths to win them over in the years after Alexander's death, even establishing a cult of Alexander in an effort to create an abstract loyalty based on the memory of their great king. On campaign the cult was set up in a tent containing a throne and Alexander's personal royal and martial accoutrements, the tent being used as a council chamber. The subordinate commanders sacrificed to him as if to a god and then joined Eumenes in open consultation under divine guidance.[44] All to no avail, for the Macedonians never truly forgave him for killing Craterus in battle or for his opposition to Antipater.[45]

After the battle Antigonus was uncertain what to do with Eumenes. Even his son Demetrius wanted him spared, but the earlier betrayal after the siege of Nora made this unlikely, especially since Antigonus did not carry clemency to such a fatal degree as Julius Caesar was to do. Out of respect for a former friend, however, he cremated the body and sent the ashes to his family. Eudamus and Antigenes, the leaders of the Silver Shields, were also put to death.[46] The Silver Shields themselves were effectively disbanded by Antigonus, who sent them off to Sibyrtius, the satrap of Arachosia, with instructions to give them such dangerous assignments that they would be destroyed.[47] At first glance that may seem surprising, since this elite unit may have been the most efficient infantry force in Greek history. Nonetheless, Antigonus did not trust

43. Ibid., 19.42–43; Plut. *Eum.* 16.4–6. Devine (1985d) 87–96.
44. Plut. *Eum.* 6.6; 13.3–4; Diod. 18.60–61; 19.15.3–4; *HM* 3 123, 132.
45. *HM* 3 133.
46. Diod. 19.44.1–2; Plut. *Eum.* 19.1.
47. Diod. 19.48.3; Plut. *Eum.* 19.2.

them and apparently felt that their unequaled fighting power, which he had witnessed on two recent occasions, coupled with a record of disloyalty, made them too dangerous to have around. They offer a clear example of the value of quality in a fighting unit when both sides employ the same tactics in battle—a type of asymmetry that is often impossible to determine when assessing reasons for victory and defeat. This fact probably leads to an excessive emphasis on tactics by modern historians in an effort to explain victory in ancient battles. In his description of the final battle between Antigonus and Eumenes, Diodorus highlights the one-sided victory of the Silver Shields over their opponents. Without loss to themselves, they defeated and routed a more numerous enemy, killing five thousand in the process. They were *formidable* in the purest meaning of the word.[48]

In the strict military sense Eumenes seems to have had the better of it, not that it mattered once treachery was more profitable than honor.[49] He simply did not represent a cause that could override the personal interests of the Silver Shields. It is once again apparent that the fighting itself yielded no decisive result in spite of the one-sided success of Eumenes' infantry and the superiority of Antigonus' cavalry and elephants. The fighting devolved into several distinct actions that show little evidence of the principle of combined arms. And once again, the reason for this lack of coordination seems to be that the opposing forces were virtual mirror images of one another, each exhibiting the same strengths and weaknesses.[50] All other things being equal, decisive victories are rare unless the strengths of one side mesh advantageously with the weaknesses of the other.

With Eumenes out of the way, Antigonus was now able to strengthen his control over the Asiatic provinces of Alexander's empire. Inevitably, this aroused suspicion and jealousy among his former colleagues: Ptolemy in Egypt, Cassander in Macedon, Lysimachus in Thrace, and Seleucus, who had fled to Egypt from Babylon after falling out with Antigonus. Technically, Antigonus' position was tenuous since his command in Asia had expired with the defeat of Eumenes. In reality, by virtue of his army and the vast financial resources of the royal treasures that he seized, he was all but a king.[51] An ultimatum

48. D.S.19.43.1; *AE* 27.
49. See also Kromayer and Kahnes (1924–31) 4:434. Billows (*ACHS* 103) gives the "main honors of the battle" to Antigonus.
50. In spite of an awareness of the superiority of Eumenes' infantry based on the Silver Shields, Antigonus could do little to counter it directly because of the overall symmetry of the two armies.
51. Perhaps as much as thirty thousand talents from Ecbatana and Susa and another ten thousand from Cyinda in Cilicia. Diod. 19.46.6, 48.8, 56.5.

from his former associates to return territory and share the contents of the treasures was ignored. From this point on Antigonus openly sought supreme command for himself, even entering into an alliance with Polyperchon, who was still at large in the Peloponnese. Both sides prepared for a war that lasted until 311.

A description of one occasion during this period permits us a glimpse of the purely physical difficulties of using horses in warfare. This occurred while Antigonus was enlarging his holdings in Asia Minor and had entrusted his son Demetrius with the defense of Syria and Palestine against the inroads of Ptolemy. The twenty-three-year-old had been provided with a substantial force comprising 12,900 infantry (including 2,000 Macedonians), 5,000 cavalry, and 43 elephants. He had also been assigned four men of great experience from Alexander's campaigns as his advisors. Although Antigonus relied greatly on Demetrius in later years, he was not completely blind to his weaknesses.[52] In 313 Demetrius learned that Ptolemy was making sea-borne raids on coastal cities in Cilicia. Leaving behind the heavy infantry, he led the cavalry and light infantry on a rapid march into Cilicia. Arriving too late to help, he immediately turned around and marched hurriedly back to his base. This impetuous foray was too much for the horses, most of which broke down, and neither the grooms nor the baggage handlers could keep up with him. Diodorus reports that he covered twenty-four stages (on the Persian road) in six days. If the average of 15 miles per stage is correct, that amounts to 360 miles at 60 miles a day.[53] A normal day's march for cavalry would be 25 to 30 miles under good conditions. Whatever the truth of these figures, Demetrius should have known better. Although he was comparatively young, he had had sufficient experience on his father's campaigns to know the capabilities of cavalry mounts. There were limits to the amount of effort flesh and bone carried on unshod hooves could endure. Thus it was incumbent on cavalrymen to balance urgent military need against the risk of rendering cavalry mounts unfit for further use. This principle of economy remained important for the armies of Europe and the Near East throughout history, because the regions could not produce the large numbers of remounts that made possible the long, rapid campaigns of the Asiatic nomads. Alexander himself seldom pushed his forces to the point of exhaustion on any given occasion, except when the prize was judged to be worth the possible loss, as was the case when he attempted to capture Darius in 330. In his army the sheer cumulative effect of

52. Ibid., 19.69.1.
53. Ibid., 19.80.1–2.

constant campaigning exhausted his men and wore down the hooves of the horses, as Diodorus records in a rare glimpse of this aspect of military life.[54]

In the following year, 312, Ptolemy—accompanied by Seleucus—marched into Syria with a large force of 18,000 heavy infantry and 4,000 cavalry.[55] Contrary to the advice of his friends, Demetrius met him near the site of Gaza with 11,000 heavy infantry, more than 1,500 light infantry, 4,400 cavalry, and 43 elephants. Demetrius stationed 2,900 cavalry on the left, his offensive wing, along with 30 elephants supported by 1,500 light troops (javelin men, archers, and slingers). There was also an advance guard of three squadrons of cavalry (*protagma*). The 1,500 cavalry on the right under Andronicus had orders to make no attack. The position of the advance guard is unclear; J. Seibert suggests that it was placed in line with the elephants and light armed troops on the left.[56] At first Ptolemy also built up his left, but the leisurely pace of Demetrius' forces as they took position allowed him time to move units to his right and thus match strength against strength. In addition to placing 3,000 of his strongest cavalry there, he also took special precautions against the elephants, which he obviously prepared for in advance, more than likely as a result of the experience he and Seleucus had had in India. The method that was employed worked especially well, because Ptolemy had no elephants of his own. Special troops moved out in front of the line and positioned some type of iron spikes connected by chains. Supporting these were javelin men and archers with orders to shoot at the elephants and their mahouts.

The battle began with cavalry actions on both wings between troops of the advance guard, Demetrius having the advantage. Since a frontal attack was precluded by the position of Demetrius' elephants, Ptolemy and Seleucus led their main cavalry around the outside in a flank attack. This failed to catch Demetrius off guard, and his troops met the enemy with an equal zeal that led to the most serious fighting of the battle.[57] In the initial contact the horsemen fought with lances, most of which were quickly shattered in what appears to have been close, vigorous combat.[58] After each side rallied they came together

---

54. Ibid., 17.94.2. This was in the eighth year of the campaign. It prompts an unanswerable question: What effect did this wear and tear have on the performance and mobility of ancient armies?

55. For the problem of Ptolemy's forces on this campaign, see especially Kromayer and Kahnes (1924–31) 4:435–38, who believe the Egyptians mentioned by Diodorus and the light–armed troops are not included in the eighteen thousand, and Seibert (1969) 166, who thinks the number is inclusive.

56. Seibert (1969) 168.

57. Ibid., 169, 180.

58. Ibid., 173. Seibert suggests that the lances were thrown, but it seems that close combat better explains the fact that they were shattered. It would also indicate a continuation of the fighting style of the Macedonian cavalry under Alexander.

a second time and fought with swords. Neither side yielded in this bloody fight, until Demetrius' cavalry were demoralized by the disaster that befell the elephants. These had advanced during the cavalry fight until they came upon the spikes, which literally stopped them in their tracks. Thus rendered harmless, the elephants and their mahouts were now easy targets for the missile troops of Ptolemy and were soon captured. At this turn of events Demetrius' cavalry collapsed and abandoned the field. Demetrius, left without support, was also forced to flee. About eight thousand of his infantry, who were scarcely engaged, were captured.[59]

The casualties on Demetrius' side are listed by Diodorus as five hundred, mostly cavalry, among whom were many friends and advisors.[60] This tends to confirm his description of a fierce cavalry fight, since horsemen who are quickly routed usually escape with few casualties. The entire account of the battle gives the impression not only that the combats of the several different arms were poorly coordinated, but that each had a dynamic of its own that should have given a general of Alexander's school fits. Yet this statement is too strong, as Ptolemy and Seleucus clearly had a battle plan involving several arms and a number of units. Demetrius, on the other hand, not only telegraphed his intentions early but—by placing his hopes in the elephants—he sacrificed any benefits he might have gained from a coordinated attack. If his more seasoned advisors offered suggestions, these were apparently ignored. They should have warned him against placing so much trust in so unpredictable an arm at the expense of confidence in their own fighting power. The close articulation of infantry and cavalry favored by Alexander is not in evidence. In this battle the experience, skill, and adaptability of Ptolemy and Seleucus meshed well with the mistakes of Demetrius to produce victory for the former.[61]

Whatever the relative merits of any particular military arm, the recovery of Babylonia by Seleucus in 312, following this battle, demonstrates that there is no substitute for boldness and skill. He departed Egypt with modest help from Ptolemy, amounting to about eight hundred to one thousand infantry and two hundred to three hundred cavalry.[62] Some additional support accrued along the way and in Babylonia itself—apparently the reward for his fair treatment of the local population while he was satrap there for four

---

59. Diod. 19.82–84.
60. Ibid., 19.85.3; Plut. *Demetr.* 5.3, who puts the casualties at five thousand.
61. The role of Seleucus is emphasized by Seibert (1983) 222–32.
62. Diod. 19.90.1; App. *Syr.* 9.54.

years.[63] Nonetheless, when Nicanor, Antigonus' general in Media, marched against him with ten thousand infantry and seven thousand cavalry, Seleucus still had a woefully inadequate force of three thousand infantry and four hundred cavalry.[64] In spite of that, Seleucus conceded nothing:

> He crossed the Tigris River; and, on hearing that the enemy were a few days' march distant, he hid his soldiers in the adjacent marshes, intending to make his attack a surprise. When Nicanor arrived at the Tigris River and did not find the enemy, he camped at one of the royal stations, believing that they had fled to a greater distance than was the case. When night was come and the army of Nicanor was keeping perfunctory and negligent guard, Seleucus fell on them suddenly, causing great confusion and panic; for it happened that when the Persians had joined battle, their satrap Evager fell together with some of the other leaders. When this occurred, most of the soldiers went over to Seleucus, in part because they were offended by the conduct of Antigonus. Nicanor, who was left with only a few men and feared lest he be delivered over to the enemy, took flight with his friends through the desert. But Seleucus, now that he had gained control of a large army and was comporting himself in a way gracious to all, easily won over Susiane, Media, and some of the adjacent lands."[65]

Seleucus' control over Babylonia was short-lived, however, for Antigonus sent Demetrius to recover it with a substantial force, and he easily scared off Seleucus' general, Patrocles, while Seleucus himself and most of his troops were away in Media. Using the Upper Satrapies as his base, Seleucus remained in the East until 301. The composition of the two armies sent by Antigonus against Seleucus seems to reflect two facts: the growing shortage of good infantry and the availability of cavalry in the eastern regions. Whereas armies that fought in the lower Balkans during the previous one hundred years fielded from 5 percent to 14 percent cavalry, Demetrius had 21 percent (fifteen thousand infantry and four thousand cavalry) and Nicanor had 41 percent (ten thousand infantry and seven thousand cavalry).[66]

---

63. Diod. 19.91.1–2.
64. Ibid., 19.92.1–2.
65. Ibid., 19.97.2–5.
66. Ibid., 19.100.4–7.

No further details of cavalry actions involving the Successors are found in the pages of Diodorus or in Plutarch until their descriptions of Ipsus, the final battle of this era, in 301. By the preceding year the power of Antigonus had become so threatening to his former colleagues that they finally agreed to concerted action against him.[67] Cassander sent part of his army, under Lysimachus, into Asia Minor while he himself marched into Thessaly to deal with the Greeks and Demetrius, who had been active there since 304. In the meantime Seleucus and Ptolemy prepared to move against Antigonus from the east and south. As soon as Antigonus realized that a coalition was gathering, he summoned Demetrius from Greece. Ptolemy's march north from Egypt began well, but his plans to join the allies were thwarted by misinformation. While he was besieging Sidon, an incorrect report arrived announcing the defeat of Lysimachus and Seleucus by Antigonus, who was said to be marching south with a large army. Ptolemy believed the report and responded in accordance with his self interest. Concluding a four-month truce with the Sidonians, he returned home to protect his kingdom. In fact only minor actions had occurred, and Seleucus was just arriving in eastern Asia Minor with a force comprising 20,000 infantry, 12,000 cavalry (including archers), 480 elephants, and over 100 scythed chariots. All the forces that had gathered in Asia Minor then went into winter quarters, expecting a decisive battle to be fought in the following year.[68]

Here ends the full narrative of Diodorus, although the result of the events at Ipsus is mentioned in the fragments of Book 21 of Diodorus as well as in Justin. Consequently, knowledge of the battle rests on the brief account in Plutarch's *Life of Demetrius*.[69]

The forces that faced each other in the battle were substantial, including the largest number of elephants ever to appear on a Hellenistic battlefield. Antigonus, now in his eighties and perhaps no longer up to the demands of a campaign, fielded 70,000 infantry, 10,000 cavalry, and 75 elephants. The allies brought together 64,000 infantry, between 10,500 and 15,000 cavalry, and 400 elephants.[70] In spite of the brevity of Plutarch's description of the battle,

---

67. Ibid., 20.106. Cassander of Macedon, Lysimachus of Thrace, Seleucus of the Upper Satrapies, and Ptolemy of Egypt.

68. Diod. 20.107–13. *ACHS* 174–80. The number of elephants has been questioned, but it is supported by Plutarch's account of the battle the following year, when four hundred were present. *Demetr.* 28.3.

69. Diod. 21.1.2–46; Justin 15.4.27; Plut. *Demetr.* 28.3, 29.3–5.

70. Plut. *Demetr.* 28.3. For discussion of the number of cavalry see *SA* 107, n. 11. *ACHS* 182, n. 34.

its salient features are discernible, making possible some observations on the tactics employed. Antigonus entrusted the most numerous and strongest of his cavalry to his son Demetrius, most likely posting them on the right. As the armies came to close quarters, Demetrius' vigorous attack against the enemy cavalry—led by Antiochus, the son of Seleucus—was so successful that he drove them off the field. At that point, according to Plutarch, he committed the mistake that cost his father both victory and his life, for he continued to pursue the fleeing cavalry and thus stripped his own phalanx of cavalry cover, in turn giving Seleucus the opportunity to move his elephants into position to block his return to the main battle. When this had been accomplished, Seleucus turned his attention to Antigonus and his phalanx. Instead of permitting the infantry to decide the issue, he sent cavalry—presumably those from the other wing—to ride around the unprotected phalanx and instill fear in the men by feigned charges. When a large part of the enemy force surrendered, Seleucus was able to rout the remainder. Antigonus fell beneath a shower of javelins.

Thus ended the last and most serious attempt to reconstitute Alexander's empire. Demetrius escaped with five thousand infantry and four thousand cavalry, but the territorial kingdom he had shared with his father was gone, soon to be divided up among the victors. Nonetheless, he still possessed a fleet which commanded the sea and numerous coastal possessions and islands, which, had he possessed his father's judgment and stability, might have been the basis of some lasting achievement. As it happened, the remaining eighteen years of his life were frittered away in ill-conceived adventures and wasted opportunities, including a stint as king of Macedon (294–288).

Only general observations can be made about the tactical intentions of the leaders on both sides of the battle of Ipsus. Billows suggests that Demetrius' aim was to drive off the cavalry opposite him and then turn in on the enemy flank and rear.[71] This required some fine judgment about how far to pursue the cavalry before turning against the phalanx. If he went too far, he might not return in time; if not far enough, he might find himself vulnerable to Antiochus' cavalry in the rear. Without superiority of number, he could not divide his forces. Modern judgment, following Plutarch, usually falls hard upon Demetrius for pursuing too far, but in fact he did return—whether in time or not cannot be said—because the elephants prevented him from reentering the fight. It was suggested by W. W. Tarn that the flight by the Seleucid

71. *ACHS* 183; n. 35.

cavalry was a calculated attempt to draw Demetrius away from the field of battle, but there is no way to evaluate this idea.[72] A fragment of Diodorus does add one more piece of information—namely, that the elephants of Antigonus and Lysimachus fought on equal terms. If true, this suggests that Seleucus committed only a fraction of his total number of elephants against those of Antigonus, leaving most available to block the return of Demetrius.[73] In any case, even if action involving infantry, elephants, and cavalry began about the same time, it is clear that cavalry could only be used against infantry (from flank and rear) when the opposing cavalry had been taken out of the fight. Thus it is in the execution of his tactics, not their conception, that Demetrius failed, and the deciding factor seems to have been the elephants. If so, this was to be the greatest achievement of war elephants in Hellenistic military history. It is noteworthy that this success came when they were being used on the defense—and this seems to be the principal lesson of this battle.

The battles of the Successors in the years from 323 to 301 present a picture that is noticeably different from that offered by the conflict between Alexander and the Persians. In part this is to be expected, since on the one hand there was the leadership of a single commander directing a largely national army against an imperial levy that was inferior in fighting power, while on the other hand there were a number of individual leaders of comparable ability and experience engaging each other with roughly identical forces. As one would expect, military principles and practices from the preceding period continued to be applied, yet due to changed circumstances these did not always bring similar results. Among the constants were close combat; high levels of organization, training and discipline; superior logistics (about which we know next to nothing); the use of offensive and defensive wings; rapidity of movement; economy of effort (that is to say, attacking a critical spot); and—although to a lesser degree—combined tactics. One practice that does not seem to have been used by the Successors is the close articulation of infantry and line cavalry on the attacking wing.

Most striking, perhaps, is the absence—or at least, the general ineffectiveness—of the coordination of the several different arms that each army contained. This is strikingly obvious in the three battles of the Lamian War, in which the Greek allies made no effort to engage their infantry, relying exclusively on the superior Thessalian cavalry. This worked twice but on the third occasion— while the two opposing cavalry forces kept each other

72. *HMND* 68–69.
73. Diod. 21.1.2.

occupied—Antipater routed the allied infantry with the superior Macedonian phalanx. Allied hopes during the war must have rested on the mistaken belief that the Macedonians would decide the restoration of their control over Greece would require more effort than it was worth. Surely they did not consider their two victories decisive, as several centuries of Greek warfare had shown that no defeat was decisive without substantial damage to the enemy phalanx.

In the two great battles fought by Antigonus and Eumenes—Paraetacene (317) and Gabiene (316)—there was no apparent effort at simultaneous coordination of infantry and cavalry. The technically decisive fighting was between the phalanxes, and in each case the edge was provided by the Silver Shields, fighting for Eumenes. The superiority of this experienced fighting unit is an example of Napoleon's dictum: "In war, the moral is to the physical as three to one." Eumenes' defeat of Neoptolemus in 322 was initially an infantry victory for the latter, but it went awry when the soldiers of the phalanx broke ranks to pursue the fleeing infantry of Eumenes, allowing his cavalry to defeat them while they were out of formation. Eumenes' victory over Craterus the following year, on the other hand, owed nothing to infantry but resulted from cavalry fights on both wings. Elephants played a decisive part on two occasions, but not in an offensive role. At Gaza in 312 Demetrius' misplaced overconfidence in his elephants contributed to a general collapse when they were defeated by Ptolemy, who had none of these animals himself. The great number of elephants that Seleucus brought to the battlefield at Ipsus enabled him to create a defensive barrier that prevented Demetrius' victorious cavalry from returning to help his father's infantry. Left without cavalry cover, Antigonus' phalanx was subject to the clearest example of simultaneously coordinated arms of the period.

The largely disjointed nature of these battles is not evidence of ignorance of the value of coordination of arms and units, something that the Successors surely observed under Alexander. It more than likely resulted from the changed circumstances under which they waged their wars. In their battles experienced, competent, and at times exceptionally able generals fought each other. They possessed similar strategic and tactical views, derived from their participation in the events of Alexander's reign. The armies they led were similar in both organization and fighting technique and most had at least a core of Alexander's veterans. Thus—except where a disparity in numbers existed—there was no significant asymmetry between the two sides. Complicating matters for the Successors was the use of elephants, whose presence on the battlefield restricted the tactical options of cavalry in particular. Because of their natural role in defense, elephants had a profoundly negative effect upon the aggressive tactics favored by Alexander. They also would have interfered with the effective use of *prodromoi*.

The troops led by the Successors also seem to have had less moral confidence about their reasons for fighting and consequently exhibited much less loyalty than had been shown to Alexander—not to mention the effect of Alexander's inimitable charisma. His principal opponents, the Persians, had been a traditional enemy whose past behavior seemed to justify a campaign of reprisal.[74] When the Successors fought each other, former comrades-in-arms often appeared on opposite sides and defeat often led, at the personal level, not to execution or slavery but to an opportunity to enroll for hire in the victorious army.

Perhaps nothing upset efforts to employ Alexander's tactics more than the existence of high-quality infantry on both sides, since frontal penetration by cavalry was impossible as long as the phalanx retained its formation. Indeed, decisive victory was unachievable unless the opposing phalanx was destroyed or effectively neutralized. Alexander had never faced this problem in Asia, because Persian infantry were inferior and the Persian leaders did not use the Greek mercenary infantry they had to best advantage.

The effect of these differences on the tactical concepts inherited from Alexander explains the changes in military practice observed under his successors. The ideal function of lance-bearing cavalry in the decades following his death was to engage their counterparts, drive them off, and then take advantage of any opportunities that presented themselves. Most important among the latter was attacking the enemy infantry in the flank or rear. In reality this seldom happened, because it was thwarted by the symmetry of the opposing armies. This resulted in virtually separate combats of infantry and cavalry with less opportunity than previously for combined arms directed against a specific weak spot in the enemy line. True line cavalry who moved forward in concert with the adjacent infantry were not found in this period. No consistent pattern of tactical success appeared, and no arm regularly outperformed the others. Local circumstances rather than tactical principles dominated the action, and successful commanders showed themselves to be versatile and adaptable in the presence of these circumstances. Tarn laments that merely the defeat of the enemy cavalry became "the regular object of

---

74. For the question of the justification of Alexander's campaigns, see *AE* chap. 5, 133–65.

Hellenistic warfare."[75] There is much truth in this, but it is truth dictated by circumstances, not concepts. A corollary is the fact that it became fairly commonplace for an army to experience victory in one arm and defeat in another. In many respects the experiences of the Successors better reflect the patterns of Western warfare than the spectacular and decisive victories of Alexander. Unfortunately, the uniqueness of Alexander's success was overlooked by many later generals, who fell under his spell without possessing his ability.

The most obvious instance of the Successors' improving upon Alexander's tactics was their success at dealing with elephants through the use of missile weapons and spikes.[76] The close combat that he used so effectively in infantry and cavalry fights was risky against elephants—even when it was successful, as at the Hydaspes—because of its lasting detrimental effect upon morale. The battle at the Hydaspes can also be viewed as a preview of conditions faced by the Successors, because Porus' elephants prevented Alexander from using the articulation of infantry and cavalry as well as a direct charge by the aggressive wing, making it a good example of the controlling influence that battlefield conditions have upon tactical concepts and principles.

---

75. *HMND* 61.
76. The ultimate ancient weapon against elephants was the Roman *carroballista*, a small catapult mounted on a cart drawn by two horses or mules. It is depicted on Trajan's Column. Veg. *Epit.* 3.24.

Chapter 14

The Hellenistic Period:
300 to 150 B.C.

WHEN ANTIGONUS, PERHAPS THE ablest of the Successors, died at Ipsus, an era came to an end. The consistently high level of leadership of Alexander's generals and the fighting quality of the armies they led would not be seen again in such comparatively narrow limits of time and space. The Hellenistic kings and generals of the following century or so would have fewer opportunities to acquire the military skills of their predecessors. Because the latter had spent their formative years on campaign with Philip and Alexander, they owed their high position far more to merit than did kings who inherited military command with their royal title or generals who were chosen by the various city-states. Although the great kingdoms founded by the most successful of Alexander's generals dominated the eastern Mediterranean region until the coming of Rome, many smaller states played an active role in the power struggles that occupied the kings. It is small wonder, then, if the battlefield scenarios of this period do not match those of the preceding half-century in spite of little change in fighting technique. The inconsistency in the application of fighting skills during this time arose naturally from the increasing importance in the eastern Mediterranean of a number of political and ethnic groups in varied geographical and economic circumstances. Military principles were applied less rigorously, and there was a decline in the overall thoroughness of preparation.[1]

---

1. See Plut. *Pyrrh.* 16.4. Here Pyrrhus, one of the greatest professional soldiers of the period, expresses amazement at Roman discipline, watches, and camp planning. Pyrrhus himself had very high standards, but the raw material out of which he was at times compelled to make soldiers (that is to say, the Tarentines) was often less susceptible to the necessary degree of discipline than either the mainland Greeks or his current enemy.

The first battle of this period for which a usable account survives, Heraclea (280), is also of more then usual interest because it offers us the opportunity to see the phalanx in action against the Roman legion for the first time. Over the next 112 years, legion and phalanx were to meet five more times in major actions: in Italy at Asculum (279) and Beneventum (276), in northern Greece at Cynoscephalae (197) and Pydna (168), and in Asia Minor at Magnesia (190).

The events in Italy that led up to these battles between Pyrrhus and the Romans may seem at first glance to be complex, but in fact they represent no departure from the traditional behavior of the Greek city-states of Sicily and southern Italy with the mother cities on the Greek mainland. On this occasion Pyrrhus responded to the appeal of Tarentum for help against the Romans, thereby joining the ranks of Gylippus, Timoleon, and his own ancestor, Alexander of Epirus. Pyrrhus departed from Greece with between 20,000 and 25,500 infantry, 3,000 cavalry, and 20 elephants.[2] During the crossing some of these forces were scattered in a storm, and there may have been losses. Once he was in Italy, Pyrrhus assembled his army and enrolled Tarentine troops. It appears that any losses he may have sustained were made up, as just prior to the battle of Heraclea he reportedly rode ahead with his 3,000 cavalry in the hopes of catching the Romans while they were crossing the Siris River. Roman numbers remain unknown but are estimated to have been approximately the same.[3]

Although Plutarch provides detailed descriptions of some events during the course of the battle, his overall narrative of the fighting is sketchy. In leading his cavalry against the Romans just after they crossed the river, Pyrrhus was apparently trying to catch them out of formation.[4] During the ensuing vigorous cavalry fight, an Italian cavalry commander by the name of Oplax made a direct attack upon Pyrrhus, striking his horse with his spear. At that very moment his own horse was struck by the spear of Pyrrhus' companion Leonnatus. Both horses went down. Pyrrhus was rescued by his own men, but Oplax' daring cost him his life.[5] A lengthy, severe engagement

---

2. The principal source is Plut. *Pyrrh.* 15–17. See also Diod. 22.6.1–3; Livy 22.59.8; Polyb. 18.28.10; Flor. 1.13.7–8; Justin 18.1.6; and Dion. Hall. 19.12.

3. Roman forces are estimated at thirty thousand in *CAH* 7, part 2 (1989) 467.

4. This stratagem had a long history. Timoleon used it earlier at the Crimisus in 341, and a medieval Byzantine treatise recommended attacking the enemy when they are in disorder. Dennis (1985) chap. 33, 105.

5. Dion. Hall. describes the same event, adding that Oplax grasped his spear with both hands (19.12).

followed until the elephants induced the Roman cavalry and legions to panic, allowing the Thessalian cavalry to rout and slaughter them.

The casualties were high on both sides, with Plutarch reporting considerable discrepancy between his two sources. The lower figures attributed to Hieronymus, seven thousand Romans and fewer than four thousand Greeks, seem more likely than the fifteen thousand Romans and thirteen thousand Greeks claimed by Dionysius. Diodorus and Livy also mention the carnage. The remark that Diodorus assigns to Pyrrhus—"If I win a victory in one more battle with the Romans, I shall not have left a single soldier of those who crossed over with me"—is the source of the term "Pyrrhic victory."[6]

One may well ask why there were so many casualties on Pyrrhus' side in a battle of phalanx and legion in which there is no evidence that the phalanx was exposed to attack upon flank or rear. In a head-on contest, the long *sarissas* of the phalanx, extending several rows in front of the first rank, effectively countered both the Roman javelin and the short sword. Such an advantage should have resulted in a more one-sided victory and fewer casualties for Pyrrhus. If there is an answer to this question it may come from Polybius, who informs us that Pyrrhus "employed not only Italian arms (ὅπλοις) but also Italian forces (δυνάμεσιν), placing cohorts (σημαίαν) of these and cohorts (σπεῖραν) composed of men from the phalanx in alternate order in his battles with the Romans."[7] Assuming this to be true, it is not easy to suggest Pyrrhus' reasons for doing so, for by adopting Italian arms and formations he reduced the advantage inherent in his phalanx. Unless this was a concession to the terrain it appears to have been a mistake, since he had three thousand cavalry and twenty elephants with which to protect his flanks—the recognized weakness in the phalanx. Although Pyrrhus was the most famous general of his day,[8] perhaps this adaptation was simply a mistake. Like the Successors, he faced enemies who were more formidable than the Persians, against whom Alexander had fought, and it is no wonder that his victories did not come more easily.[9]

---

6. Diod. 22.6.1–3; Livy 22.59.8. The quotation was more likely uttered a year later, after the battle of Asculum, as reported by Plutarch (*Pyrrh.* 21.9), whose version would seem to be derived from the same source. "If we are victorious in one more battle with the Romans, we shall be utterly ruined."

7. According to Polyb. 18.28.10, "apparently he adopted the manipular system which was evidently used by Italians as well as Romans." See also Polybius' comparison of phalanx and legion (18.29.32), where he points out that on its own terms the phalanx was unbeatable. See also *HCP* 2 586.

8. Plut. *Pyrrh.* 8.1.

9. *Kleine Pauly* (1972) vol. 4, col. 1264. "Er traf in Rom und Karthago auf Gegner, die innerlich gefestigter waren als das Perserreich, das P.' Vorbild Alexander d. Gr. zerbrach."

The victory at Heraclea owed most to the critical intervention of the elephants, with the cavalry most active in the opening moments and the rout at the end. Presumably the flanks were secure. Although this battle has been compared to Hannibal's victory at the Trebia in 218, there are noticeable differences.[10] Hannibal's infantry in the center was weaker than that of the Romans, whereas Pyrrhus' phalanx was at least their equal and probably superior. On the other hand Hannibal's advantage in cavalry was overwhelming and was the key to his success, while for Pyrrhus elephants were essential. His cavalry played only a minor part in the battle, stymied at first but useful in the rout caused by the elephants. As was commonly the case between well-matched opponents, strong infantry and symmetry of forces combined to lessen the effectiveness of cavalry.[11]

In the following year, 279—after a march on Rome as well as an offer to negotiate peace both failed—Pyrrhus fought a second battle against the Romans near Asculum.[12] This engagement, which lasted two days, fell naturally into two phases. For unknown reasons Pyrrhus was forced into battle the first day on unfavorable ground near the Aufidus, a swift river with wooded banks. His cavalry and elephants were thus not engaged, and the day's indecisive fighting was limited to infantry. The following day, after anticipating the Romans by occupying the unfavorable terrain overnight, he forced them to fight on level ground on his terms. After placing slingers and archers among the elephants, according to Plutarch, Pyrrhus vigorously led the phalanx forward in close order, "So the Romans, having no opportunity for sidelong shifts and counter-movements as on the previous day, were obliged to engage on level ground and front-to-front; and being anxious to repulse the enemy's men-at-arms before their elephants came up, they fought fiercely with their swords against the Macedonian spears, reckless of their lives and thinking only of wounding and slaying, while caring naught for what they suffered."[13] The Romans were gradually pushed back by the phalanx, but the decisive impetus came once again from the elephants, against which Roman valor alone was unavailing. Cavalry action is not mentioned, although horsemen must

---

10. *CAH* 7, part 2 (1989) 476. For Trebia, see Livy 21.54.6–56.
11. Delbrück finds the ancient accounts of this battle highly improbable. They certainly are defective, but he seems to rely too much on logic as a guide to reliability, not allowing sufficient leeway for the chaos and friction of war and its effect on rational thinking. *HAW* 298–99.
12. Plut. *Pyrrh.* 21.5–10; Frontin. 2.3.21; Diod. 20.1–3. There is much disagreement among these sources. Plutarch, probably based on Hieronymus, has seemed most reliable to the majority of modern historians and is followed here.
13. Plut. *Pyrrh.* 21.6–7.

have been present on the flanks to protect the phalanx by limiting the mobility of the Romans. According to Hieronymus Roman losses were 6,000, while those of Pyrrhus amounted to 3,505. As was obvious, the Romans could afford such losses better than Pyrrhus could, as they had much of Italy from which to recruit, whereas the highly skilled Greeks were irreplaceable.

Some decades ago T. Frank, writing in the *Cambridge Ancient History*, gave a succinct summary of the battle of Asculum that rather nicely explained Plutarch's description. He referred to Polybius' information that Pyrrhus employed Italian units. Thus, on the first day when the terrain was unsuitable for cavalry and elephants, Pyrrhus introduced Italian maniples among the companies of the phalanx, "either to attain a longer line with which to face the enlarged Roman army or to make a more flexible line in rough country."[14] The consequent similarity of the opposing forces would explain the hard-fought draw of the first day, when most of his losses would have occurred. It seems clear from Plutarch's description that the more normal compact phalanx formation was used on the following day, and that this plus the elephants proved decisive.

At this point in his sojourn in Italy, Pyrrhus was distracted by an appeal from several cities in Sicily for help against the Carthaginians, who had hopes of occupying the entire island. He responded to the call and for the better part of three years (278–275) was active throughout the island. His prestige and the hope he offered acted as a unifying force for the hitherto squabbling Greeks. The plans of Carthage were indeed thwarted, but the autocratic Pyrrhus overstayed his welcome and returned to Italy in 275 in some disgrace, reduced in forces. The Romans had put the years of his absence to good use, forcing the southern tribes of Samnites and Lucanians to submit. Consequently, in the third and final battle with Rome Pyrrhus had little local support, except for the "best troops of the Tarentines."[15]

Pyrrhus divided his army of twenty thousand infantry and three thousand cavalry (not counting the Tarentines) in order to keep the two consular armies separate and marched against the one in quarters near Beneventum. Pyrrhus' plan was to catch the Romans off guard by undertaking a night march with his strongest troops and most warlike elephants. This effort failed when the soldiers lost their way in the densely wooded terrain and daylight betrayed their descent from the heights to the hitherto unsuspecting Romans. The fact that he divided his army and then attempted this stratagem suggests

14. *CAH* 7 (1924) 647–48.
15. Plut. *Pyrrh.* 24.4. For the battle see 25.

that Pyrrhus was now inferior in number to the Romans. With time to lead out their army, the Romans, under Manius, attacked the leading units of Pyrrhus. Manius pursued them into the plain, where a more regular action apparently took place, in which the Romans were successful up to the point at which the elephants stopped them and drove them back. The Romans fled to their camp, followed by the elephants. This action around the camp became the turning point of the battle, for the fresh camp guards rushed out hurling javelins at the elephants. The missiles stopped the elephants, which turned and ran back through their own ranks with the expected harmful effect.

This decided the battle and put an end to Pyrrhus' Italian campaign. Unable to match Italian manpower and helpless against the solidarity of Rome's allies, he returned to Tarentum and thence to Epirus. He arrived in Greece with only eight thousand infantry and five hundred cavalry, providing a warning to Hannibal that went unheeded. Although cavalry undoubtedly played some part in the action, they are not mentioned in Plutarch's account. This is understandable as Plutarch had no intention of giving a complete description of the battle, especially since the serious fighting was done by the infantry and elephants. Even the success of the latter was due largely to Roman inexperience. As the Successors had learned earlier, Alexander's success with cavalry as a striking force was impossible to duplicate against good enemy infantry whose flanks were protected by their own cavalry.

In spite of the dearth of information about other battles in which Pyrrhus engaged, Plutarch does give some interesting details about an incident that occurred in 272 after a failed assault on Sparta. While en route from Sparta to Argos, his rear guard was harassed by the Spartans under King Areus. During one attack they killed Pyrrhus' son Ptolemy, and their subsequent pursuit brought them into contact with Pyrrhus' main force. Learning of his son's death, Pyrrhus led his Molossian cavalry against the Spartan infantry. Grief stricken, Pyrrhus fought like a fury, and when he saw Evalcus—the Spartan commander—he charged. Evalcus avoided the attack by moving aside while at the same time striking with his sword. He just missed Pyrrhus' bridle hand but did cut the reins. Pyrrhus reacted quickly, striking Evalcus with his spear. He fell from his horse at the same time, but continued to fight against Evalcus' comrades on foot. This action corresponds well with previous descriptions of fighting from horseback. Pyrrhus held the reins in one hand (the left) and easily manipulated his spear with his right—a spear that must have been comparatively short and light. If, as appears likely, Evalcus stepped to the left of Pyrrhus to avoid the spear in his right hand, Pyrrhus may well have brought his spear over in front of himself from right to left in order to strike Evalcus, falling from his horse in the process. The psychological element in this action is also worth noting, for Plutarch says Pyrrhus' grief lent him such ferocity that he surpassed his normally invincible and terrible feats of arms.[16]

A description by Diodorus of an action in Sicily in the 260s between Hiero of Syracuse and the Mamertines is brief, though instructive. Hiero had the numerical advantage of ten thousand infantry and fifteen hundred horse to eight thousand and forty(?) horse on the Mamertine side. (Since there was a cavalry engagement that occupied the Syracusan horsemen, the last number seems to be a mistake.) Of interest is Hiero's decision to send six hundred infantry around a hill to attack the rear of the Mamertines. The main forces of cavalry and infantry were fighting evenly and apparently separately when the fresh infantry detachment fell upon the Mamertines and decided the battle.[17] It is clear from an incident such as this that the principle of attacking an enemy's rear or flank was what mattered, not which arm carried out the attack. Cavalry might often be preferred because of their speed, but—depending upon local conditions—infantry were potentially just as useful.

From the death of Pyrrhus in 272 during an attack upon Argos until the battle of Sellasia in 222, the sources contain virtually no details regarding military events in the Greek-speaking world. Indeed, the great Hellenistic kingdoms of Egypt, Syria, and Macedon were often at odds with each other, at sea as well as on land, but no useful information about cavalry survives. A few years before Sellasia, however, two incidents show how difficult it was to preserve the level of military performance that was observed at the time of Alexander and the Successors. The first episode occurred in 225, shortly after the Spartan king Cleomenes had seized Argos. Cleomenes' enemy Aratus, general of the Achaean League, was at Corinth when he learned the news. Aware that the Corinthians were favorable to Cleomenes, he fled the city on horseback. In their haste to join Cleomenes at Argos, the Corinthians pushed their horses too hard and ruined them.[18] The distance between Corinth and Argos is about thirty miles (forty-nine km.) on the modern road, an unexceptional day's march for cavalry. Yet the ill-judged haste of the Corinthian horsemen rendered them useless, suggesting a lack of discipline and experience.

16. Plut. *Pyrrh*. 30.5–6.
17. Diod. 22.13.
18. Plut. *Cleom*. 19.2.

The second incident also involved Aratus and Cleomenes—although this time more directly. When Cleomenes attacked Megalopolis, a member of the Achaean League, Aratus came to its aid but was reluctant to fight a set battle. Even when a sally by his light infantry penetrated to the enemy camp, Aratus held his main body back, keeping a ravine between himself and the Spartans. At that Lydiades, the cavalry commander and a former Achaean general himself, disobeyed orders and led his horsemen against the Spartans. His attack routed their right wing, but he lost his head during the pursuit and found himself in country full of trees, walls, and broad ditches that disrupted his formation. Cleomenes counterattacked and in the struggle near the gates of Megalopolis—his native city—Lydiades fell. The subsequent flight of his horsemen disrupted the Achaean hoplites and assisted the Spartans in achieving victory.[19] Such insubordination is hard to imagine in the army of Philip and Alexander or under the Successors. It is perhaps explained by the fact that the office of general of the Achaean League was elective, with Lydiades and Aratus alternating in that positon for several years in the late 230s and early 220s. The battle also shows a lack of awareness of the need to coordinate arms.

In studying the battle of Sellasia, fought in southern Greece between the Macedonian king Antigonus Doson and Cleomenes, king of Sparta, one at once notices the atypical battle formations on both sides. These were dictated by the irregular terrain, which prompted both commanders—described by Polybius as "very gifted and evenly matched"[20]—to arrange their forces to take advantage of the lay of the land. The battle also serves as an example of the discrepancy between rational planning prior to an engagement and the irrational, unpredictable behavior that occurs once fighting begins.

After having made an attack upon Argos, Cleomenes retired into his own territory and awaited the invasion of Antigonus, who had been in winter quarters. Cleomenes, correctly identifying the route by which Antigonus would march south, proceeded to block it with his army near Sellasia, northeast of Sparta in the valley of the Oenus (a tributary of the Eurotas). The Spartan king had assumed a defensive position by fortifying the two hills that flanked the road and river with trenches and palisades. On the more level ground in the valley, he stationed cavalry and mercenaries on each side of the road. As Polybius describes it, "Antigonus on his arrival observed the great natural strength of the position and how Cleomenes had so cleverly occupied

19. Ibid., *Arat.* 37; *Cleom.* 6.
20. Polyb. 2.66.4.

the advantageous points with the portions of his force suitable in each case that his whole formation resembled the attitude of a good heavy-armed fighter ready for combat. For attack and defense alike nothing was wanting, the position being at one and the same time a fortified camp difficult to approach and a line of battle ready for action."[21] Since the heights precluded the use of cavalry on the outer flanks, which in any case were protected by the terrain, the horsemen were posted in the center of the line on the river plain where they had room to maneuver and could also shield the interior flanks. Cleomenes had placed his Spartan troops and the mercenaries on the rising slope of Olympus to the right. His brother Eucleidas occupied the Euas hill on the left with *perioeci* and allies. Antigonus, after several unsuccessful probes of the enemy positions, directed the attack against Olympus with the Macedonian phalanx and mercenary troops. Because of the confined space, the phalanx was apparently thirty-two ranks deep, twice the normal sixteen.[22] Antigonus had arranged to coordinate the attack in the three zones of combat—the two hills and the valley—by means of signals. A white flag was used for the troops on the opposite hill, while those in the center were to look for a red cloak raised on a *sarissa*.[23]

It is at this point that rational planning left off and the vagaries of execution took over. It appears that Antigonus' forces on Euas (his right) were not initially visible to the opposing forces under Eucleidas. Whether this was intentional—that is to say, part of an ambush, as Plutarch suggests—or due to topography is not certain. In any case a gap opened on the right during the attack on Euas, which Plutarch attributes to disobedience that occurred when some units attacked before the signal was given. Eucleidas, seeing this, sent light-armed mercenaries from the center to attack the Macedonian rear. This threat was perceived and acted upon by the young Philopoemen, who was stationed in the center with the Achaean cavalry. His part in the battle is described in some detail by both Polybius and Plutarch because of his later fame as a soldier and statesman in the Achaean League. Unable to convince his superiors of the danger, Philopoemen—on his own initiative—led an attack on Cleomenes' cavalry in the center. This caused the mercenaries to abandon their attempt on the Macedonian rear and return to their line to help their cavalry. During the cavalry fight, which had no further effect upon the

21. Polyb. 2.65.11–12.
22. Ibid., 2.66.9; *HCP* 1. The perioeci were partial citizens of Sparta who—among other things—were required to serve in the army.
23. Polyb. 2.66.12–11; Plut. *Philop*. 6.2.

outcome of the battle, Philopoemen was wounded in both thighs while fighting on foot after his horse was killed under him.[24] The honors of the day eventually went to Antigonus after vigorous fighting between the Macedonian and Spartan phalanxes on Olympus. Polybius credits the Macedonian success over Eucleidas on Euas to the initiative taken by Philopoemen.

Given the topographical circumstances, cavalry had little role to play in this battle except to protect the inner flanks of the infantry on the wings. In attacking the cavalry in the center, Philopoemen apparently assumed that the infantry would have to return there to prevent a breakthrough, since cavalry alone have a difficult time holding a defensive position. At this battle the cavalry of the Macedonians and their allies numbered twelve hundred, and since neither commander was counting on offensive success in the center, Spartan numbers were probably much the same. F. W. Walbank draws attention to the fact that the Macedonian army had a much smaller proportion of cavalry than it had had earlier when Alexander crossed into Asia.[25] Irrespective of a probable decline in Macedonian cavalry over the intervening years or current exigencies, this smaller number of horsemen was more likely to result from past experience of fighting in Greece against good infantry, in country that did not favor the mounted arm. Alexander's Persian enemies, on the other hand, placed their hopes largely in their cavalry. At Sellasia, both commanders wisely adapted their tactics to local circumstances, with the superior numbers of Antigonus probably deciding the issue.

Cleomenes escaped and fled to Egypt, where he died in 219. Nevertheless, he survived both Antigonus and his patron, Ptolemy III, by more than a year. Seleucus III had already died in 223. Thus all three great Hellenistic monarchies experienced a change of ruler about the same time, the new kings having long, active reigns characterized by military action in support of political ambition.[26] As a result of their ambition all three were involved in major battles over the next several decades. This activity plus the battle of Pydna in 168 brings the history of Greek warfare to a close.

The weakest kingdom at the time was Egypt, as Ptolemy had allowed the army to deteriorate. This state of affairs attracted the interest of Antiochus III, who hoped to expand southward into southern Syria and Palestine, then under Ptolemaic control. When he attacked Seleuceia in the spring of 219,

24. Polyb. 2.67; Plut. *Phil.* 6.2–7. For discussion of the problems, see *HCP* 1 282–84.
25. *HM* 3 357. See 353–61 for his full account of the battle. The army of Antigonus comprised 27,600 infantry; that of Cleomenes, something less than 20,000.
26. In Syria, Antiochus III, 223–187; in Egypt, Ptolemy IV, 221–203; and in Macedon, Philip V, 221–179.

Ptolemy IV's ministers, Agathocles and Sosibius, tried to buy time with diplomatic maneuvering while they corrected the army's defects. The account of these events in Polybius provides clear evidence of the high level of military sophistication among Hellenistic leaders, which survived periods of shameful neglect caused by the whims and carelessness of monarchs. Sobered by approaching disaster, the Egyptian authorities restored the situation remarkably quickly. Mercenaries were recalled, recruiting officers were sent out, and supplies were collected. Of special importance were men who had "served under Demetrius and Antigonus" and thus "had some notion of the reality of war and of campaigning in general."[27] The army was reorganized to meet the immediate danger, while the men were drilled and trained in weapons skills in the most approved Greek fashion, although many of them were Egyptians and Libyans. The officers were of Greek or Macedonian origin. A Thessalian, Echecrates, trained the Greek and mercenary cavalry—a fitting choice given his people's long-standing reputation for fielding fine cavalry.[28] Considering that the Egyptian army had been in a sorry state for many years, these efforts to resurrect it produced astonishing results; it proved to be more than a match for the more seasoned army of Antiochus in the coming battle.

For a variety of reasons, both diplomatic and military, it was June 217 before the two kings faced each other near Raphia. After five days camped in close proximity, first Ptolemy and then Antiochus led their troops out of camp. The battle lines were unexceptional in alignment, with phalanxes armed in the Macedonian manner occupying the center. On the Egyptian side these were flanked immediately by light infantry, with peltasts on the left and Gauls, Thracians, and Greek mercenaries on the right. The cavalry were posted on the outside of each wing. Ptolemy also placed 40 elephants in front of the left wing, with himself and the remaining 33 elephants in a similar position on the right. Polybius gives his numbers as 70,000 infantry, 5,000 cavalry, and 73 elephants.[29] Antiochus apparently decided to meet strength with strength, for he placed 60 of his 102 elephants and 4,000 of his 6,000 cavalry on his right, facing Ptolemy. These cavalry were grouped in two formations of 2,000 each, the outside one seemingly angled back from the battle line, possibly as a precaution against an outflanking move by Ptolemy. The remaining 2,000 cavalry and 42 elephants were stationed on the other wing.

27. Polyb. 5.63.13.
28. Ibid., 5.63.8–65.10.
29. Ibid., 5.79.2, 82.2–7. The figures for Ptolemy's infantry have been questioned. For discussion see *HCP* 1 590–92; *SA* 140–41.

Light-armed infantry filled in the line between cavalry and phalanx on both flanks. Antiochus' infantry numbered 62,000.[30]

In his description of the preliminaries to the battle, Polybius makes a remark that offers perspective on the relative importance of infantry and cavalry during this period. He says that both kings, when addressing their troops before the battle, gave most attention and encouragement to the phalangites, as they placed their greatest hopes upon these men.[31] The battle itself confirmed their importance, but it is not clear from the course of events that Antiochus really believed what Polybius credits him with saying.

The elephants initiated the action, with most of Ptolemy's smaller North African elephants fleeing from their Indian cousins and thus causing some confusion in their own lines. At about the same time Antiochus led his cavalry outside, past the elephants, and attacked Polycrates' horsemen on Ptolemy's left. The defeat of this wing was completed by Antiochus' Greek mercenaries, who attacked the peltasts already disrupted by retreating elephants. For a while the other wing was quiet, but when Echecrates—Ptolemy's commander on his right—saw his elephants refuse to advance and a dust cloud drifting toward him from the other wing, he led his cavalry around the elephants and struck the enemy horsemen in the flank and rear. As they fled, his Greek mercenaries attacked the enemy line head on. Thus each army was victorious on its own right, the elephants were largely out of the fight, and the two phalanxes were left anxiously facing each other with their flanks stripped bare. At this point the personal behavior of the two kings proved decisive. Antiochus and his horsemen continued their pursuit, leaving the phalanx to its own devices. Ptolemy, on the other hand, took refuge from his setback on the left flank by joining his phalanx. His presence and encouragement inspired his men, who lowered their *sarissas* and charged. This decided the issue. By the time Antiochus realized what was happening, it was too late to return to the fight. Polybius attributes his excessive zeal in the pursuit to his youth and inexperience, but throughout his career Antiochus seems to have had a predilection for the dash of cavalry fighting. His attitude probably owed more than a little to the experiences of the Seleucids fighting against horsemen in the East.[32]

The question of his penchant for cavalry is of some importance, as Antiochus was one of the greatest Hellenistic monarchs who—in imitation of

---

30. Polyb. 5.79.3–13; 82.8–13. *HCP* 1 607–11.
31. Polyb. 5.83.2.
32. Ibid., 5.84–85. Bar-Kochva suggests that Antiochus' pursuit of the Egyptian cavalry arose from an attempt to kill Ptolemy, who he assumed was among them. *SA* 138.

Alexander—bore the epithet "the Great." Antiochus earned this title during his own anabasis into Asia during the years 212–206. Our Mediterranean perspective and the lack of sources for these eastern campaigns distorts our picture of the events. It was a great disadvantage to face two different types of enemy, each with a different military tradition. In the Mediterranean lands to the west, infantry dominated warfare in spite of the influence of Alexander. In the vast spaces to the east, the horse cultures were more influential. It seems to have been Antiochus' tragedy that on the battlefield he was more at home in the eastern tradition, while his most dangerous enemies came from the west. Indeed, his career serves as a sort of paradigm of where and how to use cavalry. Like Alexander, he had great success in Asia, where his talents as a cavalry commander were fully realized. There, the speed and mobility of mounted troops were dominant, while infantry played a secondary role. Yet the forces that had reestablished Seleucid control in Asia proved to be deficient when matched against phalanx and legion, as Raphia and Magnesia were lost for much the same reason—overvaluation of cavalry as a striking force against a combined-arms army that was anchored by good infantry of the Greek and Roman type who fought hand to hand. Of course Antiochus also possessed a phalanx, but—at least on these two occasions—he displayed an inability to coordinate the various arms so that they fulfilled their battlefield potential.

Not a great deal of information survives regarding Antiochus' Asiatic campaigns, beyond the great impression they made on contemporary Greeks. Polybius does, however, preserve a description of an action that shows Antiochus at his best. This occurred in 208 when he was moving against Euthydemus, a Greek usurper in Bactria. The battle, which took place at Tapuria, was characterized by Cary as "a miniature Battle of the Granicus."[33]

When Antiochus learned that Euthydemus had assigned ten thousand cavalry to guard a ford across the river Arius, he broke off a siege that he was conducting and began the three-day march to the river with his army. He traveled at a normal pace for two days, but on the second evening he gathered his more mobile infantry and the cavalry and led them on a quick night march. His plan was to arrive early at the river and cross over before the cavalry arrived from a nearby town some twenty stades away where they usually spent the night. The greater part of his force was across the river before the Bactrian cavalry rode up in response to an alert from their scouts. The Bactrians attacked while Antiochus' men were still in marching order, but

---

33. Cary (1978) 71. Euthydemus, a native of Magnesia, was the founder of the kingdom of Bactria, which he ruled until 184.

Antiochus led two thousand cavalry of his immediate entourage against them after ordering the rest of his army to deploy in their usual formation. He succeeded in repulsing the first enemy hipparchy (squadron) with losses on both sides but was having some trouble against the next two hipparchies. At this point the rest of his forces advanced under Panaetotus, tipping the scales in Antiochus' favor. The Bactrians turned and fled, losing most of their men before they joined Euthydemus, who then withdrew with his army into Bactria. Polybius reports that Antiochus exhibited more personal bravery on this occasion than in any other battle. His horse was killed, while he himself was struck in the mouth and lost several teeth.[34]

Antiochus' performance in this battle was exemplary. He took advantage of the speed of cavalry and light-armed troops to arrive before he was expected; acted quickly and decisively in the face of an enemy; led picked cavalry against the attackers in order to allow time for his remaining forces to move into battle positions; justifiably placed his trust in well-trained subordinates and disciplined troops who came up to relieve him; and followed up the victory with a vigorous and destructive pursuit. Clearly the success he had on his great eastern campaign was well deserved, and it was with considerable justice that his contemporaries viewed him as a second Alexander.

Just how different the fighting in Greece proper was can be seen in the battle of Mantinea, fought in 207 between Machanidas, tyrant of Sparta, and Philopoemen, leading the Achaeans.[35] In the irregular terrain of southern Greece cavalry had a limited role in the battle itself, yet in the duel between the two generals there is a vivid description of how the spear was wielded from horseback.

As Machanidas approached Mantinea from the south, Philopoemen led the citizen levy, reinforced with mercenaries, out from the city. Each side is thought to have numbered twenty thousand.[36] Philopoemen formed up on the north side of a drainage ditch running approximately east-west about four-fifths of a mile from Mantinea. The ditch was dry and not impassable, but it was capable of disrupting a phalanx. The Spartan army took position south of the ditch, with catapults at intervals across the front. This was not a true use of field artillery, because the immobile catapults were protected by the ditch. As Polybius states, their disposition suggests that Machanidas was

---

34. Polyb. 10.49.
35. The main source is Polyb. 11.11–18, supplemented by Plut. *Philop.* 10. For critical comments, see *HCP* 2 282–94.
36. *HCP* 2 282–83.

planning to charge the Achaeans after the catapults had caused disorder in their ranks. Were the Achaeans to charge first, there was the real danger that the catapults would be overrun and destroyed, rendering them useless in any subsequent siege of Mantinea, for which they were intended. Philopoemen, however, recognized the threat of the catapults and sent mercenary cavalry, or Tarentines, from his left wing, where the ground was level and suitable for cavalry. Machanidas countered with his own Tarentines, and soon light-armed infantry were also involved. Nothing more is heard of the catapults; perhaps the mere threat represented by the Tarentines caused them to be moved out of harm's way.

A stubborn fight ensued, embracing all the mercenaries on the eastern side of the battlefield. The skill and numbers of the Lacedaemonian force proved decisive, resulting in a rout and pursuit toward Mantinea. Machanidas rashly joined in, leaving the battlefield and giving Philopoemen an opportunity to stabilize his shattered left wing, since the leaderless Lacedaemonian phalanx remained in place. Philopoemen occupied the abandoned higher ground on his left with several battalions of his phalanx and prepared to charge. The Lacedaemonian phalanx, not waiting for a command, anticipated him and charged into the ditch. When the Achaeans charged in turn, they had a height advantage over the enemy as the latter came up out of the ditch with lines in disarray. Many died there, and the rest were routed, fleeing toward Tegea to the south. Philopoemen then turned his attention to Machanidas, who found himself on the north side of the ditch. As Machanidas rode along looking for a crossing by which to escape, Philopoemen moved parallel to him on the south side. Finding a suitable spot, Machanidas turned into the ditch and spurred his horse across. He was met by Philopoemen, who struck him a mortal blow with his spear, then reversed it and stabbed him with the butt spike.[37] Machanidas' failure to respect and nullify the enemy phalanx proved to be his undoing.

In 200, at Panion near the Golan Heights, an interesting and sizable battle occurred matching Antiochus III with the Ptolemaic general Scopas. The surviving account in Polybius is unusually defective, because it is primarily a critique of Zeno's account of the battle rather than a normal Polybian narrative. Nevertheless, the principles of the battle are sufficiently apparent to warrant its inclusion.[38] The two armies were drawn up in normal fashion, with the phalanxes in the center and cavalry on the wings, while Antiochus'

37. Polyb. 11.18.; Plut. *Philop.* 10.5–8.
38. Polyb. 16.8–19. *HCP* 2 523–25. *SA* 146–57.

elephants, Tarentines, and light infantry were posted in front of the phalanx. During the battle it appears that only the phalanxes and the wings on the north side of the battle line were seriously engaged (Antiochus' right, Scopas' left). The initial attack was made by Seleucid cataphract cavalry led by Antiochus, the son of King Antiochus. He succeeded in routing the Egyptian cavalry facing him and pursued them away from the battlefield. The subsequent struggle between the phalanxes was hard fought but favored the Egyptians. Then, in virtual textbook fashion, the Seleucid cavalry returned in time to take the enemy in the rear and, together with the elephants, surround and defeat them.

The success of the cavalry on this occasion was, I think, the exception rather than the rule in Hellenistic armies. Although such tactics may have often been planned, for one reason or another they seldom worked. Most frequently the two cavalry forces on the wings of the phalanxes kept each other so busy that neither one had an opportunity to attack the enemy phalanx in flank or rear. If one cavalry force did succeed in routing the other, it was difficult and even risky to disengage and return to the battlefield, for the possible scenarios were many. Unless one had sufficient numerical superiority and could split the cavalry so that part could continue the pursuit and the other return, it remained possible for the enemy to return to the battlefield as well. At Ipsus in 301 they did return but were effectively blocked by elephants. Two years before Panion at Zama, the returning Roman cavalry sealed Hannibal's fate. Here at Panion, the Seleucids may have benefited from the fact that the younger Antiochus was leading the cavalry, since when his father found himself in similar circumstances earlier at Raphia (217) and subsequently at Magnesia (190), he proved unable to restrain his enthusiasm for the chase and thus failed to bring the cavalry back to the battlefield.[39]

In the aftermath of Hannibal's defeat in 202, which brought the Second Punic War to a close, the Romans turned their attention to Greece. Ostensibly in response to appeals from Pergamum and Rhodes, Rome decided to intervene in the Balkan Peninsula before Philip V of Macedon and Antiochus III of Syria had a chance to upset the balance of power in the East. The so-called Second Macedonian War began in the fall of 200 with the arrival in Illyria of two legions under the command of the consul Sulpicius Galba. During 199 Sulpicius attempted to invade Macedon but was thwarted by skillful maneuvers on the part of Philip, who avoided set battle. Among these actions

---

39. Bar-Kochva's topographically based reconstruction of the battle is more complex than this, but since it does not alter the crucial role of the returning cavalry, it can be passed over.

are two cavalry fights of note that offer vivid evidence of hand-to-hand combat by horsemen. On the first occasion the armies of Philip and Sulpicius lost touch with each other, leading the two commanders to send out scouting parties of cavalry. These two forces, each alerted by the approaching noise of the other, met on the same road. Thus forewarned and ready for battle, they willingly joined arms. Equally matched in number and courage, the picked troops fought hard for some time before fatigue put an end to the indecisive action. Forty men fell on the Macedonian side, thirty-five on the Roman—testimony to the often necessary futility of a "fair" fight. To add insult to injury, neither scouting party located the enemy camp, deserters eventually providing the information.[40]

This action was fought at very close quarters, as evidenced by the condition of the bodies, which Philip—thinking to honor the dead and raise fighting spirit—had brought back to camp for burial. According to Livy, they had been savagely cut apart, with arms severed from shoulders and heads from necks and with viscera lying exposed. What is not so easy to understand is Livy's comment that this carnage scared the Macedonians who saw it, because they were accustomed to fighting against Greeks and Illyrians and only used to wounds inflicted by javelins and arrows or, occasionally, a lance.[41] This is odd because the two bodies of horsemen fought for some time on equal terms, yielding only to exhaustion but not intimidated by each other while they were in combat. Furthermore, Macedonian cavalry had been using lance and sword at least since the time of Philip and Alexander. Indeed, as I have discussed earlier, it was their skill with these weapons in close combat that made them so formidable. In addition Polybius describes the Roman cavalry of his day as armed consciously on the Greek model, that is to say with spears equipped with a butt spike and strong enough to be used for more than one blow. No mention is made of swords, but Greek-style cuirasses and shields had also been adopted.[42] Given the high probability that the weapons

---

40. Livy 31.33.8–11. The comment about the noise of approaching cavalry adds a nice touch of realism. Anecdotes from the Napoleonic Wars claim that British troops sometimes detected the approach of French cavalry from downwind by the stench of saddle sores.

41. Ibid., 31.34.1–5.

42. Polyb. 6.25.3–11. Adding somewhat to the problem is Briscoe's desciption of the weapon that caused these wounds as the infantry sword. See Briscoe (1973) 140. But the sword used by the Roman infantry was a short thrusting weapon and hardly seems capable of the wounds described by Livy. The difficulty may lie in word usage, for there seems to be confusion over the correct Latin term for this sword, which was borrowed from Spain. When referring to the infantry weapon, Livy uses the phrase *gladius hispanus* (7.10.5; 22.46.5), but in this passage it is referred to as *gladius hispaniensis*. E. T. Sage, who translated the Loeb volume, identifies the weapon as a long slashing sword, which seems more likely. Sage (1953). *Livy 9, books 31–34* 100.

carried by Greek and Roman cavalry were essentially the same, the explanation may lie in the recognized ferocity of Roman war-making, which on this occasion resulted in intentional mutilation of the Macedonian dead. The subject is discussed by W. V. Harris, who suggests that the Romans "behaved somewhat more ferociously than most of the other politically advanced peoples of the Mediterranean world."[43] Polybius was aware of this behavior and suggests that the purpose of acts of atrocity, including the massacre of the inhabitants of captured cities, was "to strike terror."[44] On this occasion it seems to have worked.

Shortly afterward, Philip advanced against the Romans with twenty thousand infantry and two thousand cavalry and established camp about a mile from the camp of the enemy. Both sides remained in camp for two days. On the third day, the Romans came out to do battle. Although Philip declined the invitation, he did send out seven hundred infantry and a like number of horsemen to annoy the Roman cavalry. The Romans in turn sent out skirmishers and cavalry equal to the force of the Macedonians. According to Livy, Philip's horsemen expected to employ the typical tactics of skirmishers—riding forward, using their weapons, and then retiring—with similar sallies by the infantry, but found themselves at a disadvantage when the Romans fought as if in a normal battle line. That is, they closed for hand-to-hand fighting with swords after hurling their spears. The cavalry joined them in stationary fighting, some remaining mounted while others dismounted and joined the foot soldiers. The Macedonian cavalry, unused to stationary battle, and the infantry, lacking defensive armor, were forced to flee.[45]

If Livy's description of these events is accurate, the cavalry Philip sent out were true skirmishers, probably armed with the javelin, rather than lance-bearing line cavalry. This reluctance to engage hand to hand, however, did not extend to the phalangites and line cavalry, and the reason for the eventual defeat of the phalanx by the legion must be sought elsewhere. No regular battle occurred during the campaign of 199, but Livy does describe a number of subsequent actions in which both infantry and cavalry fought. Insufficient details of these events limit their value, although it is clear that much of the fighting was done at close quarters.[46]

In 198 the command against Philip was vigorously taken up by the new consul Titus Quinctius Flamininus, who succeeded in bringing him to the

43. Harris (1985) 51.
44. Polyb. 10.15.46.
45. Livy 31.35.
46. Ibid., 31.36–37.

conference table by occupying Thessaly. The talks fell apart when Philip refused to surrender three Macedonian fortresses—Demetrias, Chalcis, and Acrocorinth—the so-called "Fetters of Greece," which were essential for Macedonian control of the southern Balkan peninsula.

Flamininus was retained in command during the following year (197), when both sides augmented their forces and prepared to end the stalemate. In May the Roman army marched northwest from Phthiotic Thebes toward Pherae, while Philip led his forces south from Larissa.[47] Philip's army seems to have numbered twenty-seven thousand at this battle, including eighteen thousand phalangites and two thousand cavalry. The Romans were at least equal in number or perhaps slightly superior. They had more cavalry—twenty-five hundred—and an unknown number of elephants.[48] Near Pherae a vigorous skirmish occurred between cavalry and infantry from both sides, but the terrain in this area was unsuitable for a battle because it was full of trees, gardens, bridges, and walls. The next day both armies moved westward toward Scotussa, following parallel lines but kept from contact by Cynoscephalae, a range of high hills.[49] During the night of the second day of marching a severe thunderstorm broke out, and by dawn the landscape was enshrouded in a mist of low-lying clouds. Philip moved out of camp first but made little progress due to poor visibility. Consequently, he stopped his army and sent out an advance party to occupy the summits of the intervening hills. Shortly thereafter Flamininus sent out a scouting party comprising ten cavalry troops, perhaps three hundred riders, and one thousand light infantry.[50]

Unable to see in the mist, the two forces were abruptly thrown together. After some initial confusion both parties attacked, at the same time sending messengers to the commanders. The advantage in this opening action passed from side to side as reinforcements were sent forward by the two sides in turn. Thus the initial Roman setback was reversed by the arrival of five hundred cavalry and two thousand infantry. When the Macedonians were driven back upon the heights, Philip sent out the Thessalian and Macedonian cavalry and most of the mercenaries, who forced the Romans to retreat. These were saved from rout only by the exceptional spirit of the allied Aetolian cavalry. At that point Flamininus led out the main army and took up a position

47. Polyb. 18.18–27; Livy 33.6–10; Plut. *Flam.* 7.2; HCP 2 572–85; Briscoe (1973) 256–66; HM 3 436–43.
48. For a discussion of the numbers, see HM 3 436–37. Hammond conjectures that the Romans may have had a total of as many as thirty-two thousand men.
49. HCP 2 575–79 for discussion of the marches prior to the battle of Cynoscephalae.
50. Ibid., 580 for comment on the size of the cavalry units.

near the hills. Philip, for his part, had not intended to fight a battle on the site because of the mist and the difficulties of the terrain, yet he allowed himself to be persuaded by overly optimistic reports of the initial fighting and ordered his own army to move out of camp. As he occupied the heights with his well-formed right wing, he saw his advanced force retreating toward his position, followed by the Roman heavy as well as light infantry. At that point, he made the fateful decision to stand and fight in spite of the fact that the greater portion of his phalanx was still in march formation, approaching the heights. The retreating infantry and cavalry, presumably the Macedonians and Thessalians, were added to his right wing. The peltasts and phalanx on this wing were then ordered to close to the right and double their depth.[51] This accomplished, the phalanx was ordered to lower *sarissas* and advance.[52] In the ensuing battle the Macedonians, with the advantage of weight and arms and the height from which their attack originated, drove back the Romans.

Flamininus conceded defeat there and took command of his right, where he hoped for better luck against units not yet on the spot or formed for battle. With his elephants in front he led his forces against the unprepared Macedonian left, which disintegrated at first contact with the elephants and fled. But victory was still in doubt until an alert tribune detached twenty of his legion's maniples and led them against the rear of Philip's victorious right wing.[53] As the phalanx, armed with the long *sarissa* and crowded together, could not face about to defend itself, the battle was irretrievably lost. Philip, along with some Thracians and Macedonians, fled to Tempe. Losses for the Romans were about seven hundred, for the Macedonians, they included eight thousand dead and five thousand captured.

Cavalry do not seem to have played much of a role in this battle, which was decided by infantry. The Thessalian and Macedonian horsemen were on the right, apparently to protect the flank and obviously not in position to prevent the rear attack. Walbank feels there may have been six hundred on the left.[54] If so, they had no effect on the outcome, either being out of position as the left wing tried to form up or being frightened off by the elephants.

---

51. Ibid., 582. This was a change from marching order of eight deep to a battle line of sixteen.

52. Here Livy makes a notorious error (33.8.13), which raises doubts about his command of Greek. He mistranslates Polybius' καταβαλοῦσι (18.24.9), "lower" (the *sarissas*), by *positis*, "lay aside," a mistake that then compels him to add the explanation that the Macedonians fought with swords because the spears were too long. *HCP* 2 582. Briscoe (1973) 263.

53. *HCP* 2 583–84. Walbank suggests that this tribune was in command of the legion and that he acted with Flamininus' concurrence or possibly on his direct order. His identity is unknown.

54. Ibid., 583.

Ironically, the agile Roman maniples that won the battle had performed a classic cavalry maneuver in turning the enemy flank and attacking his rear, albeit an internal flank exposed by an unanticipated gap in the middle of the Macedonian line. This decisive deployment of the maniples is cited as an example of the legion's flexibility and tactical superiority, but even if that is true, a number of questions remain. Was it an act of subordination justified by success, a part of Flamininus' plan, or the kind of decision a subordinate was expected to make as the occasion arose? If the latter, it would today be called small-unit initiative.[55] Yet it would have been a meaningless potential had Philip not made the mistake of accepting battle under unfavorable circumstances before his phalanx was fully formed and ready for battle. Interestingly, the supposed weakness of the phalanx on hilly ground played no part, for where it was ready for battle on the right, it carried everything before it. Philip's failure to protect his flanks is impossible to explain using the extant sources, as he initially possessed sufficient auxiliary arms for the purpose. The phalanx proved itself superior in sheer fighting power, but Philip's error, luck, and Roman versatility determined the result.

Although they were delighted to be rid of the Macedonians, some Greek states found the Romans just as oppressive. As a result, in 192 the Aetolians—hoping to form a Greek coalition against Rome—invited Antiochus to liberate Greece. The Romans were already unhappy with him because of his campaigns in Thrace beginning in 196 and the refuge he had offered Hannibal in 195. While Philip sat idle, respecting the terms of his treaty of friendship with Rome, the consul Acilius Glabrio drove Antiochus out of Greece in 191. This did not end the matter, for the Romans had already decided that a major defeat had to be inflicted upon him to discourage further troublemaking in Greece.

Thus in the spring of 190 the new consul, Lucius Scipio, with his brother Publius—the conqueror of Hannibal—as his associate, joined the two legions already in Greece with eight thousand reinforcements. Both Livy and Appian, the main sources for the campaign, fault Antiochus for abandoning his European holdings, especially Lysimachia, which the Romans would have had to besiege before crossing the Hellespont. If he had been relying on his fleet to make this decision stand, his hopes were dashed by defeats at sea, in one of which Hannibal lost to the Rhodians. As a result the Romans, with the assistance of King Eumenes of Pergamon, landed in Asia Minor unopposed.[56]

55. For examples, see Van Creveld (1985) 169–70; 269–71.
56. Livy 37.23–31; App. *Syr.* 11.5.22–6.29.

Antiochus gathered all the forces he could and prepared to meet the Romans in battle, apparently induced by the hope of decisive victory to abandon a defensive strategy that may have been more to his long-term advantage.

For sheer spectacle the two armies that faced each other near Magnesia late in 190 had few equals in antiquity.[57] In this first appearance of the Roman legion in Asia the Roman side, with a total of about thirty thousand, was anchored on two legions and two allied alae, each of these having fifty-four hundred men. Complementing the heavy infantry were Roman, Italian, and Pergamene cavalry numbering something less then three thousand, under the command of Eumenes. Pergamenes, Achaeans, Trallians, and Cretans comprised four thousand light infantry. The Romans also had sixteen North African elephants taken from the Carthaginians after Zama. These were kept out of the battle because they were greatly outnumbered by Antiochus' Indian elephants, which also had the advantage of size.

The Seleucid army embraced a greater variety of troops, including elephants, scythed chariots, a dromedary corps, and heavily armored cataphracts, among other types of cavalry. These were part of a total force of some sixty thousand infantry and twelve thousand cavalry. As is often the case in eastern armies containing many diverse ethnic units with a variety of arms, the effectiveness of the whole was less then the numbers would suggest. On the level plain of Magnesia, Antiochus' most formidable force was the sixteen-thousand-man phalanx separated into ten sections, each thirty-two ranks deep by fifty abreast. The intervals between sections were occupied by two elephants each, totaling twenty-two, while sixteen elephants were placed on each wing for a grand total of fifty-four.

When the two battle lines faced each other, it was clear that the Romans—unlike the symmetrically arranged forces of Antiochus—were strongly overbalanced to their right. Since the left wing of the Roman army—the allied infantry *ala*—rested on the river Phrygius with its steep banks, only four *turmae* of cavalry (120 men) were posted as a flank guard. Facing them on the Syrian right beyond the phalanx were 6,700 cavalry and 21,000 infantry of various types, from heavy-armed silver shields to archers and slingers.[58]

On the other wing the forces were somewhat more evenly matched. There the Romans had Eumenes' auxiliaries and Achaean light infantry

---

57. Livy 37.37–44; App. *Syr.* 11.6.30–37. Both are based on the lost account of Polybius. *SA* 162–73 has a full discussion of the battle.

58. This follows Livy. Appian places the troops of Eumenes on the Roman left, but since they are active on the right during the battle, it should be an error. App. *Syr.* 11.6.31; 6.34.

numbering three thousand, about twenty-two hundred Roman and eight hundred Pergamene cavalry under Eumenes' command, and one thousand Cretan and Trallian infantry. Facing them on the flank of the phalanx were fifteen hundred Galatian infantry, forty-seven hundred auxiliary infantry, three thousand cataphracts, one thousand cavalry of the royal squadron, chariots and a dromedary corps in front of the line, five hundred Tarentine and twenty-five hundred Galatian cavalry, and, finally, eleven thousand auxiliary infantry of various types along with sixteen elephants.

There was a morning mist that dampened everything, according to Livy causing more trouble for the Syrian forces than for the Romans on two counts. Since the Roman line was shorter their visibility from one end to the other was unaffected, whereas that of the Syrians was restricted. In addition the moisture had softened the bowstrings, slings, and javelin thongs of the more numerous missile troops of the Syrians. Livy seems to be exaggerating this problem, because Eumenes himself used missile troops to good effect during the battle, while the most formidable troops on both sides fought with spears and swords.

The fighting began on both wings at about the same time, but with very different results. On his own right wing Antiochus took advantage of the obvious and inexplicable weakness on the Roman left by attacking their front and flank with the auxiliary infantry and the cataphract cavalry. The four *turmae* of Roman cavalry as well as some of the infantry of the Italian *ala* fled back toward their camp in the rear. Instead of turning in behind the Roman legions, however, Antiochus pursued the fugitives to the Roman camp, where a spirited defense by the camp commander, Marcus Aemilius, brought him up short.

In the meantime Antiochus' left wing had been thrown into confusion by the opportunistic Eumenes, whose previous experience with scyth-bearing chariots now served him well. He knew that these dubious instruments were useless if the horses could be frightened and made unmanageable. Consequently, he sent forward Cretan archers, slingers, javelin throwers, and some cavalry in loose order with orders to shower the chariots with missiles from all sides. This—accompanied by shouting—destroyed the charioteers' control of the horses, which rushed in all directions. Eumenes' nimble light troops easily got out of the way, but those chariots that turned back into their own line caused panic and confusion among the camels, then disrupted the cataphracts, whose heavier armor made them less mobile. He followed this with a cavalry attack, drove off the auxiliaries and cavalry on the Syrian left, and thus exposed the phalanx, which was somewhat disordered by comrades seeking refuge within its ranks. Nonetheless, the Roman legions—after hurling their javelins—had too much respect for the discipline and long spears of the phalanx to close with their swords, being content to assist cavalry and light troops in assailing them from all sides. The phalanx retired in good order until the elephants became uncontrollable, at which point it disintegrated. The ensuing rout soon became a slaughter.

Earlier, when Antiochus had pursued the Roman left to their camp, he had lost touch with the main battle. Consequently, he did not realize the immensity of the disaster until he disengaged from the camp defenders (as Appian says) or was driven off with the help of Eumenes' brother Attalus, who arrived from his right wing with two hundred cavalry (if one follows Livy). Appian suggests that until this time Antiochus comported himself as the victor but, soon realizing what had happened to his army, he fled.

There are many questions about these events. The situation on the Roman left is odd, to say the least. Cavalry in a defensive posture are incapable of holding ground, and their small number was an open invitation to the mass of horsemen facing them. The Romans would have done better to have anchored this wing directly on the river. Then there is the question of how Antiochus got behind the Roman lines. Did he simply drive off the cavalry and outflank the allied *ala*? Did he penetrate the *ala* or even a Roman legion, as Justin says? Or did some combination of these maneuvers occur?[59] The answer to these questions, I think, is to be found in the four Roman *turmae* of cavalry. Once these were driven back, fear would have done its work on the adjacent Italian infantry and caused at least some of them to flee to their camp. Why Antiochus did not use some of his victorious cavalry on the right to turn in behind the Roman line is a puzzle, as is his failure to coordinate his own attack with an advance by his phalanx. In fact both sides seem to have been hesitant to commit their heavy infantry, and the Romans would have been in trouble had it not been for the bold initiative of Eumenes. If both Scipio and Hannibal were present at this battle—as may have been the case—no evidence of it is noticeable in the course of events. The terrain, unlike that of Cynoscephalae, was ideal for the phalanx, and Antiochus' failure to use his infantry properly in coordination with his cavalry cost him the battle. As I have mentioned, his

---

59. Livy has Antiochus attack the Roman left from front and flank (38.42.7–8), whereas Appian says that he broke through the Roman line of battle (11.6.34) and Justin says that a Roman legion was routed (31.8.6). Bar-Kochva (*SA* 170) follows the latter, but Walsh correctly points out that Livy later has Roman legions (note the plural) advancing against the phalanx (1992) 169.

254   The Aftermath: 323 to 150 B.C.

success in the East had apparently fostered a fatal predilection for cavalry. If that is so, then he was precisely where he wanted to be—at the head of a cavalry charge, excited and victorious—but with hardly a thought in his head for the rest of his army.

After Magnesia, no useful battle accounts survive in the sources until the minor battle of Larissa in 171. This battle was part of a series of events leading to Pydna, the final battle in the conflict between Rome and Macedon known as the Third Macedonian War (172–168). By 171 it was clear to Perseus, the Macedonian king (179–168), that his efforts to preserve peace with the Romans were fruitless, so the decision was made to defend Macedonian freedom by force of arms. From the Macedonian perspective it was not a hopeless cause. Perseus' father, Philip, had not wasted the years of peace between Cynoscephalae in 197 and his death in 179, and Perseus continued his work.[60] The population recovered, in part from resettlement of non-Macedonians; the cities were strengthened and enlarged; agriculture and mining were encouraged; the royal arsenals were kept full; money and grain were available for a ten-year war; and the army was trained to virtually a professional level. To be sure Macedon could not win a war of attrition with Rome, but—all things being equal—its phalanx and cavalry stood a good chance against a Roman legionary army, and a Roman defeat might lead to terms that Perseus could accept.

In 171 the Roman command in Macedon fell to the consul Publius Licinius. While Perseus waited to hear from his envoys in Italy, Licinius landed at Illyris in Apollonia, moved inland, and crossed the Pindus range. Hard marching through a trackless landscape and difficult mountain passes exhausted the men and horses, and several days of rest were necessary. Perseus was to pay a high price for his delay, which had the honorable purpose of attempting to preserve the peace. A large Roman army was now on the Macedonian side of the central Balkan range, and Macedon's struggle for survival would be fought largely on its own soil.[61]

To meet the Roman force of 37,000 infantry and 2,000 cavalry, Perseus had assembled at Citium, on the western side of the Macedonian plain, an army comprising 39,000 infantry and 4,000 cavalry—a force comparable to, if not larger than, the army led into Asia by Alexander in 334.[62] Most impres-

60. See the discussion on the Macedonian recovery under Philip in *HM* 3 458–87. Livy 42.52.
61. For a succinct description of Rome's motives in this war, see Errington (1990) 214–17. *HM* 3 505–12.
62. Livy 42.50–52.

sive was the number of Macedonian cavalry on hand—3,000. This army, also much larger than Perseus' father's at Cynoscephalae, gave a clear indication of how seriously he viewed the Roman attack.

While Perseus marched south toward Thessaly, subduing some towns on the way, the Romans advanced eastward to meet him and were joined by reinforcements from the Greek states and Eumenes totaling about 2,000 cavalry and 5,600 infantry.[63] By the time Perseus appeared, the Romans had already gone into camp about three miles from Larissa. The Macedonian infantry halted about a mile from the Roman camp, while Perseus went forward with the cavalry and light-armed infantry. They soon sighted two squadrons of cavalry—mostly Gauls—and 150 light troops. Uncertain what the enemy intended, Perseus sent forward only four squadrons of cavalry and four cohorts of infantry, about equal in number to their opponents. According to Livy, "Since they were equally matched as to numbers and from neither the one side nor the other were reinforcements sent up, the battle ended in a draw."[64] About thirty of Eumenes' men on the Roman side were killed, but Livy gives no casualty figures for Perseus, who then withdrew to his camp about twelve miles away at Sycurium.

Over the next several days Perseus repeatedly led his forces to the enemy camp, but the Romans declined the invitation to fight. Then he moved his camp to within four miles of the Romans and, on the following day, marshaled his infantry at dawn. When Perseus led all the cavalry and light infantry to the enemy camp, this finally provoked a response, as the Romans also sent out all of their cavalry and light troops. The regular infantry were drawn up inside the camp. Both sides were about equal in number and similarly deployed. The commanders, Perseus and Quintus Mucius (legate for the consul), were in the center with the elite cavalry, while each wing was a mixture of light infantry and cavalry. Apparently Macedonian aggressiveness won the day, for after initial action by slingers and javelin men in front of the line, the Thracians of Perseus' left disrupted and routed their opposites—the Italian cavalry—while Perseus himself attacked the Roman center and drove it back. After the battle the Romans blamed the Aetolian cavalry for the collapse, a charge that Polybius later found suspect. There seem to be several small gaps in Livy's text, obscuring these events.[65] The Romans were spared from complete disaster on

---

63. Ibid., 42.55.7–10.
64. Ibid., 42.57.9.
65. Livy 42.58.3; 57–59 for the battle, which took place near Larissa. *HM* 3 517–18. For Polybius' exoneration of the Aetolian cavalry officers, see 27.15.14.

this occasion by four hundred Thessalian cavalry who had been posted outside the battle line on the left. They now intervened between the fleeing Roman troops and the Macedonians, where they joined Eumenes' auxiliaries and made a gradual retreat with intact ranks possible. Indeed, as the retreating Romans tightened up their formation they began to present a threat to the Macedonian cavalry, who had lost their order during the pursuit. The phalanx came up at this time, but Perseus was reluctant to storm the Roman camp and the cavalry were recalled.

Roman losses included two hundred cavalry and two thousand infantry killed and about six hundred captured. Perseus lost only twenty cavalry and forty infantry.[66] Obviously, the Macedonian cavalry were still a force to be reckoned with. The tactics employed were not fancy, as there was little opportunity for them with evenly matched forces, and good, hard fighting seems to have won the day. No flank attack was attempted, merely a straight-ahead advance by cavalry and light infantry that closed for hand-to-hand fighting. The fragmentary section in Livy mentions spears used against infantry and the maiming of horses, which indicates close combat, but whether the subjects of these acts were Macedonian or Roman, infantry or cavalry, cannot be said.[67]

Little additional detailed description of fighting survives from the years just prior to Pydna in 168, but it is clear that Perseus had considerable success against Roman armies and their consular commanders. Later, in 171, he successfully attacked foraging Romans near Crannon with one thousand cavalry and two thousaand Thracian and Cretan infantry, capturing about one thousand wagons with their teams and six hundred men. Many others were killed. Recalling his scattered cavalry, Perseus then attacked a guard detachment numbering about eight hundred that seemed to be easy prey. These sought refuge on a hill, where—although they took some casualties from missiles—their disciplined ranks, aided by the advantage of height, withstood the Macedonian attacks. Perseus' cavalry were less useful under these circumstances, and the Romans held out until a relief column appeared. Flush with his victory, Perseus challenged this larger force but was driven off with some loss.[68]

The following year Perseus attacked a Roman fleet at Oreus in northern Euboea, capturing twenty merchant ships together with their cargoes and

66. Livy 42.60.1. Plut. *Aem.* 9.2 says that twenty-five hundred Romans were killed at Larissa in a cavalry battle. This victory gained some sympathy for Perseus in Greece, since he was viewed as the underdog. Livy 42.63.1.
67. Livy 42.59.3.
68. Livy 42.65–66. Perseus lost three hundred infantry and twenty–four of his best cavalrymen. For a detailed account of these years, see *HM* 3 512–31.

four quinqueremes and sinking the remaining grain ships. He also defeated a consular army under Aulus Hostilius Mancinus as he attempted to enter Macedon; on a second occasion, when Hostilius had entered Thessaly, the Romans refused battle and withdrew.[69] Perseus' versatility and skill as a commander were also on display during the following winter after the solstice (170/169), when he conducted a remarkable campaign to the northwest of Macedon that was prompted by the defection of Uscana in Penestae. With a force of twelve thousand infantry and five hundred cavalry, Perseus captured Uscana and twelve forts—including more than two thousand Romans—in the wintery terrain of mountain ranges exceeding two thousand meters in height.

In general Perseus had the better of things again in 169, although the consul Quintus Marcius Philippus briefly occupied Dium, the southernmost Macedonian capital. In 168, however, the Romans finally showed some determination. An experienced and able commander, Lucius Aemilius Paullus, was elected consul and assigned Macedonia as his province. New troops were enrolled, while those who were unfit were dismissed, and the Senate voted that the tribunes were to be chosen only from former officeholders.[70]

The two armies contending for the fate of Macedon first faced each other across the bed of the river Elpeus just west of Dium and north of Mount Olympus in mid-June 168. For two days—the twelfth and thirteenth—there was skirmishing in the dry riverbed, but the Romans were unable to advance directly against Perseus' well-prepared defenses on the opposite bank. On the evening of the thirteenth, the consul sent Publius Scipio Nasica to seize the Petra pass to the west in order to turn Perseus' position, which was accomplished early on the fourteenth.[71] When the Macedonian king learned of it, he withdrew his army northeast to the narrow coastal plain south of Pydna. Perseus set up his camp and marshalled his forces so they faced inland, awaiting the arrival of the Romans and ready to fight as soon as opportunity offered. Aemilius apparently had not sent out scouts, because he was surprised to find the Macedonians in battle formation awaiting him as he descended the hills toward the plain. The Romans had been marching in dust and heat for half a day—it now being noon—and Aemilius thought it wise not to engage the well-prepared and fresher Macedonians. Perseus, for his part, was slow to respond, thus allowing Aemilius to establish a defensive line while a camp was laid out on a ridge to his left, inland to the west. The Romans thereupon made

69. Plut. *Aem.* 9.
70. Livy 44.21.
71. Plut. *Aem.* 16.

an orderly withdrawal into the camp. Numbers in this battle are less certain than usual, especially on the Roman side. According to Plutarch, Perseus had almost forty thousand infantry and four thousand cavalry. N. G. L. Hammond, after discussing the scattered and partial sources, reached the conclusion that the Romans were slightly inferior in infantry and about equal in cavalry. They did, however, possess elephants, of which Perseus had none.[72]

The battle, when it came, may have started by accident. The principal units of both armies were still in camp when the events that precipitated the action occurred at a stream separating the two sides. A packhorse on the Roman side got loose from its attendants, who then pursued it into the stream. It was caught, however, by three of Perseus' Thracians who were on guard there. Roman soldiers joined in, recapturing the horse and killing one of the Thracians. His compatriots, some eight hundred in number, then crossed the stream in pursuit of the Romans. While the skirmishing that followed was taking place, the two sides left camp and formed battle lines. On the level ground where the fighting began, the Macedonians had a decided advantage by virtue of their disciplined organization and long spears. In fact it was on this occasion, as reported by Plutarch, that Aemilius Paullus experienced the greatest fright of his life as he watched the dreadful effect of the massed *sarissas* of the Macedonians on his sword-bearing legions. The first Roman line was destroyed, but the second was driven back onto the mountain—an event that proved to be their salvation. The lengthy Macedonian line began to lose its cohesion as the terrain became irregular, and Aemilius had the wit to recognize an opportunity when he saw it. Now the less rigid formation of the Romans, as well as their light shields and short swords, could be used to advantage. Aemilius divided up his cohorts and ordered them to infiltrate the breaks in the enemy line, avoid the long spears, and attack the phalangites from the side. This decided the issue, for the Macedonians were routed and massacred, with between twenty thousand and twenty-five thousand reportedly killed.

This is largely the account found in Plutarch. Livy's description of the opening events of the main battle is lost, and where his account resumes, it differs from that of Plutarch in his saying that the collapse began on the Macedonian left, where an attack by the Roman elephants was followed up by the Latin allies. Livy also emphasizes the scattered attacks on a disrupted phalanx.[73] This disruption of the Macedonian line is clearly the key to Roman

---

72. Livy 44.36.1–37.4; Plut. *Aem.* 17.1–3; Frontin. *Str.* 2.3.20; *HM* 3 547–57. For numbers see *HM* 3 539–41; Plut. *Aem.* 13.9.

73. Livy 44.40–42; Plut. *Aem.* 18–21.

success, but what were the cavalry doing? They are not mentioned during the battle and obviously were not seriously engaged, since both Plutarch and Livy state that the Macedonian horsemen escaped virtually unscathed. Presumably they were protecting the flanks—their only realistic function, since they were not sufficiently superior to their Roman counterparts to drive them off and then take an active part in the battle. In any case they were not capable of attacking the Roman legions head on with much hope of success.

Given the high degree of asymmetry between phalanx and legion in respect to weapons and formation (although not relative to level of training, discipline, and willingness to fight at close quarters), a decisive victory with heavy losses on the defeated side was to be expected once an advantage was exploited. The initial success of the phalanx is also attributable to this asymmetry. The elephants mentioned by Livy may have prevented the Macedonian cavalry from attempting more than they did. This possibility had been foreseen by Perseus, who had created a unit of elephant fighters. Having no elephants of their own, they practiced against dummies, apparently to no avail. Horses have good powers of visual discrimination and often—perversely as it sometimes seems—ignore similarities between objects they do and do not shy at. Horses also have a good sense of smell, and the odor of elephants would have been impossible to reproduce.[74] Hammond assumes that Perseus withdrew his cavalry as soon as the elephants led the Roman counterattack.[75] Elephants are mentioned only on the Roman right, and it is an assumption—albeit a tempting one—that they thwarted the Macedonian cavalry on the other wing as well. Nonetheless, there is no suggestion that the Romans attempted to outflank the Macedonian line, which suggests that the cavalry were protecting the flanks for much of the battle. Even in the absence of elephants, it is unlikely that the Macedonian horsemen could have done much against the equal number of Roman cavalry. Pydna was an infantry fight from start to finish. In spite of these considerations, it does not seem unreasonable to expect greater fighting spirit on the part of the Macedonian cavalry at such a critical point in the kingdom's history. The reproaches hurled at the cavalry after the battle by Macedonian infantry who overtook them and even hurled some to the ground seem somehow justified.[76]

Perseus' previous success against the Romans, as well as that of his father, Philip, earlier in the century, suggests that the outcome at Cynoscephalae and

---

74. Livy 44.41.4; Zonar. 9.22.
75. *HM* 3 555.
76. Plut. *Aem.* 23.1.

Pydna was not inevitable, although Macedon certainly would have lost a war of attrition against a determined Rome. In both battles the phalanx itself fought at a disadvantage, and the cavalry—for one reason or another—were not used skillfully. In spite of the widely recognized versatility and tenacity of the legion, it remains doubtful that a Roman army of this period was inherently superior to a comparable Macedonian one. It is not sufficient to say that the phalanx required level ground more than the legion did. Hannibal had defeated the legion on a level battle site of his choosing at the Trebia, where he was concerned about his cavalry's ability to operate. Philip and Perseus had it within their power to do likewise, but they committed critical errors in deciding to fight in less than favorable circumstances. War, however, is not sport. Taking advantage of every opening—fair or not—is the only sensible way to proceed.

The accounts of the battle of Pydna in Livy, Polybius, and Plutarch are not the only sources of information about this last great conflict of the Hellenistic period. In the year following his victory Paullus visited Delphi, where he found an incomplete monument that had been commissioned by Perseus and converted it into a memorial to his own success. Substantial portions of a frieze from this monument survive that may, in fact, preserve a pictorial version of one or more events from the battle itself. The frieze occupied a band around the four faces of the monument near its top and just below an equestrian statue of Paullus. Twenty-eight human figures and fourteen horses, all but one bearing a rider, are recognizable in one or more scenes of combat comprising cavalry and infantry.[77] Hammond has suggested that a scene on one of the long sides—the north face—portrays the incident that led to the battle, as it shows a riderless and apparently unbridled horse in the midst of an action involving light infantry and cavalry.[78] This is extremely plausible, as is his additional comment that all four faces show the opening events of the battle. The latter seems clear based on the fact that all the scenes contain light infantry and cavalry. Thus the absence of heavy infantry of the line and the presence of cavalry, which do not seem to have played any significant role in the battle, suggest that these figures represent the auxiliaries fighting over the loose horse in the streambed. It is noteworthy that the cavalry appear to be fighting at close quarters with hand-held weapons.

The events described in the last two chapters, covering the period from 323 to 168, reflect a reasonably consistent application of cavalry that differs

77. Kähler (1965) 613–17. Pollitt (1986) 155–58.
78. *HM* 3 163.

markedly from that of Alexander—a difference that resulted from the restraint imposed upon cavalry tactics when horsemen were in the presence of good infantry as well as from the closer symmetry of the armies that faced each other. The combined arms tactics of Alexander, who advanced with articulated line infantry and cavalry directly into the Persian line and penetrated it, could not be reproduced by the Successors and their heirs. Phalanx infantry retained its normal preeminent position in Greek warfare. Nonetheless, cavalry did show greater activity on the battlefield and more willingness to fight at close quarters than was evident prior to Philip and Alexander. Furthermore, as is evident in the campaigns of Antiochus III, the mounted arm dominated fighting to the east of Greece.

In retrospect, it appears likely that these battles, rather than Alexander's experiences in Asia, offer the better analogy for what transpired at Chaeronea, supporting Rahe's argument (which I have discussed) that Alexander was in command of infantry, not cavalry, on that occasion. Given the difficulty that cavalry always had when they were facing heavy Greek infantry, it seems unlikely that Philip would have placed his trust in cavalry when his phalanx—with its near-professional level of training and longer spears—was clearly superior to the hoplite formation it faced. It is anachronistic to assume that Alexander must have been in command of cavalry at Chaeronea because that is what he did later in Asia, ignoring the difference in enemies and Alexander's genius for adapting his army to present circumstances. The failure of the admittedly meagre sources to mention cavalry at the battle of Chaeronea accordingly appears to reflect what happened rather than to indicate an omission on the writers' part.

In spite of the testimony from the ancient sources indicating that infantry retained its preeminence, the impression remains among modern historians that cavalry dominated the Hellenistic battlefield. M. Van Creveld writes: "Hellenistic sources are in any case little interested in the phalanx, since the decision invariably fell with the cavalry on the wings."[79] Spence seems to agree: "Under Philip, Alexander, and their successors, it was the cavalry and not infantry which was used as the battle winning arm."[80] Assuming similar battlefield circumstances for the period from Philip's reign through the time of the Successors is also questionable. Adcock expressed much the same opinion: "In most great battles of the Hellenistic era, cavalry had the first and last word."[81]

79. Van Creveld (1985) 287, n. 94.
80. *CCG* 157, n. 145; 177 (for quotation).
81. Adcock (1957) 52.

This view may be traceable to Tarn, who claimed that cavalry was the dominant arm during the century after Alexander.[82] Yet later in the same work he qualified this assertion, both in the case of Alexander and that of the Successors. There he correctly emphasized "the steadiness of his [Alexander's] background, the Macedonian infantry, with which the Persians had nothing to compare."[83] Tarn also lamented the fact that the object of cavalry in Hellenistic warfare was to defeat their counterparts, thereby acknowledging that the cavalry had become more limited in use after Alexander.[84] The fact that he deplores this situation suggests that he did not appreciate its virtual inevitability, which resulted from the high degree of symmetry of the Greco-Macedonian armies that faced each other during the period.

82. *HMND* 26.
83. Ibid., 61.
84. Ibid., 66.

Chapter 15

Hannibal:
218 to 202 B.C.

HANNIBAL WAS CLEARLY ONE of the great generals of antiquity—a leader of genius whose reputation as a tactician has survived intact for over two thousand years. Since he was not Greek or Macedonian, either ethnically or culturally, and did not lead a Hellenistic army, I have accordingly omitted him from the main text of this book. Nevertheless, as the son of a Carthaginian general, Hamilcar Barca, he was exposed to the military traditions of the Greeks and Romans as well as those of his ancestral Semitic culture in the eastern Mediterranean. Intimate contact with the native peoples of North Africa and Spain further broadened his military perspective. Furthermore, because of his great success with cavalry against the Romans over a period of more than fifteen years, his battles are worthy of study as part of an effort to identify the general principles of employing the mounted arm in the military environment of the Mediterranean region during the period.

Before I proceed further, however, it will be useful to look at a specific instance of Greek influence upon the Carthaginian military that occurred some decades earlier, during the First Punic War. At that time—256–255—recent Roman success had led to a decision to send an army to North Africa and confront the Carthaginians in their own backyard. Under the leadership of Marcus Atilius Regulus, consul for 256, the Romans defeated a Carthaginian army that had encamped on a hill, where their elephants and cavalry could not be properly employed. Flushed with success, Regulus lost an opportunity for peace by insisting upon excessively harsh terms. Accordingly, during the winter the Carthaginians sent recruiting officers to Greece to enlist soldiers for the next campaigning season. One of them returned with an experienced

Spartan by the name of Xanthippus. His evaluation of their recent defeat, which he attributed to their own misuse of their forces rather than Roman superiority, impressed the Carthaginian leaders so much that they placed the army in his hands for training. Apparently his Spartan methods worked well, because morale improved so dramatically that the Carthaginians regained confidence to face the Romans in open battle once again.

By the following year (255) the Carthaginians were able to field an army of twelve thousand infantry, four thousand cavalry (a comparatively high proportion), and one hundred elephants. Total Roman numbers were about equal, since Regulus had been left with fifteen thousand infantry and five hundred cavalry and had unwisely not recruited any local allies.[1] On the battlefield the Carthaginians placed the elephants in a single line in front of their phalanx. Some mercenaries were posted on the right, but the most agile joined the cavalry in front of each wing. The Romans put skirmishers in front and deepened the line, a formation approved by Polybius but criticized by modern historians, who have benefited from studying Scipio's method of dealing with elephants during the Second Punic War.[2] Yet this criticism ignores the experience of Alexander at the Hydaspes, where his phalanx successfully met the larger Indian elephants head on.[3] Needless to say, Regulus was no Alexander and does not seem to have prepared his men to face these creatures. Xanthippus, at least, was able to employ his arms effectively in order to take advantage of the weaknesses presented by the Romans. Thus his more numerous cavalry routed the Roman horse and attacked their infantry line from the rear while the elephants pushed back the center, trampling the men underfoot. The rear Roman ranks faced about to fight the cavalry but were shot down by javelins. At a cost of some eight hundred mercenaries, the Carthaginians destroyed the Roman army. Only some two thousand men plus Regulus and his entourage escaped.

All in all, this was a good preview of Hannibal's tactics in Italy, although they were clearly not modeled on those of Alexander, who preferred to penetrate the Persian line rather than to outflank it. Conceptually, this approach is very close to the tactics used by the Successors, except that they were rarely able to employ them against each other because of the high degree of symmetry in their armies. The Romans were more obliging.

---

1. Polyb. 1.32–34.

2. Ibid., 1.33.10. Criticized by T. Frank in *CAH* 7, 1st ed., 684. Scipio left lanes between the maniples, down which the elephants could pass harmlessly while themselves being subject to attacks on their flanks (Polyb. 15.12.3–4).

3. Arr. *Anab.* 5.17.

In addition to this type of influence on Carthaginian military practice in general, the possibility also exists that Hannibal himself had direct contact with Greek ideas. One of his companions on his campaigns was a Greek named Sosylus, who subsequently wrote a history of those events. Nepos describes him as Hannibal's Lacedaemonian Greek tutor. The later military writer Vegetius adds that Hannibal was able to destroy larger and stronger Roman armies by virtue of the services of a Spartan tactician—perhaps this Sosylus. In any event it seems clear that Hannibal had full access to Hellenistic military theory and practice.[4]

Examination of his campaigns against the Romans, however, shows that they are not typical examples of Hellenistic warfare of the type that took place after the death of Alexander. The army that he led against the Romans—comprising North Africans, Spaniards, and Gauls—differed more from Greek and Roman armies than the latter two did from each other. Even had he wished to do so, Hannibal could not have matched the phalanx or legion in fighting quality, since the raw material from his recruiting grounds in North Africa, Spain, and northern Italy does not seem to have been susceptible to the requisite levels of training and discipline, which were apparently the result of cultural predispositions.[5] Had he been able to recruit Carthaginians in sufficient quantity, his story might have been different, but the Carthaginians persisted in the use of mercenaries. Nonetheless, Hannibal developed his soldiers' skills to the limits of their ability. Rather than attempt to match the fighting power of the legion, he created—with the simplicity of genius—a countervailing strength in cavalry that meshed advantageously with Roman weaknesses to produce decisive victories on the battlefield. Like all great commanders, his task was to assemble an army whose superiority in one or more respects enabled him to employ flexible tactics rather than brute strength to achieve victory. Nevertheless, Hannibal was unable to transcend the purely physical limitations of his environment. He could only hope to address these limitations to better advantage than his enemies did. For many years he was successful in doing so, but in his final battle with the Romans, when he no longer possessed the necessary advantage in cavalry and faced a tactical equal, the force of circumstances proved a match for his genius.

---

4. Nep. *Han.* 13.3; Veg. *Epit.*, trans. Milner (1993) book 3, pref., 62.

5. The cultural predilection for tolerating hard work and discipline at the expense of personal freedom was a distinguishing characteristic of the Romans, which gave them a lasting advantage over the German tribes in northern Europe for centuries.

After the death of his father, Hamilcar, in 229/228, the army chose Hasdrubal, Hannibal's brother-in-law, as its commander. By the year 224 the twenty-three-year-old Hannibal held independent command over the cavalry.[6] At the death of Hasdrubal three years later in 221, Hannibal assumed command of the army. By this time the young Carthaginian would have been aware of the relative importance of infantry and cavalry in the Roman army and would have realized that the small number of horsemen insured that infantry tactics dominated Roman battle plans. He also knew that he could not transform his own infantry into a force that matched the legion in fighting power, whereas he was in a position to recruit a large number of cavalry, thereby altering the dynamics on the battlefield in his favor. By increasing their number relative to that of the Romans, he would be able to avoid the mounted stalemate so often found on Hellenistic battlefields and use cavalry as a striking force to the enemy's flank and rear. Sheer force of numbers would enable him to rout the Roman horsemen, creating this opportunity. It is significant that he did not use cavalry in a frontal attack on Roman infantry.[7] As I have pointed out, Hannibal's use of cavalry was not done in imitation of Alexander's tactics, yet the two commanders could not have agreed more in respect to coordination of arms. In Hannibal's case infantry, used in a defensive posture, had to withstand the advance of the Roman legions until the cavalry had time to complete their task. Both arms were indispensable, whereas in the Hellenistic period in Greece infantry dominated the battlefield and cavalry were often little more than a sideshow, since one side seldom had sufficient horsemen to drive the enemy cavalry from the battlefield. Usually, the cavalry on both sides were too effective in protecting the flanks, leaving the decisive fighting to the infantry.

Even though the first clash between Hannibal and the Romans in northern Italy involved only cavalry, it gave a foretaste of the tactics on which his victories and his fame would rest. In addition it offers important information about the fighting quality of cavalry on both sides.

When Hannibal debouched from the Alpine passes into the plains of northern Italy in 218, the Romans were expecting him. Nonetheless, the consul Publius Cornelius Scipio had only twenty thousand infantry and two thousand cavalry on the spot and was awaiting the arrival of the other consul, Tiberius Sempronius Longus, with twenty-four thousand infantry and twenty-

---

6. Nep. *Han.* 3.1; Livy 21.4.10.

7. See *HB* 48. This excellent study is perceptive, sober, and thorough and should be the standard treatment for years. For Hannibal's campaigns see also *HW*.

four hundred cavalry from Sicily.[8] Scipio met Hannibal quite by accident while scouting near the Ticinus River. He was leading all of his cavalry (two thousand) and some javelin men. If, as Polybius reports, all of Hannibal's horsemen were also present, Scipio was badly outnumbered. Hannibal's tactics suggest that this was in fact the case, for he placed his "bridled" and "steady" cavalry in front, with the Numidians on the wings, whence they could outflank the Romans.[9] The Romans put their javelin men and Gallic cavalry in front, but, the lines closing too quickly for the javelineers to loose their weapons, they seem to have retreated through the cavalry lines behind them—something easier to accomplish with cavalry than infantry because of the looser order. The fight that followed was indecisive for a while, and some cavalrymen dismounted and fought on foot. This changed once the Numidians began to attack the Roman rear. The consul himself was wounded in the fighting but was rescued by his seventeen-year-old son and namesake, the later Africanus.[10]

Heavy casualties were reported on both sides, which—if true—is notable, because it suggests that Hannibal's cavalry had no noticeable superiority over that of the Romans. Even if one doubts this, the battle was won by the superior numbers that gave Hannibal the tactical flexibility to attack the Roman rear. An earlier skirmish between Roman and Numidian cavalry also suggests that there was no great discrepancy in fighting quality between the horsemen of the two sides. This action occurred at the Rhone River before Hannibal reached Italy. After a hard fight, three hundred Roman and Celtic cavalry drove five hundred Numidians back to the Carthaginian camp, with serious losses to both sides—150 Romans, 200 Numidians.[11]

By December 218 Sempronius' army had joined Scipio and the two consuls were ready to face Hannibal, whose own forces had been augmented by approximately fourteen thousand Gauls.[12] Both armies numbered around forty thousand, but Hannibal still had a significant advantage in cavalry—about ten

---

8. Livy 21.17.5–9. Publius Scipio had sent his own army on to Spain with his brother Gnaius and was now commanding the forces assigned to Cisalpine Gaul. For the action itself see Polyb. 3.65; Livy 21.46.3–10.

9. *Bridled* and *steady* refer to spear- and sword-carrying cavalry similar to those of the Greeks, whereas the Numidians—armed usually with javelins—rode without bridles, as can be seen on Trajan's column from the early second century A.D.

10. Polyb. 10.3.3–7. Accepted by *HCP* 2 199. Livy 21.46.10 mentions another version, replacing the son with a Ligurian slave, which is preferred by *HB* 118. Polybius obtained his information from Laelius, the close friend and associate of Africanus.

11. Polyb. 3.41.9, 44.3, 45.1–3; Livy 21.29.1–4.

12. *HCP* 1 405. The major accounts of the battle of the Trebia are Polyb. 3.71–74; Livy 21. 54–56.8.

thousand to four thousand. What is more, he was able to choose the battlefield—a flat, treeless area near the Trebia River—as well as to plant an ambush of one thousand cavalry and one thousand infantry out of sight in a watercourse. As if that were not enough, he employed a Numidian cavalry raid to entice Sempronius and his men out of camp before their morning meal, marching through the icy river, while his own men were well fed and dry. This eagerness to fight at once rather than wait for spring supposedly went against the advice of Scipio, who was still too weak from his wound to share the command. Thus, on a cold and snowy day about the time of the winter solstice, the Romans advanced against the waiting Carthaginians, who had twenty thousand Spanish, Celtic, and African infantry in a line and ten thousand cavalry divided between the flanks. On the other side were sixteen thousand Romans, twenty thousand allies, and four thousand cavalry.

Sempronius recalled his cavalry, which had gone ahead, because the Numidians' tactics of scattering and retreating then turning about and boldly attacking proved to be too frustrating. The battle itself was initiated ineffectively by the light troops in front of each line. On the Roman side, the javelin men had already exhausted most of their weapons while the Balearic slingers of Hannibal proved to be no threat to the legions. The decisive role was performed by the Carthaginian cavalry on the flanks, with the possible help of the elephants and slingers.[13] These fresh and numerically superior horsemen stripped the cavalry from the Roman line, whereupon the Numidians attacked the exposed wings of the infantry. Nonetheless, the Roman line fought well and might have held its own had the troops lying in ambush not attacked their rear. After severe fighting ten thousand Romans broke through the Celts and Africans and escaped to Placentia. They were later joined by a small number of infantry and most of the cavalry. The Roman army was destroyed, but on Hannibal's side the losses were negligible, with most of the casualties suffered by the Celts.

Hannibal's greatness was already on display at this point; with an army clearly inferior in the fighting ability of its infantry, he achieved success by using his cavalry as a striking force. This was possible only because he realized before he departed from Spain that Roman overconfidence in their infantry could be countered by a significant numerical superiority in cavalry. He was greatly aided by the cooperative incompetence of Sempronius, which enabled him to bring his troops to battle under the most favorable conditions

---

13. Livy 21.55.6.

imaginable. Had the Romans been better led, their infantry could have put a premature end to Hannibal's invasion of Italy.

The disaster at Lake Trasimene in 217 offers no information about Hannibal's battlefield tactics.[14] It was little more than a slaughter brought on by an unusually successful ambush. Typical of Hannibal, however, it was based on sound principles—that is, knowledge of the enemy's whereabouts, in contrast with Roman ignorance; the use of surprise; the mobility of cavalry, which was used to block escape; and, not least, an army trained not to spring the trap too soon.

Cannae is another matter, for it was Hannibal's masterpiece.[15] For a time after the disasters at the Trebia and Lake Trasimene, however, the Romans were unwilling to face Hannibal in the open. Quintus Fabius Maximus, elected dictator after Trasimene, was willing to follow Hannibal at a distance and harass his foragers at every opportunity, although he had no intention of joining battle. But by the time his six-month tenure as dictator expired near the end of 217 and the consular elections for the following year were held, the mood in the city had shifted in favor of the offensive. Consequently the new consuls, Gaius Terentius Varro and Lucius Aemilius Paullus, prepared to raise and train four new legions and fill out the old ones for a total of eight, not counting an equal number of allies. Polybius gives a total of eighty thousand infantry and six thousand cavalry, while Hannibal had forty thousand and ten thousand respectively, when they fought at Cannae in August 216.[16]

On the day of the battle, when it was the turn of Varro to command, the two armies were marshalled in normal alignment, with cavalry on the wings outside the line infantry and skirmishers in front between the opposing forces. There were, however, two deviations within the infantry formations that proved to be critically important. The Romans compressed their numerically superior line infantry in the center into a deeper and closer formation than usual, whereas they should have extended their line beyond Hannibal's smaller army. Hannibal, on the other hand, thinned the Spaniards and Celts in his center and formed a crescent-shaped line projecting toward the Romans, while the Africans remained in position to right and left. The Roman cavalry on the right, commanded by Paullus, were close to the Aufidus river.

---

14. Polyb. 3.80–85; Livy 22.3–6.12; *HB* 152–56; *HW* 64–65.
15. Polyb. 3.107–17; Livy 22.40.4–49.18; Plut. *Fab.* 15–16; *HB* 191–96; Lazenby (1978) 78–85.
16. Polyb. 3.113.5; 114.5. Depending on how one calculates the number of cavalry per legion and allied *ala*, the Romans could have had as many as ninety-six hundred horsemen at Cannae. If this were the case, only six thousand took part in the battle, and the Romans made a major mistake in deploying them elsewhere. See *HB* 191–92, n. 4.

Opposite him were the regular Spanish and Celtic cavalry under Hasdrubal. Varro, with the allied horse, was on the Roman left, which was faced by Hanno and the Numidian cavalry. Hannibal and his brother Mago were in the center, where they faced Servilius, the consul of 217. Although the Spanish and Celtic infantry fought with their native weapons, a cut-and-thrust sword for the former, a slashing weapon for the latter, the Africans had been outfitted with captured Roman arms.

The opening action of light infantry proved indecisive and apparently halfhearted compared to the vigorous cavalry fight that developed near the river. Because of this barrier the horsemen found themselves crowded together more than was customary, with little room to maneuver. Thus, when they came up against each other, some dismounted and fought on foot. After hard fighting the Roman horse were defeated and the survivors fled. The infantry fighting in the center also proceeded as Hannibal intended, as the weight of the Roman advance pushed back the crescent and broke the ranks of the Spaniards and Celts, transforming the convex line into a concave one. The eager Romans continued to advance, heedless of the stationary Africans on the flanks, who then attacked from the sides at the appropriate moment. By this time Paullus had abandoned the cavalry on his right and joined the center to encourage the troops there. On the other wing the Numidian cavalry had been occupying the allied horse with their in-and out-tactics when Hasdrubal arrived with his victorious cavalry and decided the issue.

At that time the Carthaginians showed an awareness of the various skills of different types of horsemen. The Numidians were sent in pursuit of the routed cavalry, where they could best employ their particular skills of horsemanship and harassment, while the regular cavalry attacked the rear of the Roman legions, where their willingness to fight close with spear and sword would be most effective. Polybius attributes this decision to Hasdrubal, but it can be traced to Hannibal's general outlook, based on a realistic and efficient employment of his resources. It was here, in the midst of terrible slaughter, that Paullus fell, along with the consuls of the preceding year. Varro, however, was among the few horsemen to escape the Numidians, who either killed or unseated the majority. At the close of his narrative of this battle, Polybius observes that "in times of war it is better to give battle with half as many infantry as the enemy and an overwhelming force of cavalry than to be in all respects his equal.[17]

17. Polyb. 3.117.5.

Throughout their campaigns against Hannibal to date, the Romans had trusted too much in the traditional strengths of their infantry without giving any thought to adapting themselves to changing circumstances. Hannibal, on the other hand, achieved success with infantry whose fighting capacity could not match that of the Romans in either number or quality. This was no accident. He had created an asymmetry in cavalry that permitted him to deploy different arms on the battlefield in a preplanned, imaginative fashion. Seibert also draws attention to the fact that significant mistakes by the Romans contributed as much to Hannibal's victories as did his own skill. At Cannae the Roman leaders showed no understanding of how to use their numerical superiority to outflank the enemy and were instead outflanked by the smaller army. They also failed to discern the dynamics of handling very large numbers of troops.[18]

In spite of the loss of one hundred thousand men—albeit many of them allies—over two years of campaigning, the Romans refused to yield. They returned to the Fabian policy of refusing to meet Hannibal in the field while constantly dogging his tracks, interrupting his supplies, and confining him to southern Italy. Although time-consuming, this policy was successful because time was on the Roman side. When the victorious Scipio returned from Spain in 206, it was realistic to ignore Hannibal in southern Italy and consider an invasion of Africa. As consul in 205 Scipio adopted this plan, in spite of opposition from those who favored attending to Hannibal first and then rebuilding Italy. Scipio apparently thought the problem lay in Carthage itself, rather than in its general, who in any case would have to return home to defend the city.

After a year spent recruiting and training troops in his province of Sicily, Scipio sailed for Africa in 204 and landed near Utica. Rome had at last found a match for Hannibal in Scipio. He had fought in Spain from 210 to 206 and had shown himself a masterful tactician and leader. In two great battles, Baecula in 208 and Ilipa in 207, he used infantry to outflank and defeat the Carthaginian armies. This was a variation on Hannibal's use of cavalry that Scipio found possible because of the high level of training and discipline of the Roman infantry. It also resulted from Scipio's realistic appraisal of the problems he faced and his ability to remake the Roman army into a force that made better use of its inherent strengths under the guiding hand of a true master.[19]

18. *HB* 196.
19. Seibert discusses the full literature on Scipio and Hannibal in his companion volume (1993b) 57–82.

Scipio's tactical skill was even more in evidence at the first regular battle he fought in North Africa, southwest of Utica at the Great Plains, in the spring of 203.[20] The numbers involved are uncertain, probably ranging between twenty thousand and thirty thousand on each side. The Carthaginians, under Hasdrubal, placed Celtiberian mercenaries—and presumably some of their own infantry—in the center, facing the Roman legions, with cavalry on both wings. The Carthaginian cavalry were to the right facing Masinissa,[21] while on the other wing Syphax and his Numidians were opposite the Roman cavalry. As usual, the Romans were arranged in three lines: *hastati*, *principes*, and *triarii*. When the fighting started, all the cavalry on the Carthaginian side broke and fled at first contact with the enemy, but the Celtiberian infantry stood their ground and fought well against the Roman first line. Scipio then took advantage of their exposed flanks, using his second and third lines, the *principes* and *triarii*, to outflank and destroy them. This tactical variation allowed the cavalry to concentrate on their counterparts and freed Scipio from the worry that they would not be able to disengage and return to the battlefield for an attack on the enemy's rear. Such an option, available to him because of the tactical independence of the Roman lines, highlights the superior organization and flexibility of the Roman legion, which he had the skill to exploit.

The principle reason for the poor showing by Syphax's Numidian cavalry on the Carthaginian side lies in the fact that they were recently recruited farmers with little experience as cavalry.[22] This type of glimpse into the background of a fighting unit is invaluable, although rather rare. It demonstrates the importance of evaluating the quality of the troops on each side in a battle when assigning the reasons for victory and defeat as well as identifying the available tactical options.

With the return of Hannibal to Africa from Italy in 203, the stage was set for that most rare of military events, a battle between commanders of equal skill who were leading armies of roughly comparable number and quality.[23] When the battle of Zama took place the following year, not only Masinissa but most of the other Numidians were on the the Roman side as well, with the result that Hannibal had fewer cavalry than previously and was, in fact,

---

20. Polyb. 14.8.1–14; Livy 30.8.1–9; *HB* 441–42; *HW* 209–11.
21. Masinissa, the later Numidian king, had fought for the Carthaginians in Spain but had been won over to the Roman side by Scipio after Ilipa in 206. He remained a loyal—but sometimes troublesome—ally of Rome until his death in 148.
22. Livy 30.7.11, 8.8; *HB* 441.
23. Polyb. 15.9–16; Livy 30.32–35; *HW* 219–25; *HB* 466–72.

outnumbered in this arm by six thousand to four thousand. On the other hand he had the advantage in infantry—thirty-six thousand to twenty-nine thousand. These numbers were the inverse of what Hannibal was used to and preferred, and they effectively determined the tactical nature of the pending battle. Hannibal was in the unaccustomed position of having to rely on his infantry for the decision. Scipio also had to make adjustments because of the force that faced him, since on this occasion Hannibal had eighty elephants, which he placed in front of his infantry. Both armies also exhibited a triple infantry line, which was standard for the Romans, but unusual for the Carthaginians. Hannibal's first line comprised twelve thousand Ligurian, Celtic, Balearic, and Mauritanian mercenaries. Behind them were the native Libyans and Carthaginians, while Hannibal's veterans from Italy formed the third line some six hundred feet back.

Hannibal hoped to disrupt the Roman infantry with the elephants, but Scipio was ready for them and had lined up the maniples of the three lines one behind the other rather than in the usual formation that was similar to the black squares on a checkerboard. The spaces between the maniples were occupied by light-armed *velites*. When the elephants charged, noise from the Roman horns frightened some, causing them to turn back against their own lines. The rest advanced into the spaces between the maniples as Scipio had planned and fought with the *velites*, who took the casualties. Some of the elephants passed through the lines, while others were driven off to the right or left, suffering from javelin blows along the way. The Roman line itself remained completely intact and soon joined battle with the Carthaginian infantry.

Meanwhile the Roman and Numidian cavalry routed their opponents and drove them from the battlefield. Numerical superiority on the Roman side made this possible, just as it had earlier for Hannibal in Italy. If, as on previous occasions, Scipio planned to envelop the Carthaginian line with his *principes* and *triarii*, this was thwarted by Hannibal's veterans, who had been held back as a reserve. As both leaders knew, the cavalry action would probably decide the issue. Hannibal could only hope that his fleeing horsemen could occupy the Roman cavalry long enough to give him at least a chance to use his more numerous infantry to good advantage. Scipio, on the other hand, could entertain at least the possibility that his cavalry would destroy or disperse the enemy quickly enough to allow a return to the battlefield and the opportunity to strike them from behind. Since Hannibal had already used his elephants against the infantry, they were not at hand to block the return of the cavalry as had been the case against Antigonus in 301 at Ipsus. Even that might not have been of use, because the horses of Scipio's Numidian cavalry were more accustomed to elephants.

Despite some casualties, the Roman infantry advanced successfully against the Carthaginian mercenaries in the front line. When they gave way and tried to escape, they came to blows with their own second line—the Carthaginians—who refused to receive them. In spite of the resulting confusion they engaged the Romans, while the remnants of the mercenaries fled to the sides. Confusion in the sources makes the details of what followed unclear, but the Roman *hastati*, now probably outnumbered, were most likely aided by some of the *principes*. In any event the Carthaginians were also routed and driven off to the sides, as Hannibal would not allow them to disrupt his veterans in the third line. Then there was a pause in the fighting. Scipio recalled the *hastati* and reformed his men into a single line, placing the *principes* and *triarii* on the flanks of the *hastati*. Hannibal more than likely added the remnants of his Carthaginians to his veterans, and battle was the joined once again. The two sides are described as equal in spirit, number, and courage. The struggle was hard fought and of some duration, with no clear advantage to one side or the other until Laelius and Masinissa returned with the cavalry to deliver the coup de grace. Polybius describes their arrival as δαιμονίως, marvelously [timed], but Livy omits the qualifying adjective.[24] The timing may indeed have been most fortunate, but the tactics were intentional. It was merely a question of whether Scipio's horsemen could disengage themselves without risk. The subsequent slaughter of the Carthaginian forces was great, although Hannibal himself escaped. Further resistance was impossible, however, and this battle brought an end to the Second Punic War.

Zama presents us with exceptionally important insights into the operational limitations of cavalry during this period in the Mediterranean region. In spite of some differences in organization, battle formation, and character and quality of individual units, the great symmetry of the two armies—including their exceptional leadership—precluded any attempt to employ flexible tactics of the sort each commander had relied on for victory in the past. Scipio's preparation rendered Hannibal's elephants ineffective, while Hannibal's reserve third line prevented Scipio from using his second and third lines in an outflanking move. Before the battle Hannibal could give no thought to his usual use of cavalry, because on this occasion he was inferior

24. Polyb. 15.14.7; Livy 30.35.1.

in his cavalry arm, and his previous success with it as a striking force depended absolutely on numerical superiority. The employment of elephants against the Roman line suggests some doubt about the mercenaries, although Hannibal's infantry numbers were greater overall than those of the Romans. There is no clear indication of the outcome of the battle had Laelius and Masinissa not reappeared. Given the high performance of Hannibal's cavalry on previous occasions, it is likely that they did their best—even though they were outnumbered—to prevent the Roman cavalry from returning. They, if anyone, would know the danger.

The preparation for and course of the battle show clearly that each commander had a thorough understanding of the reality facing him and that both made whatever adjustments the circumstances allowed. This was the foundation of their previous victories, and it is proof of their greatness. Recognizing the difference between actuality and perception is an absolute prerequisite of military success. To that should be added the ability to adapt one's tactics to the reality one faces rather than forcing the issue by using what was successful in the past. The result is the essence of generalship. Until the return of the Roman cavalry, both generals must have been discouraged at the prospect of a drawn-out, face-to-face infantry fight with its attendant losses. Each had been fortunate not to have faced an equal in his earlier battles, for then the tactical options would have been restricted and the victories fewer and less spectacular.[25] Their campaigns clearly demonstrate the limitations as well as the potential of cavalry on the ancient battlefield.

---

25. Awareness of this fact is attributed to Hannibal in Byzantine military treatises. See Maurice's comment in Dennis (1984) 91: "An army is judged by the spirit of its general. Hannibal the Carthaginian understood this well, for when he had learned that Scipio was commanding the Romans, he spoke highly of the disposition of their army. Some of them criticized him for being so slow to march out and fight against those whom he had often defeated. He defended himself by saying: 'I would prefer to deal with a troop of lions commanded by a deer than with a herd of deer under the leadership of a lion.'" Whether authentic or not, it fits the dilemma he faced at Zama.

Conclusion

IT IS IMPOSSIBLE TO SAY when true cavalry first appeared in Greece. Reasonably clear evidence in the form of historical narrative begins in the fifth century B.C., although vase painting, coins, and sculpture offer some evidence prior to that. Two broad statements can be made at the outset, however. Against a background of changing attitudes about both the nature and the purpose of war, the mounted arm was transformed from an aristocratic monopoly that had almost no place in Greek phalanx fighting into an integral part of virtually every army in the lower Balkans, while the preexisting cavalry forces of Thessaly and Macedon were raised to a level of operational performance probably unsurpassed in Greco-Roman antiquity. Concurrently, the individual cavalryman was converted from what was, by infantry standards, a rather timid javelin-throwing annoyance on the battlefield to an aggressive, spear-wielding, hand-to-hand mounted fighter. In short cavalry had become useful for virtually any battlefield task except a direct frontal assault on an unbroken phalanx.

Before proceeding to offer conclusions about the operational place of cavalry on the Greek battlefield, I should say a word about the causes of military success and failure. Although human leaders who prepare soldiers and armies for combat obviously strive to win, their efforts do not always—perhaps not even often—achieve the desired result. When two incompetent generals, of whom there have been many in history, face each other in battle, one usually comes off victorious, possibly for reasons unrelated to his generalship, perhaps—to quote a friend—because he "outstupefied" the enemy. That being the case, the historian should resist the temptation to assign victory only to the skill of military leaders. Instead, all possible nonhuman causes of victory must be examined before one attempts to identify the role of generals. This will contribute both to historical accuracy and to our understanding of military problem solving. Once the contributing and convergent causes have been identified, the general's role—as expressed through his ideas, orders, and actions—can be evaluated.[1]

Among the various battlefield conditions that affect the outcome, terrain is one of the most important. Terrain often determines where battles are fought (that is, Boeotia in central Greece), can contribute to the outcome (that is, Pydna), and may determine the marshaling of troops (as at Sellasia, where the cavalry were in the center on the level and the infantry on the heights to either side). Other influences include the relative levels of training, discipline, technology, and morale; accident and luck, such as weather; and the loyalty of the troops. When generals and armies are closely matched in ability, the skill of the leaders may express itself in stalemate, each denying victory to the other until some extraneous force intervenes, as may have happened with the return of Scipio's cavalry at Zama. The result was very different at Ipsus, where returning cavalry were denied access to the battlefield by elephants.

To return to the cavalry, it is clear that in spite of numerous examples of vases depicting mounted warriors during the Archaic period before 500, there is little we can say with certainty about their role in combat. Worley's claim that they were able to decide "the outcome of the battle by shock if necessary" is unproved and unlikely.[2] Prior to the rise of hoplite infantry sometime after 700, aristocratic horsemen more than likely did have a proportionately more important role in city-state fighting, but it is beyond our power to know whether they even fought from horseback. Once hoplite tactics and the phalanx were adopted, however, cavalry had virtually no place on the battlefield, and there appear to have been no formal cavalry units in existence in central and southern Greece until the fifth century. The acceptance by the Greeks of this limited type of warfare—consisting of short face-to-face infantry battles without the use of reserves, flank attacks, or pursuit—positively discouraged any attempts to find a use for other arms such as cavalry or light infantry. The economic cost of keeping horses in Greece and the widespread democratic bias against the aristocrats, who were among the few able to afford them, are further reasons for the absence of cavalry during this period. Few, if any, perceived a need for them. Furthermore, as long as phalanx tactics were found

1. See Lloyd (1996), in Lloyd, 187–98.
2. *HCAG* 58. See discussion above, part 1, chap. 3.

to suffice for warfare between two city-states, the operational dimension was not in use.

While this is true for warfare in central and southern Greece, it never applied to Thessaly, Macedon, and the rest of northern Greece or to those Greeks who migrated to overseas colonies as early as the late eighth century, where they had to adapt their style of fighting to that of their new neighbors. The emphasis upon hoplite tactics that can be found in modern histories of Greece owes much to the focus placed on Athens due to its extraordinary cultural legacy. The events that affected its history have attracted a disproportionate amount of interest ever since antiquity. This distortion obscures the fact that elsewhere in the Mediterranean military practice was quite different and arms other than infantry assumed a role commensurate with their inherent qualities. In Sicily, for example, the Greek colonists fought against the indigenous Sicels and Sicans as well as the Carthaginians who had settled in the western parts of the island. Cavalry and other arms played a more important part in Sicily from an early date, this more challenging military environment prompting the invention of the catapult around 400 in Syracuse, which was perhaps the largest Greek-speaking city at that time.

An even more vivid example of the way external pressure can modify the military outlook of a people can be seen in the case of Rome. Early in its history Rome apparently did use the hoplite system, but under the military pressure of a variety of enemies—Etruscans city-states to the north, tribal peoples in the hills to the east and southeast (Sabines, Volsci, Samnites), and the agriculturalists of Campania to the south, not to mention the Greek city-states on the coast—Rome had to adapt to survive. The common plundering raids it faced were better met by a less formalized response than the phalanx. Lighter troops and cavalry proved to be more useful in central Italy in general, although the Romans responded primarily by changing their infantry formation to the legion, which combined the javelin as a missile weapon with the short sword for close fighting. This solution to the necessity of fighting different types of enemy proved to be highly successful and was one of the reasons why Rome eventually conquered the Mediterranean area. Whether consciously or not, the Greeks in the homeland ignored these diverse fighting styles and the evolutionary changes that conflicts among the different peoples of the region fostered.[3]

3. This subject is well treated by Raaflaub (1996), in Wallace and Harris, 273–314, esp. 283–84.

Nevertheless, by the end of the Peloponnesian War, there had been great changes even in Greece. This conflict had precipitated a variety of modifications in force structure with respect to weapons technology, command, organization, level of training and discipline, and increased use of light infantry and cavalry. Attempts were also made to create and exploit asymmetry and to bring forces to the battlefield that could employ maneuvering tactics. The use of combined arms led to a form of operations whereby good commanders chose those tactical options that were best suited to the particular battlefield circumstances that they faced.

To some extent the traditional outlook began to change by 500, as the Greeks increasingly came into contact with their horsey neighbors to the north and the Persians to the east. In Thessaly and Macedon infantry remained secondary to cavalry, whose existence was more natural in a setting of open, grassy plains. Although the Spartans had clashed with Thessalian cavalry as early as 511/510, they did not establish a cavalry force until 424, during the Peloponnesian War. The two encounters between these peoples, one favoring infantry, the other cavalry, demonstrate a lasting military principle even at this early date: numerical superiority is more valuable than an advantage in the type of arm one employs, other factors such as morale or level of training generally being equal. In this instance the Thessalian cavalry won one battle, the Spartan infantry the other, and the reason in each case was superiority in number.

Shortly after this, during the Persian Wars, the Greeks confronted an enemy who possessed cavalry in considerable numbers. Yet the almost complete absence of horsemen from the armies of central and southern Greece (the vantage point from which we view the events of these years) prevents us from discerning their importance for the Persians and their Theban allies. The fact that the Greeks came off the victors and the significance attached to their victories tend to obscure the extremely precarious position in which they had found themselves. The Persian defeat likewise prompts us to discount the contribution of cavalry to their army. It is a fact, however, that Greek awareness of the enemy cavalry greatly affected their choice of the battle site at Plataea as well as their strategy and tactics. Specifically, the Persian horsemen harassed the Greek front line with impunity by launching missiles from a distance and then retiring before they could be brought to bay; they drove the Greeks from water; they destroyed disorganized enemy infantry; and they protected the retreat of their own infantry. Nevertheless, the importance of these significant accomplishments should be tempered by the fact that the

Greeks could put no cavalry of their own into the field as a counter. Furthermore, the Persian cavalry were incapable of fighting at close quarters with infantry and consequently played no part in the decisive action.

In the decades that followed, down to the outbreak of the Peloponnesian War in 431, no advances in cavalry operations can be detected in the admittedly scanty sources. It was not until the 450s that Athens created even a small mounted force of about three hundred horsemen, a number that had increased to one thousand by the late 430s at the beginning of the Peloponnesian War. This great conflict, which convulsed the Greek world for almost thirty years, accelerated changes in military practice that had already begun. The breakdown in the concept of limited war was obvious when Pericles refused to allow the Athenian army to meet the Spartans in the field because he feared a decisive defeat. His strategic decision to adopt a policy of attrition ultimately encouraged both sides to seek military advantage wherever it might offer itself rather than on a single battlefield. An obvious option was to exploit the potential of hitherto less-utilized arms such as cavalry and light infantry. Pericles' strategic decision was made possible by the great superiority of Athens' fleet and the fact that the city and its harbor were well protected by walls.

Perhaps the most surprising result of this change in military outlook was the brilliant adaptability to new conditions exhibited by Spartan commanders overseas, in particular Gylippus in Syracuse and Brasidas in the north Aegean. Given the traditional view of the Spartans as unimaginative, hidebound conservatives, these two generals are a revelation, for they showed genius in evaluating their immediate circumstances and in employing local forces to good effect, including better cavalry than they were used to at home.

Concomitant with this broadening of outlook was a corresponding increase in fighting skill brought about by the amount of fighting itself and a growing awareness of the need to train for higher levels of performance. Cavalry began to fight more like infantry, in the sense that they were less reluctant to engage hand to hand as they traded in the javelin for lance and sword. This obviously led to new tactics and organization as well as the development of different types of cavalry with specific functions. Greater specialization of fighting skill and an increase in the types of combatants led—perhaps naturally—to the coordination and combination of arms on the battlefield, where each type of fighting force had more or less specific functions. This, in turn, required more ability on the part of the generals, who had to know the capabilities of each arm and the way to employ each best, both singly and in combination. A solid appreciation of this new reality was essential for success.

The length of the Peloponnesian War and the fact that it involved most of the Greek-speaking world insured that there would be intense reflection on the art of war and wide dissemination of ideas and newly acquired skills. During this period cavalry came into its own, but that was only part of a much broader advance in military sophistication that was to have important consequences in the following century. Cavalry operations took on many forms. Early in the war, under Pericles' leadership, the Athenians raided the coast of the Peloponnese by landing cavalry from ships. This was particularly effective because the Spartans did not employ cavalry until 424, when they created a mounted force possibly in response to these very incursions. Closer to home, the Athenian horsemen found ample employment protecting Attica from Spartan raids. After the enemy seized and fortified Deceleia in 413 they were pressed into daily use, resulting in the constant lameness of some horses because of the rocky ground.[4]

By this time cavalry had become a normal component of most armies. They not only clashed with other cavalry but also showed a greater willingness than previously to attack light infantry when conditions were favorable. In combination with light infantry, they occasionally ventured to attack hoplites. Often it was a case of taking advantage of fleeting opportunities, yet there is no doubt that as time passed they showed greater boldness—the result of intensified experience coupled with discipline and better training. At Delium in 424 the Athenians had an unfulfilled plan to use cavalry in reserve while the Boeotians employed a successful coordination of cavalry and hoplites that was followed up by a vigorous and bloody pursuit of the vanquished. The tactics of this battle, which seem much in advance of their time, probably arose from the skillful application of principles to a local situation. Two years later at Amphipolis cavalry and peltasts attacked a hoplite army on its right, unshielded side, causing it to break and flee, and then followed up this success with a vigorous pursuit. It was in Sicily, however, that the mounted arm had its most decisive effect upon the outcome of the war.

Time and again in the three years from 415 to 413, military decisions were forced upon the Athenians because of their lack of cavalry. In spite of Nicias' warning before the expedition sailed and some effort to add cavalry after their arrival in Sicily, the Athenians were never able to match the Syracusans in this arm. Perhaps they simply underestimated the number and

    4. Thuc. 7.27.5.

quality of horsemen they would have to face in the west. If so, there was little excuse, for cavalry had always played a more prominent role in warfare there than in Greece proper.

The success of the Syracusan cavalry began with the first raid that the Athenians launched from their ships, which were based in Catana. Unlike their earlier ship-borne raids against the Peloponnese, in this raid they came up against local cavalry and were driven off. A weakness in cavalry also forced them to abandon their first camp near Syracuse in 415. In short, Syracusan cavalry made essential contributions to almost all subsequent victories, somehow even succeeding in routing Athenian hoplites. The only significant defeat experienced by the Syracusans was attributed by their commander, the Spartan Gylippus, to his own mistake in fighting under circumstances that precluded the use of cavalry. When the end finally came in 413, the mobility of the cavalry prevented the Athenians' escape and—working in concert with the missile troops—doomed the expeditionary force to destruction.

Subsequently, in the final decade of the Peloponnesian War, there was much fighting in the northeast around the approaches to the Black Sea in which not only the presence of cavalry but their use in combination with infantry were taken for granted. Yet when the war came to an end in 404, it was Spartan naval power subsidized by the Persian Cyrus that forced Athens to surrender. The dominance of hoplite tactics as a regular means of settling disputes among the Greek city-states was over. Now that their eyes were opened to the possibilities offered by unrestrained employment of their military resources, the Greeks responded with their usual creativity, with the result that the fourth century is the period of greatest military advance in the ancient world.

The end of the Peloponnesian War did not bring peace for long. Thousands of men used to fighting had little else to do and thus sold their services, even to Persian paymasters. Some ten thousand of these joined Cyrus the Younger in his attempt to overthrow his brother, the Persian king. This military adventure, described in Xenophon's *Anabasis*, made a lasting impression on the Greeks in spite of its failure at Cunaxa in 401. Isocrates later referred to it on more than one occasion as evidence of the weakness of the Persian royal army.[5] It also demonstrated the effectiveness of combining well-trained hoplites with good cavalry.

The trend toward more active employment of cavalry and their combination with infantry continued during the first four decades of the following

---

5. Isoc. *Paneg.* 145–46; Isoc. *Phil.* 90–93.

century. In Asia Minor, Agesilaus found it impossible to campaign without adequate cavalry in 395–394, although on mainland Greece the major battles were decided exclusively by infantry. Cavalry also played an essential role in all field operations around Olynthus in the late 380s.

During the 370s and 360s the Thebans showed how effective well-handled cavalry could be against infantry in the brilliant success of Pelopidas at Tegyra (375) and Cynoscephalae (364) and in Epaminondas' epochal victories at Leuctra (371) and Mantinea (362), for neither of which a clear reconstruction of events is possible. These last examples sum up the essential improvements in the use of cavalry that resulted from an increase in the fighting skills of individual horsemen and the bolder and more imaginative employment of cavalry units as integral parts of armies on the battlefield. An example of the increased confidence arising from greater individual skill can be seen in the intensity of the cavalry action prior to Mantinea that was exhibited by travel-weary Athenians, Thebans, and Thessalians.

Lest it be thought that these changes in military practice were confined to clashes in the open, mention should be made of the Greeks' application of the same principles of integration and coordination to defenses designed to protect cities and territories. Since disputes were no longer regularly settled by formal battle, considerable thought was given to defending one's land against whatever type of attack might occur. The best examples seem to come from Attica, although archaeological remains of the physical portions of defensive systems have been found throughout Greece. The Athenian system was fully in place by the 370s, in response to the threat from Sparta, and was institutionalized in the following decade because of the rising power of Thebes. None of the individual elements in the system were particularly new, but their integration was. This included a mix of physical structures and operational activity by a variety of troops, combining "watchtowers, barrier walls, light infantry and cavalry patrols, and garrison forts—into a system of territorial defense adequate to the needs of Athens and Attica under conditions of war."[6] The importance of cavalry in this system is well attested. Xenophon cites an instance in which cavalry unexpectedly rode out through a sally port and caught Spartan horsemen and peltasts off guard.[7] The sophisticated military thinking evident in these activities reflects the intense intellectual endeavors of the Greeks at the time, which was also exemplified

6. Munn (1993) 187. See also Ober (1985).
7. Munn (1993) 53; Xen. Hell. 5.4.39.

by the works of philosophers, rhetoricians, pamphleteers, and scientists, including specialized treatises on almost every imaginable subject.

As is well known, the Macedonian kingdom, which played such an important part in Greek history from the mid-fourth to the mid-second centuries, was the creation of Philip, the father of Alexander. The combination of military and diplomatic skills that found expression in his person was virtually unique in Greek history, one of his legacies being a type of army that dominated the battlefields of the eastern Mediterranean for almost two centuries. Of course Philip did not start from scratch. Macedon, like Thessaly, had a tradition of high-quality cavalry, whereas infantry had been neglected by both peoples. Philip—strongly influenced by his stay in Thebes—changed that. In view of what seem to be the cavalry-dominated campaigns of Alexander, it is easy to forget that Philip had to create a first-rate infantry army before he was able to become a player among the Greek city-states to his south. It is important to note that Philip did not simply copy the Greek hoplite but rather created a new type of infantry, with less body armor, a smaller shield, and a longer spear. The longer spear (*sarissa*), especially, changed the dynamics of massed infantry fighting.

No small part of Philip's military success was due to the fact that he "demanded a degree of training unprecedented in the Greek world," as E. Carney has expressed it.[8] This level of training, given to *sarissa*-bearing infantry who worked closely with the fine Macedonian cavalry, resulted in a degree of asymmetry relative to other contemporary armies that was decisive, and this asymmetry increased as the army gained experience on the battlefield. Yet this was not all that Philip bequeathed to his son, for the personal relationship the Macedonian king enjoyed with his soldiers was an essential element in their morale and willingness to fight and could be found in no other large state at the time.[9] Philip's contribution to the Greek military legacy that Alexander inherited must be kept in mind when attempts are made to explain Alexander's legendary success in Asia. In the new army both infantry and cavalry were trained to fight regularly at close quarters with hand-held weapons. This practice had been normal for Greek infantry for centuries and was becoming more common for cavalry even before Philip's time. When it was joined to Philip's innovations and the traditional Macedonian fighting skills, the result was an army that must have presented a more formidable and savage impression than contemporaries had seen before.

8. Carney (1996) 24–25. See Diod. 16.3.1–3.
9. Carney (1996) 31, 42.

The army was especially effective against the Persians, whose soldiers relied more on missile weapons and were not well prepared psychologically for the aggressiveness of the Macedonian style of fighting. Unprotected archers were particularly susceptible to panic if charged, because they could not protect themselves at close quarters. An observation by Keegan about Custer is very much to the point here: "Custer was ferociously brave, with the sort of ostentatious bravery that actually diminishes risk in hand-to-hand combat because its display instills fear into opponents."[10] Something akin to this accounted for part of the Macedonian fighting power that Alexander used so effectively against the Persians.

It is unfortunate that the sources for Philip's reign are so defective that any effort to reconstruct his tactics must be based on considerable conjecture. One cannot assume that Alexander simply continued his practices. For one thing, the enemies Philip and Alexander fought were too different. It does seem likely, however, that Philip—when facing Greek infantry with cavalry on the wings—would engage infantry with infantry while trying to drive off the enemy horse so that his cavalry could attack the enemy infantry in flank and rear. At Chaeronea, however, the confined nature of the battlefield probably prevented this, resulting in a battle decided by infantry. What is clear, if these were indeed Philip's *ideal* tactics, is that Alexander fought very differently against the Persians. It should be noted at the outset that—to judge by his actions—Alexander did not consider himself primarily a cavalry commander. He exhibited an exceptional ability to use the individual arms to best advantage, either singly or in combination. The first glimpse we get of this practice is in 335 in the battle against the Triballians. There Alexander displayed what was virtually a signature practice—the advance on the center right of infantry and cavalry units *side by side*. These were literally cavalry and infantry of the line. Other cavalry units were assigned the function of attacking the flank. On this occasion the Triballians, who preferred missile weapons, collapsed as soon as the Macedonians closed for close combat, which demonstrates the psychological advantage of hand-to-hand fighting.

Flank attacks against the Persians were precluded by their advantage in numbers. In fact Alexander had to be careful lest he himself be encircled. Consequently, in all three major battles against the Persians, he penetrated the Persian line, creating new interior flanks, and then turned in an appropriate direction to wreak havoc. While the right side of Alexander's army

---

10. Keegan (1995) 316.

advanced to the attack, the left fought mainly a holding action. Success there was absolutely essential, and it demanded lengthy, difficult, skilled fighting. Mounted skirmishers (*prodromoi*), varying in type over the years, drew first blood and softened up the enemy for the right wing, which would then be fresher and better formed than the enemy. This use of *prodromoi* suggests a brilliant appreciation of the nature of cavalry actions, which are quite exhausting, demanding short bursts of high energy. Sending them into action first against the enemy's regular cavalry would force the latter to expend energy against the *prodromoi* that would put them at an additional disadvantage when they faced the line cavalry. Such tactics were not de rigueur, however, for there were usually some adjustments prompted by enemy dispositions and battlefield topography. At the Granicus and Gaugamela, infantry and cavalry units advanced in line, while at Issus, a more rapid advance—possibly to avoid missiles—left the infantry behind and opened a gap in the Macedonian line. This was a mistake, for the Persians drove through it and headed for the baggage train, a failure to exploit an advantage that was lucky for Alexander. Had they been more alert to their options, they could have given the Macedonians serious trouble in their rear.

Once he was in India Alexander faced a different enemy—one who deployed a significant number of war elephants. Darius seems to have had fifteen of these animals at Gaugamela, but no mention of them is found in the battle narratives. At the Hydaspes, against King Porus, Alexander found the enemy infantry drawn up behind a long line of elephants, perhaps as many as two hundred. This prevented penetration by cavalry and infantry, as horses would not behave normally in the presence of elephants. Alexander had anticipated this problem by training the infantry to face elephants, so they were sent against the Indian center. The cavalry worked their way around the right flank and eventually surrounded the enemy, who were apparently numerically inferior.

Throughout his eastern campaigns Alexander showed himself to be extremely adept at using a variety of arms to supplement the infantry and cavalry of the line. Only elephants seem to have been left out of the mix. In spite of their success at some later battles such as Ipsus, his decision may have been correct—at least within his immediate environment. Alexander's understanding of the capabilities of each arm and his skill at appropriately employing them is unsurpassed in antiquity. Nevertheless, in spite of the deservedly high praise for his military skills, it must be remembered that his eastern enemies were in many respects inherently inferior to the Macedonians. As

Bosworth correctly observes, Alexander's veterans became "the most adept and proficient fighters seen in the ancient world."[11] Thus his conquests were not due solely to his genius but resulted from his ability to apply the strengths of the exquisite fighting force created by his father, Philip, to the weaknesses of his eastern enemies. It is unlikely that his ability arose out of some sort of inspired intuition, although that may have played a part during the battle itself. More probably he possessed the rare ability to recognize the reality of his military environment and prepare accordingly. The fact that he never faced a properly deployed Greek phalanx in open battle precludes a complete picture of his military ability.

The difficulties Alexander would have faced are apparent from the moment he died and the fighting began, both the fighting for independence in Greece and among the Successors for domination. Satirical criticism of the unworthiness of Alexander's enemies appears in Lucian's *Dialogues of the Dead* in the second century A.D. The critical words are put into the mouth of Philip, who chides his son for conquering only cowards "armed with nothing better than bows and bucklers and wicker shields." These enemies are contrasted specifically with Boeotians, Phocians, Athenians, Thessalian cavalry, Elean javelin men, Mantineans, Thracians, Illyrians, and Paeonians, all of whom were dealt with by Philip. In another *Dialogue* Hannibal makes the same charge.[12] No doubt some of the criticism is due to ethnic bias, but it is soundly based on fact. Nevertheless, Alexander was unique in his ability to apply his skills so absolutely to warfare. This is clear from a comparison with battles in the Balkans and Near East immediately before and immediately after his reign. Fighting became an end in itself for him, and the intensity and ferocity with which he fought and expected his men to fight was incomprehensible to Greeks and Persians alike.[13] Even his father might not have understood him in this regard, for Philip was always alert to the political goals at hand and was willing to temper his use of violence if it furthered those goals, often preferring diplomacy or bribery to fighting. Not even the Successors—those generals who had fought their way east under his leadership and had shared his danger as well as his dinner table—were able to match his complete dedication

---

11. *AE* 27.

12. Lucian *Dialogues of the Dead*, "Philip and Alexander," 2; "Alexander, Hannibal, Minos, and Scipio," 2–3.

13. *AE* 28 and chap. 5. Bosworth (1996) 28 describes this behavior in vivid, unsparing language: "These men [that is to say, the Macedonian soldiers] were dangerous and none of them more than Alexander himself. . . . He gloried in battle and killing, and had an awesome proficiency in the technique of slaughter . . . and sent his lethal cavalry against populations which took to flight rather than submit."

to fighting. Nor did they wish to do so, though upon his death they fought each other for power and a piece of the empire he had conquered. The army was divided among them and its like was not seen again. It is little wonder, then, that none of the Successors was his equal.

The change was immediately apparent in the battles of the Lamian War, between the Greek states and Macedon under the regent Antipater. In the first meeting of the two sides in 323, the defection of the Thessalian cavalry to the allied side gave them an overwhelming advantage in numbers and decided the issue. Although technically a victory for the allies, it had no lasting result because the Macedonian infantry were allowed to withdraw to safety. Maintaining their superiority in cavalry, the allies had similar success against Leonnatus' reinforcements in 322, but they could not prevent his infantry from joining Antipater. The third battle, at Crannon in 322, saw the Macedonians more numerous in both infantry and cavalry. Nonetheless, the allies still placed their hopes of victory in cavalry, while Antipater realized that a decision could only be achieved by defeating the enemy infantry. While the cavalry fought each other, the infantry ended the war. These battles betray little of the coordination of arms or intensity of fighting characteristic of Alexander, while the allies' emphasis on cavalry seems inexplicable in purely military terms. Is it possible that the stories of Alexander's success so distorted the part played by cavalry that the Greeks thought that this arm could win on its own? Plutarch provides a different explanation for the allies' lackluster performance, incidentally highlighting some reasons for the lower level of fighting quality in the armies of the Greek city-states. He describes the defeat at Crannon as not severe, with few casualties, and attributes it to the men's lack of obedience to their young commanders and Antipater's tempting overtures to the individual cities.[14] This sounds reasonable, since it is inherently improbable—no matter how high the stakes—that the Greek city-state hoplites could match the hardened Macedonian veterans.

The struggle among Alexander's successors in Asia Minor and the Near East was much more intense than the halfhearted struggle for independence in Greece. Although there was traditionally a greater reliance on cavalry in these regions, the Successors always sought to acquire Macedonian infantry for their armies in the apparent conviction that success was inconceivable without them. In that sense they agreed with Alexander, but the circumstances they faced were so different from his that their effect upon battlefield

---

14. Plut. *Phoc.* 26.1.

dynamics was profound. Significant changes included: the armies' more evenly matched leadership, type, and overall quality—that is to say, greater symmetry; the loss of a strong bond between king and soldier, leading to a decline in loyalty and morale; the loss of a sense of fighting for national or personal survival, since defeated soldiers were usually viewed as a welcome asset to the victor's army; and the fact that since most of the fighting was the result of personal ambition, the death of a general cancelled any obligation to continue the fight. The fact that Macedonians were often fighting each other also lessened their martial ardor. Thus there is no reason to expect the Successors to match Alexander's achievements in Asia, even if we were to ignore his personal genius. One of the most telling facts about the battles in the two decades following his death is the number of them decided by treachery or carelessness.

The career of Eumenes is most instructive in this respect. In 321 Eumenes' infantry were routed by Neoptolemus' Macedonians, but he salvaged victory when the latter broke ranks to pursue. That gave Eumenes' victorious cavalry a chance to catch them out of formation and force a surrender. In his clash with Craterus and Neoptolemus, a short time later only cavalry were engaged. After both of these opponents were killed in the battle—Neoptolemus in a duel with Eumenes—their infantry surrendered. A year later Antigonus defeated Eumenes at Orcynii when the latter's cavalry deserted during the battle. The last two battles between Eumenes and Antigonus, Paraetacene (317) and Gabiene (316), exhibit the defining characteristics of large-scale Hellenistic warfare. In both instances the cavalry and infantry fought separately against each other. Eumenes' qualitatively superior infantry twice defeated those of Antigonus. Credit for this went to an elite unit that was formerly part of Alexander's army—the Silver Shields. At Paraetacene, however, the Silver Shields advanced too quickly in pursuit of their opponents and opened a gap on their right. When Antigonus took advantage of it with his cavalry, he turned left into the flank of Eumenes' horse rather than right against the infantry, probably for fear these previously unengaged cavalry would strike him in the rear. The overall result was a draw. The result the following year at Gabiene was similar up to a point, as the fighting ended in a draw. The difference lay in Antigonus' decision to use his victorious cavalry to capture the enemy baggage train rather than to attack the infantry. In fear of losing their families and possessions, the Silver Shields handed over Eumenes to Antigonus. In a purely military sense, the victory should have gone to Eumenes. The Silver Shields were again successful and Eumenes tried to mount an attack to recover the camp, but the cavalry commander refused to carry out the order. It is noteworthy that when Antigonus sent cavalry against the isolated Silver Shields, it was thwarted by the discipline and experience of these infantry, who retreated to safety. Once again the comparison with Alexander is telling, both in respect to the quality of the enemy and the loyalty of subordinates.

At Gaza in 312 Ptolemy and Seleucus faced Demetrius in what was primarily an engagement of cavalry on both flanks of rather inactive infantry. The severe mounted action with lance and sword ended when Demetrius fled after his elephants were stopped by caltrops. Since Demetrius was greatly outnumbered in infantry and only he had elephants, it looks as though he wished to decide matters with elephants and cavalry alone. It is unclear why his opponents did not use their more numerous infantry more vigorously. Perhaps it was simply not necessary, since eight thousand of Demetrius' eleven thousand infantry surrendered.

Ipsus, the final battle of this era, is unusual because of the great superiority in elephants enjoyed by the allies against Antigonus. Although war elephants were perhaps the least reliable of arms, they may have decided one of the most important battles of the Hellenistic period on this occasion. The opening stages of the battle present us with the ideal of Hellenistic tactics. Demetrius, the son of Antigonus, drove the enemy cavalry of the left wing from the battlefield and then returned to support his father, only to find his way blocked by the elephants. That gave Seleucus his opportunity, but he did not engage his infantry vigorously as one might have expected. Instead, he used his remaining cavalry to ride around the enemy infantry and intimidate them with feigned charges. Perhaps he knew something about their loyalty, for a large number of them surrendered, allowing him to rout the remainder.

That readiness to surrender was decidedly not present in the three battles fought between Pyrrhus and the Romans in the years from 280 to 275. One possible reason for this might have been their different ethnic backgrounds, supporting professionalism on the Greek side and defense of home territory on the Roman. These were hard-fought infantry clashes in which the invader's elephants seem to have decided the issue in the first two "Pyrrhic" victories. On the third occasion the Roman camp guards drove off the elephants and reversed the decision. Cavalry had a relatively small part to play during this campaign, although when mounted action did occur it exhibited the hand-to-hand combat with spears that was typical of the period. In spite of differences in respect to organization, equipment, and fighting style between the Greeks and Romans, both fought with a high level of skill and determination that resulted in high casualties on both sides—a result that was less common when Greek armies of the period fought each other.

A good example of the importance of applying military principles based on battlefield reality and employing each arm to best advantage appears in the battle between Hiero of Syracuse and the Mamertines in Sicily in the 260s. Although cavalry and infantry fought separately, as was typical during this period, Hiero decided the issue by sending six hundred infantry around a hill to attack the Mamertines in the rear. Because of their greater speed and mobility, cavalry would have been the obvious choice for such an assignment, but on this occasion Hiero apparently realized that infantry could succeed.

At Sellasia in 222 topography dominated the thinking on both sides. Cavalry were stationed in the center of the line, where a river valley offered the most level terrain, while the phalanx was split between the adjacent hillsides. Although Philopoemen, acting with the cavalry on his own initiative, saved the Macedonian rear, the decision itself lay with their phalanx. In retrospect one may ask why the numerically inferior Spartans formed their line athwart the river rather than parallel to it on the rising land to one side, thus using the riverbed and heights as a defense. Perhaps they feared that the Macedonians would have easy access to the city to the south via the undefended side of the valley, although they would have been exposed to a flank attack. The lie of the land was also a factor at Mantinea in 207, a ditch disrupting the Lacedaemonian phalanx.

Antiochus III, the Seleucid king in Syria, is worth more individual attention because of his long reign and active military career, during which he faced both enemies to the east with strong mounted traditions and Mediterranean armies to the west that were anchored by good infantry. His campaigns offer a good example of the difficulty of using the mounted and infantry arms appropriately. Although Seleucus, the founder of the dynasty, focused most of his attention on the Mediterranean to the west, Antiochus hoped to expand his realm in both directions and recapture previously held territory. In the military sense his outlook seems to have been most influenced by the eastern tradition, his title of "Great" resulting from his own anabasis as far as India, in imitation of Alexander. In spite of this the Seleucid army was based on the Macedonian phalanx. It was apparently his misfortune to possess the mentality of a cavalry general. Against his eastern enemies that worked to his advantage, and his title was well deserved. Polybius' description of his fight at Tapuria in 208 could almost serve as a chapter in a military treatise on how to conduct a cavalry battle.[15] Yet Antiochus did not exhibit such mastery when he faced Greek or Roman infantry. At both Raphia (217) and Magnesia (190) his single-minded cavalry charges, not coordinated with infantry action, and his failure to engage his phalanx aggressively probably cost him the victory. It is ironic that at Magnesia it was the opportunistic but appropriate use of cavalry by Eumenes II of Pergamon that handed victory to the Romans, while Antiochus—with little thought for his own phalanx, which the Romans feared—was leading his misdirected cavalry attack.[16] Once again, as is often the case, error on the battlefield obscures our ability to make a purely military evaluation of the two sides.

The same situation applies in the great struggle between Rome and Macedon, who faced each other at Cynoscephalae (197) and Pydna (168) with the two finest armies of Greco-Roman antiquity. The Roman victory was not as obvious as it seems in retrospect, as unfortunately sketchy accounts of the campaigns preceding these battles suggest that the Macedonians more than held their own. During these two battles, however, mistakes by the Macedonian kings allowed the phalanx to fight at a distinct disadvantage, while the cavalry—for no obvious reason—were used ineffectively or not at all. On both occasions, wherever well-formed phalanx and legion met, the phalanx was locally superior, and it seems apparent that on an open battlefield, with the several arms of both armies performing to their potential, the Macedonians usually would have dominated. It is likely that Macedon could no longer produce as many cavalrymen as it had previously, but that does not explain their failure to protect the flanks in these battles. The much-praised flexibility of the Roman legion would have been of no avail had mistakes not been made on the other side. Perhaps when we look back at the poor decisions made by generals who commit their armies to battle under unfavorable circumstances, we should think of Keegan's observation that the tension among men facing each other may reach a point at which everybody merely wants to get the whole thing over with.[17]

I included Hannibal's major campaigns in this book as something of a control, since his fame rests largely on his adroit use of cavalry, with which he seems to have accomplished things that others—Alexander excepted—

---

15. Polyb. 10.49. Great cavalry leaders, some at least, seem to be a type. In addition to the physical courage necessary for the inherent danger of riding under battle conditions, they exhibit a fearless, reckless, flamboyant behavior that sets them apart. Examples are Seydlitz, who fought under Frederick the Great, and Custer.

16. *HMND* 66.

17. Keegan (1995) 135.

failed to do. The question is, did he do anything essentially different or, like Alexander, did he take advantage of a compliant enemy? Although what he did on the battlefield may look different, I do not think that it was. He did not add any tricks to the prevailing Hellenistic military outlook. Rather, Hannibal offers a classic case of a commander who recognized reality and adapted himself and his forces to it. That was the basis of his genius, whereby he ably exploited the Hellenistic legacy to the full—especially widely accepted and enduring military principles that found their expression in tactics designed for a specific military environment. Unit for unit, his cavalry were not demonstrably superior to those of the Romans and their allies, and his infantry were inferior. His victories rest upon his decision to use a numerical superiority in cavalry that permitted him to engage the mounted arm against the legion's flanks and rear *free of interference from the enemy*. The idea of attacking an enemy's flank and rear goes back at least to the Peloponnesian War, but it was difficult or impossible to accomplish when one's opponent had skilled infantry and cavalry and possessed approximate numerical parity. Alexander found his solution by penetration of a weaker line with better infantry and cavalry, since his numbers did not offer him the chance to outflank the Persians. Hannibal took advantage of the Romans' comparatively indifferent attitude toward the mounted arm and somewhat justified overconfidence in their infantry, as well as their poor leadership, to achieve some of the most spectacular victories in history.

At Cannae, for example, his smaller army outflanked and encircled the more numerous Roman forces, and it is likely—as Seibert suggests—that the Roman commanders had not yet learned how to handle such large numbers of men to the best advantage.[18] On the same occasion he ordered his African infantry to attack the Roman flank while the regular cavalry struck the legions in the rear and the Numidians pursued the Roman horse, an effective division of labor based on intrinsic fighting skills. As I noted in the chapter devoted to Hannibal, Polybius observed, when reflecting on Cannae, that it was better to be weaker in infantry and much stronger in cavalry than to be numerically equal to one's enemy.[19]

While this seems to explain the outcome at Cannae, it should not be applied as an absolute principle; variables arising from local circumstances usually determine the outcome on any given day. This is convincingly shown by the later battle of Pharsalus between Caesar and Pompey in 48. At Pharsalus

18. *HB* 196.
19. Polyb. 3.117.5.

Pompey had the advantage in both infantry and cavalry and was so confident his seven thousand horsemen could carry the day that he seems to have held back his infantry. His plan was to have all his cavalry on the left rout their one thousand opponents and then turn in behind Caesar's legions. But Caesar, immediately seeing through Pompey's plan, was not as obliging as his predecessors had been to Hannibal. Withdrawing six cohorts from his third line, Caesar posted them on his right and instructed them as to the way to deal with Pompey's cavalry. When the cavalry attacked and routed Caesar's horsemen, the fourth line of cohorts waited until they were given the signal and then attacked so vigorously that Pompey's cavalry galloped away in panic. After killing some archers and slingers, the cohorts turned in behind Pompey's line and initiated the destruction of his army. Caesar credited the cohorts with the victory.[20] In each of these battles the victor outgeneraled his opponent through a realistic evaluation of the circumstances that allowed him to take advantage of enemy mistakes and make appropriate adjustments. Caesar clearly had a better grasp of Pompey's intentions than Pompey had of his, while his appreciation of the relative strengths and weaknesses of the infantry and cavalry on the ground that day decided the issue. Had Pompey's horsemen been more battle hardened, the result might have been different. His more experienced troops had been lost in Spain the previous year.[21]

The inconsistent results achieved by the Greek and Macedonian generals during the Hellenistic Period can be attributed more to circumstances than lack of ability, even if we admit that none of the generals possessed the military genius of Alexander and Hannibal. The same applies to success with cavalry. In spite of some showy displays by the mounted arm and occasional success, infantry—of necessity—dominated the Hellenistic battlefield. But while the efforts of one arm or another may have been decisive on any given occasion, it was the result of all of them in concert that produced the victory. During that time it proved too difficult to achieve the necessary degree of asymmetry that Alexander and Hannibal were able to exploit to advantage. These two famous generals also benefited from a closer relationship with their soldiers, which in turn seems to have produced a greater willingness to fight on their behalf. There is no doubt about their genius—a genius that was acutely attuned to a reality to which, in turn, they adapted their armies and operational plans.

One aspect of the reality of Hellenistic battlefields that does not lend itself to easy analysis is the presence of elephants. Their initial employment,

20. Caes. *B. Civ.* 3.84–98.
21. App. *B. Civ.* 2.76, and Plut. *Caes.* 45 describe Pompey's cavalry as young and inexperienced.

at least, would seem to offer an opportunity to achieve significant asymmetry. Yet although they did occasionally contribute to victory, at first glance their overall record seems disappointing. While the use of elephants in warfare after the time of Alexander is not in doubt (as has been shown in the foregoing battle narratives), the question is whether they were worth the effort. And effort it truly was, for it required a great deal of support for each side in a battle to keep 50 to 100 elephants in the field. A total of between 150 and 200 elephants on a battlefield was not rare, and at Ipsus there were 475. Although it is folly to assume that human decisions are always made rationally, one must ask why so much effort was expended on bringing these animals to the battlefield when, it is possible to argue, they were not very useful. Some of the expense of keeping elephants was avoided by capturing young adults from wild herds rather than breeding them in captivity and waiting fifteen or so years for them to mature.[22] Technically they are not domestic animals and have not been genetically transformed by controlled breeding as have all true domesticates. Maintaining a good supply of these animals may have been a greater problem than insuring suitable care and fodder. Indeed, their number on the battlefield declined in the third century, when contact with India decreased as the Seleucids lost their eastern possessions. Nonetheless, feeding them must have been a quartermaster's nightmare; one need only recall that as recently as World War I, fodder for cavalry horses and draft animals was the largest logistical item. It is reasonable, therefore, to assume that there was some military reason for including the elephant corps in Hellenistic armies.

Seibert, however, is not convinced. He points out that the true military geniuses of antiquity (Alexander, Scipio, Caesar) did not include them in their operational plans and suggests that the lesser generals were overly impressed by their power.[23] The first half of the statement is certainly correct, but each of the three leaders did take serious measures to counter elephants when their troops had to face them, and their failure to use them may have owed something to availability. Furthermore, many of the Successors and later Hellenistic kings who regularly employed elephants were good generals in their own right. Among the several excellent generals who did use them are Seleucus, Antigonus, Eumenes, Pyrrhus, and Hannibal. Indeed, just prior to the battle

---

22. Diamond (1997) 169. For a general discussion of domestication see 160–75. Some instances of captive breeding may have occurred in antiquity, as textual references to mothers and calves as well as pictorial representations exist. Scullard (1974) 112, fig. 2, pl. vii, ix.

23. Seibert (1973) 361.

of Gabiene in 217, Antigonus made a notable effort to intercept a group of Eumenes' elephants that failed only because Eumenes sent out a timely and effective rescue detachment. The fact that the best generals had to devise a counter to elephants before their troops could face them with some confidence suggests that they were indeed a threat. The problem lay in determining how to use them properly to achieve some desirable military goal, but that is the problem with any type of arm or weapon and is not peculiar to the elephant corps. Under the right conditions their presence was decisive—for example, at Ipsus, in Pyrrhus' two victories against the Romans, and in the Carthaginian defeat of Regulus, among battles I have described.

I have not yet mentioned the famous "elephant victory" won by Antiochus III in Asia Minor against the invading Gauls in 275. Facing inexperienced troops, his sixteen elephants frightened off the cavalry and destroyed the infantry, in the process gaining a fame that survived for centuries into the Roman period.[24] This degree of success was not typical, however, and for most of the battles in which elephants appeared from the death of Alexander to the mid-second century the record was uneven and their contribution seldom decisive. Nonetheless, to be fair, it must be admitted that cavalry during this period had little more to show for their efforts on the battlefield, and for much the same reason—the armies that fought each other were too similar, and all the players, soldiers and commanders alike, well understood the offensive and defensive strengths and weaknesses of every arm. It also seems clear that the elephant corps was more likely than the cavalry to be in a low state of readiness and thus not capable of exhibiting its potential on the battlefield.[25] Furthermore, in view of the broad range of behavior shown by elephants in battle—from fright and turning back on their own to ferocious aggression—it should always be kept in mind that these are living animals and not machines.

In short it would appear that the elephant corps was a legitimate arm during this period, capable of contributing to or even creating the asymmetry always sought by good commanders. Against inexperienced cavalry mounts, as at Ipsus, it could have devastating success. Like any other arm, its employment had to be adapted to the circumstances of each battlefield. Individually, elephants—by virtue of their size and small total number—were more valuable than horses. Their size also means that they could be more easily targeted by missile weapons, which were probably the single best counter to them. Although horsemen had more uses off the battlefield, in

---

24. Lucian, *Zeux.* 8–11. Scullard (1974) 122–23.
25. Scullard (1974) 195–96.

combat the record of elephants is not significantly worse than that of cavalry. Yet because of the difficulty of obtaining and supporting them, they were not as common on the battlefield as cavalry. After the Peloponnesian War it was almost unthinkable to field an army without the mounted arm, whereas elephants—once they became available after Alexander's death—remained something of a military luxury.

Whether elephants could tolerate battlefield conditions as well as horses cannot be clearly demonstrated, although a close reading of the sources suggests that their endurance of pain in the heat of battle was lower than that of horses.[26] It must be emphasized that—except possibly in the cases of Alexander and Hannibal—infantry remained the single most important arm in Hellenistic warfare, so that it is unrealistic to expect either cavalry or elephants to perform marvels. It is probable that some commanders expected them to do so, but they were bound to be disappointed. Nonetheless, the distinct impression remains that something is missing from our understanding of the dynamics of Hellenistic battlefields. Specifically, it seems that elephants should have had more success in neutralizing cavalry. At Ipsus perhaps it was their number, as much as anything, that kept Demetrius' horsemen at bay. One can only conclude that it was not an insurmountable task to accustom horses to the sight and smell of elephants, as it is only in clear cases of a lack of prior experience that modest numbers of them could be effective. At the

26. The reason for this difference is described in a short story by Rudyard Kipling entitled "Her Majesty's Servants." In the tale a British soldier in India (who understands camp-beast language) overhears a discussion about bravery carried on by a baggage camel, a trooper's horse, an artillery mule, two gun bullocks (oxen), and an elephant. In the course of the animals' relating their respective duties and skills, the question of bravery in battle arises. The bullocks consider the elephant a coward, because he balks as soon as he has brought the big guns close to the front, so they must take his place and bring them into position. The elephant admits that the bullocks are brave but attempts to explain his behavior by the fact that he can see inside his head what will happen when a shell bursts. To make matters worse, he thinks about it. The horse can also see this to some extent, but he tries not to think about it, which he succeeds in doing if there is a trustworthy rider on his back. The bullocks are the bravest of all precisely because they are utterly devoid of this type of imagination. The difference between the elephant, which balks, and the horse, which fights at the front, is the latter's capacity to trust a rider—a capacity that the elephant lacks because of its greater intelligence. The elephant admits that "you could put a whole regiment of [trooper] Dicks on my back, without making me feel any better" (Kipling [1895], 185). It is precisely this understanding of animal behavior, based on long experience, that we have lost since the advent of the internal combustion engine. It has not been completely forgotten, however, and a modern veterinarian, Michael Schäfer, recognizes precisely this difference in intelligence even among different breeds of horses. He observes that an intelligent breed—the Arab, for example—is more reluctant to do dangerous and boring things than a duller breed would be. Schäffer attributes what we call courage in animals to a lack of imaginative capacity. He recognizes that some of this reluctance in an intelligent horse can be overcome through trust in the rider, but suggests that excessive trust of this sort is an indication of a lack of (survival) intelligence (Schäfer [2000], 97–100).

Hydaspes Alexander solved the problem by having his cavalry avoid them. Cavalry were clearly more maneuverable and quicker than elephants and could operate more effectively on their own. Most often elephants were protected by a screen of light infantry comprising some combination of archers, javelin men, and slingers.

Another puzzling aspect of events on the battlefield is the relative ineffectiveness of missile troops against cavalry. The fact that sling bullets and arrows were unsettling to horses is not in doubt, and there are a number of references in the ancient sources either recommending or describing their use against cavalry.[27] Some of the most useful examples come from Xenophon. Following the death of Cyrus at Cunaxa, as the Greeks attempted to withdraw northward away from the Persian army, a number of clashes occurred that highlight the strengths and weaknesses of missile troops, especially slingers. During their retreat it took the Greeks a while to work out an appropriate defense against the Persian troops who persisted in harassing them. On the first occasion the Persian commander, Mithradates, inflicted significant casualties on the Greek rear guard with about two hundred horsemen and four hundred archers and slingers. Asymmetry—in the form of disparity in the range of missile weapons—was the reason in this case, for the Cretan bowmen had a shorter range than their Persian counterparts and the Persian slingers outshot the Greek javelin men. A charge by hoplites and peltasts was useless, since the enemy withdrew and the Greeks had no cavalry for rapid pursuit.[28] In this situation the Greeks showed the value of adaptability. On the recommendation of Xenophon, two hundred slingers and fifty horsemen were organized from among the mercenaries, who included men from Rhodes—an island famous for its slingers. Previous skill with this weapon was essential, because it required years of practice to perfect its use. The horses were those abandoned by the cavalry that had deserted to the Persians and animals captured along the way.[29]

Encouraged by early success with such small numbers, Tissaphernes had given Mithradates one thousand horsemen and some four thousand archers and slingers, hoping to deal with the Greeks once and for all. On this occasion, when the Persians caught up with them and began to loose their missiles, the Greeks charged with infantry and cavalry upon a prearranged signal. Surprise as much as anything caused the Persians to flee, and the

27. Pritchett has collected the references (especially those to slingers) in *GSW* 5 1–67.
28. Xen. *An.* 3.3.6–11.
29. Ibid., 3.3.16–20.

Greeks were able to inflict some casualties in the pursuit.[30] As the enemy made no appearance for a while afterward, the Greeks proceeded unmolested for several days. Then Tissaphernes himself arrived with a much larger force. Although unwilling to risk formal battle, he ordered his missile troops to fire upon the Greeks. Upon being met with a damaging volley from the Rhodian slingers, they withdrew. The reason for this lay in the fact that the Rhodians used lead bullets, which traveled farther and did more damage to flesh than the stones used by the Persians and even outranged their arrows.[31] This pattern of skirmishing lasted for some time, the Greeks suffering casualties before the Persians abandoned the pursuit, but they were able to inflict enough injury on the enemy to prevent them from risking battle. Although these events show the value of slingers, the immediate reason for the survival of the Greeks was their temper and mettle. The Persians could not match their morale and individual skill and at times even had to be driven to fight with the lash.[32] Once again, it was the immediate circumstances that permitted the successful employment of a specific weapon and appropriate tactics. In spite of instances such as these, missile troops always remained fragile elements of a Greek or Hellenistic battle line, as they possessed too little defensive armor and skills to resist determined infantry and cavalry who could often easily overrun them.

An interesting example of the interplay among different types of forces is found at the battle of Paraetacene between Antigonus and Eumenes in 317. On Eumenes' right wing a numerically superior force of mounted archers attacked his elephants, which were protected by archers and slingers. Although the cavalry were incapable of making a frontal assault, because of their number and mobility they inflicted serious damage upon the elephants. When Eumenes realized this, he summoned light cavalry and ordered them to charge the flanks of the mounted archers. Aided by light infantry and followed by the elephants, they easily routed the mounted archers, matching their mobility while showing the superiority of hand-held weapons and the threat of close combat.[33] This was always the weakness of missile troops and would seem to explain why they did not prove to be more effective against either cavalry or infantry. The relative ease with which archers and slingers could be overrun by determined infantry and cavalry wielding hand-held

30. Ibid., 3.4.3–5.
31. Ibid., 3.4.14–17.
32. Ibid., 3.4.25–26.
33. Diod. 19.28–30.

weapons strongly suggests that these missile troops were incapable of the sustained, concentrated fire that would itself have provided a defense. One problem was that of supply, for arrows and lead sling bullets could be rapidly exhausted.

The symmetrical armies of the Hellenistic period usually did not permit the type of success that Xenophon had with the slingers or the effective coordination of arms that marked the campaigns of Alexander and Hannibal. The very different enemies they faced offered opportunities not open to Hellenistic generals, who probably did as much as was possible in the environment in which they found themselves. Yet an awareness of the effect of symmetry has not always been recognized as a determinant of tactical options. Tarn, for example, thought that changes in the use of cavalry arose from the "accident that, at the battle of Raphia in 217 between Antiochus III and Ptolemy IV, the two wings [that is to say, the cavalry] cancelled out and the battle was decided by the heavy infantry in the center."[34] It was no "accident," but rather the almost inevitable result of the similarity or symmetry of the two armies. That being the case, allowance must be made for the possibility that the commanders understood it and expected cavalry to fight each other until or unless some more dramatic opportunity presented itself. Cavalry and the other arms retained their importance as part of a whole that was truly effective only when the individual elements were properly coordinated by a skilled general.

At first glance it seems surprising that the Macedonian kings made such poor use of cavalry against the Romans at Cynoscephalae and Pydna, since the first of these battles occurred twenty years after Hannibal's first victories, which showed how cavalry could be used effectively against the legion. Since Philip had been in touch with Hannibal, he must have known something of these victories, but we have no record of it; clearly much has been omitted from the surviving sources. Admittedly, the two Macedonians allowed themselves to be drawn into a fight under less than ideal conditions, so they may not have been able to employ their cavalry wisely. Still, the cavalry had held their own against the Romans in actions prior to those battles and should have been more effective.

It also appears that once asymmetry had been achieved by one side, the opportunity for the successful use of coordinated arms increased, because individual arms had more freedom of movement and could be applied offensively

---

34. *HMND* 26.

more easily. The battle of Zama where neither side came to the battlefield with a significant superiority, clearly shows what happens when that is not the case. The result on that occasion was that both Scipio and Hannibal had to abandon any hope of using their formerly successful tactics, which rested upon asymmetry and coordination of arms. It may be disappointing to us that neither of these exceptional generals displayed evidence of their previous tactical brilliance at Zama, but we should applaud the perceptiveness with which each faced reality and the fact that they made the best adjustments that the local conditions allowed. It is a sign of their greatness that they resisted the temptation to use previously successful tactics under circumstances that precluded their effective employment.

It seems clear from the military actions I have presented in this book that successful cavalry tactics, more than those of the infantry, are ad hoc applications of fundamental military principles against a specific enemy on a specific battlefield.[35] They may be sketched broadly well in advance, as Hannibal did against the Romans, or adjusted just prior to battle, as Alexander did against the elephants of Porus. Flexibility and adaptability are essential amidst the unpredictable behavior that occurs on the battlefield. It should also be noted that many ingredients—some obscure—lie behind the tactics that can be observed in battle. Every military generation transmits a great body of knowledge and skill to the next, whether through the apprentice system of military training or in written documents such as the military treatises that survive from the fourth century B.C. to the Byzantine decline a millennium and a half later. This knowledge may be conceptual, behavioral, or technological in form, and the skilled military leaders of each age use it, adapt it, and enlarge upon it with their creative faculties. Certain prerequisites must be in place, however, before individual tactics can be conceived and applied. For example, the willingness and ability of cavalrymen to fight hand-to-hand with spear and sword predated the tactics of having them attack infantry in the flanks and rear, or—as they did under Alexander—penetrate a weaker enemy line. But their physical inability to penetrate the Greek and Mace-

---

35. These principles are timeless, and when they are applied to cavalry are found into modern times in spite of the change from cutting and thrusting weapons to firearms. An example that receives too little attention occurred on the third day at Gettysburg. Lee sent J. E. B. Stuart with his cavalry around the Union right with orders to come in behind the enemy when Pickett was making his advance against the Union front. Brig. Gen. David Gregg, commander of the Second Cavalry Division, receiving word of Stuart's movements and determined to protect the Union right and rear, moved against him with the brigades of Custer and McIntosh. After heavy fighting near Rummel Farm, especially by Custer's Michigan brigade (on loan from the Third Division), Stuart was stopped. Had that not happened, Gettysburg might have had a different ending. See Urwin (1990) 73–82.

donian phalanx frontally produced outflanking tactics as an alternative that was contrary to the traditional Greek concept of frontal attack that had dominated warfare for the two hundred years prior to the Peloponnesian War. The great geniuses—Philip, Alexander, and Hannibal—exploited these tactics to the full and further increased their chances of success by applying new levels of intensity to training and discipline, so that at times it was as if professionals were facing amateurs.

Assuming that this interpretation is correct, one may well ask whether the military men of antiquity were consciously aware of what a modern reading of the ancient sources suggest that they did. Fortunately, the answer seems to lie in the ancient military treatises, which were—at the very least—intellectual ruminations on military skills and practices, and—at their best—serious attempts to identify and codify principles of military success. Although it may be impossible to demonstrate their direct influence upon history, they do record ideas that were current at the time of composition, and their literary influence can be traced well into the Byzantine period. Furthermore, we know that some military leaders did think highly of them. Plutarch, for example, reports in a statement about Philopoemen that "among other writings, he was most devoted to the *Tactics* of Evangelus, and was familiar with the histories of Alexander, thinking that literature was conducive to action."[36] Pyrrhus had his friend Cineas prepare an epitome of Aeneas Tacticus and himself wrote a treatise that is now lost.[37] Xenophon's *Cyropaedia* was also popular, being the vade mecum of Scipio Africanus on his campaigns.[38] Caesar had also read this work and was familiar with the historical works on Alexander the Great as well.[39] Even Cicero claims to have found opportunity to apply Xenophon's lessons when he was governor of Cilicia.[40]

Of the formal treatises of this period, two survive in complete form while a third is represented by a single book from an original eight. The first two are Xenophon's works, *The Cavalry Commander* and *On Horsemanship*, while the third is Aeneas Tacticus' book, *On the Defense of Fortified Positions*.[41] In addition—and perhaps most important—there is the *Cyropaedia* of Xenophon.

36. Plut. *Phil.* 4.4.
37. Ael. *Tac.* 1.2.
38. Cic. *QFr.* 1.1.23.
39. Suet. *Div. Iul.* 87; Plut. *Caes.* 11.
40. Cic. *Fam.* 9.25.1.
41. For a survey of all the ancient treatises, see Jähns ([1889]1965) 13–136; for Xenophon, *AGH* 155–80; for Aeneas, Oldfather (1923) 1–17. For a recent translation and commentary of Aeneas see Whitehead (1990).

Although it is frequently described as a historical romance, in reality it is a serious attempt by Xenophon to present his mature ideas on education and military science in the guise of a (largely fictitious) narrative about Cyrus the Great.[42]

The surviving part of Aeneas, which concerns the defense of cities, can be dealt with quickly, since it adds nothing to our knowledge of the use of cavalry in battle. Nevertheless, several references to this arm suggest its importance in other contexts.[43] It is unfortunate that Aeneas' work on tactics does not survive, although it was used by later writers, including Pyrrhus, Polybius, and Aelian.[44] On the other hand Xenophon's two works on horsemanship, which continue to be admired by modern writers on the subject, detail a level of equitation that was most likely higher than that practiced by the typical cavalryman.[45]

Excluding tactics, which are discussed separately below, Xenophon's comprehensive treatment is clear from the following list of topics to be found in his works.

> From *The Cavalry Commander*: Selecting, conditioning, and training the horse (1.3–6), including conditioning of the feet, which was especially important in the absence of horseshoes (1.16). Riding over different types of terrain to improve the seat (1.18). The value of sham fights (3.12-13). Guidelines for marching (4.1–6). Qualities of a cavalry commander (6.1–6). Training horses and men to jump ditches and walls, and to ride up and down hill (8.3).
>
> From *On Horsemanship*: Selecting and judging horses (1.2–17; 3.1–12). Stable management (4.1–14). Grooming (5.1–6.16). Mounting (7.1–2). The proper seat (7.5–7). Riding skills and exercises at the various gaits and on different terrain (7.10–8.9). Hunting as exercise for war (8.10). Horse psychology (9.2–12). Different bits and their uses (10.6–11).

---

42. Anderson (1970) 11–12; Hirsch (1985) chap. 4.
43. For example, the way in which to render land unfit for cavalry (Aen. Tac. 8.4); the use of cavalry for reconnaissance, seizing heights, and preventing surprise (15.1); and the way in which to deal with foragers (16.7).
44. Only Aelian's treatise survives. See Devine (1989b) 31–64.
45. Chenevix-Trench (1970) 23–27, and 30 for especially positive comment.

Xenophon's own extensive military experience provides the basis for his writings, making him an invaluable observer of the military practices current during his lifetime. To be sure, that is not to say that he understood and appreciated all that was happening, as his reserve regarding the accomplishments of Epaminondas and Pelopidas seems to indicate. Nevertheless, he was not blind to new ideas if he was convinced of their value, a fact that is clear from the influence the Persians had upon his thinking.[46] Much of the advice that he offers on military practices and tactics was commonplace in his own day, although it was no less important for that reason. Incidentally, his *Anabasis* is the best eyewitness account of military operations that survives from antiquity, whereas the *Cyropaedia* is its theoretical counterpart. The latter work, in spite of its inferior style and lack of philosophical content, may be considered as a military analogue to Plato's works of political theory, *The Republic* and *The Laws*. Among Xenophon's recommendations are the use of deception and ambush; raiding parties of cavalry employing hit-and-run tactics against an invader when the full levy is not available; and attacking the enemy when they are out of formation—for example—at meals or while crossing a river.[47]

Other recommendations of Xenophon's seem to foreshadow the work of Philip and Alexander. Examples are his advice to use one's whole force even when the enemy is obviously weaker and thereby to achieve an overwhelming victory (through asymmetry); to use the best men when one is forced to fight and retire at a disadvantage; and, when one is facing a body of cavalry equal to one's own, to charge with forces divided in two parts in order to unsettle the enemy and make their task more difficult.[48] Complete victory was a hallmark of Alexander's strategy, and where circumstances permitted his pursuits were relentless. He also used more than one cavalry force when his right wing advanced to the attack.

By its very nature as a work of fiction the *Cyropaedia* offered Xenophon an opportunity to present his thoughts in ideal form, and because it was written near the end of his life it contains his mature reflections on the military arts as he understood them. The work is also of interest because Xenophon projected his thoughts upon a much larger military stage than battles of the

---

46. Hirsch (1985) 90. A specific example is his recommendation to adopt the Persian slashing sword and javelin. Xen. *On Hors.* 12.11–12. Xenophon's preference for the javelin was not shared by Greeks and Macedonians, but the slashing sword (*kopis*) was used effectively by Alexander and his companion cavalry. Cf. Arr. *Anab.* 1.15.7–8.

47. Xen. *Cav. Cmdr.* 4.9–5.15; 7.7–12.

48. Ibid., 8.10; 12–16; 17–18.

Greek and smaller armies, envisaging battles that involved hundreds of thousands of combatants. It is generally agreed that the tactics attributed to Cyrus are not those of the barbarian king but of the author himself, as he saw them in use by the Greek phalanx.[49] He may even have introduced ideas that he had never seen in practice. In addition to the pursuit and destruction of the enemy army, he recommends that cavalry be prepared for hand-to-hand combat. Previously, in *On Horsemanship*, he had recommended that cavalrymen carry two Persian javelins made of cornel wood, one to be thrown and the second for close work. There he included advice on how to throw the javelin from horseback.[50] In the *Cyropaedia* he equips the cavalry of Cyrus with a heavy lance and has them mentally well prepared for close combat. He even suggests that the enemy infantry will have to sustain a charge of steel backed by the impetus of horses.[51] This point is most interesting, because there is no evidence that it was ever successful on a Greek battlefield, raising the possibility that Xenophon saw it as feasible against a foreign army but not a Greek one. Certainly, Alexander later was to apply the principle with a vengeance.

In portraying the battle between Cyrus and Croesus in the seventh book of the *Cyropaedia*, Xenophon created a hypothetical operational setting in which his ideas could play themselves out during the course of the action.[52] Although the manner in which the battle resolved itself is altogether too rational to be realistic, individual recommendations have great merit. These include his use of cavalry as one among several arms whose coordinated efforts produce victory. Present on the battlefield were heavy infantry, javelin men, archers, cavalry, a camel brigade, chariots, and towers containing archers.[53] Cyrus stationed some cavalry and infantry behind his line with instructions to take Croesus' wings, which were bent forward at a right angle to their center in an effort to encircle the Persians. Thus Croesus' army began the attack on three sides at once. It failed on the two bent wings, because Cyrus was able to strike their flanks in turn and cause panic. He himself led the cavalry on the right, while camels went forward on the left and frightened the enemy cavalry. Cyrus initiated a pursuit, only to be stopped when it became apparent that Croesus' best infantry—the Egyptians—were advancing unbroken

49. *GSW* 1 129.
50. Xen. *On. Hors.* 12.2–13.
51. Xen. *Cyr.* 6.2.16; 4.18.
52. Ibid., 7.1.23–40. The battle is discussed at length by Anderson (1970) chap. 9.
53. Xenophon had a high regard for the combination of arms; twice elsewhere in his writings he describes as ideal an army that comprises hoplites, cavalry, peltasts, archers, and slingers. Xen. *An.* 5.6.15; Xen. *Oec.* 8.6.

against his center. Realizing the weak spot in the phalanx, Cyrus led his cavalry around behind the Egyptians. Assaulted on all sides, they surrendered, accepting the generous terms offered by the Persian king.

Anderson criticizes Xenophon for not having Cyrus "pursue instantly and relentlessly immediately after victory" in the manner of Alexander.[54] This, however, ignores the great danger inherent in leaving the enemy phalanx intact on the battlefield, as Alexander himself realized when he destroyed the Greek mercenaries at the Granicus. The basic operational plan of Cyrus' victory is very similar to the later Hellenistic ideal, that is to say, the infantry fighting each other in the center while one's cavalry clear the enemy horse from the wings and attack the infantry from the rear. Although this plan seldom worked during the Hellenistic period because the armies were too symmetrical, it was the basis of Hannibal's success against the Romans in Italy.

Scholarly judgment varies regarding Xenophon's influence on the military arts. M. Jähns found him far in advance of his time as a tactician because of his willingness to abandon the long, solid line of the phalanx in rough country for the flexibility of tactical units of one hundred men; his introduction of a reserve; and his realization that the organic combination of different arms represented a true advance.[55] Delbrück, on the other hand, disagreed completely, feeling that the "practical soldier" at this point "falls off into impractical theorizing."[56] Jähns, I think, has the better of this argument, for it seems perverse to deny that Xenophon had something of value to say, not only—as Delbrück himself admits—in regards to "the psychological and morale aspects" of war[57] but also concerning the value and use of cavalry, the principle of combined arms, and the value of pursuit. The host of details regarding organization, training, and discipline in his work should also not be overlooked. These latter, which appear so frequently in military manuals of all periods, may appear at an intellectual level to be quite simple, even "stupefyingly obvious,"[58] but they are quite the opposite when they are institutionalized and put into practice at the operational level. Then they are a facet

---

54. Anderson (1970) 190.
55. Jähns ([1889] 1965) 20–24. See Xen. An. 4.8.9–10 for what Jähns sees as an anticipation of Roman maniple tactics; 6.5.9–11 for the use of reserves. Support for Jähn's statement on Xenophon's use of coordinated arms is found in Rahe (1980) 95, where it is suggested that Xenophon learned it from Cyrus the Younger's dispositions at Cunaxa and that he in turn influenced Agesilaus during his campaigns in Asia Minor in the early 390s. See also Hirsch (1985) 87 for Persian influence upon Xenophon.
56. HAW 160.
57. Ibid., 159.
58. Gray (1986) 180 on the subject of the theory of crisis management.

of genius. Indeed, on one occasion Alexander so intimidated his enemies by a dazzling display of drill maneuvers that they fled as soon as he advanced against them.[59]

A study of Xenophon's military writings as well as of the battles fought prior to 360 clearly shows the conceptual level of military thinking and awareness of principles that existed when Philip appeared on the scene and applied his genius to this material. As a hostage in Thebes during the years 367–365 Philip had the opportunity to observe and perhaps even meet the two greatest military leaders in Greece—Epaminondas and Pelopidas—and to learn the value of combining highly trained, well disciplined infantry with good cavalry to achieve victory on the battlefield.[60] Although the Greeks preferred to think of the Macedonians as barbarians, they were indeed a branch of the Greek people, and nowhere did they exhibit this relationship more than in the application of the Greek principles of rational, systematic organization to the creation of a national army. This they did with a single-mindedness and determination that even the Spartans could scarcely match. The capstone was the creative flair possessed by both Philip and Alexander, which produced the finest single army in the ancient world.

The success of this army was achieved not by the slavish imitation of borrowed tactics but by a realistic appraisal of its strengths and weaknesses relative to those of the enemy. This principle, as applied to the immediate battlefield, had been expressed earlier by Xenophon in his work *The Cavalry Commander*: "It is always necessary for the commander to hit on the right thing at the right moment, to think of the present situation and to carry out what is expedient in view of it."[61] With this as a starting point, Philip transformed the Macedonian army. The transformation was, in fact, an ongoing process that lasted to the end of Alexander's life. The foundation lay in general principles, which in turn found expression in tactics that were based on contemporary fighting styles and technology. The reliance upon principles rather than specific tactics must, I think, be stressed. It is found clearly expressed in the military manuals of the Roman period and is one of the hallmarks of later Byzantine military science. These treatises are all part of a single tradition, and they contain much that goes back to the Hellenistic period, although none of the originals of that period survive.

---

59. Arr. *Anab*. 1.6.1–4. This underscores the perennial advantage that well trained troops had over less disciplined, less well-organized forces, no matter how brave they were.

60. *HM* 2 204–205.

61. Xen. *Cav. Cmdr*. 9.1.

The work of Onasander, of the first century after Christ, is typical of the better treatises.⁶² It recommends a high dose of reality and emphasizes versatility. Onasander recommends for example, that: "The general will arrange his cavalry not as he wishes but rather as he is compelled;"⁶³ "If the enemy are superior in cavalry, the general should choose if possible a locality that is rough and hemmed in, near mountains which are least suitable for riding, or he should avoid battle so far as he may until he finds an appropriate place, adapted to his own circumstances";⁶⁴ and "The sight of present circumstances demands expedients based on the exigencies of the moment, which the necessity of chance rather than the memory of experience suggests."⁶⁵ The late-fourth-century Roman military writer Vegetius offers similar advice: "Let him [that is, the general] call a council of war and judge between his own and the enemy's forces, . . . If he finds himself superior in many particulars, let him be not slow to enter a battle favorable to himself. If he recognizes that the enemy is stronger, let him avoid a pitched battle."⁶⁶ Two maxims from the Byzantine period, from the *Strategikon* of Maurice, written around A.D. 600, reflect the same outlook: "A good general is one who utilizes his own skills to fit the opportunities he gets and the quality of the enemy"; and "A wise commander will not engage the enemy unless a truly exceptional opportunity or advantage presents itself."⁶⁷

Of course the mere awareness of these principles does not mean that they could be automatically applied. Good commanders who recognized reality were often frustrated by the force of circumstances and the necessity of having to fight under less than ideal conditions, as happened to Hannibal at Zama. This realization must have been particularly annoying in the case of cavalry, because their mobility and striking power in close combat offered the potential for quick, decisive results. During the Hellenistic period, because of the symmetry of evenly matched armies and generals, this opportunity was

---

62. Onas. *Gen.*, in Oldfather et al. (1923) 343–527. Although Onasander was described as a philosopher, his principles "apply to almost any army at any time" (Ibid., 350). This is very different from the work of the first century B.C. writer Asclepiodotus, which is a theoretical study of phalanx tactics bearing little evidence of practical military knowledge (ibid., 231–33).

63. Onas. *Gen.* 16, 443.

64. Ibid., 31.1, 473.

65. Ibid., 32.10, 481.

66. Veg. *Epit.* 3.9. The translation is from Milner (1993) 82.

67. Maur. *Strat.* 8.2.13, 86. The translation is that of Dennis (1984) 84, 90. These statements represent principles identical to those of the fourth-century B.C. Chinese military writer Sun Tzu—that is to say, realism (Griffith [1963] 3.31, 84), deception (1.17, 66), and asymmetry: "Troops thrown against the enemy as a grindstone against eggs is an example of a solid acting upon a void" (5.4, 91).

seldom present. Alexander and Hannibal were true exceptions to this situation, for by virtue of their genius they were able to recognize and exploit the asymmetry between their armies and those of their enemies to achieve decisive victories with seemingly spectacular cavalry tactics. Their influence upon later generations of military commanders was therefore limited. The principles they applied still survive, but the precise tactics they used were suited to specific situations and could be used successfully only under similar circumstances. Infantry dominated Hellenistic battlefields for good reasons, and when generals attempted to use cavalry inappropriately, failure was to be expected—as Antiochus III learned at Raphia and Magnesia.

In general cavalry came into their own during the Peloponnesian War and were a more important military arm from that time until the rise of Macedon than is commonly recognized. On the other hand modern historians tend to overestimate cavalry's contribution to victory after the time of Alexander; in fact, this was mainly achieved by infantry. Cavalry were an integral part of all great armies of the time, for they were combined-arms forces. Thus one should never seek the cause of victory in the action of one arm alone, for the contribution of each is essential. By trusting exclusively in cavalry during the Lamian War, the allied Greeks sealed their fate. The rise of cavalry to importance in the last quarter of the fifth century seems to be based largely on a growing willingness to dispense with missile weapons and engage in close combat with spear and sword. This meant the giving and receiving of nasty wounds from edged weapons, which reflected a mentality that conferred superiority on those who possessed it over less bloody-minded opponents. It stands in stark contrast to the fighting style of the mounted steppe nomads, who practiced hit-and-run tactics with missiles, often saving themselves in battle by running away.

It appears that the good generals of the Hellenistic period did understand the military principles expressed in the literature and observed on the battlefield. The self-restraint that they exhibited when faced by formidable opponents suggests that they understood all too well the limitations of the possible tactical options and realized what would not work. The rigidity of Hellenistic tactics was the result more of reality than of theory. The tactical versatility of the medieval Byzantine army, for example, resulted less from a more sophisticated military outlook than from the fact that they fought against enemies of different ethnic and cultural character who presented the Byzantines with both the necessity and opportunity for innovation. Pure fighting power rather than tactical sleight of hand, usually determined victory in the Hellenistic period, however. Hard fighting by all the arms—not just by the infantry, which often decided the issue—was essential, with cavalry playing an especially important part in protecting the infantry's vulnerable flanks and rear. Their primary job was to allow the infantry to do what it did best—that is, to direct its attack forward against the enemy line. If cavalry were able to rout their opponents, then their particular qualities of speed, mobility, and intimidation could be brought to bear against suitable parts of the enemy formation. Alexander and Hannibal understood that early on, against enemies whose weaknesses meshed well with their own strengths. The Hellenistic generals were less fortunate, because too often the opposing forces were similar to each other in type and quality. Nevertheless, these commanders often possessed a coup d'oeil that allowed them to take advantage of fleeting opportunities as they arose.

Obviously, there is much that we will never know about cavalry fighting in antiquity. Perhaps its most elusive facet is the degree to which the simple pleasure of riding and the prestige associated with it resulted in a greater use of the horse in war than its intrinsic military value warranted. Certainly, there is a mystical and irrational quality to the relationship between man and horse, which Dick Francis nicely describes in one of his novels: "I'd loved horses always: it was hard to explain the intimacy that grew between horses and those who tended or rode them. Horses lived in a parallel world, spoke a parallel language, were a mass of instincts, lacked human perceptions of kindness or guilt, and allowed a merging on an untamed, untamable mysterious level of spirit. The Great God Pan lived in racehorses."[68]

---

68. Francis (1995) 68.

List of Battles Discussed in the Text

PART 2

Chapter 4

511 B.C. Phalerum
510 B.C. Southern Attica
494 B.C. Malene
490 B.C. Marathon
479 B.C. Plataea

Chapter 5

457 B.C. Tanagra

Chapter 6

429 B.C. Spartolus
425 B.C. Solygeia
424 B.C. Delium
422 B.C. Amphipolis
418 B.C. Mantinea
414 B.C. Syracuse

Chapter 7

401 B.C. Cunaxa

Chapter 8

395 B.C. Sardis
394 B.C. Near Corinth and Sicyon
394 B.C. Coronea
390 B.C. Lechaeum

Chapter 9

375 B.C. Tegyra

Chapter 10

371 B.C. Leuctra
370–366 B.C. Phlius
364 B.C. Cynoscephalae I
362 B.C. Mantinea II

PART 3

Chapter 11

340 B.C. Crimisus [River]
358 B.C. Illyrians
357 B.C. Crocus Plain
338 B.C. Chaeronea

Chapter 12

334 B.C. Granicus
333 B.C. Issus
330 B.C. Gaugamela [Arbela]
326 B.C. Hydaspes

PART 4

Chapter 13

323 B.C. Lamia
322 B.C. Lamia
322 B.C. Crannon
321 B.C.. Eumenes vs. Neoptolemus
321 B.C. Eumenes vs. Craterus and Neoptolemus
317 B.C. Paraetacene
316 B.C. Gabiene
312 B.C. Gaza
301 B.C. Ipsus

Chapter 14

280 B.C. Heraclea
279 B.C. Asculum
275 B.C. Beneventum
222 B.C. Sellasia
217 B.C. Raphia
207 B.C. Mantinea III
200 B.C. Panion
197 B.C. Cynoscephalae
190 B.C. Magnesia
171 B.C. Larissa
168 B.C. Pydna

Chapter 15

218 B.C. Ticinus [River]
218 B.C. Trebia [River]
216 B.C. Cannae
203 B.C. Great Plains
202 B.C. Zama

Note to the Maps and Battle Plans

SEVERAL MAPS AND BATTLE plans have been included to add clarity to some points made in the text. The relief map of the Balkan peninsula should help explain the traditional preference for infantry in the rugged terrain of central and southern Greece and the prominence of cavalry on the plains of Thessaly and Macedon. The maps showing battle sites give some indication of the influence of topography and political importance on the choice of battlefields, the best example of which is Boeotia in central Greece. The effect of Alexander's conquest of the Persian Empire, which drew Greek and Macedonian armies to the east for almost two centuries thereafter, is also obvious.

I must admit that it is more difficult to present accurate information in battle plans, and the lack of confidence they inspire has prevented me from including many of them. Even if a reasonably accurate narrative of an ancient battle exists, it almost never gives complete information regarding the depth of infantry and cavalry lines, the number of combatants present, the precise geographical location of the battle (not to mention changes in surface topography, vegetation, and river courses since antiquity), or the identity and movements of specific units. The map of a nominal battle formation is intended merely to give an approximation of it, with some attention to proportion in a few common features such as infantry with a depth of sixteen and cavalry with a depth of four in an event unaffected by the realities of time, place, and participants. The battle of Chaeronea provides an example of the use of natural obstacles to protect the flanks, while the battle of Sellasia offers an extreme case of the influence of local topography, forcing a reversal of the normal positions of infantry and cavalry.

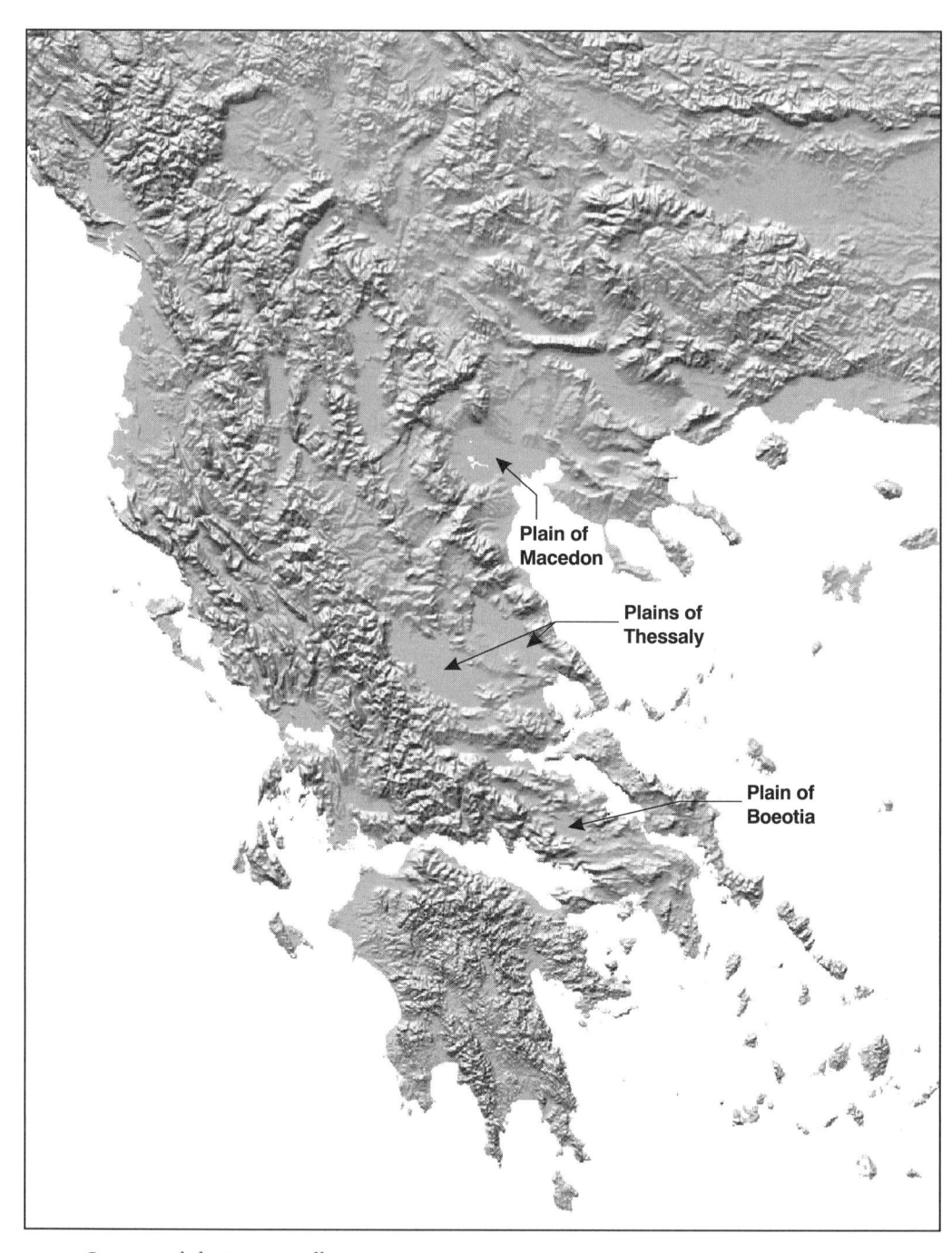

Greece and the Lower Balkans

Battle Sites in Central and Southern Greece

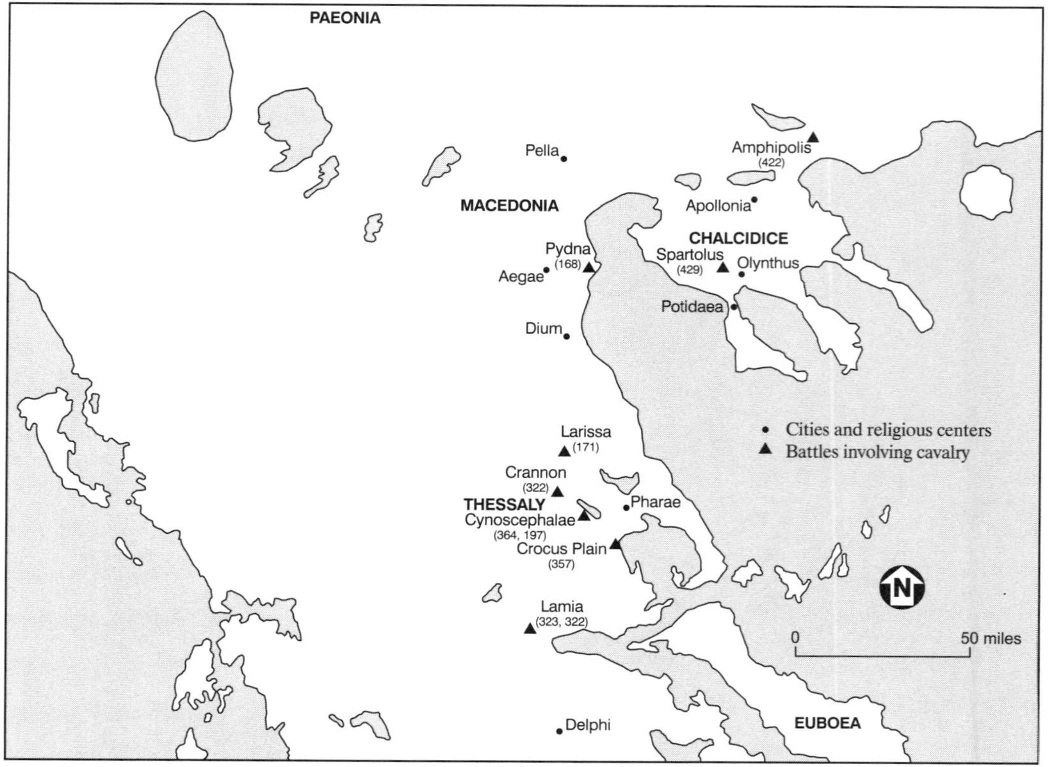

Battle Sites in Northern Greece

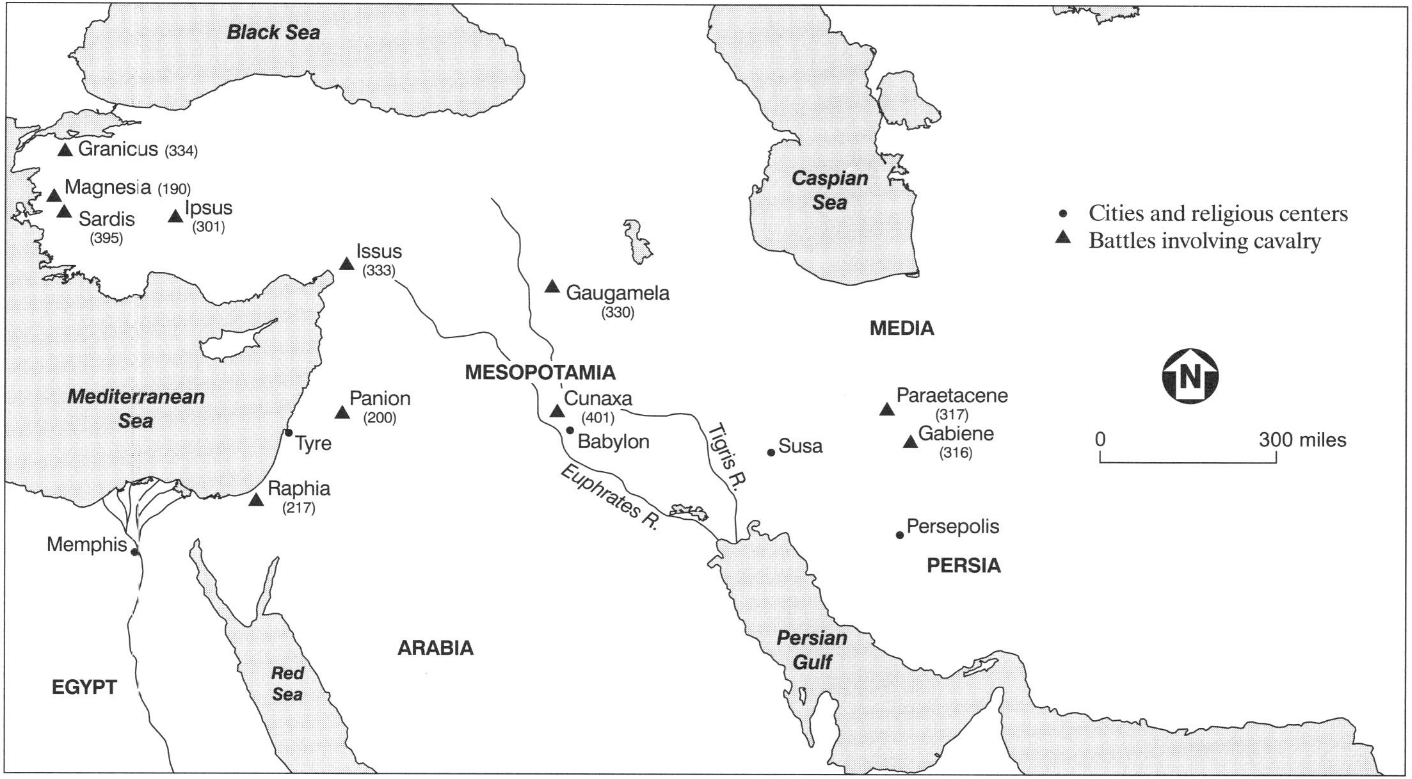

Battle Sites in Lands to the East of Greece

Forces on Each Side

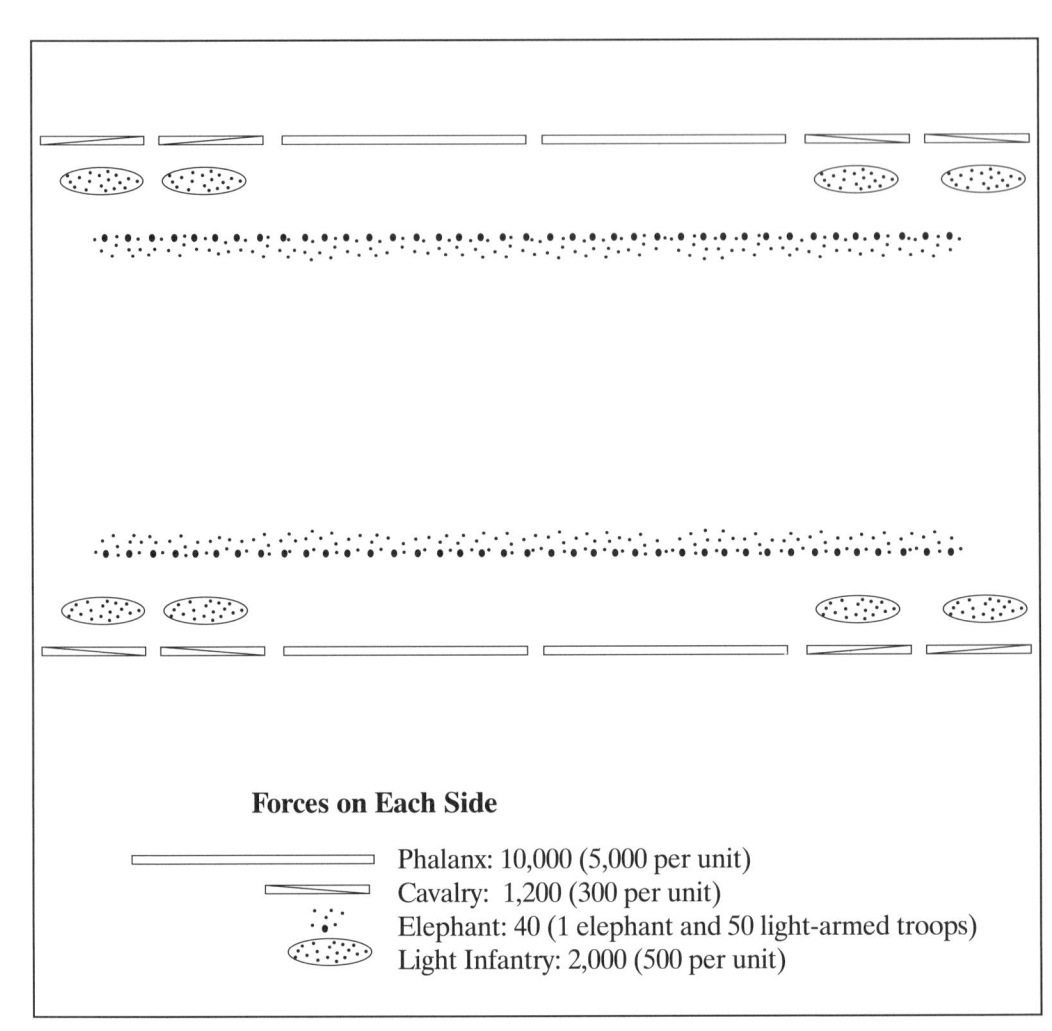

- Phalanx: 10,000 (5,000 per unit)
- Cavalry: 1,200 (300 per unit)
- Elephant: 40 (1 elephant and 50 light-armed troops)
- Light Infantry: 2,000 (500 per unit)

Nominal Order of Battle in the Hellenistic Period

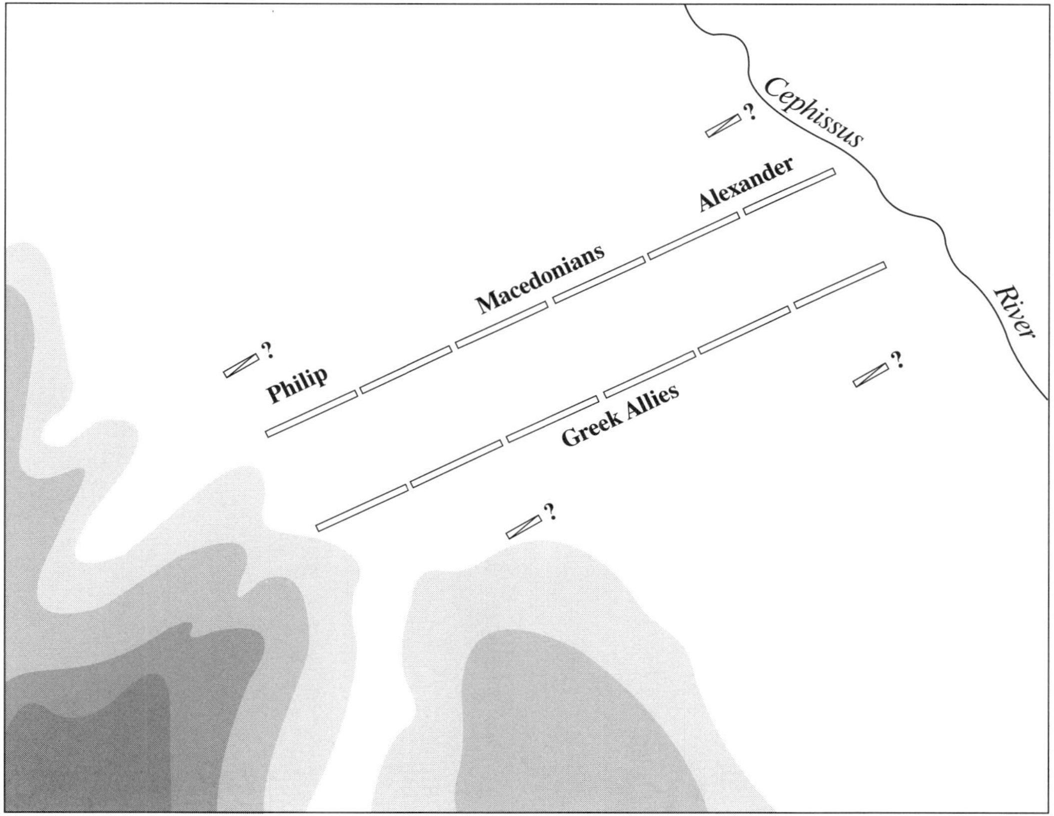

Battle of Chaeronea, 338 B.C.

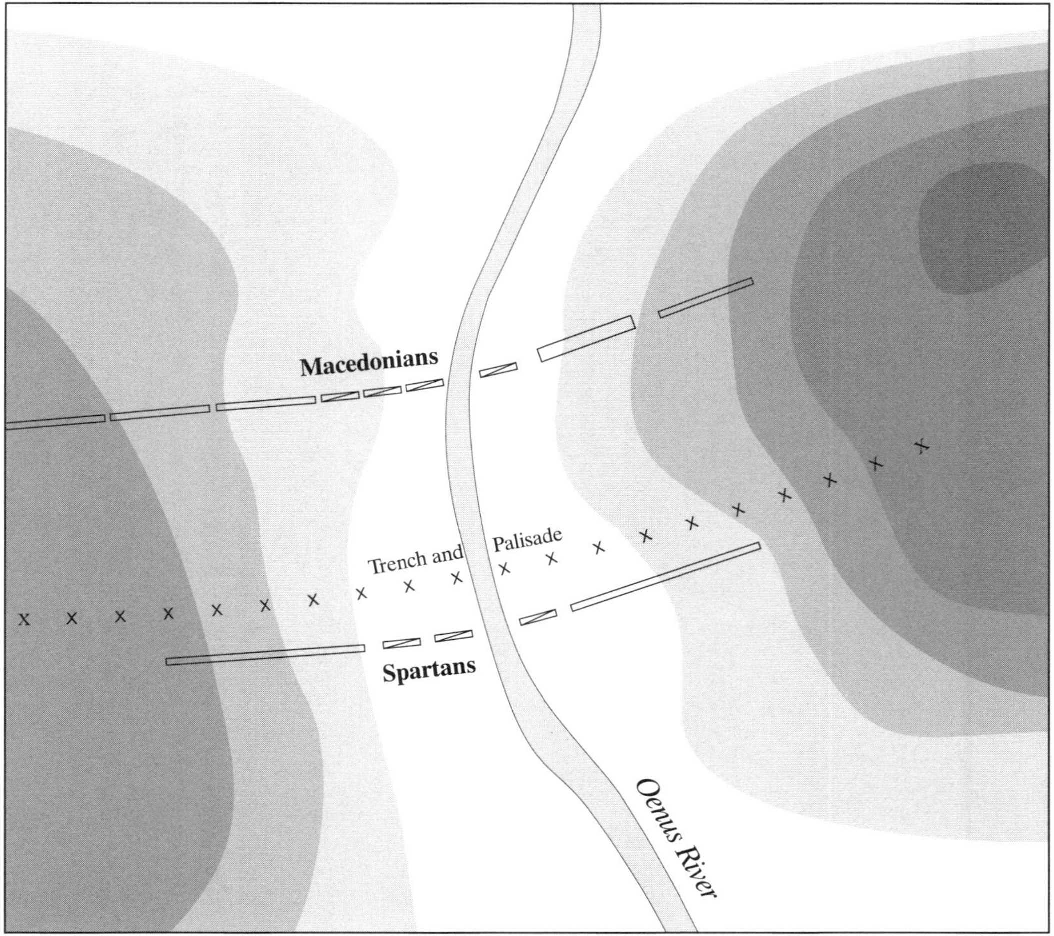

Battle of Sellasia, 222 B.C.

Glossary

In the following entries (G) and (L) indicate words originating in the Greek or Latin language.

Agrianians. Tribal group living northeast of Macedon. Allied with Alexander, for whom they provided a light-infantry unit.

ala. (L) Troop or squadron of cavalry from the time of Augustus. Earlier allied infantry or cavalry stationed on the wings of the legion.

akon. (G) Throwing spear, javelin.

anabasis. (G) Literally a "going up." Used by both Xenophon and Arrian as the title of a military expedition into the Near East from the western coast of Asia Minor.

aspis. (G) Greek hoplite shield.

caltrop. Four-spiked metal device used on the battlefield to impede cavalry and elephants. When it was thrown on the ground, one of its four sharp spikes always projected upwards.

cohort. (L) Subdivision of the Roman legion comprising three maniples, each of two centuries (that is, 360 to 600 men), that could be used as a separate tactical unit.

cuirass. Upper-body armor made of a variety of materials, for example, leather, linen, bronze, or iron.

Delian League. Originally an alliance against Persia of mostly Ionian cities of the Aegean established in 478/477 B.C. under the leadership of Athens. By midcentury it was virtually an Athenian empire.

dory. (G) Spear, usually the Greek hoplite spear.

gladius. (L)	Short cut-and-thrust legionary sword.
hamippoi. (G)	Infantry who fought alongside cavalry.
harmost. (G)	Spartan military commander/governor outside of Sparta.
hasta. (L)	Spear.
hastati. (L)	Infantry forming the first line of a legion.
hipparch. (G)	Commander of a cavalry squadron.
hipparchy. (G)	Cavalry squadron.
hippeus. (G)	Horseman.
hippotoxotes. (G)	Horse archer.
hoplite. (G)	Heavily armed Greek infantryman who fought in the phalanx.
ila. (G)	Cavalry squadron.
kontos. (G)	Long spear.
kopis. (G)	Curved short sword designed for cutting, perhaps identical with the machaera.
legion. (L)	Roman infantry formation comprising four thousand to six thousand men in three lines: *hastati*, *principes*, and *triarii*. Armed with a javelin (*pilum*) and short sword (*gladius*) and protected by a helmet, body armor, and a long shield (*scutum*).
machaera. (G)	Curved cutting sword, perhaps identical with the kopis.
maniple. (L)	Subunit of the legion, thirty in number.
mora. (G)	One of six divisions of the Spartan army.
Paeonians.	Tribal group dwelling north of Macedon, which furnished Alexander with an often-mentioned cavalry unit.
palton. (G)	Light spear often carried by Persian cavalry, used for both throwing and thrusting.
peltast. (G)	Light infantry, possibly originating in Thrace, armed with a javelin and wicker shield (*pelte*).
pelte. (G)	Light wicker or wooden shield.
Pentecontaetia. (G)	Name given to Thucydides' account of the period of approximately fifty years between the end of the Persian Wars and the beginning of the Peloponnesian War (479–431).
perioeci.	Subjects or half-citizens of Sparta with local political rights who lived in the mountains and coastal regions. Although often serving in the Spartan army, they were not subject to the collective military discipline of the full citizens.
phalangite. (G)	*Sarissa*-bearing line infantry of the Macedonians.
phalanx. (G)	Greek and Macedonian infantry formation, usually eight or sixteen men deep, with a maximum of fifty men. Philip's Macedonian version was equipped with less protective armor and a longer spear, the sarissa.

pilum. (L)	Javelin of the Roman legionary.
principes. (L)	Second line of a Roman legion.
prodromoi. (G)	Cavalry squadrons used by Alexander to initiate action on his right wing. Four were Macedonian, one Paeonian.
psiloi. (G)	Light infantry with little defensive armor. Archers, slingers, and javelin men.
sabre.	Curved cavalry sword for cutting.
Sacred Band.	Elite, three-hundred-man infantry unit at Thebes. Destroyed at Chaeronea in 338.
sarissa. (G)	Long Macedonian infantry spear introduced by Philip. Originally about fifteen or sixteen feet long, it was later extended perhaps up to twenty-one feet.
sarissophoroi. (G)	Macedonian cavalry who may or may not have carried the *sarissa*. Their exact function is not clear.
Scythian.	Term used by the Greeks to describe seminomadic people residing northeast of Greece from the Danube to lands north of the Black Sea.
tagus. (G)	Highest civil and military magistrate among the Thessalians.
taxis. (G)	Major subunit of the phalanx. At Athens one of ten tribal divisions of infantry. In Macedon there were twelve in the phalanx, each with fifteen hundred men.
toxotes. (G)	Archer.
triarii. (L)	Third line of the Roman legion.
trophy.	Greek military monument to victory originally set up on the battlefield, consisting of a suit of captured enemy armor placed on a stake at the site where the enemy turned in flight. By the fourth century stone monuments in the form of towers and buildings were constructed in cities.
turma. (L)	Troop of cavalry, thirty strong.
velites. (L)	Light infantry associated with the legion.
xiphos. (G)	Straight sword.
xyston. (G)	Spear.

Bibliography

Adams, W. L., and E. N. Borza, eds. 1982. *Philip II, Alexander the Great and the Macedonian Heritage*. Washington, D. C.: University Press of America.

Adcock, F. E. 1957. *The Greek and Macedonian Art of War*. Berkeley: University of California Press.

Afshar, A., and J. Lerner. 1979. "The Horses of the Ancient Persian Empire at Persepolis." *Antiquity* 53: 44–47.

Alexander, C. 2000. "Ancient Greece, Part 3." *National Geographic* 197, no. 3 (March): 42–75.

Amschler, W. 1935. "The Oldest Pedigree Chart." *Journal of Heredity* 26: 233–38.

Anderson, J. K. 1961. *Ancient Greek Horsemanship*. Berkeley: University of California Press.

———. 1967. "Philopoemen's reform of the Achaean Army." *Classical Philology* 62: 104–105.

———. 1970. *Military Theory and Practice in the Age of Xenophon*. Berkeley: University of California Press.

———. 1974. *Xenophon*. New York: Scribner.

———. 1975. "Greek Chariot-Borne and Mounted Infantry." *American Journal of Archaeology* 79: 175–87.

Anthony, D. W. 1991. "The Domestication of the Horse." In *Equids in the Ancient World*, vol. 2, ed. R. H. Meadow and H. P. Uerpmann, 250–77. Wiesbaden: Ludwig Reichert.

Atkinson, J. E. 1980. *A Commentary on Q. Curtius Rufus' Historiae Alexandri Magni Books 3 and 4*. Amsterdam: J. C. Gieben.

Azzaroli, A. 1985. *An Early History of Horsemanship*. Leiden: E. J. Brill.

Badian, E. 1977. "The Battle of the Granicus: A New Look." *Ancient Macedon* 2: 271–93.

Barker, E. 1962. *The Politics of Aristotle*. New York: Oxford University Press.
Bar-Kochva, B. 1976. *The Seleucid Army*. Cambridge: Cambridge University Press.
Barnett, R. D., and M. Falkner. 1962. *The Sculptures of Aššurnasir-apli II, Tiglath-pileser III and Esarhaddon from the Central and South-West Palaces at Nimrud*. London: Trustees of the British Museum.
———. 1976. *Assyrian Palace Reliefs in the British Museum*. Oxford: British Museums Publications.
Baynham, E. J. 1994. "Antipater: Manager of Kings." in *Ventures in Greek History*, ed. I. Worthington, 331–56. Oxford: Clarendon Press.
Beal, R. H. 1992. *The Organization of the Hittite Military*. Heidelberg: Universität Verlag Carl Winter.
Best, J. G. P. 1969. *Thracian Peltasts and Their Influence on Greek Warfare*. Groningen: Wolters-Noordhoff.
Biblical Archaeology Review. 1993. 19, no. 4 (July/August): 16.
Billows, R. A. 1990. *Antigonus the One-Eyed and the Creation of the Hellenistic State*. Berkeley: University of California Press.
———. 1995. *Kings and Colonists*. Leiden: Brill.
Blumenson, M. 1985. *Patton*. New York: Quill/Morrow.
Bokovenko, N. A. 1995. "Scythian Culture in the Altai Mountains." In *Nomads of the Eurasian Steppe in the Early Iron Age*, ed. J. Davis-Kimball, V. A. Bashilov, and C. T. Yablonsky, 285–97. Berkeley: Zinat Press.
Bosworth, A. B. 1980–95. *A Historical Commentary on Arrian's History of Alexander*. 2 vols. Oxford: Oxford University Press.
———. 1988. *Conquest and Empire*. Cambridge: Cambridge University Press.
———. 1996. *Alexander and the East: The Tragedy of Triumph*. Oxford: Oxford University Press.
Braun, K. 1972. "Die Dipylon-Brunnen B 1, die Funde." *Mitteilungen des Deutschen Archäologischen Instituts* (Ath. Abt.) 85: 129–269.
Breasted, J. H. 1912. *A History of Egypt*. New York: C. Scribner's.
Brereton, J. M. 1976. *The Horse in War*. New York: Arco Publishing.
Briscoe, J. 1973. *A Commentary on Livy, Books 31–33*. Oxford: Clarendon Press.
———. 1981. *A Commentary on Livy, Books 34–37*. Oxford: Clarendon Press.
Bruce, I. A. F. 1967. *An Historical Commentary on the Hellenica Oxyrhynchia*. Cambridge: Cambridge University Press.
Brunt, P. A. 1976–83. *History of Alexander and Indica*. 2 vols. Cambridge, Mass.: Harvard University Press.
Buckler, J. 1980a. "Plutarch on Leuktra." *Symbolae Osloenses* 55: 75–93.
———. 1980b. *The Theban Hegemony 371–362 B.C.* Cambridge, Mass.: Harvard University Press.
———. 1989. *Philip II and the Social War*. Leiden: E. J. Brill.

———. 1990. "Χωρὶς ἱππεῖς; A Note on the Battle of Chaironeia in 338 B.C." *Teiresias* 20, supp. 3: 75–80.

———. 1995. "The Battle of Tegyra, 375 B.C." *Boeotia Antiqua* 5: 45–58.

Bugh, G. R. 1988. *The Horsemen of Athens*. Princeton: Princeton University Press.

Burkert, W. 1985. *Greek Religion*. Translated by John Raffan. Cambridge, Mass.: Harvard University Press.

Burn, A. R. 1965. "The Generalship of Alexander," *Greece and Rome*, 2nd Series 12: 140–54.

Burnett, E. D. 1976. *Assyrian Palace Reliefs in the British Museum*. Oxford: British Museum Publications.

Camp, J. M. 1986. *The Athenian Agora*. New York: Thames and Hudson.

Campbell, D. A. 1988. *Greek Lyric*. Cambridge, Mass.: Harvard University Press.

Carney, E. D. 1994. "Olympias, Adea Eurydice, and the End of the Argead Dynasty." In *Ventures in Greek History*, ed. I worthington, 331–56. Oxford: Clarendon Press.

———. 1996. "Macedonians and Mutiny." *Classical Philology* 91, no. 1 (January): 19–44.

Cartledge, P. 1977. "Hoplites and Heroes. Sparta's Contribution to the Technique of Ancient Warfare." *Journal of Hellenic Studies* 97: 11–27.

———. 1987. *Agesilaus and the Crisis of Sparta*. Baltimore: John Hopkins University Press.

Cary, M. 1978. *A History of the Greek World: 323–146 B.C.* London: Methuen.

Cawkwell, G. 1972. "Introduction and Notes." In *Xenophon: The Persian Expedition*, trans. R. Warner, Harmondsworth: Penguin.

———. 1978. *Philip of Macedon*. London: Faber and Faber.

———. 1997. *Thucydides and the Peloponnesian War*. London: Routledge.

Chadwick, J. 1976. *The Mycenaean World*. Cambridge: Cambridge University Press.

Chenevix-Trench, C. 1970. *A History of Horsemanship*. New York: Doubleday.

Chilver, G. E. F. 1979. *A Historical Commentary on Tacitus' "Histories" I and II*. Oxford: Clarendon Press.

Chilver, G. E. F., and G. B. Townend. 1985. *A Historical Commentary on Tacitus' "Histories" IV and V*. Oxford: Clarendon Press.

Churchill, Winston S. 1931. *The World Crisis 1911–18*. Abr. and rev. ed. London: Thornton Butterworth.

Clabby, J. 1976. *The Natural History of the Horse*. New York: Tablinger Publishing.

Connolly, P. 1981. *Greece and Rome at War*. Englewood Cliffs, N.J.: Prentice Hall.

———. 1987. " The Roman Saddle." *British Archaeological Reports*. Inter. Series 336: 7–27.

Cook, J. M. 1983. *The Persian Empire*. New York: Schocken Books.

Crouwel, J. H. 1981. *Chariots and Other Means of Land Transport in Bronze Age Greece*. Amsterdam: Allard Pierson Museum.

Dalley, S. 1984. *Mari and Karana: Two Old Babylonian Cities*. London: Longman.
Davis-Kimball, J., V. A. Bashilov, and L. T. Yablonsky, eds. 1995. *Nomads of the Eurasian Steppe in the Early Iron Age*. Berkeley: Zinat Press.
Delbrück, H. 1920. *Geschichte der Kriegskunst, Erster Teil: Das Altertum*. Berlin: G. Stilke.
———. 1975. *History of the Art of War*. Vol I. Translated by W. J. Renfroe. Westport, Conn.: Greenwood Press.
de Lee, N. 1976. *French Lancers*. London: Almark.
Denison, G. T. 1913. A *History of Cavalry from the Earliest Times*. 2nd ed. London: Macmillan and Co.
Dennis, G. T. 1984. *Maurice's Strategikon*. Philadelphia: University of Pennsylvania Press.
———. 1985. *Three Byzantine Military Treatises*. Washington, D. C.: Dumbarton Oaks Research Library and Collection.
Dennis, G. T., and E. Gamillscheg. 1981. *Das Strategikon des Maurikios*. Vienna: Verlag der Österreichischen Akademie der Wissenschaften.
Dent, A. 1977. "The Pre-Domestic Horse." In *The Encyclopedia of the Horse*, edited by E. H. Edwards, 12–14. New York: Crescent Books.
de Rocca, A. J. M. 1990. *In the Peninsula with a French Hussar*. London: Greenhill Books.
Desroches-Noblecourt, C. 1963. *Tutankhamen*. New York: New York Graphic Society.
Detienne, M. 1968. "La Phalange: Problèmes et controverses." In *Problèmes de la guerre en Gréce ancienne*, ed. J. Vernant, 119–42. Paris: LaHaye Mouton.
Devine, A. M. 1975. "Grand Tactics at Gaugamela." *Phoenix* 29: 374–85.
———. 1983. "Embolon: A Study in Tactical Terminology." *Phoenix* 37, no. 3: 201–17.
———. 1985a. "The Strategies of Alexander the Great and Darius III in the Issus Campaign (333 B.C.)." *Ancient World* 12, nos. 1 and 2: 25–38.
———. 1985b. "Grand Tactics at the Battle of Issus," *Ancient World* 12, nos. 1 and 2: 39–59.
———. 1985c. "Diodorus' Account of the Battle of Paraetacene." *Ancient World* 12, nos. 3 and 4: 75–86.
———. 1985d. "Diodorus' Account of the Battle of Gabiene." *Ancient World* 12, nos. 3 and 4: 87–96.
———. 1986. "Demythologizing the Battle of the Granicus." *Phoenix* 40: 265–78.
———. 1988. "A Pawn Sacrifice at the Battle of the Granicus." *Ancient World* 18, nos. 1 and 2: 3–20.
———. 1989a. "Alexander the Great." In *Warfare in the Ancient World*, ed. J. Hackett, 104–29. New York: Facts on File.
———. 1989b. "Aelian's Manual of Hellenistic Military Tactics." *Ancient World* 19: 31–64.

———. 1991. Review of *Conquest and Empire*, by A. B. Bosworth. *Ancient World* 22, no. 1: 61–66.

Diamond, J. 1997. *Guns, Germs, and Steel*. New York: W. W. Norton.

Disston, H. 1973. *Beginning Polo*. South Brunswick, N.J.: A. S. Barnes.

Dixon, K. R., and P. Southern. 1992. *The Roman Cavalry: From the First to the Third Centuries A.D.* London: Routledge.

Edwards, E. H. 1980. *A Standard Guide to Horse and Pony Breeds*. New York: McGraw-Hill.

———, ed. 1977. *The Encyclopedia of the Horse*. New York: Crescent Books.

Edwards, I. E. S., C. J. Gadd, and N. G. L. Hammond, eds. 1971. *The Cambridge Ancient History*. Cambridge and New York: Cambridge University Press.

Ellis, J. R. 1976. *Philip II and Macedonian Imperialism*. London: Thames and Hudson.

Engels, D. W. 1980. *Alexander the Great and the Logistics of the Macedonian Army*. Berkeley: University of California Press.

Ep'hal, I. 1984. "On Warfare and Military Control in the Ancient Near Eastern Empires." In *History, Historiography and Interpretation*, ed. H. Tadmor and M. Weinfeld, 88–106. Leiden: E. J. Brill.

Errington, R. M. 1969. *Philopoemen*. Oxford: Clarendon Press.

———. 1990. *A History of Macedonia*. Berkeley: University of California Press.

Evans, J. A. S. 1987. "Cavalry at the Time of the Persian Wars." *Classical Journal* 82, no. 2: 97–106.

Faulkner, R. O. 1958. "The Battle of Kadesh." *Mitteilungen des deutschen archäologischen Instituts, Abteilung Kairo* 16: 93–111.

Ferrill, A. 1985. *The Origins of War*. New York: Thames and Hudson.

Forrer, L. 1975. *The Weber Collection, Vol. II. Greek Coins*. New York: Attic Books.

Foss, C. 1977. "The Battle of the Granicus: A New Look." *Ancient Macedonia* 2: 495–502.

Francis, D. 1995. *Come to Grief*. New York: G. P. Putnam's Sons.

Fraser, A. F. 1992. *The Behavior of the Horse*. Wallingford: CAB International.

Frederiksen, M. W. 1968. "The Campanian Cavalry." *Dialoghi di Archeologia* 2: 3–31.

Frost, F. J. 1997. *Greek Society*. 5th ed. Boston: Houghton Mifflin Co.

Fuller, J. F. C. 1958. *The Generalship of Alexander the Great*. London: Eyre and Spottiswode.

Galili, E. 1976–77. "Raphia, 217 B.C.E. Revisited." *Scripta Classica Israelica* 3: 52–126.

Gardiner, A. 1969. *Egypt of the Pharaohs*. Oxford: Oxford University Press.

———. 1975. *The Kadesh Inscriptions of Rameses II*. Oxford: Griffith Institute Ashmolean Museum.

Garlan, Y. 1975. *War in the Ancient World*. New York: Norton.

Garoufalias, P. 1979. *Pyrrhus: King of Epirus*. London: Stacey International.

Gelb, I. J., B. Landesberger, A. L. Oppenheim, and E. reiner, eds. 1961—. *The Assyrian Dictionary*. Chicago: The Oriental Institute.

Ghirshman, R. 1964.*The Arts of Ancient Iran*. New York: Golden Press.

Glubok, S., and S. Tamarin. 1976. *Olympic Games in Ancient Greece*. New York: Harper and Row.

Goldsworthy, A. K. 1996. *The Roman Army at War: 100 B.C.–A.D. 200*. Oxford: Clarendon Press.

Gomme, A. W. 1945–56. *A Historical Commentary on Thucydides, Vols. 1–3*. Oxford: Clarendon Press.

Gomme, A. W., W. Andrewes, and K. J. Dover. 1960–81. *A Historical Commentary on Thucydides, Vols 4–5*. Oxford: Clarendon Press.

Goralski, W. J. 1989. "Arrian's Events after Alexander." *Ancient World* 19: 81–108.

Grainger, J. D. 1990. *Seleukos Nikator*. London: Routledge.

Grant, U. S. 1989. *Personal Memoirs of U. S. Grant*. Edited by E. B. Long. Norwalk, Conn.: Easton Press.

Gray, C. 1986. *Nuclear Strategy and National Style*. Lanham, Md.: Hamilton Press.

Green, P. 1974. *Alexander of Macedon*. Harmondsworth: Penguin.

———. 1999. *From Alexander to Actium*. Berkeley: University of California Press.

Greenhalgh, P. A. L. 1973. *Early Greek Warfare*. Cambridge: Cambridge University Press.

———. 1980. "The Dendra Charioteer." *Antiquity* 54: 201–205.

Grenfell, B. P., and A. S. Hunt. 1908. *The Oxyrhynchus Papyri*. London: Egypt Exploration Fund.

Griffith, G. T. 1935. *The Mercenaries of the Hellenistic World*. Groningen: Boumas' Boekhuis. Reprint, Chicago: Argonaut, 1969.

———. 1947."Alexander's Generalship at Gaugamela." *Journal of Hellenic Studies* 67: 77–89.

———. 1980. "Philip as a General and the Macedonian Army." In *Philip of Macedon*, ed. M. B. Hatzopoulos and L. D. Loukopoulos, 58–77. Athens: Ekdotike Athenon.

Griffith, S. B. 1963. *Sun Tzu: The Art Of War*. Oxford: Oxford University Press.

Grmek, M. D. 1989. *Diseases in the Ancient Greek World*. Baltimore: Johns Hopkins University Press.

Groenewegen-Frankfort, H. A., and B. Ashmole. 1972. *Art of the Ancient World*. New York: Harry N. Abrams.

Grundy, G. B. 1948. *Thucydides and the History of His Age*. 2nd ed. 2 vols. Oxford: B. Blackwell.

Gurney, O. R. 1954. *The Hittites*. 2nd ed. Baltimore: Penguin Books.

Hamilton, C. D. 1979. *Sparta's Bitter Victories*. Ithaca: Cornell University Press.

Hamilton, J. R. 1969. *Plutarch, Alexander: A Commentary*. Oxford: Clarendon Press.

Hammond, N. G. L. 1959. *A History of Greece*. Oxford: Clarendon Press.
———. 1980a. *Alexander the Great*. Park Ridge, N.J.: Noyes Press.
———. 1980b. "The Battle of the Granicus River." *Journal of Hellenic Studies* 100: 73–88.
———. 1980c. "Training in the Use of the Sarissa and Its Effect in Battle, 359–333 B.C." *Antichthon* 14: 53–63.
———. 1989. *The Macedonian State*. Oxford: Clarendon Press.
Hammond, N. G. L., and G. T. Griffith. 1972–79. *A History of Macedonia*. 2 vols. Oxford: Clarendon Press.
Hammond, N. G. L., and F. W. Walbank. 1988. *A History of Macedonia*. Vol. 3. Oxford: Clarendon Press.
Hansen, K.1992. "Collection in Ancient Egyptian Chariot Horses." *Journal of the American Research Center in Egypt* 29: 173–79.
Hanson, V. D. 1988. "Epameinondas, the Battle of Leuktra (371 B.C.) and the Revolution in Greek Battle Tactics." *Classical Antiquity* 7: 190–207.
———. 1989. *The Western Way of War*. New York: Oxford University Press.
———. 1995. *The Other Greeks*. New York: Free Press.
———. 1999. *The Wars of the Ancient Greeks*. London: Cassell.
———, ed. 1991. *Hoplites: The Classical Greek Battle Experience*. London: Routledge.
Harris, W. V. 1985. *War and Imperialism in Republican Rome, 327–70 B.C.* Oxford: Clarendon Press.
Harrison, E. B. 1972. "The South Frieze of the Nike Temple and the Marathon Painting in the Painted Stoa." *American Journal of Archaeology* 76: 353–78.
Hatzopoulos, M. B., and L. D. Loukopoulos, eds. 1984. *Philip of Macedon*. London: Ekdotike Athenon.
Hendricks, B. L. 1995. *International Encyclopedia of Horse Breeds*. Norman: University of Oklahoma Press.
Hignett, C. 1963. *Xerxes' Invasion of Greece*. Oxford: Clarendon Press.
Hirsch, S. W. 1985. *The Friendship of the Barbarians: Xenophon and the Persian Empire*. Hanover, N.H.: University Press of New England.
Hodge, A. T. 1975. "Marathon: the Persians' Voyage." *Transactions of the American Philological Association* 105:155–73.
Hope, C. E. G., and G. N. Jackson, eds. 1973. *The Encyclopedia of the Horse*. New York: Viking Press.
Hornblower, J. 1981. *Hieronymous of Cardia*. Oxford: Oxford University Press.
Hornblower, S. A. 1987. *Thucydides*. Baltimore: Johns Hopkins University Press.
———. 1991–96. *A Commentary on Thucydides*. 2 vols. Oxford: Clarendon Press.
How, W. W., and J. Wells. 1912. *A Commentary on Herodotus*. 2 vols. Oxford: Clarendon Press. Reprint, Oxford: Clarendon, 1967, 1968.
Humble, R. *Warfare in the Ancient World*. London: Cassell, 1980.

Hyland, A. 1990. *Equus: The Horse in the Roman World*. New Haven, Conn.: Yale University Press.
———. 1993. *Training the Roman Cavalry from Arrian's Ars Tactica*. Washington, D.C.: Grange.
———. 1994. *The Medieval Warhorse*. Dover, N.H.: Alan Sutton.
Jacoby, F. [1923–58] 1954–69. *Die Fragmente der griechischen Historiker*. Leiden: E. J. Brill.
Jähns, M. 1889. *Geschichte der Kriegswissenschaft, Abt. I*. Munich: R. Oldenbourg. Reprint, Hildesheim: Georg Olms, 1965.
Jankovich, M. 1971. *They Rode into Europe*. London: Harrap.
Johnson, D. 1989. *The French Cavalry: 1792–1815*. London: Belmont Publishing.
Jones, A. 1989. *The Art of War in the Western World*. Oxford: Oxford University Press.
———. 1992. *Civil War Command and Strategy*. New York: Free Press.
Junkelmann, M. 1990–92. *Die Reiter Roms*. 3 vols. Mainz: Verlag P. von Zabern.
Justin. 1994. *Epitome of the Philippic History of Pompeius Trogus*. Translated by J. C. Yardley. Atlanta, Ga.: Scholars Press.
Kagan, D. 1974.*The Archidamian War*. Ithaca, N.Y.: Cornell University Press.
———. 1981. *The Peace of Nicias and the Sicilian Expedition*. Ithaca, N.Y.: Cornell University Press.
Kähler, H. 1965. *Der Fries vom Reiterdenkmal des Aemilius Paullus in Delphi*. Berlin: Mann.
Kammenhuber, A. 1961. *Hippologia Hethitica*. Wiesbaden: O. Harrassowitz.
Keegan, J. 1977. *The Face of Battle*. New York: Vintage Books.
———. 1987. *The Mask of Command*. New York: Viking.
———. 1995. *Warpaths*. London: Hodder and Stoughton.
Keegan, J., and R. Holmes. 1986. *Soldiers*. New York: Konecky and Konecky.
Kidd, J. 1985. *International Encyclopedia of Horse Breeds*. London: H. P. Books.
Kienast, D. 1973. *Philipp II. von Makedonien und das Reich der Achaimeniden*. Munich: Wilhelm Fink Verlag.
Kilby, E. 1987. "Foxfield!" *Equus* (April) 64–70, 113–15.
Kilian, K. 1982. "Mycenaean Charioteers Again." *Antiquity* 56: 205–206.
Kipling, R. 1895. *The Jungle Book—The Second Jungle Book*. The New World Edition of the Works of Rudyard Kipling. Garden City: Doubleday, Page, and Co.
Köchly, H. A., and W. Rüstow. 1853–55. *Griechische Kriegsschriftsteller*. 2 vols. Leipzig: Engelmann. Reprint, Osnabrück: Biblio Verlag, 1969.
Kroll, J. H. 1977. "An Archive of the Athenian Cavalry." *Hesperia* 46: 83–140.
Kromayer, J., and E. Kahnes. 1924–31. "Drei Diadochenschlachten." In *Antike Schlachtfelder*, ed. J. Kromayer and G. Veith, 391–424. Berlin: Weidmann.
Kromayer, J., and G. Veith. 1903–31. *Antike Schlachtfelder*. 4 vols. Berlin: Weidmann.

———. 1922. *Schlachtenatlas zur antiken Kriegsgeschichte*. Leipzig: H. Wagner.
Kromayer, J., and G. Veith. 1928. *Heerwesen und Kriegführung der Griechen und Römer*. Munich: C. H. Beck. Reprint, Nördlingen: Beck, 1963.
Lane Fox, R. 1975. *Alexander the Great*. New York: Dial Press.
Launey, M. 1940–50. *Recherches sur les armées hellénistiques*. 2 vols. Paris: E. de Boccard.
Lawford, J. 1976. *The Cavalry: Techniques and Triumphs of the Military Horsemen*. New York: Crescent Books.
Lazenby, J. F. 1978. *Hannibal's Wars*. Warminster: Aris and Phillips.
———. 1991. "The Killing Zone." In *Hoplites: The Classical Greek Battle Experience*, edited by V. D. Hanson, 18–109. London: Routledge.
———. 1993. *The Defense of Greece: 490–479 B.C.* Warminster: Aris and Phillips.
Lewis, L. D. 1995. *Feeding and Care of the Horse*. 2nd ed. Baltimore: Williams and Wilkins.
Liddell, H. G., R. Scott, and H. S. Jones. 1940. *A Greek-English Lexicon*. Oxford: Clarendon Press.
Ling, R., ed. 1984. *The Cambridge Ancient History*. Plates to Vol. 7, Part I. Cambridge and New York: Cambridge University Press.
Littauer, M. A. 1969. "Bits and Pieces." *Antiquity* 43: 290, 298–300.
———. 1972. "The Military Use of Chariots in the Aegean in the Late Bronze Age." *American Journal of Archaeology* 76: 145–57.
———. 1981. "Early Stirrups." *Antiquity* 55: 99–105.
Littauer, M. A., and J. H. Crouwel. 1979. *Wheeled Vehicles and Ridden Animals in the Ancient Near East*. Leiden: E. J. Brill.
———. 1983. "Chariots in Late Bronze Age Greece." *Antiquity* 57: 188–89.
———. 1985. *Chariots and Related Equipment from the Tomb of Tut'ankhamun*. Oxford: Griffith Institute.
———. 1996. "The Origins of the True Chariot." *Antiquity* 70: 934–39.
Lloyd, A. B. 1996. "Philip II and Alexander the Great." In *Battle in Antiquity*, ed. A. B. Lloyd, 169–98. London: Duckworth.
Luckenbill, D. D. 1927. *Ancient Records of Assyria and Babylonia*. Vol. 2. New York: Greenwood Press. Reprint, New York: Greenwood Press, 1975.
Luttwak, E. N. 1985. *Strategy and History*. New Brunswick: Transaction Books.
McNeill, W. H. 1982. *The Pursuit of Power*. Chicago: University of Chicago Press.
Macqueen, J. G. 1986. *The Hittites*. London: Thames and Hudson.
Malbran-Labal, F. 1982. *L'armée et l'organisation militaire de l'assyrie*. Geneva: Librairie Droz.
Manti, P. A. 1983. "The Cavalry Sarissa." *Ancient World* 8, nos. 1, 2: 73–80.
Margiotta, Franklin D., ed. 1994. *Brassey's Encyclopedia of Military History and Biography*. Washington, D.C.: Brassey's.
Markham, S. D. 1969. *The Horse in Greek Art*. New York: Biblo and Tannen.

Markle, M. M. 1975. Review of *Alexander the Great*, by J. R. Hamilton. *Classical World* 69, no. 2: 141.

———. 1977. "The Macedonian Sarissa, Spear, and Related Armor." *American Journal of Archaeology* 81: 323–39.

———. 1978. "Use of the Sarissa by Philip and Alexander of Macedon." *American Journal of Archaeology* 82: 483–97.

———. 1982. "Macedonian Arms and Tactics under Alexander the Great." In *Studies in the History of Art* 10: 87–111.

Marsden, E. W. 1964. *The Campaign of Gaugamela*. Liverpool: Liverpool University Press.

———. 1969. *Greek and Roman Artillery: Historical Development*. Oxford: Clarendon Press.

———. 1971. *Greek and Roman Artillery: Technical Treatises*. Oxford: Clarendon Press.

Martin, A. 1887. *Les Cavaliers Athéniens*. Paris: E. Thorin.

Meadow, R. H., and H. P. Uerpmann, eds. 1986–91. *Equids in the Ancient World*. 2 vols. Wiesbaden: Ludwig Reichert.

Miller, S. G. 1982. "Macedonian Tombs: Their Architecture and Architectural Decoration." *Studies in the History of Art* 10: 152–69.

———. 1993. *Lyson and Kallikles*. Mainz: P. von Zabern.

Milner, N. P., trans. 1993. *Vegetius: Epitome of Military Science*. Liverpool: Liverpool University Press.

Milns, R. D. 1967. "Philip II and the Hypaspists." *Historia* 16: 509–12.

Mitchell, S. 1996. "Hoplite Warfare in Ancient Greece." In *Battle in Antiquity*, ed. A. B. Lloyd, 87–105. London: Gerald Duckworth.

Moore, M. B. 1968. "Horses by Exekias." *American Journal of Archaeology* 72: 357–68.

Moorey, P. R. S. 1970. "Pictorial Evidence for the History of Horseriding in Iraq before the Kassite Period." *IRAQ* 32: 36–50.

———. 1986. "The Emergence of the Light, Horse-drawn Chariot in the Near East, 2000–1500 B.C." *World Archaeology* 18, no. 2: 196–215.

Morgan, J. D. 1981. "Sellasia Revisited." *American Journal of Archaeology* 85: 328–30.

Mørkholm, O. 1991. *Early Hellenistic Coinage*. Cambridge: Cambridge University Press.

Morris, D. 1988. *Horse Watching*. New York: Crown.

Munn, A. H. 1993. *The Defense of Attica: The Dema Wall and the Boiotian War of 378–375 B.C.* Berkeley: University of California Press.

Murray, O. 1983. *Early Greece*. Stanford: Stanford University Press.

Noble, D. 1990. "Assyrian Chariotry and Cavalry." *State Archives of Assyria Bulletin* 4, no. 1: 61–68.

Ober, J. 1985. *Fortress Attica: Defense of the Athenian Land Frontier 404– 322 B.C.* Leiden: Brill.

O'Connell, R. L. 1989. *Of Arms and Men*. Oxford: Oxford University Press.

Oldfather, W. A., and the Illinois Greek Club, trans. 1923. *Aeneas Tacticus, Asclepiodotus, Onasander*. Cambridge, Mass.: Harvard University Press.

Osborne, R. 1996. *Greece in the Making*. London: Routledge.

Palmer, L. R. 1965. *Mycenaeans and Minoans*. London: Faber.

Parke, H. W. 1933. *Greek Mercenary Soldiers from the Earliest Times to the Battle of Ipsus*. Oxford: Clarendon Press.

Petrenko, V. G. 1995. "Scythian Culture in the North Caucasus." In *Nomads of the Eurasian Steppe in the Early Iron Age*, ed. J. Davis-Kimball, V. A. Bashilov, and C. T. Yablonsky, 5–22. Berkeley: Zinat Press.

Piggott, S. 1983. *The Earliest Wheeled Transport*. Ithaca: Cornell University Press.

Podhajsky, A. 1980. *Reitkunst*. Hamburg: Rowohlt.

Pollitt, J. J. 1986. *Art in the Hellenistic Age*. Cambridge: Cambridge University Press.

Powell, T. G. E. 1971. "The Introduction of Horse-Riding to Temperate Europe: A Contributory Note." *Proceedings of the Prehistoric Society* 37: 1–14.

Price, S. T., and C. Kauffman, 1989. *The Polo Primer*. Lexington, Mass.: S. Greene Press/Pelham.

Pritchett, W. K. 1965–80. *Studies in Ancient Greek Topography*. 3 vols. Berkeley-Los Angeles: University of California Press.

———. 1971–91. *The Greek State at War*. 5 vols. Berkeley: University of California Press.

Raaflaub, K. S. 1996. "Born to Be Wolves? Origins of Roman Imperialism." In *Transition to Empire: Essays in Greco-Roman History, 360–146 B.C. in Honor of E. Badian*, ed. R. W. Wallace and E. M. Harris, 273–314. Norman: University of Oklahoma Press.

———. 1997. "Soldiers, Citizens and the Evolution of the Early Greek Polis." In *The Development of the Polis in Archaic Greece*, ed. Lynette G. Mitchell and P. J. Rhodes, 49–59. New York: Routledge.

———. 1999. "Archaic and Classical Greece." In *War and Society in the Ancient and Medieval World*, ed. K. S. Raaflaub and N. Rosenstein, 129–61. Washington, D.C.: Center for Hellenic Studies.

Rahe, P. A. 1980. "The Military Situation in Western Asia on the Eve of Cunaxa." *American Journal of Philology* 101: 79–96.

———. 1981. "The Annihilation of the Sacred Band at Chaeronea." *American Journal of Archaeology*, 85: 84–87.

Reich, J. J. 1963. "The Horse-Head Ideogram in the Proto-Elamite Script and Minoan B." *Kadmos* 2: 151–52.

Rice, T. T. 1957. *The Scythians*. London: Thames and Hudson.

Richter, W. 1968. *Die Landwirtschaft im homerischen Zeitalter*. Göttingen: Vandenhoeck and Ruprecht.

Rivet, A. L. F. 1979. "A Note on Scythed Chariots," *Antiquity* 53: 130–32.
Robinson, C. E. 1965. *History of Greece*. New York: Thomas Y. Crowell.
Roe, F. G. 1979. *The Indian and the Horse*. Norman: University of Oklahoma Press.
Rolle, R. 1976. "Rote Pferde-goldene Reiter. Betrachtungen zu den Pferden der Skythen." In *Festschrift R. Pittioni*, 756–76. Vienna: Deuticke, Horn, and Berger.
———. 1980. *Die Welt der Skythen*. Luzern: C. J. Bucher.
Roux, G. 1966. *Ancient Iraq*. Hammondsworth: Penguin.
Rudenko, S. I. 1970. *Frozen Tombs of Siberia*. Berkeley: University of California Press.
Ruspoli, M. 1987. *The Cave of Lascaux*. New York: Abrams.
Sage, M. 1996. *Warfare in Ancient Greece*. New York: Routledge.
Sallares, R. 1991. *The Ecology of the Ancient World*. London: Duckworth.
Schäfer, M. 2000. *Handbuch Pferdebeurteilung*. Stuttgart: Kosmos.
Scheit, V. 1973. *Textes de Comptabilité Proto-Elamites, Mémoires de la Mission Archéologique de Perse*. Vol. 17. Paris: E. Leroux.
Schiele, Erika. 1975. *Pferde der Puszta*. Munich: BVL Verlagsgesellschaft.
Scott, H. C. 1861. *Military Dictionary*. New York: D. Van Nostrand. Reprint, New York: Greenwood Press, 1968.
Scullard, H. H. 1974. *The Elephant in the Greek and Roman World*. Ithaca, N.Y.: Cornell University Press.
Sealey, R. 1976. *A History of the Greek States: 700–338 B.C.* Berkeley: University of California Press.
Seibert, J. 1969. *Untersuchungen zur Geschichte Ptolemaios I*. Munich: C. H. Beck.
———. 1972. *Alexander der Grosse*. Darmstadt: Wissenschaftliche Buchgesellschaft.
———. 1973. "Der Einsatz von Kriegselefanten. Ein militärgeschichtliches Problem der antiken Welt." *Gymnasium* 80: 348–62.
———. 1983. *Das Zeitalter der Diodochen*. Darmstadt: Wissenschaftliche Buchgesellschaft.
———. 1993a. *Hannibal*. Darmstadt: Wissenschaftliche Buchgesellschaft.
———. 1993b. *Forschungen zu Hannibal*. Darmstadt: Wissenschaftliche Buchgesellschaft.
Severin, T. 1991. *In Search of Genghis Khan*. London: Hutchinson.
Shaw, I. 1991. *Egyptian Warfare and Weapons*. Princes Risborough: Shire Publications.
Shrimpton, G. 1980. "The Persian Cavalry at Marathon." *Phoenix* 34: 20–37.
Silver, C. 1976. *Guide to Horses of the World*. New York: Exeter.
Simpson, G. G. 1961. *Horses*. Garden City, N.J.: Doubleday.
Snodgrass, A. M. 1965. "The Hoplite Reform and History." *Journal of Hellenic Studies* 85: 110–22.
———. 1967. *Arms and Armour of the Greeks*. London: Thames and Hudson.
———. 1980. *Archaic Greece*. Berkeley: University of California Press.
Soteriades, G. 1903. "Das Schlachtfeld von Chäronea." *Athenische Mitteilungen* 28: 301–30.

Spence, I. G. 1990. "Pericles and the Defense of Attika during the Peloponnesian War." *Journal of Hellenic Studies* 110: 91–109.

———. 1993. *The Cavalry of Classical Greece: A Social and Military History*. Oxford: Oxford University Press.

Sponenberg, D. P. 1996. *Equine Color Genetics*. Ames, IA: Iowa State University.

Spruytte, J. 1983. *Early Harness Systems*. London: J. A. Allen.

Szeliga, G. 1983. "A Representation of an Archaic Greek Saddle-Cloth from Sicily." *American Journal of Archaeology* 87: 545–47.

Talbert, R. J. A. 1974. *Timoleon and the Revival of Greek Sicily 344–317 B.C.* Cambridge: Cambridge University Press.

Tarn, W. W. 1930. *Hellenistic Military and Naval Developments*. Cambridge: Cambridge University Press.

———. 1948. *Alexander the Great*. 2 vols. Cambridge: Cambridge University Press.

Tuplin, C. 1993. The Failings of Empire. *A Reading of Xenophon "Hellenica"* 2.3.11–7.5.29. Stuttgart: Franz Steiner.

Twelveponies, M. 1982. *There Are No Problem Horses, Only Problem Riders*. Boston: Houghton Mifflin.

Urwin, G. J. W. 1990. *Custer Victorious*. Lincoln: University of Nebraska Press.

Vainshtein, S. 1980. *Nomads of South Siberia*. Cambridge: Cambridge University Press.

Van Creveld, M. 1982. *Fighting Power.* Westport, Conn.: Greenwood Press.

———. 1985. *Command in War.* Cambridge, Mass.: Harvard University Press.

———. 1991. *Technology and War.* London: Brassey's.

Vanderpool, E. 1966. "A Monument to the Battle of Marathon." *Hesperia* 35: 93–106.

Vernant, J., ed. 1968. *Problèmes de la guerre en Grèce ancienne*. Paris: Lattaye, Mouton, and Co.

Vranopoulos, E. A. 1975. "War Elephants of the Hellenistic Period" (Greek with English resume). *Platon* 27: 130–46.

Wace, A. J. B., and Stubbings, F. H. 1962. *A Companion to Homer.* London: Macmillan.

Wade-Gery, H. T. 1933. "Classical Epigrams and Epitaphs." *Journal of Hellenic Studies* 53: 71–104.

Wagoner, D. M., L. W. Chalkley, and W. R. Cook, eds. 1978. *Equine Genetics and Selection Procedures*. Dallas: Equine Research Publications.

Walbank, F. W. 1940. *Philip V of Macedon*. Cambridge: Cambridge University Press.

———. 1957–79. *A Historical Commentary on Polybius*. 3 vols. Oxford: Clarendon Press.

———. 1990. Review of *Conquest and Empire*, by A. B. Bosworth. *Journal of Hellenic Studies* 60: 254–55.

Walsh, P. G. 1992. *Livy Book 37*. Warminster: Aris and Phillips.

Warner, R., trans. 1972. *Xenophon: The Persian Expedition*. Harmondsworth: Penguin.

Weigley, R. 1991. *The Age of Battles*. Bloomington: Indiana University Press.

Wheeler, E. L. 1979. "The Legion as Phalanx." *Chiron* 9: 303–18.
———. 1991. "The General as Hoplite." In *Hoplites*, ed. V. D. Hanson, 121–70. London: Routledge.
White, L. 1962. *Military Technology and Social Change*. Oxford: Clarendon Press.
Whitehead, D. 1990. *Aineias The Tactician*. Oxford: Clarendon Press.
Wiesner, J. 1968. *Fahren und Reiten*. Göttingen: Vandenhoeck and Ruprecht.
Woodward, Sir Llewellen. 1967. *Great Britain and the War of 1914–1918*. London: Methuen and Co.
Worley, L. J. 1994. *Hippeis: The Cavalry of Ancient Greece*. Boulder: Westview Press.
Wreszinski, W. 1935. *Atlas zur Altägyptischen Kulturgeschichte*. Vol. 2. Leipzig: J. C. Hinrichs.
Yalichev, S. 1997. *Mercenaries in the Ancient World*. London: Constable.
Zarins, J. 1986. "Equids Associated with Human Burials in Third Millenium B.C. Mesopotamia." In *Equids in the Ancient World*, ed. R. H. Meadow and H. Uerpmann, 164–93. Wiesbaden: Ludwig Reichert.
Zeuner, F. E. 1963. *A History of Domesticated Animals*. New York: Harper and Row.
Ziegler, K., W. Sontheimer, and H. Gärtner, eds. 1964–75. *Der Kleine Pauly*. Stuttgart and Munich: A. Bruckenmüller.

Index

Aemilius Paullus, Lucius, 269–70
Aemilius Paullus Macedonicus, Lucius, 257–60
Aeneas Tacticus, 303–304
Agesilaus, 117–21, 125–26, 137–38
Alcetas, 210–11
Alexander (son of Polyperchon), 212
Alexander I of Epirus, 231
Alexander IV, 201
Alexander Mosiac (Pompeii), 169–171
Alexander of Pherae, 133–34, 136, 146
Alexander Sarcophagus (Sidon), 170
Alexander the Great, 159–96; at Chaeronea, 155, 156n.43; contrasted with Successors, 205–206, 226–29, 288–90; cult of, 218; at Gaugamela, 186–87; at Granicus, 183–85; at Hydaspes, 188–90; inheritance from Philip, 157–58; at Issus, 185–86; legacy of, 160, 200–201, 286–89; military practices of, 179–80, 182–83, 190–96, 228, 286–88, 310–11; personality of, 159, 160n.4, 190–91, 288n.13; use of Companions, 174–77, 180–81, 184–88; use of mounted skirmishers, 172–78, 179n.89, 180–84
Amphipolis (422 B.C.), 100–101
Anacreon, 56
Antigonus I Monophthalmus, 209–12, 223; at Gabiene, 216–18, 227, 290, 297; at Ipsus, 224–46, 291; at Paraetacene, 213–16, 227, 290, 300–301
Antigonus III Doson, 237–39
Antiochus I Soter, 225
Antiochus III, 239, 242, 292–93; at Magnesia, 251–54; at Mantinea, Third, 243–44, 292; at Panion, 244–45; at Raphia, 240–41, 293, 301
Antiochus IV, 245
Antipater, 201–205, 209, 289
Apobates, 42
Aratus, 236–37
Archers, mounted, 49, 92, 153–55, 162n.14, 177–78
Aristotle: *History of Animals*, 24–25, *Politics*, 56–57
Armor, 28–29, 111, 161
Arms, coordination of: decisive use of, 100, 127–28, 146, 148–49, 194–96, 301–302; lack of, 205, 219, 222, 237, 253, 293
Arrhidaeus, 201
Artaxerxes II, 110–11, 146
Atilius Regulus, Marcus, 263–64
Artillery. *See* Catapults
Asculum (279 B.C.), 233–34
Asymmetry: cavalry and, 185, 191, 271, 285; principle of, 4n.2, 5, 68, 299, 301–302. *See also* Symmetry

Bardylis, 148
Beneventum (275 B.C.), 234–35
Brasidas, 100–101
Bridles, 25–26, 51

Cannae (216 B.C.), 269–71, 294–95
Cassander, 211–12, 219, 224
Catapults, 144n.2, 151, 187, 188n.118, 243–44
Cavalry, 14–15, 31; against infantry, 57, 98, 106, 112, 126–27, 155–56, 261; armor of, 28–29, 111, 161; asymmetry and, 158, 191, 271, 285; Athenian, 59–60, 85–89, 93–99, 108–109, 133–35; charge of, 127–28, 145, 156n.44, 179, 180n.91, 181n.94, 293; close combat and, 158n.52, 162–63, 164n.19, 165–68, 179–81, 246–47, 302; commander of, 5–6, 293n.15, 303–304, 308; Companions, 168, 172, 174–77, 180, 181n.95, 184–88; in coordination, 100, 127–28, 146, 148–49, 150n.18, 194–96, 301–302; formations of, 118, 158n.51, 181n.98, 182; in combined-arms army, 95–96, 104, 106, 119, 131n.9, 136, 149n.16, 188, 191–92, 283–84, 306n.53; javelin, 29, 48–49, 54, 118, 162, 164, 305n.46; lance, 29, 161, 162n.13, 163, 164n.19, 165; management of, 23, 93n.11, 210; marching rates of, 138n.31, 210n.26, 220–21, 242–43; missile troops against, 102, 104, 299–300; Persian, 53–55, 183–87; pursuit by, 136–37, 148, 182, 183n.106, 193; remounts for, 157–58, 209; as shock forces, 9, 40, 41n.41, 57, 91n.4, 106, 156; Spartan, 88–89, 120, 127–31; spear, 54, 91, 118; sword, 161, 164n.19, 168, 247; symmetry and, 121, 205, 261–62, 274; Syracusan, 102–108, 282–83; tactical units of, 172–73, 181n.95, 253–54; terrain and, 65, 84, 126–27, 184–85, 243, 292; Thessalian, 87, 132, 174n.62, 191, 226; types of, 173nn.61,63, 174n.22, 175, 192, 228, 286–87. *See also* Skirmishers, mounted; Warriors, mounted
Chaeronea (338 B.C.), 154–55, 156n.43, 157, 261

Chariotry, 32–43, 46–48; Assyrian use of, 48–49; Carthaginian use of, 145–46; Egyptian use of, 35–36; Hittite use of, 36n.24, 37–38; Indian use of, 189; Mycenaean use of, 39–42; Persian use of, 145, 186–87; Scythian use of, 35; Seleucid use of, 252; Sumerian use of, 34
Cleombrotus, 130–32
Cleomenes, 236–39
Cleon, 100–101
Coenus, 190n.127
Companion Cavalry, 181n.95; tactical use of, 174–77, 180–81, 184–88; weaponry of, 168, 172
Corinth vs. Sicyon (394 B.C.), 120
Corinthian War (395–386 B.C.), 116–123
Cornelius Scipio, Publius, 266–68
Cornelius Scipio Africanus, Publius, 267n.10, 271–74
Coronea (394 B.C.), 121
Crannon (322 B.C.), 203–205, 289
Craterus, 203, 207–208, 218, 290
Crimisus River (340 B.C.), 145
Crocus Plain (375 B.C.), 152
Croesus of Lydia, 53–54, 306–307
Cunaxa (401 B.C.), 111–12, 283
Cynoscephalae, First (364 B.C.), 136–37, 140, 284
Cynoscephalae, Second (197 B.C.), 248–50, 259–60, 293, 301
Cyrus the Great, 53–54, 60, 303–307
Cyrus the Younger, 73, 110–12, 116–17, 283, 307n.55

Darius I, 153
Darius II, 54, 110
Darius III, 185–87
Delian League, 86n.19, 95
Delium (424 B.C.), 97–100
Demetrius, 217–18, 220–27, 291
Demosthenes (general), 98, 107–109
Demosthenes (Greek orator), 152, 155
Derdas, 124–25

Elephants, 296n.22; decisive use of, 224–28, 232–34, 264, 291, 297; intimidation by, 232, 249, 259; as military arm, 189–90, 241, 273–74, 287, 295–97,

298n.26, 299; tactics against, 212–13, 229n.76, 264n.2, 273
Epaminondas, 130n.5, 131–34, 137–40, 150n.18
Equitation. *See* Horsemanship
Eucleidas, 238–39
Eumenes II, 250–56
Eumenes of Cardia, 206, 209–210, 218–19, 290–91; vs. Craterus and Neoptolemus, 207–208; at Gabiene, 216–17, 227, 297; at Paraetacene, 213–16, 227, 300–301
Eumenes vs. Craterus and Neoptolemus (321 B.C.), 207–208
Eumenes vs. Neoptolemus (321 B.C.), 207
Euthydemus I, 242–43

Formations, cavalry: diamond, 118; square, 181–82; wedge, 118, 158n.51, 181n.98, 182

Gabiene (316 B.C.), 216–18, 227, 290, 297
Gaugamela (330 B.C.), 162–63, 186–87
Gaza (312 B.C.), 221–22, 227, 291
Gelon, 82–83
Granicus (334 B.C.), 162–63, 183, 184n.112, 185
Great Plains (203 B.C.), 272
Gylippus, 105–106

Hamilcar (general), 83
Hamilcar Barca, 263, 266
Hamippoi, 139–40
Hannibal, 263–75; at Cannae, 269–71, 294–95; at Great Plains, 271–72; at Ticinus River, 266–67; at Trebia River, 267–68; use of cavalry, 293–95, 301–303, 310–11; use of elephants, 273–75; at Zama, 272–75, 302
Hasdrubal (brother-in-law of Hannibal), 266
Hasdrubal (officer at Cannae), 270
Hasdrubal (son of Gisgo), 272
Heraclea (280 B.C.), 231–33
Hiero of Syracuse, 236, 292
Hippeis, 178
Homer, 55–56
Hoplites: against cavalry, 63, 102–103, 134, 283; aristocratic, 58–59, 63n.1, 278; as combined arm, 104, 119; limited warfare of, 65–67, 68n.15, 69, 70n.19, 111, 114–15, 122, 131, 278–79; reforms under Iphicrates, 122–23; suitable terrain for, 68, 84; weaponry of, 58n.44, 164
Horsemanship: bareback seat, 10–12, 28, 91, 165–66; collection, 29–31, 166nn.29,30, 167n.31; figured evidence for, 14, 44–46, 56; leg yield, 184; shoulder barging, 167. *See also* Horses; Xenophon
Horses: armor of, 28–29, 111, 161; association with wealthy, 10, 23, 55–56, 278; Assyrian type of, 49–50; domestication of, 32–34; equipment of, 11–12, 25–28, 44, 47, 51, 54–55, 91; figured evidence for, 13–14, 20, 22, 52–53; Greek type of, 19–23, management of, 23–27, 37, 38n.31; Persian type of, 49; Scythian type of, 13–14, 52–53
Horseshoes, 28
Hydaspes (326 B.C.), 188–90

Illyrians (358 B.C.), 148–49
Iphicrates, 121–22, 132–33
Ipsus (301 B.C.), 224–26, 291
Issus (333 B.C.), 185–86

Jason of Pherae, 132
Javelin. *See* Weaponry
Javelinmen, mounted, 162n.14, 176–78, 188

Kadesh Relief of Rameses II (Luxor), 35–37
Kikkuli Text (Anatolia), 37–38
Kinch's Tomb (Naoussa), 170–171

Lake Trasimene (217 B.C.), 269
Lamia, First (323 B.C.), 202, 289, 310
Lamia, Second (322 B.C.), 202–203, 289, 310
Lance. *See* Weaponry
Larissa (171 B.C.), 254–56
Lechaeum (390 B.C.), 121–23
Legion, Roman, 272–74, 291–93
Leonnatus, 202–203, 289
Leosthenes, 202
Leuctra (371 B.C.), 129–32

Lucian, 288
Lydiades, 237
Lysimachus, 205, 206n.13, 219

Macedonian War, Second (200–196 B.C.), 245–47
Macedonian War, Third (172–168 B.C.), 254
Machanidas, 243–44
Magnesia (190 B.C.), 251–54, 293
Mago (brother of Hannibal), 270
Malene (494 B.C.), 63
Mamertines, 236, 292
Mantinea, First (418 B.C.), 101, 104
Mantinea, Second (362 B.C.), 139–40, 150n.18, 284
Mantinea, Third (207 B.C.), 243–44, 292
Marathon (490 B.C.), 70–72
Mardonius, 74–75, 77–78
Masinissa, 272n.21
Masistius, 75–77
Maurice, 153n.32, 154, 309
Military treatises: Aeneas Tacticus, 303–304; Maurice, 153n.32, 154, 309; Onasander, 309n.62; Vegetius, 309; Xenophon, 12, 24, 113n.7, 118, 140, 303–308
Mithradates, 299

Neoptolemus, 206–208, 290
Nicias, 102–108

Onasander, 309n.62
Onomarchus, 150–52
Oplax, 231

Paeonians, 172–75, 177–79, 184–87
Pagondas, 99–100
Panion (200 B.C.), 244–45
Paraetacene (317 B.C.), 213–16, 227, 290, 300–301
Paullus Monument (Delphi), 260
Pausanius, 78–79
Pazyryk Tombs (Altai Mountains, Central Asia), 25, 52–53
Pelopidas, 127–28, 133, 136–37, 140
Peloponnesian War, First (c.460–446 B.C.), 86–87

Peloponnesian War (431–404 B.C.), 90–109, 280–83, 310
Peltasts, 91; against cavalry, 96, 106–107, 112; mobility of, 95, 106, 120–23, 152
Perdiccas, 146, 206–207, 209
Pericles, 92–93, 95–99
Perseus: at Larissa, 254–56; at Pydna, 257–60
Persian Wars (500–479 B.C.), 63–80, 280–81
Phalerum (511 B.C.), 64–65
Pharsalus (48 B.C.), 294–95
Philip II, 143–58; Greek influence on, 150; introduction of *sarissa*, 147–48; legacy of, 157–
58, 285–86; transformation of Macedonian army, 147–49
Philip V, 245–49
Philopoemen, 243–44, 292
Phlius (370–366 B.C.), 134–35
Plataea (479 B.C.), 74–79
Plutarch, 224
Polyperchon, 211–13, 220
Porus, 188–90
Prodromoi, 172–77, 178nn.83,85, 179,184–87, 287
Ptolemy I Soter, 219–20, 221n. 55, 222
Ptolemy III, 239
Ptolemy IV Philopater, 239–40, 301
Punic War, First, 263
Punic War, Second, 264
Pydna (168 B.C.), 257–60, 293, 301
Pyrrhic victory, 232n.6
Pyrrhus, 230n.1, 231, 232n.6, 234–36, 291

Quinctius Flamininus, Titus, 247–50

Raphia (217 B.C.), 240–41, 293, 301

Sacred Band, 127, 155–56
Sacred War, Third (353 B.C.), 150–52
Saddlecloth, 27–28, 44, 47, 54–55
Saddles, 11–12, 27–28, 91; Roman, 11n.16; Scythian, 11n.13, 25; treed, 11, 27
Sardis (395 B.C.), 118, 119n.7
Sarissa: figured evidence for, 169, 169n.45, 170, 170n.47, 171, 171n.53; infantry use

of, 154n.37, 155–56, 168, 232, 241, 249, 285; Macedonian adoption of, 147, 164; Physical nature of, 148, 168nn.36,39, 169n.45, 172n.56, 173; *prodromoi* use of, 178n.85
Sarissophoroi, 172–73, 176, 188
Scopas, 244–45
Seleucus, 219, 221–27, 291
Sellasia (222 B.C.), 237–39, 292
Seuthes, 205–206
Silver Shields, 213n.32, 219; destruction of, 217–18; under Eumenes of Cardia, 213–14, 219n.50, 227, 290–91
Skirmishers, mounted: archers, mounted, 49, 92, 153–55, 162n.14, 177–78; javelinmen, mounted, 162n.14, 176–78, 188; Paeonians, 172–75, 177–79, 184–86; *prodromoi*, 172–77, 178nn.83,85, 179, 184–86, 287; *sarissophoroi*, 172–73, 176, 188. *See also* Cavalry; Warriors, mounted
Slingers, 104, 114, 149, 183, 268, 299–300
Socrates (philosopher), 92, 108
Socrates (soldier), 174
Solygeia (425 B.C.), 93–94
Southern Attica (510 B.C.), 64–65
Spartolus (429 B.C.), 95–96
Spear. *See* Weaponry
Stirrups, 11, 12n.21, 27, 91
Successors, 288–91, 295; lack of coordinated arms, 205, 216n.40, 219, 222, 226–27, 253, 293; military inheritance of, 199–201, 208, 221–22, 226; use of elephants, 201, 212–17, 224–29, 296–97. *See also under individual names*
Sword. *See* Weaponry
Symmetry: Hannibal and, 274–75; principle of, 149n.16, 261–62, 301–301, 309–310; Successors and, 219n.50, 226–28, 288–90. *See also* Asymmetry
Syracuse (414 B.C.), 104–106

Tanagra (457 B.C.), 87–88
Tarentines, 216–17, 230n.1, 244–45
Tegyra (375 B.C.), 127–28
Teleutias, 124–25
Ten Thousand, The, 110–115, 119

Terentius Varro, Gaius, 269–70
Terrain, effect of, 70; on cavalry, 65, 73, 84, 126–27, 184–85, 243, 292; on infantry, 65, 68, 84
Thermoplyae (480 B.C.), 73
Thucydides, 90, 108; *Histories*, 88–89; *Pentecontaëtia*, 84
Ticinus River (218 B.C.), 266–67
Timoleon of Corinth, 143–46
Tissaphernes, 116–17, 299–300
Trebia River (218 B.C.), 267–68

Vegetius, 309

Warfare, Homeric, 65–66
Warriors, mounted, 14; Assyrian use of, 49–51; figured evidence for, 29–30, 48–49; rise of, 46–47; Scythian use of, 51–53; weaponry of, 48n.17, 49. *See also* Cavalry; Skirmishers, mounted
Weaponry: javelin, 29, 48–49, 54, 118, 162, 164n.19, 305n.46; lance, 29, 161, 162n.13, 163, 164n.19, 165; *sarissa*, 147–48, 154–56, 164, 168–73, 178; spear, 48–49, 91, 118; sword, 29n.56, 163n.17, 164n.19, 168, 246n.42, 267n.9, 305n.46

Xanthippus, 264
Xenophon: on cavalry equipment, 12, 29, 47, 118, 164; on cavalry tactics, 11, 117–18, 132–33, 164; on cavalry training, 12–13, 24, 26, 126–27; on combined-arms army, 306n.53; on *hamippoi*, 140; on horse management, 20, 23; on horsemanship, 12, 27–28, 29–31, 165, 166n.29, 167n.31; influence on Philip II, 150; military principles of, 303–308; with the Ten Thousand, 112–15. Works: *Anabasis*, 110; *Cavalry Commander, The*, 140, 303–304, 308; *Cyropaedia*, 113n.7, 303–307; *Hellenica*, 108; *On Horsemanship*, 24, 118, 303–304, 308
Xerxes I, 73–74, 82

Zama (202 B.C.), 272–75, 302